AF599400

THE KNIGHT WHO GAVE US KING ARTHUR

CECELIA LAMPP LINTON, PH.D.

THE KNIGHT WHO GAVE US KING ARTHUR

Sir Thomas Malory, Knight Hospitaller

Christendom College Press
Front Royal, VA

Cover by Niall O'Donnell

On the cover: "Gallos" by Rubin Eynon at Tintagel
Castle in North Cornwall (Alamy P13D3C)

All inquiries should be addressed to:

Christendom College Press, Front Royal, VA 22630.

Distributed by Sophia Institute Press, Box 5284, Manchester, NH 03108.

hardcover ISBN 979-8-9868157-2-5

ebook ISBN 979-8-9868157-3-2

Library of Congress Control Number: 2023934738

First printing

In gratitude to my amazing family,
without whose help and encouragement this book would not have been written:

to Larry Linton, my husband, who traveled with me to Yorkshire and photographed the haunts of the Malorys, and to Cambridge and Oxford Universities to enable me to examine some medieval manuscripts in their keeping; and who navigated the convolutions of The Computer to produce good copy, revision after revision; and

to our sons, Jeb, Kit, and Coby Linton:

to Jeb, for developing the Artificial Intelligence based on deep neural networks which is required to verify objectively that there is "not a whiff of Warwick" in *Le Morte Darthur*; to Kit, for serving as my map and chart aide;

and to Coby, for sharing my excitement and helping with my research; and

to Dr. Robert C. Rice,
for his faithful friendship and countless hours of expert copy editing; and

to Dr. James W. Spisak,
noted Malory scholar and new friend, who immediately saw the worth of

the argument in this book and generously set out to
help me improve its presentation; and

to that skeptical inquirer Dr. William Matthews —
this book is humbly dedicated.

Contents

Section Four

But What about Newbold Revel?

Section Five

Wrap-Up

I find in it, sometimes implicit, sometimes explicit, an unforced reverence not only for courage (that of course) but for mercy, humility, graciousness, and good faith.... In such passages, and indeed almost everywhere, we meet something which I chiefly hesitate to call "morality" because it is so little like a code of rules. It is rather a civilization of the heart (by no means of the head), a fineness and sensitivity, a voluntary rejection of all the uglier and more vulgar impulses.... It makes the *Morte* a "noble" as well as a "joyous" book.

C. S. Lewis, "The English Prose Morte," in *Times Literary Supplement* (June 7, 1947), 274.

If a shaky theory is repeated frequently enough with increasing emphasis, it will convince the masses.

Lotte Hellinga, *Caxton in Focus* (London: The British Library, 1982), 39.

FOREWORD

James W. Spisak

THE QUESTION OF which Sir Thomas Malory wrote *Le Morte Darthur* has puzzled scholars for over a century. And this puzzle is a relatively modern one: no serious effort to attach a person to the name was made until the late nineteenth century, more than four hundred years after the *Morte* was written. It seems odd indeed that the author of a work that has been popular from its earliest days — and in fact was an early work issued by William Caxton when he brought printing to England — could live in name only for so long.

The leading contenders for authorship of the *Morte* are Sir Thomas Malory of Newbold Revel, first put forward by G. L. Kittredge in 1894 and subsequently endorsed by Edward Hicks in 1928 and P. J. C. Field in 1993, and Thomas Malory of Hutton Conyers in Yorkshire, put forward by William Matthews in 1966 and here championed by Cecelia Lampp Linton. While the Newbold Revel knight has become the default candidate, there have always been reservations about him. The Yorkshireman, albeit with scholarly credibility, never gained traction as a serious candidate because there was no evidence put forth, until now, that he was a knight. In Linton's study, David of Yorkshire once again takes on Goliath of Newbold Revel.

Most scholars have stayed away from the authorship question, and understandably so, since the evidence for one candidate or another has been incomplete, contradictory, or otherwise inconclusive.

One result of this is that the fragmented evidence we do have is asked to carry more weight than it can reasonably sustain. Another is that ancillary evidence, both positive and negative, has been brought to bear. While some of this has been relevant, none of it has overwhelmed. The scholarship in this area has also been decidedly one-sided: much more energy has been spent trying to garner acceptance of the Newbold Revel knight than to give open and honest consideration to the Yorkshireman.

The present study by Professor Linton goes a long way toward filling some gaps, resolving some inconsistencies, and even toward solving the puzzle. She presents an abundance of new evidence, forces us to question some beliefs that have become sacrosanct, and enables us to envision an author about whom we have known so little. Along the way she provides illustrative historical contexts for various parts of her argument, from the Cistercian underpinnings of the Knights Hospitaller and Crusades to the frequently shifting alliances during the Wars of the Roses. Linton also offers some highly illuminating readings of key passages in the *Morte,* drawing clear connections between the author and his favorite character, Lancelot.

The arguments Linton puts forth for the Yorkshire Malory as author of the *Morte* are compelling. First, she presents strong evidence that the Thomas Malory of Hutton Conyers was indeed a knight — one of the known and documented Malory Knights of St. John, Hospitaller — thus addressing the most serious and common charge against his acceptance as the author. This is an absolute game changer. It also provides a simple and clear explanation as to why we know so little about the author: as a knight of the church, a monk, he would be naturally excluded from most of the records in which we would be looking for him.

In making her case, Linton discusses the Malory family, their ancestors, and their properties in great detail, and makes a strong case for why Thomas Malory of Hutton Conyers would have entered the order of St. John, Hospitaller. She also provides a credible explanation of why he would have been imprisoned at the time the *Morte* was written.

Another persuasive argument comes in her discussion of the provenance of the Ribston *Suite du Merlin,* one of Malory's sources, and a version of the *Estoire du Graal,* which was bound together with the *Suite.* Linton also provides a methodical discussion of the dialect issues that so many scholars have quietly sidestepped. Discussions of this Malory's role in the Wars of the Roses and his exclusion from a pardon issued by Edward IV provide additional evidence that the Yorkshireman was the most likely person to have written the *Morte.*

Linton also carefully reviews the arguments against the Newbold Revel Malory as author of the *Morte.* Most of these are familiar: he would not have had access to the numerous works Malory used to write the work; the language of the *Morte,* and some of its English sources, would have been difficult at best for the Newbold Revel knight to use as easily as the author did; his character was not commensurate with that of someone who would write an English romance "briefly drawn" from various French sources; he was not imprisoned at the time the work was written; and 70ish, as Matthews put it, is "no age at all" to be writing the *Morte.* In discussing these arguments, Linton does not gloss over the inconsistencies but, when there's doubt, asks us to use common sense instead of automatically giving the benefit.

Linton's identification of a Knight Hospitaller as the author of the *Morte* buttresses her discussion of Malory as a writer. Her insightful readings of the text, particularly where it varies from his sources, reveal a connection between the writer and his work that is engaging rather than perplexing. She provides numerous examples of original material that illuminate Lancelot's character, especially in his regard for and relationship with Guinevere. When Morgan le Fay and her cohorts cast a spell on him, giving him the ultimatum of choosing one of them as his paramour or dying in their prison, Lancelot chooses prison without hesitation and further rebuffs Morgan's suggestion that he's saving himself for the queen. Here and elsewhere, Linton shows how he not only avoids an adulterous relationship with Guinevere, but also defends her honor and loyalty at every opportunity.

Linton's discussion of Lancelot draws clear parallels, and distinctions, between his development as a secular knight and his spiritual growth, based on the author's deep roots in the Cistercian tradition. As long as Lancelot is known as the best knight in the world, pride prevents him from being able to accept divine intervention. His pride eventually leads him to engage in wrongful quarrels, and once he does this, his secular prowess is destroyed; only then can his spiritual journey begin in earnest. Humility is the vehicle for his spiritual growth, based on recognition of his misdeeds and penance and with clear encouragement by Guinevere. Once he has renounced worldly fame, and has avowed divine rather than secular values, he is able to heal Sir Urry, a miracle taken from the Hospitallers' playbook. Readers who accept the Yorkshire Knight as author of the *Morte,* even provisionally, will find a clear consistency between the man and his work, with no spurious assumptions or explanations needed.

Linton here revisits the authorship question with wit and intelligence. The evidence she presents in support of the Yorkshireman forms the foundation of her reading of the *Morte* as a monumental work written by a humble Knight Hospitaller. Debate will no doubt continue, but the arguments and evidence put forth here demand serious consideration. As a student and collaborator of William Matthews, my bias has always been toward the Yorkshire Malory. But like others, including Matthews, I was bothered by the fact that there was no evidence, until now, that he was a knight. Thanks to the painstaking work done by Linton, that worry can be put to rest, and Sir Thomas Malory of Hutton Conyers can take his rightful place in the company of literary giants.

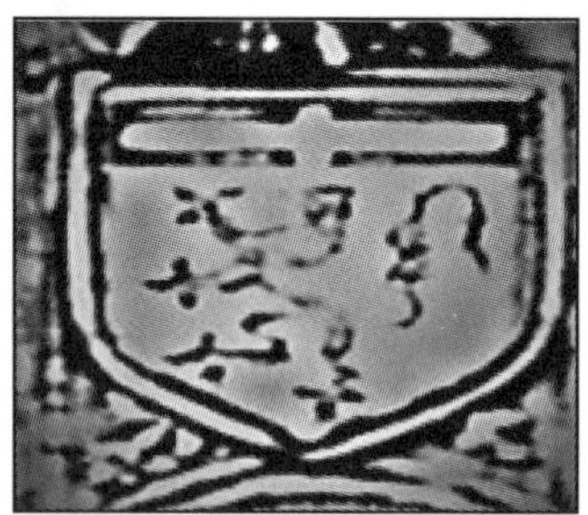

Detail, the Malorys as a Hospitaller family: Malory coat of arms beneath the feet of Christ on Knights Hospitaller processional cross donated to the order in 1439 by Prior Robert Malory. Courtesy of the Museum of the Order of St. John, London, Curator Abigail Cornick

Preface

IT HAS BEEN 125 years now since George Lyman Kittredge proposed that the author of *Le Morte Darthur* must have been Sir Thomas Malory of Newbold Revel, Warwickshire. Kittredge's major point of evidence was that this man was the only Thomas Malory he had been able to unearth who was without doubt a knight when *Le Morte* was written, and its author had claimed in the book that he was a knight. Since then, Malory readers have gradually come to accept the Newbold Revel man as the author, so that nowadays critical judgment of *Le Morte* almost always begins with the a priori assumption that the Newbold Revel man wrote the book.

I don't believe he did.

I used to think so, not because I had found any evidence for his authorship but just because I trusted that other people had. Now, after years of research concerning this question, I am convinced that many other scholars approach the identity issue the way I used to do: they themselves have not discovered any evidence, but they trust that others have. The whole case has become an argument from authority.

My doubt set in when I read two books on the subject — William Matthews's *The Ill-Framed Knight,* which argued for a man from Yorkshire as the author and caused me to doubt what I thought I knew about the Warwickshire man; and P.J.C. Field's *The Life and Times of Sir Thomas Malory,* which absolutely set the seal on my doubt. It was the latter book that showed me how meager the evidence is for Malory of Warwickshire.

Field has become the major Malory authority in our time. In *Life and Times,* he set himself the task of proving that the Warwickshire man had to be our author, because the only other candidate left standing was Matthews's Yorkshireman, and he could not possibly have been a knight. Unfortunately, Field had only one recorded fact that he might be able to use, one solid piece of information upon which to hang his argument. However, he was undaunted; he used what he had. That one fact was that Thomas Malory of Yorkshire was left out of his parents' will. From that, Field deduced that the other Malory, the one from Warwickshire, must be the author. This is how his reasoning goes:

Thomas Malory of Yorkshire was not
mentioned in his parents' will,
ergo,
he must have been a bastard
(or, as Field says, a "byblow"),
ergo,
nobody would ever have made him a knight,
ergo,
Thomas Malory of Warwickshire was
the only knight of that name,
ergo,
Malory of Newbold Revel, Warwickshire, wrote the book.
Q. E. D.

Professor Field has taken what looked initially like an outrageous non sequitur—Malory of Yorkshire was disinherited, therefore Malory of Warwickshire wrote *Le Morte Darthur*—and made it into the winning argument. I believe there are very few Malory scholars today who have actually examined the basis of Field's case. He remains the leading proponent of Sir Thomas Malory of Warwickshire; nobody has bested his argument for this Malory, for no one has found any better evidence. After 125 years, it appears that there is none to be found.

Field's argument comes in the first chapter of *Life and Times,* concluding on page 20. When I read it, I was astonished — could this possibly be the foundation of our almost universal assumption that Sir Thomas Malory of Newbold Revel, Warwickshire, wrote *Le Morte Darthur*? I found it completely unconvincing, and I felt sure that others would, too, if they looked closely at Professor Field's argument. I knew immediately that I had to study the issue further, and I set out to do so. I learned that there is very little real, firm evidence in the case for the Newbold Revel man, so scholars tend to stretch it to the breaking point, in many cases not even seeming to realize that that is what they are doing.

Fortunately, Professor Field inadvertently gave me a pathway to a much stronger case for the other candidate, the Thomas Malory who was supported by William Matthews half a century ago, in *The Ill-Framed Knight*. This book presents a new investigation of that man as one of the Malory Knights of St. John of Jerusalem, Hospitallers.

Malory scholarship proliferates today. Scholars have studied at length virtually every aspect of *Le Morte Darthur*: its sources, its dialect, its influence, its author, its place in the history of romance and of English prose, its place in the hearts of readers, its errors, its anachronisms, its … everything else. Lovers of *Le Morte* have worked long and hard; some have spent entire careers in the study of Malory. I realize that in presenting this new view of his identity I am putting myself in the unenviable position of someone who tips over the table in the middle of a hard-thought and hard-fought chess game. Nobody loves a table tipper — the pieces go everywhere and chaos is come again. But the very chaos brings excitement, for there is sure to be a brand-new game. If we adjust our thinking about Malory and the kind of knight he was, we see things in the *Morte* that we have never seen before. Imagine how many articles, how many lectures, how many midnight discussions are waiting to get started. Even those scholars who still believe in the man from Newbold Revel may be inspired to try to find some new and better evidence in his favor, for now that his old opponent is revived, the competition can start again in earnest. Let the Great Conversation begin.

Readers who expect a literary-critical discussion as a matter of course in a book about a famous author will not find much of that here; my purpose is historical rather than literary. Of the twenty-two chapters, only four (13–16) are focused on the *Morte* itself; these four look at Malory's book for clues to his identity. This book is a down-to-earth study of a real person with all the accoutrements of a lived human life—family, home, religion, work, and so forth. It is not abstract. There are no fallacies of logic or flights of unsubstantiated speculation. Hypothesis is of course at the heart of reasoned investigation, but when a passage is hypothetical, that fact is clearly announced. Nothing is under the rug. There is no spin. There are a few historical documents that Professor Field used to support his candidate; every one of these is presented clearly and Field's treatment of it is shown to readers so that all can evaluate his case for themselves.

Most important of all, in making this argument I have tried never to violate plain common sense. My readers will judge whether I have succeeded.

THE KNIGHT WHO GAVE US KING ARTHUR

INTRODUCTION

IT IS IMPOSSIBLE to exaggerate the influence of Sir Thomas Malory, the author of *Le Morte Darthur,* Although the whole panoply of chivalry and romance embodied in Le Morte originated in medieval France as a huge random assortment of tales, it was Malory who tackled that conglomeration and worked it into the greatest 15th-century literary work in English, the prototype of our beloved modern genre, the novel.

And until now, all we have known about the author has been his name and his knightly rank. This book offers the first complete and coherent identification of the man who gave us the doomed Round Table, the mythical king, and the best-loved love story ever told, of Guenevere his Queen and Sir Lancelot his greatest knight. The author is identified at last, as a member of the Order of Knight Hospitallers of St. John of Jerusalem, who were monks as well as knights, and dedicated healers as well as intrepid warriors.

SECTION ONE

Backdrop

1

The Mystery: Contentions and Contentiousness

THERE WAS GEOFFREY Chaucer, with God's Plenty, and there was William Shakespeare, with his peerless plays and his linguistic razzle-dazzle, and, right there in between them, there was Thomas Malory, playing midwife to the wobbly infant that, in due time, would develop into the great literary genre of our own era, the Novel. And we don't know who he was. What is more, we don't know why we don't know who he was. That such an important author would be unknown and unnoted in his own time and for five hundred years since is an astonishing fact. Why, during the fifteenth century, when his book was an immediate hit, and during the next hundred years, when it went through printing after printing, when everybody knew *Le Morte Darthur,* did nobody know who wrote it? Why, today, over five hundred years later, when everybody still knows *Le Morte Darthur,* does nobody yet know who wrote it? The mystery is one of the best whodunits in all of English literature.

It is not much like a Sherlock Holmes, nor an Agatha Christie. It is more like a good Barbara Vine, which tells readers right at the beginning who was hanged for the murder, and then gives clues to help them figure out the rest of the story. We know the author's name and rank: Sir Thomas Malory, Knight. We know that he finished his book in the ninth year of the reign of King Edward IV — that is, between March 4, 1469, and March 4, 1470. We know he was a prisoner when he finished it. All of this we know because Malory has told us, in his book, but that's about all Malory told us. And, up until 1934, we didn't even know that much, for the Caxton edition, upon which everyone relied until that year, did not tell us that Malory was a prisoner.

William Caxton, the first printer in England and the first printer of Malory's work, declined to say much about the author. Caxton's preface runs to about 1,765 words; buried somewhere in among them are these: "Sir Thomas Malory did take [it] out of certain books of French, and reduced it into English."[1] That is all he has to say concerning Malory. The rest of the preface concerns speculations about whether Arthur actually lived or not; homiletics on taking what is good in the Arthurian material and discarding the rest; and a lengthy outline of his plan for printing: so many chapters for this tale, so many chapters for this other, and so forth.

Naturally, much inquiry and ink have been spent on the search for information about the author's identity. Scholars have seen a few hints embedded in *Le Morte* itself; for example, there is the commentary on the vicissitudes of captivity. In a passage describing the illness of Trystram while he is in prison, the narrator laments that a prisoner may suffer a great deal in various ways, but as long as he has good health, he can bear his troubles with fortitude. However, if he becomes ill, he suffers so much that he wishes for death, and "than may a presonere say all welth is hym berauffte, and than hath he cause to wayle and wepe. Ryght so ded sir Trystram whan syknes had undirtake hym, for than he toke such sorow that he had allmoste slayne hymselff."[2] This passage sounded irresistibly like the voice of personal experience, making scholars wonder whether perhaps Thomas Malory the author was himself a prisoner. Adding to their speculation on this point was

1 William Caxton, preface to Sir Thomas Malory, *The Works of Sir Thomas Malory*, ed. Eugene Vinaver, 1 vol., 2nd ed. (Oxford: Oxford University Press, 1967, repr. 1970), xvii. Further citations of this work will be in parentheses in the text.

2 Sir Thomas Malory, *The Works of Sir Thomas Malory*, ed. Eugene Vinaver, 1 vol., 2nd ed. (Oxford: Oxford University Press, 1967, repr. 1970), 404. All citations of Malory's work will be from this edition and henceforth will be by page number in parentheses in the text, by the title *Works*.

the fact that more than once in his book he had asked his readers to pray that God would send him "good delyveraunce," using the phrase that usually meant in those days "release from captivity" (Malory, *Works*, 133, 273, 623, 816, 883). Yet there was no proof.

In 1894, George Lyman Kittredge, a Harvard scholar, proposed as the author of *Le Morte Darthur* a certain Sir Thomas Malory of Newbold Revel manor in Warwickshire, and he gained much favorable attention for his proposal. Little was known about this Thomas Malory at the time, only what was included in an entry in Sir William Dugdale's encyclopedic book, published in 1656, *The Antiquities of Warwickshire*. Dugdale was a man who loved old things, and who loved his home county, Warwickshire. He had traveled about the county interviewing people, studying church records, making rubbings of gravestones, sketching anything that interested him, and in any other way available, attempting to preserve the history of his county, because he had been warned by a friendly agent of the king that Parliament had a plan to destroy all such evidence of old papist times. *The Antiquities of Warwickshire* reported that a certain Sir Thomas Malory of the parish of Monks Kirby served at Calais as a soldier in Richard Beauchamp's force during the reign of Henry V (1413–1422); that he took with him one lance and two archers; that he was paid twenty pounds per annum and food for his one lance and one of the archers, and ten marks and no food for the other archer. Further, Dugdale noted that in later years Malory served as a member of Parliament for Warwickshire, and that he died in 1470 and was buried in the Greyfriars church in London.[3] It had turned out that Dugdale's advance notification of destructive intentions in the Parliament, concerning old papist records, was accurate, and most of the records of those days were indeed destroyed, along with other treasures architectural, artistic, devotional, literary, and who knows what-all, meaning that this entry in Dugdale's old book was all we knew about this Sir Thomas Malory for centuries. And most

3 Sir William Dugdale, *The Antiquities of Warwickshire* (London: Thomas Warren, 1656), 55.

people, of course, because most people do not read books like *The Antiquities of Warwickshire,* did not know even that much. And then Kittredge, late in the nineteenth century, taking his hint from Dugdale's almost forgotten book, proposed that this man may have been the author of *Le Morte Darthur*. He made quite a satisfactory candidate, this Malory, because of his knightly derring-do with Beauchamp at Calais, his service to his county, and his burial at the Greyfriars elegant and aristocratic church, with an elegant and aristocratic grave marker, duly recorded in time by Dugdale before it was destroyed by "reformers":

HIC JACET DOMINUS THOMAS MALLERE
VALENS MILES
OB 14 MAR 1470
DE PAROCHIA DE MONKENKIRBY IN
COM WARWICI[4]

Kittredge's argument on behalf of this man was thoughtful and convincing, and seemed to be well-researched. The point that clinched the matter, however, and effectually stopped all further searching for another candidate for author, was Kittredge's declaration that he had comprehensively searched all pertinent records, he had followed all avenues of inquiry, and there simply was not alive in England, at the time *Le Morte* was written, another Thomas Malory who could possibly have written it. Therefore, this Malory had to be the author: "There is absolutely no contestant," said he, "and until such a contestant appears, it is not unreasonable to insist on the claims of this Sir Thomas."[5] So Kittredge's argument, and his candidate, were mostly accepted.

4 Quoted in William Matthews, *The Ill-Framed Knight: A Skeptical Inquiry into the Identity of Sir Thomas Malory* (Berkeley and Los Angeles: University of California Press, 1966), 33. Transcript of the epitaph is found in B.L. MS. Cotton Vitellius F.xii, fol. 284r. Further citations of this work will be in parentheses in the text.

5 George Lyman Kittredge, "Who Was Thomas Malory?" in *Harvard Studies and Notes in Philology and Literature,* vol. 5 (Boston: Ginn, 1896), 97.

However, as satisfactory as the Warwickshire Malory seemed as the author of the definitive romance of King Arthur and his knights, there were some problems. For one, Dugdale, in his sketch of the life of the Warwickshire knight, had not said a word about *Le Morte Darthur.* And then there were those hints in the book that its author might be a prisoner. Kittredge had said nothing about that possibility, but some scholars were uneasy. If only there could be some verification that the Warwickshire man had been in prison in 1469, it would go a long way to ease any doubts raised by Dugdale's failing to mention what would surely be the crowning achievement of any man's life, writing *Le Morte Darthur.* The hunt was on for some evidence that Kittredge's man was not only a knight but also a prisoner. It seemed that if any verification of the identity were to be found, it must be found among public records of the English jails of the fifteenth century. There was a great deal of material to be searched, and searching through it was a laborious task, but the first scholar to find the prison record of Sir Thomas Malory would earn for himself quite a handsome feather for his cap. Kittredge was at Harvard, far away in Massachusetts, and was uncomfortably placed for rifling through medieval court records in England, so he stood by.

And then, after what must have seemed a very long time, the evidence started coming in, first in drops, and then the deluge. The culmination of the meticulous search of the English court records of the fifteenth century came in 1928, when Edward Hicks published his findings in a speculative biography, entitled *Sir Thomas Malory, His Turbulent Career,* which incorporated some prison records that Hicks had uncovered. There was left no doubt at all that this Thomas Malory of Newbold Revel in Warwickshire had spent upwards of ten years in His Majesty's prisons between 1443 and 1461, charged with various crimes.[6] Kittredge wrote a jubilant preface for Hicks's book, and sent

[6] Edward Hicks, *Sir Thomas Malory, His Turbulent Career* (Cambridge, MA: Harvard University Press, 1928). Hicks's findings concerning Malory's career of crime and incarceration are presented throughout his book. All further citations of this work will be in parentheses in the text.

him a letter of heartfelt thanks for his diligent searching and reporting. There was now only the celebrating left to do; it seemed that the author of *Le Morte* had been found. Even scholars who had been hesitant about accepting Kittredge's candidate gave Malory of Warwickshire their consent. But here the story takes a surprising twist.

Six years later, in 1934, W. F. Oakeshott of Winchester College in England was asked to put together some sort of library display to impress a group of visitors. He went looking around in storage rooms and forgotten piles of stuff in various locations in the college, searching for something interesting, and he found something, in the warden's bedroom: he found a lost medieval manuscript of the King Arthur stories by Sir Thomas Malory.[7] The world of Malory scholarship suddenly changed. It appeared that Caxton had done more than merely print Malory's book; he had edited it significantly, and one of the passages that he had deleted was right there in the Winchester manuscript, just as the author had written it:

> And this booke endyth whereas sir Launcelot and sir Trystrams com to court. Who that woll make ony more lette hym seke other bookis of kynge Arthure or of sir Launcelot or sir Trystrams; for this was drawyn by a knyght presoner, sir Thomas Malleorre, that God sende hym good recover. Amen. (Malory, *Works*, 133)

It was immediately evident that Caxton had in his imprint omitted a key bit of information about Thomas Malory; he was, indeed, a prisoner, as he had hinted in the phrase "good deliverance," and thus aroused the curiosity of scholars. It seemed that there was no more to be said on the subject; Sir Thomas Malory of Newbold Revel, Warwickshire, was known to have been a prisoner during the best part of ten years of his life; the author declared himself to have been a prisoner;

[7] Walter Oakeshott, "The Finding of the Manuscript," in *Essays on Malory*, ed. J. A. W. Bennett (Oxford: Clarendon Press, 1963), 4.

therefore, Sir Thomas of Newbold Revel must have written *Le Morte Darthur*. Few objected, and their voices were almost drowned out. Even Eugene Vinaver, engaged in producing his vast edition of Malory's work, and having resisted up until now, surrendered the point and accepted this man as the author.[8]

Then, a generation later, in 1966, the voice of a skeptic was heard in the land. William Matthews, who called his book a "skeptical inquiry" into the identity of Thomas Malory, was engaged in comparing Malory's version of the Roman War episode in the *Morte* with the alliterative *Morte Arthure*, an English poem that was Malory's source, when, he tells us, he was struck by an unorthodox question: "Could the author of *Le Morte Darthur* possibly have written like this, and really been from Warwickshire?" The problem was "certain peculiarities in dialect" (Matthews, 75). Those peculiarities inspired Matthews to a wide and intensive study of the language in the *Morte*, which led him to conclude that it was definitely not the language of Warwickshire but a dialect of the north and North Midlands. Matthews went on from the language study to a study of allusions, places, and probable reading experiences of the author, and found that "they all point firmly to the probability that the author was a northerner" (Matthews, 107).

From there, Matthews went looking for "another man of the same name," having conceived a suspicion that Kittredge's investigation of possible other candidates was not so thorough as Kittredge had claimed, and that his declaration that there was absolutely no other suitably qualified Thomas Malory alive in England at the right time to write *Le Morte*, was not so guileless as Kittredge had hoped we would believe. What kind of English family, Matthews asked himself, would

8 William Matthews (42–43) quotes Vinaver as saying in 1929 that although it may be true that there could be only one Thomas Malory in prison in 1469–1470, it cannot be proved, and therefore "our author's identity must be a little less than certain." However, as Matthews points out, Vinaver, "cautious in 1929, accepted the identification without question in his edition of 1947." Matthews does not cite his source of the Vinaver quotation.

not have somewhere a boy they called Tom (Matthews, 114)? The diligent search that followed led Matthews to a Thomas Malory the son of William and Dionisia Malory of Studley and Hutton Manors in Yorkshire (Matthews, 122–125). Matthews presented a reasoned and convincing argument for this Yorkshire man as the author, ending by acknowledging that the man is not designated either a knight or a prisoner in any records he found, but claiming that in every other way he is a far better candidate than the Newbold Revel knight. Perhaps, said Matthews, this Thomas Malory was knighted on the battlefield and therefore left no record for us to read. And perhaps the author was not imprisoned in a jail for criminals; perhaps he was a political prisoner or a prisoner of war (Matthews, 153).

The adherents of the Warwickshire man, aware of course of the difficulty readers had had in crediting with the authorship a thoroughgoing scoundrel like Sir Thomas Malory of Newbold Revel, in and out of jail for years on criminal charges, took this last suggestion of Matthews's and ran with it. Maybe *their* candidate was not a scoundrel at all but merely someone who had attracted unfavorable attention by his political views. If so, that fact could possibly be made to redirect attention away from the by-now-obvious fact that the prison records of the Newbold Revel man abruptly stopped on October 24, 1461, when a pardon with Malory's name on it was granted, and that after that, try as the advocates of this Malory might, they were never able to learn that he ever went to jail again; nor were any more criminal charges ever brought against him. All of this, of course, worked against their case, because the author specifically states in his book that he finished his book as a prisoner, in 1469–1470, long after any record of imprisonment of Malory of Newbold Revel stopped.

That is where the argument stood for a few years after Matthews's 1966 publication. Many scholars were convinced by Matthews's argument; many others were not. Then, in 1993, P. J. C. Field published his *Life and Times of Sir Thomas Malory,* skirting around Matthews's arguments for the Yorkshire man and going back to the Warwickshire man from Newbold Revel, previously backed by

Kittredge. Field based his support for this man solely on the fact that the author himself had told us he was a knight, and the fact that the Warwickshire man is the only Thomas Malory called a knight in the public records of his time. Therefore, says Field, he must be the author. Field adds a great deal of ancillary information about this man's ancestors and descendants, to expand the very small amount of information actually known about Malory himself, into a book-length work, and therefore the book ends up being more about the *Times* than the *Life* of Sir Thomas. Professor Field tells us, for example, a great deal about the situation in England in the fifteenth century with two factions striving for the crown; and the later parts of his book are devoted to the generations of Malorys after Sir Thomas himself was dead. He also considers a few pertinent documents, which mention a Thomas Malory, and interprets them to relate to his candidate from Newbold Revel, always basing his argument on the fact that this man is the only recorded knight. We will be saying more about Field's arguments as we continue; suffice it to say that as of right now his candidate, the Warwickshire man, is the top contender for authorship. In his review of Field's *Life and Times*, Mark Adderley declared, "Field has demonstrated that the body of evidence points beyond all reasonable doubt away from Matthews' conclusion."[9]

Beyond all reasonable doubt.

But surely the correct response to that sort of valediction forbidding further inquiry is obvious: not so fast.

9 mark-adderley.com.

2

FIELDING A CLASH OF KNIGHTS

PROFESSOR P. J. C. FIELD is the most prominent Malory scholar of the late twentieth and early twenty-first centuries. He supports Sir Thomas Malory of Newbold Revel Manor in Warwickshire as candidate for authorship of *Le Morte Darthur,* basing his firm belief in that candidate solely on the insistence that there existed no other English knight named Thomas Malory in the fifteenth century who could possibly have written the book, and the author claimed to be a knight. Ironically, Field's argument turned out to be the very thing that convinced me that William Matthews's candidate for authorship was indeed a knight and the author of *Le Morte.* I had read Matthews and was impressed by his meticulous research and persuasive details. I was the ideal reader for his book, having no particular opinion about the identity of Malory. Matthews's argument was convincing, and I was convinced — almost. I still wanted to see how a refutation of Matthews would look. When I learned that Field had written a later study, arguing for Kittredge's old candidate from Warwickshire, I was eager to see how he refuted Matthews. I picked up his book.

On the very first page of *Life and Times,* Professor Field makes the requisite statement concerning the author of the *Morte,* that "all that is known for certain about him comes from his book. Its closing words say its author was called Thomas Malory, that he was a knight and a prisoner, that he wanted his readers to pray for him, and that he finished his book between 3 March 1469 and 4 March 1470."[10] However,

[10] P. J. C. Field, *The Life and Times of Sir Thomas Malory* (Woodbridge, Suffolk: D.|S. Brewer, 1993), 11. Further citations of this work will be in parentheses in the text.

on page 11, Field says that there is certain information about Thomas Malory of Yorkshire that Matthews did not use, and that "the remainder of this chapter will attempt to show that that information fatally undermines the case for Thomas Malory of Hutton having written the *Morte*. The next chapter will argue that that information also excludes all other Thomas Malorys, known or as yet unknown, except one, and shows who did write the *Morte Darthur*" (Field, 11). What he means, it turns out, is that he plans to try to prove that there is no chance that Malory of Studley and Hutton could possibly have been a knight, and therefore the only man who could have written *Le Morte* was Sir Thomas Malory, Knight, of Newbold Revel. After a brief discussion to eliminate a few other candidates for authorship whose cases had come up at various times, Field turns his attention to the family of Thomas Malory of Yorkshire, the candidate backed by Matthews in his "skeptical inquiry." A little Malory family background is in order before we look at Field's argument.

This man's parents were William Malory, sometimes called knight and sometimes called esquire in public records, and his wife Dionisia Tempest Malory (Matthews, 125.) Both were of knightly and prosperous families of Yorkshire, and both inherited manors and other property, so that their joint holdings were large. William's mother was Joan Plumpton, daughter of Sir William Plumpton and Lady Lucy DeRos; his grandmother was Katherine Nunwick, heiress of Sir Ralph Nunwick and wife of Thomas's grandfather the first Sir William Malory; his great-grandfather was Sir Christopher Malory, who married Joan Conyers the heiress of Robert Conyers, and thus brought into the Malory family the manor of Hutton Conyers. Dionisia Malory was the daughter and heiress of Sir William Tempest of Studley and Eleanor Washington, daughter of Sir William Washington (the Washington family home, Washington Hall, was one of the properties that Dionisia Malory inherited; these Washingtons later emigrated to Virginia and became the ancestors of George Washington). Our William and Dionisia Malory joined, by their marriage, extensive properties of these two ancestral lines. They also had a large family, eight sons and six daughters (Matthews, 161–165); it is therefore not surprising that the disposition of their manors and other properties should be complex. There are two documents still extant, a settlement signed in 1462 and a will signed in 1472, which show how William and Dionisia planned for their many children to inherit, in an orderly fashion that precluded the dissolution of the property (Matthews *Inquiry*, 126; Field, 12ff).

Professor Field studied these documents closely and gives us an analysis of their implications for the many children, particularly the sons, of the Malorys. First, Field explains the Malorys's complex scheme for their sons' inheritance, and he tells us that Thomas is not mentioned either in the 1462 settlement or the 1472 will (Field, 16), even though we do know, from pedigrees and other documents, that there was a Thomas among the children of William and Dionisia Malory. Field's search of the public records of Yorkshire yielded little fruit; the family dispositions of property, and other records, tell much about the standing of each of the other sons, but, Field says, "Thomas presents a quite different picture.... Of his seven brothers, only Robert, who died as a child, is recorded fewer times than Thomas, and four who had no rank higher than esquire or gentleman are much better recorded than Thomas is. This group of records is an unpromising basis for belief that Thomas was knighted" (Field, 16).

Next, Professor Field begins his list of all the explanations he could think of, why Thomas, alone of all the Malory sons except Robert, who is thought to have died as a child, should be ignored by William and Dionisia in the disposition of their property. He comes up with these possible explanations:

First, he might have been dead. But this explanation won't work, says Field, because Thomas is mentioned in a Hutton Conyers manor document in 1471.

Second, he might have been thought dead. Maybe this would work for the first settlement, Field tells us, but it will hardly work for both; parents are unlikely to believe mistakenly for ten years that their son is dead, especially since he is mentioned in the manor document above, between the two settlements of property.

Third, he might have been disinherited: "There is no direct evidence, but it would be untypical of the age, and an estate that would provide for six sons would provide for seven" (Field, 17).

Fourth, he might have been the eldest son, to whom primogeniture would have guaranteed his inheritance whether or not he was listed in his parents' will. Not likely, says Field; we know that John was the first because we know that John inherited both Hutton and Studley, and became Sir John.

Fifth, Thomas may have been given his share of the inheritance already, making it unnecessary to mention him. But, says Field, "if Thomas did have an early, large, and complete settlement, it is even more difficult to see why he did not witness the 1462 and other land settlements, to safeguard the rights of his brothers" (Field, 17).

Sixth, Thomas might have been William's son by a previous marriage, although Field had already posited that William was likely married to Dionisia at age five. He goes on to say that in view of William's extreme youth when he married Dionisia, an earlier marriage is "highly improbable" (Field, 17). Indeed, it seems impossible that a boy of three or four could marry, beget a child, and become a widower in time to marry again at age five. Nevertheless, Field considers the possibility, and concludes that that explanation won't work because, in that case, far from being eliminated from inheritance, Thomas would have been the rightful heir of all the Malory property.

Seventh, Thomas might have been William's illegitimate son. And unlike the other possibilities, this one is given no refutation. Professor Field makes it obvious that this is what he believes; he goes on to support this proposition: "Illegitimacy would explain why Thomas was neither a beneficiary nor a witness in the 1462 settlement, although William and Denise had then at most two legitimate adult sons to ensure the continuance of their family" (Field, 18).

It would also explain, says Field, why they were so meticulous in saying "our" sons when they named the other five. And it would explain why the Malorys, in case the lawful heirs of Dionisia's body failed, in other words, in case there were no male Malory heirs in succeeding generations, left the residue of the family property to the Tempest relatives of Dionisia.

Field acknowledges that proposing illegitimacy for Thomas contradicts the family genealogies, but he feels justified in doing so because he thinks illegitimacy would explain the uncertainty in birth order in those genealogies; they list Thomas variously as first, third, fourth, and sixth among the sons. And last:

Eighth, Thomas might have been the child of neither William nor Dionisia but simply a young Malory relative they took in to rear as their own. "His surname, however, shows that his father was a Malory, and there is no trace of any other Malory family in Yorkshire at the time" (Field, 19), and anyway, argues Field, if he was merely a sort of foundling, it is hard to see why the genealogies repeatedly describe Thomas as William and Dionisia's child. Then he goes on to say that it is unlikely in any case that there would be two knights of the same generation in one family, because of the high cost of knighthood.

That is the end of Field's study of possible reasons why Thomas Malory of Studley and Hutton in Yorkshire is not mentioned in any property settlement of his parents. He explains it by saying Thomas was a "byblow," a nothing, who "was and would remain nothing" (20). And that is also the sum total of evidence that the other Sir Thomas Malory, the one from Newbold Revel in Warwickshire, is the author of the *Morte*. With that, the argument for the Newbold Revel man ends; Field considers his theory proven and no further evidence required. From this point on in the book, Sir Thomas of Newbold Revel is simply assumed to be the author of *Le Morte*.

I found myself completely unable to believe in such an argument.

However, the puzzle becomes easy to solve — not only as to why the Yorkshire Malorys did not provide for their son Thomas in their will but also as to why Thomas would be called a knight — if he was not a secular knight at all but a knight of Christ. Everything offered to support the thesis that Malory was illegitimate would support as well his identification as a religious knight. In that case he would not be a beneficiary; having taken a vow of poverty, he would be forbidden to own property. He would not be a witness, either; he had retreated from the secular world of such legalities. The term "our sons" in the settlements simply means "our sons," with no sly suggestion that there is, in spite of all the pedigrees that call Thomas the son of both Dionisia and William, another boy in the family who is not Dionisia's son but only William's. The possible remaindering of the property to the Tempests is normal; after all, most of it came to the Malorys from William's marriage to Dionisia Tempest in the first place, and there is no reason why it should not go back to the Tempests if the Malory line ran out. If Thomas was not mentioned because he had had an early and complete settlement before the death of his parents, that would simply have been according to the customary arrangement for a person entering religious life; the legacy would have been given to the religious order he was entering, rather than to himself, at the time of his entry. And the point that knighthood was too expensive for a family to support two knights at the same time simply vanishes if Thomas was a member of a religious order of knights of Christ.

That point apparently didn't occur to Professor Field, but that doesn't mean he was unaware of the possibility of religious knighthood. In fact, he actually has a footnote, on the very same page as his conclusion, which refers to another religious knight in the Malory family, the prior of the Order of Knights Hospitallers in England, Sir Robert Malory. In that footnote, Field explains that "his knighthood is a consequence of his membership of his order, not of the status of his family" (Field, 20n). Yet even though he knows that the title *knight* sometimes refers to membership in the Order of Knights Hospitallers, he failed to connect that information with Thomas Malory of Yorkshire, who was, like all the Malorys, a kinsman of the prior Sir Robert. Perhaps Field's dedication to the Newbold Revel Malory prevented him from making the connection.

As to the question of Thomas's illegitimacy, that is not subject to an examination of evidence, because there isn't any. We cannot study a record that hints of such an irregularity, because there is none. We cannot compose a valid syllogism, based on any available records, by which we are forced to deduce that Thomas Malory was illegitimate. Only those Malory records that do actually exist are subject to our examination and argument, and they are few. We know little about Thomas's father, William Malory. It is not certain whether he was a knight, for the records disagree. In some documents, such as his will, he is called armiger, that is, esquire, but in others he is called knight, so William Matthews told us in 1966 (Matthews, 122). Field as well as Matthews mentions two sources that disagree on whether William Malory was esquire or knight (Field, 14, 14n). And that is where the question still stands today. We do know, however, that he was married young, to a neighboring girl, and that they had fourteen children. We know that they were both from knightly families, and that when she came into her inheritance and it was added to the holdings of her husband, they became very wealthy indeed; William Malory, who was in his own right the Lord of Studley and Lord of Linton in the county of York, became as well, by right of his wife, the Lord of Washington, the Lord of Trefford in the Durham bishopric, and the Lord of Hutton Conyers, also in Yorkshire County; but that is only the beginning of the extensive holdings of William Malory.[11] Moreover, we know that his descent from knights of several generations, "of fadir syde and modir syde," meant that he was eligible for knighthood. We know that he was a devout Christian who generously shared his goodly means with donations, legacies, and oratories, and that he kept a chapel in his home at Studley for family devotions. In short, what we know from the records indicates that this William Malory lived a decent, honorable

[11] Matthews (120), as well as others, has listed the vast properties of William and Dionisia Malory and remarked that "these extensive and widespread tenures, and their marriage alliances with the most important Yorkshire families, establish them as being several rungs higher on the social and economic ladders than their Warwickshire namesakes; the annual rental [value] of Hutton alone was as great as that of Sir Thomas Malory of Newbold Revel." As for the property of the Newbold Revel Thomas Malory, when he died, probate certified that he owned no property in the county. It appears that he had never owned the manor at Newbold Revel; it seems to have passed from his mother to his wife to his grandson (Field, 190).

life, doing his duties both secular and religious. There is much in the record that does him credit, and nothing that discredits him. Certainly there is nothing to suggest that he was an adulterous husband and the father of an illegitimate child, whom he acknowledged but disinherited anyway because, after all, the boy was a bastard.

~ 3 ~

Thesis: Le Shyvalere

IN OUR TIME, Malory scholars are well aware that William Caxton, Malory's first printer and publisher, was quite freehanded with his editing, even to the point of deleting passages from Malory's text when he chose. But before 1934, the liberties he took were not known, for there was no other version of *Le Morte Darthur* than the Caxton with which it could be compared. But that year, when Oakeshott found the Winchester manuscript, Malory studies changed dramatically. After some time and some contention among the scholars, the newly discovered text was acknowledged to be older than the Caxton and thus closer to what Malory actually wrote.[12] We have already seen one passage deleted by Caxton that is greatly significant to the search for the identity of the author: "This was drawyn by a knyght presoner, sir

[12] This consensus was not immediate. The studies of Lotte Hellinga and Hilton Kelliher as to the Winchester manuscript's age and relation to Caxton convinced scholars that the manuscript had actually been in Caxton's print shop as he was producing his edition of Malory's work. Telltale signs in the Winchester: "There are traces that could indicate that the manuscript had been in Caxton's printing house: a fragment of an indulgence printed by Caxton was used to repair a leaf; and more intriguingly, there were smudges of printing ink, and some very faint offsets of printing types which only Caxton possessed" (Hellinga, *Caxton in Focus*, 90). Both the Pierpont Morgan manuscript of Caxton's *Le Morte Darthur* and the Winchester manuscript were on display, next to each other, in the Caxton quincentenary exhibition in 1976. An abstract of that exhibition noted, "A certain piquancy was added to their temporary conjunction here by the suggestion, then only recently put forward, that the two volumes had once before occupied premises together, namely Caxton's office at Westminster during the 1480s" (*The British Library Journal* 3, no. 2 [Autumn 1977]).

Thomas Malleorre." Because that passage confirmed the suspicion that Malory had written at least part of his book in prison, since 1934 it has been given intense attention.

But there is another passage, deleted by Caxton but recovered in Winchester, which has even more bearing on the search for Malory's identity than the "knyght presoner" passage, yet it has hardly been noticed. It comes right after the "Tale of Lancelot and Guenevere":

> And here on the othir syde folowyth the Most Pyteuous Tale of the Morte Arthure Saunz Gwerdon *Par le Shyvalere Sir Thomas Malleorre, knyght.* (emphasis mine; Malory, *Works,* 816)

Scholars have assumed that Malory is merely being redundant here, possibly accidentally or possibly for emphasis of his knightly rank; they have not considered the word *Shyvalere* to be anything except an unnecessary iteration of *knyght.* But it is far more than that. With the word *Shyvalere,* Malory claims his identity.

It is not customary today to call an English knight a chevalier, and it was not customary in the fifteenth century either. *Chevalier* is, of course, a French word, designating a certain rank in the hierarchy of French nobility, equivalent to the English designation *knight.* The two words may have been used interchangeably during the two centuries or so after the Conquest when the French language, along with the conquerors, took over England, but that time had long passed when Malory was alive. English, with all its various dialects to be sure, was the language of Malory's England. His very project, translating old French texts into English, testifies to that fact. In his day, an English knight was called a knight. He was so called in life, and his fictional equivalent was so called by Thomas Malory in *Le Morte Darthur.* Even Sir Launcelot du Lac, whom readers know very well to be a Frenchman, is called a knight in *Le Morte.* That is his proper title, for he serves an English king; he is a member of Arthur's Round Table, and the fact that he is a Frenchman is rarely mentioned. Certainly he is not called a chevalier, and neither is any other of Arthur's knights. In the body of *Le Morte Darthur,* Malory uses the word *knight,* in singular and plural forms, 4,505 times. He also uses the word *chevalier* eight times, in the following instances.[13]

First, when Lancelot has accepted the humiliation of being banished from court by Guenevere, and embraces his penance, he hides and goes by an assumed French title as a disguise, in order to divorce himself from the great fame of Lancelot, the greatest knight. The name that he uses is "Le Shyvalere Ill Mafeete." It appears in the text six times. Three of those times, Malory translates it for us; he says the phrase means "the knyght that hath trespassed." The very fact that Malory offers a translation is evidence that his readers would not have found *chevalier* and *knight* interchangeable words. Those are the only times Malory uses the word *chevalier* in referring to one of his characters (Malory, *Works,* 826–832).

Then, in giving us the title of one of his sources, Malory uses the word twice: "Than, as the Freynsch booke sayth, sir Launcelot was called many dayes aftyr 'The Shyvalere de Charyott,' and so he ded many dedys and grete adventures. And so we leve of here of 'Le Shyvalere Le Charyote,' and turne we to thys tale" (Malory, *Works,* 800).

In fact, Malory follows standard English usage. He uses the French *chevalier* only eight times, and only in particular cases: in one alias assumed for disguise, and in one book title. He uses *knight* thousands of times. He was an Englishman, and that was the way the English spoke of knights in his day.

However.

There was one band of knights, in England and elsewhere, who were customarily called the Chevaliers. They were the Order of St. John of Jerusalem, the Knights Hospitallers. The appellation *Chevalier* was apparently taken over from the Templars; in its history of the Templars, the Royal Australian Historical Society tells us, "The original Knights who joined the Order (known as Chevaliers) came from the North of France as members of the First Crusade under Godfrey of

13 Kato Tomomi, *A Concordance to "The Works of Sir Thomas Malory"* (Tokyo: University of Tokyo Press, 1974).

Bouillon who captured Jerusalem on the 15 July 1099." Today it is the practice in the reconstituted brotherhood that claims descent from the original Hospitaller order, the Americas Priory of the Knights Hospitaller of Malta, for notables to be given the title *Chevalier,* in recognition of that ancient usage among the knight-monks of the Hospital. In 1629, the French government tried to restrict by ordinance the use of the title by anyone not qualified by lineage and by his particular place in a noble family to assume the title of a chevalier; "a younger son, however, who could not claim a title by other means might be admitted to the Order of the Hospital of St. John (Knights of Malta) and thereby assume the title of chevalier."[14] From its beginning, the order classified its members into three ranks—priests, Knights of Justice, and serving brothers—however, the government of France recognized all members as Chevaliers. The title belonged to the order at large, just as the castle that is today called the Crac des Chevaliers, built by the Hospitallers in 1140, partially on the foundation of a previous building, and formerly called le Crac de l'Ospital, belonged to the order at large. The Hospitallers were known as the Chevaliers.

14 *Encyclopaedia Britannica Online,* s.v. "chevalier," www.britannica.com/topic/chevalier.

English knights in Malory's time were not called Chevaliers, unless they were Hospitallers, all of whom by custom held that title. Sir Thomas Malory told us, right there in his book, that he was one of the Chevaliers, and he told us his standing within the order, knight. It could not be plainer. His book was written "Par le Shyvalere Sir Thomas Malleorre, knyght." We simply have not had eyes to see.

And so to the thesis of this book. I contend that Thomas Malory of Yorkshire, identified in 1966 by William Matthews as the author of *Le Morte Darthur*, is the author, and that he was a professed knight of the monastic Order of St. John of Jerusalem, the Knights Hospitallers. On the day of his profession in the order, he was given the rank *Knight of Justice*, the title *Knight*, and the appellation *Sir Thomas Malory*. The title was a function of his standing in his order rather than his place in the secular social hierarchy. We began by saying that not only do we not know who Malory was, but we don't know why we don't know who he was. Note well: this identification of Sir Thomas Malory as a Knight Hospitaller not only tells us who Malory was; it also tells us why we have not known. It is difficult — maybe impossible — to think of any other role in life that would explain the invisibility of our author, but his membership in a monastic order perfectly explains it. The Knights Hospitaller were not only knights; they were monks, living in their monasteries when they were not actually at war, largely isolated from society. They were enjoined by their order not to seek attention for themselves. The following chapters will present evidence that the elusive Thomas Malory, author of *Le Morte Darthur*, was one of these monk-knights, a member of the monastic Order of St. John of Jerusalem, a Hospitaller — a Chevalier.

SECTION TWO

Taking a Closer Look

4

Who Were the Hospitallers? Who Were the Cistercians?

THE MALORYS OF Yorkshire had strong ties to two great religious orders, the Knights Hospitallers of St. John of Jerusalem, and the Cistercians, which blend together in their influence on the Malory family and thus on Thomas Malory and *Le Morte Darthur,* so that it is impossible to separate them. From their inception, both orders were tremendously influenced by the same man, Bernard of Clairvaux. Bernard was born in 1090 of the highest level of nobility in France, in the same region that gave rise at the same time to the flowering of Arthurian legends, chivalry, and *fin amour,* or courtly love, so dominant in medieval European culture. Bernard was born "in the family castle"[15] near Dijon and Troyes, the son of devout parents of seven children. His mother dedicated each one of them at birth to God and the Church. Both parents died when Bernard was young, his father while on crusade. Bernard apparently hated the life of privilege and luxury to which he was heir, and after his mother died, he resolved to leave it for a life of contemplation, silence, and prayer — in short, to become a monk. He became in time the flower of the Cistercian Order.

The other religious order with tremendous significance in the story of the Yorkshire Malorys is the Order of Hospitallers of St. John

15 Helen Walker Homan, "Cistercian Order of the Common Observance." In *Knights of Christ,* 25–41. Englewood Cliffs, NJ: Prentice-Hall, 1957. Catholic Culture. https://www.catholicculture.org/culture/library/view.cfm?recnum=4425. Further citations of this source will be in parentheses in the text.

of Jerusalem, established in the Holy Land at about the time of the First Crusade. And like the influence of the cloistered and contemplative Cistercians, the influence of the warrior Hospitallers permeates *Le Morte Darthur*. Both of these orders trace their early history to the influence of Bernard.

Cistercians were essentially disaffected Benedictines. The great old order of St. Benedict, whose Rule of Life was laid down in 533, had become lax and worldly, in the eyes of some of its members, who longed for a return to the old stringent discipline of silence and austerity. In 1098 Robert, abbot of Molesme in France, one of those so moved, left his monastery, taking with him a handful of like-minded monks including one Alberic and the Englishman Stephen Harding. They set up a new home in the swampy land nearby, on a site that they had successfully begged from its viscount owner, who apparently considered it useless to himself. The reeds growing in the marsh there were called *cistels*, and they gave the name *Cisteaux* or *Citeaux* to the new foundation, in Latin *Cistercium*, and *Cistercians* to the men who lived there among the reeds. Times were rough, not surprisingly, for a few years. The population of the new monastery declined. Their first prior, Robert, was recalled by the pope to his former Benedictine house at Molesme; Alberic, the second prior, died. Stephen Harding became the third and was struggling to hold together his little band of monks when, in 1112, Bernard showed up with his brothers and his friends. Prior Stephen answered a summons to the door, and

> without the portals waited a company of thirty-one horsemen, elaborately mounted and richly dressed — all

> young noblemen of Burgundy. Their leader was the winning Bernard of Fontaines, twenty-one years of age.... Deeply religious, [he] had been drawn as a magnet toward Citeaux. The extraordinary thing was that upon announcing his decision to become a monk, all his four brothers, all his cousins, and many gay young men of his acquaintance declared in a body that they too would become monks and would follow him ... [to] Citeaux. Abbot Stephen could scarcely believe his ears as Bernard, dismounting from his horse, knelt in the dust and begged that the company of thirty-one be admitted as postulants. It was the saving of Citeaux (Homan).

That was in 1112. By 1115, three new Cistercian houses had been established, and Bernard, now twenty-five years old, was sent out by Abbot Stephen to establish another, this time in a deep, wide valley called the Valley of Bitterness. On June 25, 1115, Bernard renamed it the Valley of Light, Claire Vallee, which shortly came to be called Clairvaux, and Bernard eventually became known by the name of this first house of his own founding. That was only the beginning of the career of the man who is widely held to be the most important man of twelfth-century Christendom. He became a statesman, diplomat, theologian, writer, friend of popes, and a dozen other things, even eventually a canonized saint and a Doctor of the Church. But the role that concerns us here is his founding of monasteries. Homan continues: "Under the sweep and power of his inspiration, the Order spread out from France into most of contemporary Europe, establishing foundations in Italy, Germany, England, Austria, Belgium, Switzerland, France, Scotland, Portugal, Hungary, Ireland, Poland, Bohemia, and all Scandinavia. When Bernard died in 1153 ... there were some 350 Cistercian houses scattered over the Continent" (Homan). Bernard was the primary inspiration and founder of monasteries of the Cistercian Order. One of them was Fountains Abbey in Yorkshire, a few yards away from the home of Thomas Malory's ancestors and, eventually, his own home; indeed, the family donated some land to the monastery in 1347.

It was typical of the Cistercians founding a new house that a group of disgruntled members of existing Benedictine monasteries, longing for a firmer discipline, a return to the old austere rules, would band together and start over under the guidance of Bernard. These Benedictines came in time to be a new order, the Cistercians. So it was with the monks of Fountains Abbey in Yorkshire. In 1131, a group of Benedictine monks at St. Mary's Abbey in York, longing for silence, solitude, prayer, and a stricter observance of St. Benedict's Rule, decided to leave and start over. This time, the remaining monks and their abbot tried to prevent those few from leaving, actually coming to blows and much discord. However, with the help of Archbishop Thurston of York, who sheltered them in his own house for a short time and donated a piece of land for their new home, they succeeded in breaking away. They went out to the country nearby, to a place called Skelldale on the banks of the little river Skell, and set up their camp on the site that the archbishop had given them. Although the monks were grateful for the gift, "the spot of ground had never been inhabited, unless by wild beasts, being overgrown with wood and brambles, lying between two steep hills and rocks, covered with wood on all sides, more proper for a retreat for wild beasts than the human species."[16] For nearly two years they lived a primitive life, their only food what they could procure with their hands and donations of loaves of bread from the archbishop, and their only shelter the overhanging rocks along the river bank that formed little caves, and the trees.

The first tree to shelter them was a mighty elm, but soon they turned instead to a copse of yews, which history has since named the Seven Sisters.[17] Tim Hills, writing about these remarkable trees, notes that "anyone who has sheltered beneath the thick foliage of a healthy yew will have experienced how rain is deflected to the outer extremity of the canopy, and be aware that a grove could provide

[16] John Burton, *Monasticon Eboracense* (1758), quoted in William Gilpin, *Remarks on Forest Scenery and Other Woodland Views* (Edinburgh: Fraser, 1834).

[17] Etching by Jacob George Strutt, *Sylva Britannica* (London: Henry G. Bohn, 1822–1826).

shelter for many people."[18] Also, he continues, our knowledge of the great ages of some yews means that there is no reason why a grove could not date from the twelfth century. "Two yew trees now grow at the Seven Sisters site," and one of them "is certainly one of the original trees"; a second may be another. These were alive well into the twenty-first century, in the care of the National Trust. The Seven Sisters and the caves along the river offered shelter to the monks for two years. The winters were rough. Some of the men died. Still, they had left their home abbey by their own choice, and only one of them turned back. They had achieved the austerity they wanted, and it was indeed austere. Finally, the deprivation and exposure wore down their spirits, and they decided to write to Bernard at Clairvaux and ask permission to join him there. He invited them to come.

But then, providentially, as they were preparing to depart for France in 1132, Hugh, Dean of York and a wealthy man, asked permission to join the Cistercians at Skelldale and was accepted with joy. He brought with him his possessions, including "many books which he had collected at considerable cost."[19] These books became the germ of the library and the scriptorium at what was destined to be the great Fountains Abbey. The tide had turned in favor of the new Cistercians, and the growth of their prosperity had begun; eventually Fountains became one of the greatest monasteries in all of England, claiming its foundation from the Frenchman Bernard of Clairvaux, always maintaining its allegiance to his Cistercian Order.

This is the order that has long been recognized as the governing influence in the mystical story of the quest of the Holy Grail, as related in the early thirteenth-century prose Vulgate Cycle. Pauline Matarasso, translator of *The Quest of the Holy Grail,* mentions the influence of St. Bernard on the *Quest* legends, and comments that "the author's view is essentially monastic, since monks and hermits, and most of them

[18] Tim Hills, "The Fountains Abbey Yews," 6, quoting Dr. John Burton, *Monasticon Evorancese,* 1758, quoting William Gilpin, *Remarks on Forest Scenery,* 1834, https://www.ancient-yew.org/pdfs/Fountains%20Abbey.pdf.

[19] *Fraser's Magazine for Town and Country 14* (1876): 349.

white-robed ones [Cistercians wear white habits], are spiritual guides to the questors."[20] In great detail, in his 1934 "The Cistercian Influence in *The Quest of the Holy Grail*," Edmund J. McCorkell also explicates the influence he sees.[21] Discussing possible authorship of the Grail story, he says that it "has long been a matter of dispute, but recent studies have made it possible to say that the evidence points to a Cistercian monk, or at least a writer who came under the influence of the Cistercian movement.... The *Queste del Saint Graal* as a whole incorporates those mystical ideas which radiated from Citeaux." St. Bernard, McCorkell says, by "his eloquent tongue and pen produced and propagated a science of mystical theology which was taken up in the many monasteries which sprang up in nearly every country of Western Europe. The Cistercian movement, in short, produced Cistercian mysticism" (McCorkell, 7). This he describes as Catholic mysticism of any age but peculiarly intense, and with added discipline first propagated by St. Bernard — asceticism, detachment, humility, resistance of natural cravings, irrevocable devotion to God that entails cutting oneself off from ties to family. "That the quest of the Holy Grail as told by Malory is filled with these and other general mystical ideas, who can doubt?" asks McCorkell (McCorkell, 8). Then he goes on to give examples from Malory's work: the Grail, symbolizing grace, makes its first appearance at Pentecost, "and they were all alighted of the grace of the Holy Ghost" and set off on their quest.

> A note of severe asceticism is sustained throughout. When Lancelot endeavors to begin aright by confession, he is given, as a penance, a hair shirt, perpetual abstinence from meat, and daily attendance at Mass. Bors, following confession, goes on a diet of

[20] *The Quest of the Holy Grail*, trans. Pauline Matarasso (Middlesex: Penguin Books, 1969), 21. Further citations of this work will be in parentheses in the text.

[21] Edmund J. McCorkell, C.S.B. "The Cistercian Influence in *The Quest of the Holy Grail*," *The Pamphlet* 29 (Toronto: The Institute of Medieval Studies, University of Toronto, 1934), 5–15. Further citations of this work will be in parentheses in the text.

> bread and water … and sleeps on the bare floor; and all this because he has committed one sin in his past life…. Further, all knights-errant are guided by hermits…. They have dreams and visions which only hermits can interpret…. In brief, the quest of the Grail is a pilgrimage of grace (McCorkell, 9).

And there are specific elements in Malory's telling of the quest story that remind the reader of Cistercian life, such as Galahad's being found at an abbey "in a great valley," like Clairvaux; the white habit worn by Malory's hermits, like the white habit of the Cistercians; and "the striking circumstance of so many deserted chapels which the knights-errant stumble upon, which indicated that religious life is in need of the rejuvenation which the Cistercians gave it" (McCorkell, 10). Malory makes full use, as well, of the Bernardian doctrine of humility as explicated in the saint's homiletic treatise *De Gradibus Humilitatis,* steps to humility, when Lancelot realizes that his pride has kept him from union with God. "Cistercian mysticism following St. Bernard puts the greatest emphasis upon humility as the foundation of Christian knighthood," points out McCorkell. In addition to this particularly Cistercian view of humility found in the quest, there is also the detailed analysis of the way the Three Persons of the Blessed Trinity operate on the human soul, to lead men to Truth; all of this is specifically Cistercian. And finally, there is the presence of Solomon in the quest tale, reminding the reader that St. Bernard's chief published work was his sermons on the *Canticles of Solomon* (*Song of Songs*). McCorkell quotes Malory's renowned editor Eugene Vinaver, saying that he "committed himself to the opinion that the whole Lancelot-Grail cycle, except the Merlin section, 'was the product of a religious man steeped in the doctrines of Citeaux'" (McCorkell, 14). Karen Ralls goes further; she simply states that the *Queste* was written, in 1215, by a Cistercian monk.[22]

[22] Karen Ralls, *The Templars and the Grail* (Wheaton, IL: Quest Books, 2003),138. Further citations of this work will be in parentheses in the text.

And then there is that other religious order that interests us, the Knights of St. John, the Hospitallers. Whereas Bernard of Clairvaux had tremendous influence on the Cistercians, it appears that in the case of the Hospitallers the order is reversed, and they significantly influenced Bernard, by way of the other monastic-military order, the Knights of the Temple. The Hospital was born in the Holy Land at about the time of the First Crusade, which was also about the time that Bernard was born in France, in the 1090s. This order, which became in time the greatest order of fighting monks, started as a loosely connected group of men led by one Peter Gerard, men who devoted themselves to nursing wounded Crusaders and pilgrims. In 1104, Baldwin I, king of Jerusalem, recognized and confirmed the Hospitallers as an order of monks.[23] This was just eight years before the young Bernard of Clairvaux joined the Cistercians. The new Order of Hospitallers flourished, eventually becoming Crusader knights as well as monks. Twenty-four years after the Hospitallers' founding, in 1128, at the Council of Troyes, a now older Bernard presided over the foundation of a brother order, the Knights of the Temple of Jerusalem, the Templars; he wrote the rule for the new order himself. That order, being also an order of fighting monks, was inevitably closely associated with the Hospitallers, and in time, when the Templars no longer existed as a recognized separate entity, the remnants of it fused with the Order of

Hospitaller Grand Master Guillaume de Clermont defending Acre in 1291; Dominique-Louis Papety

[23] Richard Broun, *Synoptical Sketch of the Illustrious and Sovereign Order of Knights Hospitallers of St. John of Jerusalem, and of the Venerable Langue of England* (London: Printed for the Order, 1857), 13. Further citations of this work will be in parentheses in the text.

Hospitallers. In about 1136, Bernard wrote, at the request of Hugh, Master of the Templars, what became one of his most famous compositions, a letter "In Praise of the New Knighthood," praising the new monk-knights and exhorting them to persevere on their chosen path. That path was to keep their religious vows of poverty, chastity, and obedience, but to combine their vocation as monks with a new vocation as warriors. Bernard begins thus: "A new knighthood seems recently to have appeared on the earth, and in that part of the world which the Orient from on high once visited in the flesh. As he then drove out the powers of darkness by the strength of his mighty hand, so he now drives out their supporters, the children of disbelief."[24] The reader will recognize the acclaim for the Crusader; it is more specifically the monk warriors who are being praised by Bernard. The Order of Templars was one of Bernard's great projects, and this letter was written to their leader, to praise and encourage the new brotherhood. However, this order was not the first order of fighting monks; that distinction belongs to the Hospitallers.

In 1118, ten years before the establishment of the Templars at the Council of Troyes, when Raymond du Puy became the second leader of the Knights of the Hospital, he instituted a great change in the mission and identity of the order: henceforward, while keeping to their sacred task of nursing the sick and injured and offering hospitality to the poor, they would, additionally, take up the sword for Christ, in defense of the holy places. Raymond's words, in instituting this new role and identity, were these: "I desire, therefore, that every brother, who shall engage himself in the service of the poor, and in defense of the Catholic Church, shall maintain and observe, by the grace of God, the three vows which they have made.... The soldiers of Jesus Christ are destined to fight only for his glory.... After a due exercise of charity, they should take the sword in hand, for the extermination of Mahometans, and of all who abandon the true

[24] St. Bernard of Clairvaux, *In Praise of the New Knighthood: A Treatise on the Knights Templar and the Holy Places of Jerusalem*, trans. M. Conrad Greenia, O.C.S.O., with an introduction by Malcolm Barber, Cistercian Fathers Series 19B (Kalamazoo, MI and Spencer, MA: Cistercian, 2000), 33. Further citations of this work will be in parentheses in the text.

religion."[25] The Hospitallers were present but loosely organized at the First Crusade in the 1090s, nursing the wounded. Under their first leader, Peter Gerard, shortly after this crusade, they became a formal order, the patriarch of Jerusalem hearing their vows and clothing them in their new habit. Pope Paschal II shortly after that formally approved the establishment of the Hospitallers by a bull in 1113 (Porter, vol. 1, 3). The new identity of the order, as warriors as well as monks, came in 1118 under their second leader, Raymond du Puy. Under Raymond, the monks were invested as knights, and have been called such ever since, even to the present day. It is easy to identify passages in St. Bernard's famous letter to the Templars that indicate he was familiar with Raymond's words to the Hospitallers when they took on their new role as fighter monks. Most striking is this one:

Raymond: "From the moment they shall have devoted themselves to this sacred cause, they should animate themselves by the example of the Maccabees; those holy soldiers and martyrs, who combated so gloriously, in the maintenance of their religion, and who, though few in number, have often, by the assistance of God, overthrown the most formidable armies" (du Puy, quoted in Porter, vol. 1, 31).

Bernard: "They are mindful of the words of Maccabees, *It is simple enough for a multitude to be vanquished by a handful. It makes no difference in the sight of God of heaven whether he grants deliverance by the hands of few or of many; for victory in war does not depend on a big army, but bravery is the gift from heaven*" (St. Bernard, 47).

It is not remarkable that Bernard should have been aware of the Hospitallers, or that he in some ways should invite the Templars to emulate them. The Hospitallers were a sort of older brother order to the Templars, engaged in similar enterprises in the Holy Land, for as long as the Order of the Temple lasted. It lasted until 1311, 183 years; the Order of Hospitallers goes on. When the Templars were disbanded, all of their landed property was given to the Hospital, by decree of Pope Clement V,

[25] Raymond du Puy, quoted by Whitworth Porter, *History of the Knights of Malta, or the Order of St. John of Jerusalem*, 2 vols. (London: Longman, Brown, Green, Longmans, and Roberts, 1858), 1:31. Further citations of this work will be in parentheses in the text.

and many surviving members of that order joined the Hospitallers. But the two orders were always closely connected. They can be seen as brothers, fighting shoulder to shoulder to defend the Holy Land against the encroachments of the Muslim. Despite the sort of sibling rivalry that almost inevitably grew up between them, and the mission of hospitality that belonged to the one order and not to the other, they were such close kin that when one died, the other inherited, and even today the two orders are frequently confused.

However, although it is not remarkable that Bernard knew both orders of fighting monks, there is something remarkable about this story—that is, that the saint who fostered the two religious orders should have had his birth and beginning at the same time and place as the birth and beginning of the stories of the quest for the Holy Grail, and from them the whole chivalric tradition including King Arthur, and that the same saint should have propagated those stories and that tradition even as he propagated his religious orders. Pete Craft comments that "the Grail Quest in *Le Morte D'Arthur* relies chiefly upon the Cistercian-influenced morality that later found its way into the French Vulgate Cycle. This set of values sprang primarily from St. Bernard.... According to Bernard, spiritual knights should conscientiously differ from worldly knights ... by not taking wives or having children, not owning personal property, and striving to look the same as their fellow Templars.... In other words, Bernard viewed the new knighthood as an essentially ascetic monastic order whose martial battles glorified God."[26] After the dissolution of the Order of Knights of the Temple, all that was left of the Templars was to be found in the houses of the Hospitallers. For our investigation, the most important item of that inheritance is the rich trove of Arthurian lore that eventually found its way into *Le Morte Darthur*.

Something new was in the air in Clairvaux, in Troyes, in the twelfth century, something that influenced not only the holy man Bernard as he spoke to the Council of Troyes and submitted his proposed knightly rule

[26] Pete Craft, "Malory's Conflicting Conceptions of Knighthood," April 12, 2001, pages unnumbered, vault.hanover.edu/~battles/arthur/lancelot/htm.

Fountains Abbey viewed from Studley Royal Garden, Malory home

for the new order of Templars, something that spread out across France, across Europe, across England. It was not merely chivalry but quest, the quest of holiness symbolized by the Grail. Alongside that theme was love, not only love of God and neighbor but *courtois, fin amour,* the courtly love of the romances. It seeped into the court of Eleanor of Aquitaine, the daughter of a troubadour father, even as Bernard was doing spiritual battle with her for her soul; from Eleanor it went to the court of her daughter Marie de Champagne; from there it spread to the lais of Marie's devoted troubadours and to the tales by Chrétien de Troyes that Marie commissioned, and to the literature of the world. But it started and began to flourish in Clairvaux, in Troyes, in the same places and at the same time as the knightly order of Templars and the mystical order of the Cistercians. That something in the air gave us both the brotherhood of warriors of the Round Table and the mystical quest of the Holy Grail.

At this point the reader may be wondering what all this discussion may have to do with our own quest, for the identity of the author of the *Morte.* The answer is, quite simply, everything. G.K. Chesterton tells the anecdote of a man who sets out on a journey in search for Truth, travels far and wide in his pursuit, and eventually ends up back where he started, and finds the Truth in his own backyard. Our search for the identity of Sir Thomas Malory has similarly led us far and wide, into the histories of Bernard and Marie and Chrétien and others. But after all the wandering, it leads us inevitably back to England, to Yorkshire, to the Cistercian monastery at Fountains Abbey, which is not figuratively at all but quite literally in Thomas Malory's own backyard.

5

WHO WERE THE MALORYS?

IN OCTOBER OF 1451, in accordance with the working-out of the terms of the will of her father, Sir William Tempest, Dionisia Tempest Malory came into her inheritance. According to the probate documents, she was thirty-six years old at the time, by which we calculate that she was born in late 1414 or in 1415. She married William Malory, who may or may not have been Sir William; records disagree. Both the Tempests and the Malorys were long-established and well-connected families; they had had and were to have a noble history. Dionisia's grandmother was Eleanor Washington, of the family who became the ancestors of George Washington, the ranking general of the American Revolution, who led his ragtag force to victory over the British army and became the first president of the United States of America. As for the Malorys, John Bennett Boddie traces their pedigree back to the Magna Carta, and further back to the kings of Scotland (958 Malcolm, King of Scotland; 1043 Bethoc (Beatrix), daughter of Malcolm and Queen of Scotland; and so on), and forward down to the Malorys we know, of Hutton Conyers and Studley Royal manors.[27]

And they were prosperous, these Malorys. Hutton Conyers, which had come to them by the marriage of William's great-grandfather Sir Christopher Malory to Joan Conyers, was a fortified and moated manor set in a twelve-hundred-acre park, probably much like

[27] John Bennett Boddie, *Virginia Historical Genealogies* (Redwood City, CA: Clearfield, 1954; repr., Baltimore: Genealogical, 1990, 1996, 1999, 2005), 103–107. Further citations of this source will appear in the text in parentheses.

Markenfield

its neighbor Markenfield Hall. Hutton is gone, but Markenfield is still very much the same as it was in the fifteenth century; in 2012, it celebrated the seven hundredth anniversary of its fortification; and anyone interested in seeing how Hutton probably looked can tour Markenfield on certain days. It is interesting to trace the gradual disappearance of the old Malory manor of Hutton Conyers in the comments of various reporters over the last century. In 1905, the publication of the Virginia Historical Society reported, as still standing, on the home of our Malorys: "A picturesque gable on the north side, and richly ornamented ceiling (the lion of the Mallory arms is displayed in the compartments) in a neglected apartment in the southeast wing remain of this date," showing that the house, then in use as a farm, had once been the home of the lords of the manor. The reporter goes on to say that, by tradition, the house was attacked during the Civil War by Parliamentarians; the Sir John Mallory of that time was a zealous Royalist. "Several cannon balls and some weapons of war have been found in the fields around.... The mansion is shaded by a goodly show of great sycamores, which give it a pleasing

From a recent drawing. HUTTON CONYERS, YORKSHIRE, ENGLAND. See Oct. 1905 Mag., p. 218.

air of solemnity, and seem still to assert its claims to a rank above that of an ordinary farm house."[28] That was in 1905. In 1966, the house was gone, reported William Matthews; all that was left of Hutton was a scar on the ground, the ghost of its moat, and from that he deduced that the manor had been somewhat larger than Markenfield (Matthews, 122). Today, even the ghost is gone. *British History Online* notes: "Just north of the village [of Hutton Conyers] is the site of Hutton Hall, the old moated manor-house of the Conyers, and subsequently of the Mallorys. There is no trace of the park which once surrounded it."[29]

There is another manor, still thriving today, which was probably much like Hutton Conyers; that is Norton Conyers. Boddie tells us this: "About 1200 a division of the Conyers' estates was made between Roger, son of Robert de Conyers, the right heir, and his uncle Roger. Hutton was allotted to the elder branch" (Boddie, 103) and Norton to the younger. In the fourteenth century, Joan Conyers, heir of Robert

28 "The Mallory Family," *The Virginia Magazine of History and Biography* 13 (October 1, 1905): 218, https://archive.org/stream/jstor-4242740/4242740_djvu.txt.

29 "Hutton Conyers," in *A History of the County of North York Riding*, vol. 1, ed. William Page (London, 1914), 403–405.

Conyers of Hutton, married Sir Christopher Malory, bringing Hutton Conyers into the Malory family. After that time, that manor was always a Malory holding but with strong familial ties to Conyers until time erased the house at Hutton from the landscape. In fact, our Thomas Malory's aunt, his mother's sister Isabella Norton, was the wife of Richard Norton; their son and thus Thomas's first cousin was Sir John Norton alias Conyers (the "alias" was the result of a Conyers of a previous generation's having married a Norton and taken the surname of his bride). Norton Conyers is still prospering, barely two miles away from the scar on the ground that is all that is left of Hutton. It is in the care of Sir James Graham, eleventh Baronet Graham, and Lady Halina Graham. Sir James and Lady Halina open their home to visitors on certain days, and they are most kind and welcoming in relating the history of their ancient house. In Thomas Malory's day, the families of Norton and Hutton Conyers undoubtedly spent much time in each other's home. Hutton is gone, and after centuries of changes to Norton Conyers, the chief feature remaining from medieval times is the outline of its great hall, and even that has been shortened somewhat; however, it is gratifying to stand in that room and think that we are standing in the footprints of the author of *Le Morte Darthur*.

Sir James and Lady Halina Graham

But in the fifteenth century, Hutton Conyers was the home of a large and lively family of Malory children, and their home was considerably expanded when their mother received her legacy. The home of the Washingtons, Washington Hall, came to Dionisia Malory as part of it, along with Studley, Trefford, and other properties; a probate document lists them: "divers lands, etc in the same places and at Brompton near Northallerton, Coppedhewyk, Aldfeld, Winkesley, Wodhous and Grantley, five messuages in Westgate in Ripon, and three acres of land adjoining them, 6s. of annual rent out of the tenements of John Whixley, jun., in Ripon, 8d. of rent out of the ten't of John Crouper there, and 14d. of rent out of the ten't of Wm. Roche there, to her and the lawful heirs of her body."[30] Thus William Malory, Dionisia's husband, who was already lord of the manor of Hutton Conyers in his own right, became a great deal richer, and became Lord of Studley, Lord of Washington, and Lord of Trafford as well, by right of his wife. Matthews comments that "John Leland, reporting on Northallertonshire in

30 John Richard Walbran, *Memorials of the Abbey of St Mary of Fountains, including a Genealogical Account of the Lords of Studley Royal, 1841*, vol. 2, part 1, The Publications of the Surtees Society, vol. 57 (Ripon: William Harrison, 1876), 69. Further citations of this work will be in parentheses in the text.

Norton Conyers

1535, declared that the gentlemen of most name in that wapentake were the Strangways of Harlesey, the Nortons of Norton Conyers, and the Malorys of Studley and Hutton" (Matthews, 119). Matthews says further, "At the time *Le Morte Darthur* was being written, [the Malorys] owned land and messuages at these places within four miles of Ripon: Woodhouse, Studley, Grantley, Sawley, Aldfield, Mackershaw, Winksley (Winkelsey as they sometimes called it). Studley and Sawley were manors, and twelve miles west of Ripon,they also owned a manor at Linton-in-Craven" (Matthews, 120). Within Ripon, they also owned several properties, plus land in Sharow and Copt Hewick, property at Dishforth, a manor at Sand Hutton, more property in Thornton-le-Street, a manor at Hackforth, another at Trafford in Durham, another at Piercebridge, and still another at Hylton Floghen near Inglewood Forest, "the locale of some of the better Arthurian romances written in the North just before [Thomas] Malory's day" (Matthews, 120). And that is not all. They had a half share in the manor of Upper Helmsley (Helmsley, in ancient times called Hamelak, was the seat of the DeRos family, ancestors of William Malory, since before 1100),

Studley in the eighteenth century, replaced medieval house

and several other properties, and — what may be significant to Thomas Malory's dialect — possibly interests in Lincolnshire as well (Matthews, 120). Altogether these Malorys were wealthy and prominent members of Yorkshire society; Matthews tells us that "these extensive and wide-spread tenures, and their marriage alliances with the most important Yorkshire families, establish them as being several rungs higher on the social and economic ladders than their Warwickshire namesakes: the annual rental of Hutton alone was as great as that of all the holdings of Sir Thomas Malory of Newbold Revel" (Matthews, 120). However, the family manors that interest us the most are Studley and Hutton, because of their location, so close to the grounds of the great abbey of Fountains. In fact, if we google "Studley Royal" today, we see that that manor, now in National Trust care, is billed as "Studley Royal, including the ruins of Fountains Abbey." The National Trust, current owner of the old Malory manor at Studley, considers it and Fountains Abbey the same place, with the one included in the other. Studley remained a Malory holding until late in the seventeenth century; Mary Malory, the daughter of John Malory, inherited the manor in 1666. She married an Aislabie, thus passing Studley into Aislabie ownership. Studley and Fountains Abbey were joined in 1693, when Mary Malory Aislabie's son John Aislabie, heir to Studley, bought the abbey ruins in order to expand his garden. The other family home of William and Dionisia Malory, Hutton Conyers, was not adjacent to Fountains but still not far away, close enough for the family to have gone freely between the childhood home of the mother and that of the father. The abbey is situated more or less between those two manors.

So what do we know about the fifteenth-century Malorys, who made their home here and are claimed to be the family of Sir Thomas Malory who wrote *Le Morte Darthur*? We know that William and Dionisia were country neighbors from their birth. Possibly they were promised in marriage by their two families even as babies, or possibly their ages were more divergent, so that they "found" each other later. Their wedding date is not known; nor do we know William's birth date; various researchers put his birth at various dates. Professor

Field speculates that they were married when William was five years old and Dionisia a little older. He points out that Dionisia's father brought a lawsuit on William's behalf in 1422, with the implication that at that time William was both a minor and already married to Dionisia. He then goes on to say that something in the "ruling seems to imply that they thought that William's minority had sixteen years to run" (Field, 12). He does not tell us what is in the document that leads him to this conclusion; he merely gives us his conclusion. It may be true. However, he then puts Dionisia's age at the birth of her first baby at twenty, and that doesn't seem right. A girl who is married when she is a little older than five — six? seven? — if she proves capable of bearing children, will begin soon after puberty, and Dionisia Malory was certainly capable of bearing children. She had fourteen babies: sons John, William, Thomas, Robert, Christopher, Henry, George, and Richard; and daughters Margaret, Jane, Isabel, Elizabeth, Joanna, and Eleanor. We know that Dionisia was born about 1415. She died between 1472, when her husband's will names her as his executor, and 1475, when his will was proved and she did not fill that office, leading us to conclude that she died before her husband. So let us, somewhat arbitrarily but reasonably, put her age at first childbirth at about fifteen, in 1430. In a noncontraceptive world, the average family produces a new baby about every two years; Dionisia presumably had a baby on average every two years for twenty-six years. That would mean that the birth dates for her children were approximately 1430, 1432, 1434, 1436, 1438, 1440, 1442, 1444, 1446, 1448, 1450, 1452, 1454, and 1456. That puts Dionisia's age at her last child's birth at forty-one. Even today, most mothers are finished with their childbearing by that age, and medieval people aged faster than do moderns, so a maternal age of forty-one seems acceptable for the last Malory baby to be born. If this schedule is approximately correct, then Dionisia died when her youngest child was in the late teens. The will of her husband William Malory, written May 1, 1472, bequeaths to his daughters Joanna and Margaret, each, one hundred marks for her marriage; this bequest seems to indicate that both of these daughters were as yet unmarried, and in fact we know that Margaret married John Constable in 1475. Joanna and Margaret may have been the two youngest children. All of this is speculative, but reasonable. We do not know the birth order of the girls, nor whether their births were interspersed among the boys', but it is normal to assume that they were. It would be an unusual family indeed that had, for example, eight baby boys in a row and then six baby girls in a row. We do know that John was the first son, because he was the heir, and William the second son. Let us assign them the birth dates, respectively, of 1430 and 1432, just to get them out of the way, so to speak. After that, we have the information, from conflicting pedigrees, that Thomas was either the third, the fourth, or the sixth son, but that does not necessarily mean that he was either the third or fourth or sixth child. Nevertheless, just for convenience and without any more solid evidence than this for his birth date, let us say that he was born between 1432 and 1442. Remember that all of this is speculation, but reasonable, and this sort of birth date would make him a plausible age in the late 1460s to write *Le Morte Darthur*.

So we know that the Malory family was large, active, and wealthy. We know that they belonged to the minor nobility, having noble ancestors on both sides, and made their home adjacent to Fountains Abbey. We also know that they were devout Christians. They were generous donors to the religious foundations in Yorkshire: Fountains, Ripon Cathedral, the four orders of friars in York, Franciscans at Richmond, and the monastery of St. Robert of Knaresborough. They had a chantry chapel in their home at Studley, and "established and maintained oratories and chantries at Ripon, Hutton, Studley, and other places" (Matthews, 120). When they died, they were laid to rest in the Malory chapel within the cathedral at Ripon, with suitably impressive monuments over them, described by John Leland. Monuments to the fifteenth-century Malorys have not survived, although the chapel has, together with some monuments to Malorys of later times. The Malory children were at home in both of the family manors closest to Fountains. After the Malorys acquired Studley, they did not abandon their home at Hutton but continued to frequent it until the end of the sixteenth century.[31] Studley and Hutton manors more or less flanked the abbey. Situated as their homes were, could anyone seriously doubt that the Malory boys, and possibly their half a dozen sisters as well, were always all over the monastery grounds as they were growing up?

During the three-hundred-plus years that had passed since a handful of monks had left their monastery in York because it had seemed too worldly for them, and founded a more ascetic communal home for themselves, much had changed at Fountains by the time our Thomas Malory was born. The astringent life of that original monastery had attracted much favorable attention; many men had joined the community; a great and thriving enterprise had been the result. As Matthews points out, the only reward the world can give to voluntary poverty is worldly prosperity (Matthews, 11), and so it had been with Fountains. Walbran says, "It will be remembered that, at the time of the Reformation, the abbey of Fountains was one of the most magnificent and extensive structures, as well as one of the most powerful and wealthy monastic foundations in the kingdom" (Walbran, appendix, 107). Today, the very ruins testify to its greatness. As the great overweening edifice and enterprise of the Malorys's neighborhood, and a center of Yorkshire society and thus a significant part of their lives, Fountains Abbey must have had an incalculable influence on the children growing up in its shadow.

Presumably, Studley and Hutton as well were busy places, but the monastery held special added attractions. There was, for example, the corn mill, still a popular tourist diversion today, with visitors invited by the National Trust to "Have a go at grinding some corn and see the water wheel in action as you explore."[32] Can anyone doubt that the Malory children next door knew how to pester the millers to let them "have a go at grinding some corn"? And there was the sheep operation; Fountains was one of the greatest wool-producing locations in

[31] *Virginia Historical Magazine*, vol. 13, 218

[32] British National Trust, https://www.nationaltrust.org.uk.

England, for export to the wool markets of Europe. The inventory of livestock that was made at Fountains by the dean of York and the abbot of Rievaulx when the English monasteries were dissolved counted 1,326[33] sheep; the number in the mid-fifteenth century was probably similar; and every single one of those sheep had begun its life as a wooly and cuddly newborn lamb, as irresistible to neighbor children as they would be to children today. There were all sorts of industries at Fountains having to do with husbandry, and, in the manner of children everywhere and always, the many young Malorys were doubtless always underfoot — common sense tells us that much.

Common sense can also tell us more: children are not all alike. Some may have found the very idea of the library and scriptorium just as intriguing as the farmyard. Fountains had had a library since 1132, when Hugh, dean of York, joined the Cistercians there and brought with him his books (Burton, 134–138). Modern excavations have proved, if there were any doubt, that it also had a scriptorium, located upstairs, away from the communal fireplace in the refectory, which may have threatened the books. The scriptorium was possibly on the decline in the fifteenth century, since the advent of a class of private scribes; still, maybe one of the Malory boys was drawn to the high, cool, silent room where the monks did their writing. Maybe he was permitted to enter and watch. And, if so, maybe this lad learned, standing as still as he was able in the hushed room, that writing was not only beautiful and mysterious; it was an important thing, a thing that a man could turn his hand to doing.

It appears that sometimes there was hired entertainment at Fountains; quite likely, the lay brothers who worked at the various abbey enterprises and their families, and the other neighbors, were allowed to see the show. Possibly the show was planned especially for them; we do not know. In the bursar's book, reports Walbran, in the fifteenth

[33] Janet Burton, "Houses of Cistercian Monks: Fountains," in *A History of the County of York*, vol. 3, ed. William Page (London, 1974), 134–138, pages not numbered individually. Further citations of this work will appear in parentheses in the text.

century, we find a record of these entertainers and their fees. Scattered among the meticulous listings of various household expenses, such as, "Paid to Robert the sadler, for repairing the abbot's harness, 2 od.; … red wax, 1d; … a boar from William boon of Baldersby, 5s; … horse bread for Sir James Strangewayes's horses, 2d," we also find the following:

> to a blind minstrel, del.
> to the players of Topcliffe, 4d.
> to the minstrel of William de Plumpton, 8d.
> to a fool from Byland, 4d.
> players from Thirsk, 4d.
> to the minstrel of the Earl of Northumberland, 8d.
> to a story teller (fabulator) whose name was unknown, 6d.
> to the minstrels of Beverley, 16d.
> the minstrels of Lord Arundell, 16d.
> the minstrels of Lord Beaumont
> of Lord Fitzhugh
> to the king's minstrels, in part, 3s 4d.
> to the fabulator or story teller of the Earl of Salisbury, 12d.
> to the players of the Earl of Westmerland, 2d.
> to the players of Ripon, 2d.
> to a fool called Solomon (who came again), 4d. (Walbran, 90)

We notice all the story tellers and players, and we can't help wondering what stories they told or acted, and which were favorites of the audience, and whether Arthur and his knights figured in any of them.

And then there was school. We do not know where the Malory children were educated. It is possible that they were schooled at home, by tutors brought in for the purpose. Possibly they were sent away from home, as were many children of the upper social orders, to acquire a wider command of culture than they would absorb at home; to make desirable social connections; and to avert the threat of growing too dependent on parents and home comforts. But it is also possible, and considering the convenience and the large number of their children, it even

seems likely that they were schooled at Fountains. Normally, a great abbey would conduct two schools: a music school for training the monks themselves in liturgical music, and a grammar school for the children of lay employees of the monastery and neighbor children. Several manuscripts surviving from the library at Fountains attest to the teaching of music, and a bestiary hints at lessons for children in the exotic animals of the world.[34] George Hodges thinks it likely that "Fountains, like other great houses, maintained a grammar school for the sons of the neighbours. The master of such a school would not be a monk,"[35] he says, but a secular person employed by the abbey. The Cistercian vocation was not teaching; these monks worked the land with the help of lay brothers; they conducted hospitals for the community, and grammar schools for the neighbors, but their vocation and their desire was silence, as much as possible. However, going to school to a master hired by the monks could probably guarantee that the education he offered would be seriously influenced by the monks. For one thing, the philosophy and religious point of view would presumably mirror the monks' own; for another, the boys would almost certainly be comfortable with French. Richard Ingham, indeed, holds that children of the literate classes in late-medieval England would begin grammar school at age seven already having learned French at church schools when they were even younger. He believes that they would learn it as a "second native language," at the very young age when children are able to pick up a language without effort, and then be trained later in the more difficult

[34] Medieval Manuscript Images, Pierpont Morgan Library, Fountains Abbey bestiary, MS M.890 folio 1r.

[35] George Hodges, *Fountains Abbey: The Story of a Mediaeval Monastery* (London: John Murray, 1904), 73–74.

aspects of French, in the grammar schools.[36] At any rate, Fountains probably offered the Malorys a suitable early education for their boys, and possibly they accepted it. The Malory children, hardly knowing when they were playing on their own parents' land and when they were on Abbey grounds, would have ample room to run races, climb, wrestle, shoot at targets, fight, dig, ride, see ghosts, tell stories, make things, destroy things, swim, explore, read, watch work being done, study, build "forts," make noise, learn. In short, the home of the Malorys of Hutton and Studley, abutting as it did the grounds of Fountains Abbey, provided a paradise of a playground for growing boys. First there was the land itself; then there was the industry of the place; then there was the school, so that a lad need hardly leave home to have everything he required.

But there was, of course, a third element of influence in this playground, which makes this whole picture relevant to our search for the author of *Le Morte*. The Malory children grew up in the heart of Cistercianism; they were steeped in Cistercian thought, as Vinaver thought the author of the Grail *Quest* had to be. But what is it? Is it anything besides the mysticism of St. Bernard, anything that a child could see and understand? Of course, a child could see the distinctive white habit, and learn to associate it with the hospital at the gate of the abbey;[37] that hospital was not intended nor operated just for the monks; it was a charity for anyone in need of it. Most of the injured knights in the *Morte*, the reader will remember, were taken to a monastery of white monks (we read: Cistercians) to have their wounds tended; this little detail is lifted from reality in the Middle Ages. The Cistercians also were agricultural workers; their houses were supposed to be established in desert places, far from the press of man, but although each house may have been begun in such a place, the Cistercian

36 Richard Ingham, "Multilingualism in the Middle Ages" (lecture, Birmingham City University, Birmingham, England, 2007).

37 George Lawton, *The Religious Houses of Yorkshire* (London: Simpkin, 1853). Lawton tells us, "There was an hospital at the gate of the great abbey at Fountains for the poor, and travellers, founded as early as the reign of Richard I" (83). Further citations of this work will be in parentheses in the text.

practice of clearing and tilling and reaping soon transformed it to something at the heart of human intercourse: farming. And all of that enterprise served charitable ends; the Cistercian abbey had a house for the reception of the poor as well as an infirmary for the sick, and "in them all received a generous hospitality and remedies for the ills of soul and body."[38] There was also an intellectual side of the Cistercian character. An abbey was a home for books and the writing of books. St. Bernard himself began his adult life as a student of literature; he wanted to learn how to read and interpret books so that he would be better equipped to tackle the Scriptures. He spent his lifetime using persuasive words both spoken and powerfully written, in the courts of Christendom as well as among his own monastic brothers.

All of this, and more, is part of Cistercian thought; some of it a child would see and know what he was seeing; some of it would gradually take hold of his mind without his realizing that he knew it. It is difficult to imagine a way in which anyone could have come under a stronger Cistercian influence than the Malory children. They were exposed to it from the age when they could first toddle across the grass toward the great abbey, which even in its ruins today is such an overwhelming sight. And a significant part of Cistercian thought, even from the abbey's inception, had been transmitted by means of the stories in the Arthurian tradition. *The Quest of the Holy Grail* is a Cistercian product. The children who grew up at Studley and Hutton and Fountains, likewise, were virtually a Cistercian product. We can be sure that they knew those old stories the way they knew Fountains Abbey and its ways — like the backs of their hands. And one of them was named Thomas Malory.

[38] Marie Gildas, "Cistercians," in *The Catholic Encyclopedia*, vol. 3 (New York: Robert Appleton, 1908), https://www.newadvent.org/cathen/03780c.htm.

6

The Making of a Monk-Knight

WE CAN SAY that it would solve a great many investigative problems if Sir Thomas Malory were a knight of the Church, a Knight Hospitaller, but that simply raises the question of whether there is any evidence that he actually was one. And when we look carefully, we find a great deal of evidence both circumstantial and non-circumstantial to support our case.

For example, it is easy to see a major difference between the Malorys of Yorkshire and their cousins in other counties, families that also produced sons named Thomas Malory, candidates for authorship of *Le Morte*. The Yorkshire Malorys seem to have had no interest in involving themselves in civic affairs. Hyonjin Kim comments on this peculiarity in his comparison of the Malorys of Yorkshire with other Malorys; he says that "unlike their distant cousins in Warwickshire and Cambridgeshire ... they had never undertaken any local office of higher prestige, which reflects their uncharacteristic detachment from local politics." Speaking of three Thomas Malorys — one who was a member of Parliament, one who was a tax collector, a distributor of relief money, and possibly also a member of Parliament, and Thomas Malory of Yorkshire — Hyonjin Kim tells us that "with the exception of the Yorkshire man, they seem to have been reasonably active in local politics, as their administrative or parliamentary duties attest," but as for the Yorkshire Thomas Malory, "his life is veiled in complete mystery."[39] He seems never to have

[39] Hyonjin Kim, *The Knight without the Sword: A Social Landscape of Malorian Chivalry*, Arthurian Literature 45 (Cambridge: D.|S. Brewer, 2000), 5.

done anything at all. The answer to this puzzle is not hard to find, however. The Yorkshire Malorys's lodestar was different: it was God. If we want to see any record of their lives, we must look not to the Parliament, and not to the records of civil service, but to the Church and the monastery. Moreover, as Hyonjin Kim does not seem to realize, the very fact that the life of Thomas Malory of Yorkshire is veiled in complete mystery ought to be a significant clue: the life of the author of *Le Morte Darthur* as well, for five hundred years and more now, has been veiled in complete mystery.

John Richard Walbran, in his memorials of Fountains Abbey, describes the abbey as a social center for the noble families of Yorkshire, including the Malorys:

> Not only in the tedious route or the enjoyment of the chace [*sic*] there gathered in this princely hall, Percy, and Mowbray, Nevill and Scroop, Marmion and Fitzhugh, Lacy and Rolle, Markenfield, Norton, Mallory and Mauleverer and the bearer of many a noble name still sounding like trumpet music in the antiquary's ear, leaving their noisy followers, when the bounteous repast was followed by retirement and repose, to select their beds on the straw-strewn floor; for when monastic austerity admitted of mirthful relaxation, how often did not its walls resound with the jocund applause that greeted the feats of mimics and jesters, or with the strains of the errant minstrel, that never turned to a monastic home without the assurance of a welcome and liberal reception. (Walbran, 174)

Walbran also gives us a description of some family arms carved into the stone of the abbey gateway; it was decorated, he says, with the arms of Percy, Vavasour, "and a third, with the arms of Mallory of Studley Royal, with the quarterings of Tempest of Bracewell, Conyers and Washington impaling Constable of Halsham. On the south side

---

Further citations of this work will be in parentheses in the text.

is a fine but headless statue of the Virgin and Child ... inscribed in black letter: 'S'CTA MARIA ORA PR'NOBIS'" (Walbran, 174). Note: Tempest, Conyers, Washington, and Constable are all part of the extended family of Thomas Malory of Yorkshire.

Judging from the mores of the time and place in which William and Dionisia Malory lived, we see a strong probability that one or two of their sons belonged to a religious order. They were devout Catholics. Most people, of course, were Catholic in England in the fifteenth century, but not every family had an oratory or a chapel in their house; in fact, that required Church permission, which the Malorys were given: "On October 25, 1458, Archbishop Booth granted an oratory for three years to William Malory, esq., Dionisia, his wife, and their children (Reg. 204 a) which privilege was renewed to them for the same period on Nov., 17, 1467 (Reg. 57 a). This was the beginning of the Chapel of the Blessed Virgin at Studley."[40] The Malorys's religious devotion is similarly attested by their giving so generously of their worldly goods to the Church; this generosity continued over several generations of the family. By a deed of 1347, Sir Roger Conyers (our Thomas's great-grandfather) and Sir Christopher Mallore, as Lord of Hutton (Thomas's great-great-grandfather), granted lands at Lynton to Fountains Abbey; this deed was confirmed for tenements in Melverbie, Balderwick, Dishforth, and Rainton in 1536 by Sir William Malory. William Malory, the father of our Thomas, in his will of 1472, left money to the four orders of friars in York and the monastery of St. Robert of Knaresborough. William Matthews tells us that "Ripon Cathedral, Fountains Abbey ... the Franciscans at Richmond, and all the orders of friars of York were [also] recipients of their bounty" (Matthews, 120). As we have seen, the Malorys had their final resting place in the Malory chapel within the Ripon Cathedral, "just under the library in the southeast transept" (Matthews, 119), further testimony to the family piety, even in death. And even more: several members of their family

[40] *Virginia Historical Magazine,* vol. 13, 218.

belonged to the Corpus Christi Guild in York, which presented plays acting out the doctrines and the moral teachings of the Church for the edification of the townspeople yearly on the feast day celebrating the mystery of the Holy Eucharist. Thus the Malory family of Yorkshire demonstrated their piety.

And William and Dionisia had eight sons, in addition to their six daughters. There was a strong tradition in the Middle Ages, in families with many sons, to "give back to God" one of them, by devoting him to the Church. We are speaking here not of the practice of child oblation, by which a young child would be "donated" to a house of religion, in the expectation that the monks would rear him and that he would eventually take monastic vows and join their order. That practice had virtually died out by Thomas Malory's time, and the Order of Knights Hospitaller amended their rule to forbid it in 1433, laying down the new regulation that a postulant could not be accepted under the age of fourteen. We are speaking here simply of the general expectation in large Catholic families that one of their children would choose the priestly or monastic life. That would not be the first boy, who would be expected to take over his father's role; and it would not be the second, who would be expected to remain in secular life in case of the untimely death of the first. The third or subsequent son was eligible for the religious life. Today, devout Catholic parents of a large family possibly may hope for a religious vocation among their children, but medieval parents in that situation would likely just arrange it. It was part of the normal, acceptable, good care of their children for parents to arrange their lives for them — marriage, career, admission to a monastery, if that was what parents deemed a child's calling to be. The pious Malorys very likely dedicated at least one of their many children to the Church. It was not their eldest son, John, who became Sir John and died as a young married man. It was not William, usually assumed to be the second son; he too was married. Thomas was either the third or subsequent son; therefore, he was eligible by custom for the religious life.

Added to the custom of "giving back" a son to God, there was also a strong monastic influence in these children's lives. They grew up in the shadow of the great Cistercian monastery, Fountains Abbey. They saw and heard, as they grew, all the enterprises of the monks. They saw the sheep raising, the hospital, the schools, the almsgiving, the corn mill, the entertainments, the fields and gardens, the scriptorium, the library. They heard, as part of the normal sounds of daily life, along with the noises of husbandry and industry, the music, as the monks practiced their chants and went to and from Mass and other liturgical celebrations. All of this, we may assume, was the warp and woof of the young Malorys's childhood. The result of this nearness was, of course, that the Malory boys absorbed the ordinariness of monastic life. It was as normal and accepted for them as the lives of their parents, their other kinsmen, their servants, their friends. They knew the religious life of the monastery not as mysterious or peculiar but as simply a good option for a man's career. All things considered, it seems more than likely that at least one, if not more, of the Malory sons pursued the religious life, and probably Thomas because of his place in the lineup of boys.

But supposing we are convinced that Thomas Malory of Hutton and Studley was a member of a religious order, why would he not be a Cistercian? Is there any reason to believe he chose the Order of St. John of Jerusalem, the Knights Hospitallers? There is no rule, of course, that an aspirant to the religious life must choose any particular order. In Yorkshire alone, there were, in addition to the Cistercians in the Malorys's backyard, other Cistercian houses, Benedictines, Carthusians, Franciscans, Augustinians, Canons of the Holy Sepulchre, Dominicans, Crouched Friars, Trinitarians, Carmelites, and Hospitallers, to mention the best-known orders, and at least sixteen other orders less well known (Lawton, in discussions throughout his book). Why should Thomas Malory, having all these to choose from in his own county, choose to be a Hospitaller? Essentially, the answer is twofold and easy: first, because, as we know from the *Morte,* Thomas did not love meditation and solitude, he loved battle; and second, because that is simply what Malorys did. His family was attached to the Order of Hospitallers in a special way. The Malorys in England comprised one large family with several branches; everyone with the surname Malory was kin to everyone else with that name, although the degree of kinship between one and another is usually not ascertainable. Together, this clan Malory made up one of the well-known "Hospitaller families," families that gave disproportional support to that order, in the forms of money, property, and — most notably — sons. In the time just previous to our Thomas's and probably extending into his lifetime, the grand prior of all of England was his kinsman, the Hospitaller knight Sir Robert Malory. There were as well, besides Sir Robert, other Malorys who were knights just before and just after Thomas's time: one serving brother, John Malory, and one knight, Sir John Malory, whose lifetime overlaps his. Moreover, given that most English Hospitallers were from the north of England and there was a tight web of family connections among the northern families, it is not difficult to find other cousins of the Malorys, with different surnames, in the order. For one example, the Hospitaller knight Thomas Plumpton of Yorkshire, commander of Carbrooke, appears to have been first cousin to our Thomas Malory, whose grandmother was Joan Plumpton. And there is a strong possibility that there was a Hospitaller who was very close kin indeed to our Thomas, his own brother. Here is what we know:

William and Dionisia Malory had eight sons — John, William, Thomas, Christopher, George, Robert, Richard, and Henry. Of these eight, one, Robert, has been said to have died in childhood. In his introduction to a Surtees publication of 1830, *Visitations of the North Circa 1480–1500*, editor F. W. Dendy notes that a "copy made by Robert Glover (1544–88) … of an old manuscript, now lost, which may have been the official record of an heraldic visitation of the northern counties made in the later part of the fifteenth century," in its pedigree of the Yorkshire Malorys, has *obit puer* after Robert's name. Thus, a student of the Malorys would be justified in assuming that Robert died young, basing that inference on the Glover copy. However, there is better evidence that Robert lived and became in time a member of the Order of St. John, Hospitallers. If that is so, then the Yorkshire

Malorys, like so many of their kin, had the closest possible connection with that order, and that close connection makes it all the more likely that Robert's brother Thomas was also a member of the Hospital. Let us look at the evidence.

First, the assumption that Robert Malory died as a child comes from a pedigree of his family, made late in the fifteenth century, but it is well known that the Malory pedigrees that list the children of William and Dionisia Malory are wildly inaccurate and therefore not reliable evidence of Robert's early death. Some examples of pedigree error: William Flowers's pedigree of 1563–1564 omits sons William and Robert altogether; the one in the Church of St. Peter in York lists William but omits Henry as well as Robert; the *Visitation of Yorkshire* in 1563 and 1564 (edited by C. G. Norcliffe) lists only eight of the Malorys's fourteen children; Robert Glover's pedigree of 1584–1585 lists all fourteen children but notes *obit puer* after Robert's name; a pedigree by John Richard Walbran, in *Memorials of Fountains Abbey*, lists thirteen children but makes no mention of Robert. The most prominent Malory of the fifteenth century, the prior of the English Language of Hospitallers from 1433 to 1440, Sir Robert Malory, does not appear at all in any of the pedigrees of his family. Anyone depending entirely on those documents would not even know that this man had existed, and yet a great deal is known about his life; P. J. C. Field has written a concise biography of him for the *Dictionary of National Biography* (2004).

However, there are other records, more accurate than the Malory pedigrees, to give us clues about the life of William and Dionisia Malory's son Robert. Several men were called Robert Malory during Thomas Malory's lifetime, and they show up in various records doing various things. Two of those records hold particular interest for us because they connect a Robert Malory with the prominent Hospitaller Sir John Langstrother, and one of those records actually states that Robert Malory lived in the same house as Langstrother, the Hospitaller monastery at Clerkenwell, near London, which was the main priory of the order in England. Those records are these:

On April 7, 1463, the Yorkist King Edward commissioned five men — Sir John Langstrother, Sir James Strangways, Geoffrey Middleton, the mayor of York (Thomas Scawsby, although he is not named in the commission), and Robert Malory to go to the north of England and fetch the Lancastrian rebel Humphrey Neville back to the king.[41] This errand entailed a long journey to Northumberland, where Neville was helping to hold three castles for the deposed Lancastrian king Henry VI, and a long journey back. For the length of those two journeys, Langstrother the Hospitaller and Robert Malory, as well as the other three men, ate, slept, and rode together in close association. There is no record that the errand entailed any warfare. Neville went peaceably with those sent to fetch him; and when he was delivered to the king, the king issued him a pardon and knighted him. More about this presently.

In 1469, after the Battle of Edgecote, fought bitterly between the Lancastrian supporters of the deposed king Henry VI and the Yorkist supporters of the current king Edward IV, two members of King Edward's family were beheaded. They were the father and the brother of King Edward's wife, Queen Elizabeth, and thus the husband and son of the queen's mother, Jaquetta, Duchess of Bedford. After the battle, Jaquetta, the king's mother-in-law, accused thirty-five men of having murdered her husband and son.[42] The incident in question took place right after the battle, and the very fact that the duchess accused so many seems to indicate that the deaths were not really murder but deaths on the battlefield, and no legal charges were ever brought. In fact, Jaquetta's husband and son were apparently executed by the orders or at least with the approval of Richard Neville, Duke of Warwick, who was at that time leading the rebellion against King Edward. Among the thirty-five names listed in the accusation brought by the queen's mother were two of the same names included in the Northumberland commission mentioned

41 British Public Record Office, London, *Rotuli Parliamentorum*, v. 478, 511; *Calendar of Patent Rolls* (1461–1467), 122, 267, 279.

42 British Public Record Office, London, KB 27/836, m. 61d.

above, Sir John Langstrother and Robert Malory. Langstrother was by that time the prior-elect of England of the Order of Hospitallers. This time, the address of John Langstrother and Robert Malory is given on the document accusing them of murder. Both are said to reside at the same address, at the Hospitaller Priory at Clerkenwell. Robert Malory is identified by Jaquetta with the title *esquire*. The fact that he resided at the priory strongly suggests that this Robert Malory was a member of the order. The fact that he was designated esquire is no deterrent to that conclusion; not every member of the order was a professed knight. There were three divisions, or classes, of Hospitallers: Knights of Justice, religious chaplains, and serving brothers. There were more serving brothers in the order than knights, and these brothers were designated esquires to the knights.[43]

Now we must go back in time from that point, to April 7, 1463. On that date, remember, Sir John Langstrother, Knight Hospitaller, Robert Malory, and three others were commissioned by King Edward to go and find a certain Lancastrian, Humphrey Neville, who had been engaged in irregular harassment raids against Edward, and bring him to the king. Neville was King Edward's cousin, close to his own age. In 1463, the young Edward was still hoping to engage Neville and others of the nobility on his side of the contest with Henry VI for the throne. Langstrother was one of the notables of the Order of Hospitallers, and, although nobody knew it yet in 1463, he was destined to become prior of England after the death of the current prior, Robert Botyl. Although Botyl had supported Lancastrian Henry until Henry's mind failed, in 1463, he was supporting Yorkist Edward, and Edward had no reason not to trust Botyl's underling Langstrother with the important embassy of fetching Humphrey Neville.

43 It is possible that this Robert Malory, who lived in a monastery and bore the title *esquire*, was the son of William Malory, the father of Thomas who is the subject of this book. If so, and if William the father of Robert was also a lay member of the Order of Hospitallers, that could explain the confusion about whether his proper title was *knight* or *esquire*, discussed above in chapter 2, "Fielding a Clash of Knights."

The commission to fetch Neville does not give any identifying information about the Robert Malory mentioned in the document, but we do have some clues to his identity. During most and possibly all of the 1460s, the lieutenant of the Constable of the Tower of London is known to have been a man named Robert Malory. There is no record of the exact dates of his service. So now we have two Robert Malorys to consider: the Robert Malory who is named in the two documents listed above as associated with John Langstrother, and in one of these documents actually said to reside in the same house as Langstrother, in the monastery at Clerkenwell; and the Robert Malory who was at some time during that decade an officer of the Tower. But there is a third Robert Malory in the case, the son of Sir Thomas Malory of Newbold Revel. Because it seemed to P.J.C. Field obvious that a Tower officer would be appointed to go along on such an errand as fetching Neville, he argued that the Robert Malory associated with Langstrother, named in the king's commission, and Robert Malory the officer of the Tower, are in fact one and the same Robert Malory. Then, he tried at some length to demonstrate that these two Robert Malorys — the one associated with Langstrother and the one who was the Tower official — were not only the same man but that that man was also identical with the third Robert Malory, the son of Thomas Malory of Newbold Revel, Field's candidate for the authorship of *Le Morte Darthur*.

However, the attempt to make these three men — Robert Malory living in a monastery, Robert Malory officer of the Tower, and Robert Malory son of Sir Thomas Malory — into the same man ran into trouble. Field's effort entangled him in an argument that depends on his supposition of a scribal error in an official document. Robert Malory son of Thomas Malory of Newbold Revel, according to his father's inquisition postmortem in 1471, was too young to be the Tower official. That inquisition says that Robert was twenty-three years old at the time his father died, in 1470, and that means he would have been thirteen, possibly fourteen, years old when a man by the name of Robert Malory was first recorded as holding the position of lieutenant. Anyone can see that fourteen is too young for a boy to be put in charge of the Tower of

London. However, says Field, there could have been a scribal error in the inquisition: "a single error of viginti (say) for triginti would have been easy to commit" (Field, 160). Field says that the scribe may have written *viginti* (twenty) for *triginti* (thirty), and thus stated young Robert of Newbold Revel to be ten years younger than he actually was in 1470, thirty-four. That would have made it more reasonable to appoint him lieutenant in 1461, at twenty-four. However, Field, in making his argument, makes something in the nature of a "scribal error" himself. The Latin word for *thirty* is not *triginti* but *triginta,* meaning that the sleepy or careless scribe, in writing *viginti* when he meant to write *triginta* would have had to make not one but two errors, two substitutions of letters in a single word, in order to support Field's argument. That seems unlikely. Since this proposed "scribal error" is the only bit of support Field offers for his theory that the Robert Malory of the two official documents was the son of his favorite Thomas Malory, the argument loses credibility; this Malory's son Robert was at most fourteen years old when Robert Malory the lieutenant of the Constable of the Tower is first recorded as holding that position.

But here is a possible answer to the mystery. Professor Field, in attempting to identify all of these Robert Malorys, eliminated all the men of that name in that century who, for one reason or another, seem not to fit into the puzzle, and one of those he eliminated was Robert the son of William and Dionisia Malory of Yorkshire, who was said in a family pedigree to have died as a child. Field apparently eliminated him because of a trusting attitude in this instance toward the Malory genealogies, even though he was well aware of their wildly erratic nature, having written the *Oxford Dictionary of National Biography* (2004) entry for the famous prior Malory, who is completely missing from his family pedigrees. The Robert Malory who went with Langstrother on the commission to arrest Humphrey Neville could well have been William and Dionisia's son Robert, not dead as a boy but, on the contrary, living as a monk or a lay brother at the Hospitallers' monastery at Clerkenwell, performing his esquire duties to the knights of his order. This son could have been the same man who shared that same address with Langstrother in 1469.

There is no evidence that a Tower official went along on the errand to arrest Humphrey Neville, and there is no apparent reason why the lieutenant of the Constable of the Tower of London would live in a monastery. The commission simply says "Robert Malory." Field assumed that that person was the lieutenant, probably because it seemed reasonable to him that King Edward would send a Tower official along to arrest a renegade. However, this "arrest" of Neville was not for the purpose of jailing him or executing him; it was for the purpose of wooing him to Edward's (Yorkist) side. When Langstrother and the others delivered Neville as directed to Edward, Edward issued him a pardon and knighted him. Moreover, Neville had been safely ensconced in one of the mighty castles of Northumberland, and the fact that he accompanied the handful of men who came to get him, without any apparent fear or struggle, argues that the errand was peaceful. In fact, it argues that the king deliberately sent on this embassy men who were already known to Neville as friends.

If the Robert Malory who went with Langstrother to find Humphrey Neville, and then, years later, was seen to be living in the Hospitallers' monastery along with Prior Langstrother, was in fact the brother of our Thomas Malory of Yorkshire, then he is another close link joining the Yorkshire Malorys with the Knights Hospitallers. If Robert did not die in childhood but simply vanished from the family home because he went to join the Hospitallers, that fact would explain some things: first, why he lived in a monastery (because he was a monk!); second, why his parents did not mention him in their will (not because he was dead but, again, because he was a monk); and finally, if he was a serving brother, why Jaquetta called him esquire in her accusation of the murder of her husband and her son. Moreover, Robert Malory thus is demonstrated in the public records to have been closely associated with Prior John Langstrother: they lived in the same house at the same time. He is also demonstrated, in the king's commission, to have been acquainted with Humphrey Neville; he was one of the handful of men who escorted Neville through the length of England from Northumberland to the king in court, probably in London. Those associations will be shown to be greatly significant as we examine other documentary evidence in our search for the identity of the author of *Le Morte Darthur*. However, already we can see that evidence points to the conclusion that this Robert Malory was the son of Dionisia and William Malory of Yorkshire, because such a keen scholarly attempt, by such an eminent Malory scholar, was devoted to identifying him as someone else, and it failed. And if he was their son, the link between these particular Malorys and the Order of Hospitallers was of the closest possible kind.

Membership in the Hospitallers was a sort of family profession for the medieval Malorys. It seems probable, as we see above, that Robert Malory of Yorkshire was a Hospitaller. In any case, the Yorkshire Malorys were almost sure to have had sons in the order, because of their piety and because they had so many sons, and because the great Fountains Abbey was such an intimate and constant part of their experience that a monk's life was inevitably commonplace to the Malory children as they grew up. Thomas was the third or subsequent son out of their eight, so the heir-and-a-spare policy would comfortably allow him to follow a religious vocation and to embrace the family profession by joining the Knights Hospitallers. I believe he did.

7

Of Manors and Manuscripts, Part 1

THE STORY OF the influence of Bernard of Clairvaux on *Le Morte Darthur* not only conflates the stories of the two monastic orders, contemplative Cistercians and warrior Hospitallers, but also encompasses the story of the Malorys, who eventually became known as one of the "Hospitaller families" because of their unusually close association with that order. And that association leads us to one of the most important bits of evidence in the whole search for the identity of Thomas Malory, because it is not circumstantial. All the scholars who have inquired into the writer's identity have posited arguments for various candidates and offered various bits of evidence for this man or that one, but all the evidence they have offered is wholly circumstantial. Circumstances will allow this or that candidate to be the author, but that is as far as circumstantial evidence can go; it cannot show that, in fact, he *is* the author. But there are two pieces of evidence not offered until now as proof of Malory's identity, not hypothetical, not circumstantial, but solid and direct. We have seen one of them, the author's claim in the pages of his book that he was a Chevalier, a Hospitaller knight. The second is a fifteenth-century document, which states Thomas Malory's name and rank, and calls him the author, and places him in a monastery of the Knights Hospitaller in Ribston, Yorkshire. Here it is:

In slightly clumsy French, in a hand not so far seen anywhere else, tucked away in the dust of centuries " 'in an old hide trunk, together with all the old deeds and seals relating to the property back to the 12th century, at Ribston Hall, Wetherby, Yorks,' " (Matthews, 109), a monastery of the Hospitallers, and presumably having always been there, we find this, written in the margin of an ancient romance: First, the signature Hospitaller cross, standing in as asterisk to point out the exact beginning of the book, then "Ci comence le livre que Sir Thomas Malori Chr reduce in Engloys et fuist emprente par Willm Caxton" (*La Suite du Merlin,* Cambridge University Library Add. MS 7071, Vinaver, 1280)—"Here begins the book that Sir Thomas Malory, Chevalier, reduced into English and had printed by William Caxton."

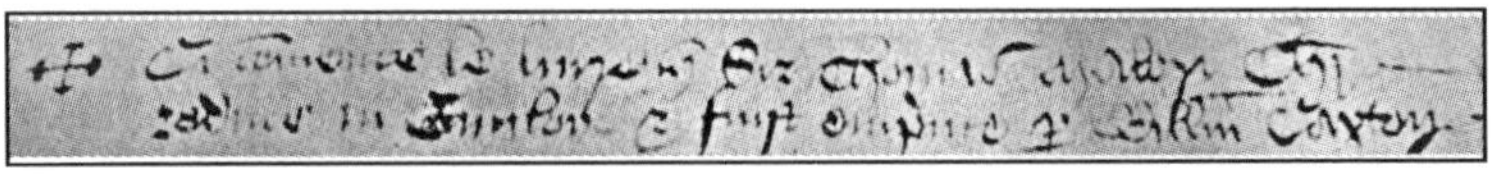

The book in question begins exactly where Malory begins *Le Morte Darthur*. It could not be easier or more clear: Here is the book that Malory translated and had printed by Caxton—if only we were able to read the notation and accept its literal meaning. But alas, some Malory scholars up until now have not been able to do so. Many do not know that the manuscript exists, or, if they do, take the word *book* to mean "story"—here begins the story that Malory translated—and of course, even though English allows that interpretation, that reading shifts the meaning off to something else entirely from what the marginal notation actually says. Moreover, T.C. Rumble established a long time ago that Malory used the term *tale* to refer to his own telling of a particular segment of the *Morte,* but he used the word *book* when he was referring to his source: "the freynsch booke."[44] Whoever wrote the French margin notation in the Ribston manuscript follows the same practice—"Ci comence le livre": "Here begins the book."

When Eugene Vinaver was evaluating this book in 1947 for the Cambridge University Library as a proposed acquisition, he had recently, after resisting for some time, allowed himself to be persuaded that the author of *Le Morte* was Sir Thomas Malory of Newbold Revel,

44 T.C. Rumble, "The First *Explicit* in Malory's *Morte Darthur,*" *Modern Language Notes* 71, no. 8 (December 1956): 565–566

Warwickshire. He advised the officials of the university to purchase the manuscript, and they did, but he withheld judgment as to whether it was actually used by Malory. Of course, Vinaver would have known that it was unlikely that Malory of Newbold Revel had made his way north to Yorkshire and to a small monastery there, got himself imprisoned in the monastery, and used the Ribston manuscript in his translating project. However, if someone had told Vinaver that Sir Thomas Malory, a knight of St. John, a Hospitaller, had written *Le Morte*, and that this man grew up within a morning's walk of the Hospitaller house at Ribston, and that he was actually living in that same house at the appropriate time, likely Vinaver's judgment would have been affected by that information. He would have been able to see what we can see, that the margin note means just what it says: not the Sir Thomas Malory who lived far away in Warwickshire but the Sir Thomas Malory who lived right there under the same roof reduced this book into English and caused it to be printed by William Caxton.

Consider for a moment the remarkable history of this manuscript — not the textual history with variant readings and influences and all such as that — that history has been amply studied. Consider the history of the book as Thing: a thing laid away with other things of the same general nature in an old trunk in an old house. The old house, Ribston Hall, belonged to Lord Robert DeRos in the twelfth and early in the thirteenth century. In 1217, Lord DeRos donated it to the Order of Knights Templar of Jerusalem. The deed of gift was laid away in a hide trunk along with some other writings, including the *Suite du Merlin*. In 1312, the Order of Templars was disbanded and their property, including Ribston Hall, became the property of the Knights Hospitallers; the old trunk with its contents stayed where it was. In the sixteenth century, the monasteries of England were dissolved and the house came into the possession of Charles Brandon, First Duke of Suffolk and a courtier of Henry VIII. The trunk with its contents, again, stayed right where it was. In 1542, Brandon sold the property to Henry Goodricke. After three centuries in Goodricke ownership, in 1836, it was sold to Joseph Dent, and it has remained in the Dent family. In the 1940s, the owner of Ribston Hall was Major J. G. Dent. The *Suite du Merlin* manuscript was still in the house, and still in the trunk. Major Dent, in correspondence with a bookseller, Mr. H. Eisemann, regarding the manuscript, told Eisemann, "It was found in an old hide trunk, together with all the old deeds and seals relating to the property back to the 12th century, at Ribston Hall, Wetherby, Yorks, by my grandfather, and had presumably always been there."[45] Among the old deeds in the trunk with the manuscript was the deed of gift of Ribston from Lord DeRos to the Templars, dated 1217.

The remarkable fact about the provenance of this book is that it stayed where it was put for more than seven hundred years. This particular seven hundred years is a long time in anybody's history of the world. Kingdoms rose and fell; the Black Death devastated Europe; people moved to town; the machine age began and throve; Columbus discovered a new world; the Church broke up into rival sects; the monasteries of England were destroyed and their treasure hoard of books stolen; the mechanical clock was invented; the telephone was invented; Joan of Arc heard voices; the fields of England were enclosed for sheep; the very notion of monarchy wavered, then toppled; the Magna Carta was signed; the Declaration of Independence was signed; the assembly line system of manufacture was invented; the automobile was invented; Wilbur and

45 Harry Speight, late in the nineteenth century in *Nidderdale and the Garden of the Nidd: A Yorkshire Rhineland* (London: Elliot Stock, 1894), before the discovery of the manuscript in question, gives us a fulsome history of the house at Ribston where it was kept, remarking that "the charters and documents preserved at Ribston Hall are ... very numerous, and some of them (of exquisite calligraphy) yet remain to be deciphered" (167). He goes on: "Rarely indeed do we find so complete and well-proven record of facts as exists at Ribston, illuminating by deed and charter the dim ages of the remote past," and "in the library are preserved the old charters from which our history of Ribston is mainly derived, besides various rare and curious books" (189, 196). The story of the Ribston ownership of the manuscript is told briefly by William Matthews in *The Ill-Framed Knight*, 108–110, except that Matthews mistakenly says that the Templars owned the house until 1540; actually that order was disbanded in 1312 and ownership passed to the Hospitallers. Matthews quotes the letter mentioned above, from Dent to Eisemann, describing the history of the manuscript in the house at Ribston.

Orville Wright in North Carolina showed the world that man can fly; the English longbow was invented; the atomic bomb was invented; the Nazis murdered millions of Jews; the whole world went to war, and then it went to war again—and so forth. And all the time, as the centuries went by with all their multitudinous doings, this manuscript stayed tucked safely away. There is evidence that it was taken out of its old trunk at least once, to replace some damaged pages sometime in the fifteenth century, but it was put back. There is no evidence at all that it was ever taken out of its old house. The chain of custody is unbroken. The only surprise is that it has been hardly noticed by Malory scholars.

When Malory used this book, he used it at Ribston Hall, Wetherby, Yorkshire, which was at that time a monastery of the Knights Hospitaller. The Hospitallers owned the book, and they kept it in that house. Remarkably, even after the dissolution of the monasteries, after Ribston was in private hands, for a few more centuries, the manuscript stayed in its trunk, right where it was. This is the only existing more-or-less full copy (folios 269–273 and 335–343 recto are fifteenth-century replacements of presumably damaged pages) of the *Suite du Merlin*, which forms the first part of *Le Morte Darthur*, except for a Picard dialect copy that was in French ownership and stayed in France until after 1869 when Henry Huth bought that one from a bookseller in Paris. His son eventually published an edition; the manuscript now belongs to the British Museum. But while the Huths were dealing with their copy of the *Suite*, the Ribston copy stayed put, right where it had always been. Its provenance is undisputed.

The owner of Ribston Hall, and thus the Ribston manuscript, in the mid-twentieth century, Major Dent, decided to share the treasure with the world. It went to Christie's auction house in 1944 and was purchased by H. Eisemann, who offered to sell it to Cambridge University. The syndics of the Cambridge Library, in need of expert advice about whether to buy the old book, approached Eugene Vinaver. Vinaver was in the midst of work on his monumental three-volume edition of Malory, but he took time to examine the manuscript. He knew that it had lain in its trunk, together with the Ribston deeds and other documents, for centuries; the earliest property-related documents in that trunk with it were dated from the 1100s. Vinaver recommended that the university should buy the book. Accordingly, it became the property of Cambridge University and was given the designation "Cambridge Add. 7071"— thus obscuring the fact of its origin, Ribston Hall in Yorkshire. The seventy or so years that the book has now spent at Cambridge has caused the scholarly world to forget the seven hundred that it spent in the old hide trunk at Ribston. Nevertheless, when Malory was writing his book, that manuscript was owned by the Knights Hospitaller and housed not at Cambridge but in the monastery of the Hospitallers at Ribston, in Yorkshire.

Enclosed within the same boards as the *Suite du Merlin* is another book, a prose version of the Grail story, called *L'Estoire del Saint Graal*, by Robert de Boron. This book is not rare, nor was it rare in Malory's day; there are many medieval copies still extant of *L'Estoire*. Interestingly, although Thomas Malory apparently had the Ribston copy of *L'Estoire*, bound within the same cover as the *Suite du Merlin*, in his hands, and although he translated the *Suite du Merlin* from that copy, and although he was interested in the Grail legend and eventually gave us his own telling of that story, Malory did not use the particular version of the story of the Grail found bound with the Ribston *Merlin* when he wrote his "Tale of the Sankgreal" in the *Morte*. More about that later.

Eugene Vinaver had little to say about the Ribston manuscript in his 1947 edition of *The Works of Thomas Malory*; it came into his hands too late. However, he commented fully on it in his second edition of the *Works* in 1967. He tells us:

> The Cambridge MS., as it is now called, has several claims to the attention of students of Arthurian romance: it fills the lacunae in the Huth MS., it contains some of the material which has hitherto only been known through a late fifteenth-century fragment, and it includes, after the story of Arthur's coronation, a long account, drawn from the *Estoire de Merlin*, of Arthur's wars against the rebel kings. It thus supplies the source of Malory's

> pp. 17–41 to which there is no parallel at all in the Huth MS., and which have hitherto been thought to be a direct borrowing from the *Estoire de Merlin*. In the sections which are represented in both the Huth and the Cambridge MSS., the latter offers many distinctly more acceptable readings and often helps to emend some of the hopelessly corrupt passages. (Malory, *Works*, vol. 3, 1280–1281)

In notes on pages 1281 and 1282, Vinaver gives us further information, specifying many places where the Ribston ("Cambridge") manuscript supplies passages not found in any other possible French source; here I expand Vinaver's notes for easier reading:

> In my first edition I called attention to the fact that [*sic*] Malory's description of the villein "all befurred in blacke shepis skynne" (Vinaver, vol. I, 38). I hardly expected to find exactly the same description in the Cambridge MS: *le sorcoz estoit furre d'une grant penne de moton noire*. The following words and phrases which I have not so far been able to find in any of the French versions may well belong to the same category:
>
> 7. 3 in Cornewaill
> 15. 19–20 on twelfth day
> 32. 30–31 he was a passynge good knyght and but a yonge man
> 41. 32 to putte hit oute of thought
> 47. 20 under a cloth
> 47. 22 of dyvers coloures
> 48. 25 be my fadirs soule Uther
> 49. 6 for all thy crafftis
> 50. 24–25 all the place thereas they fought was ovirbledde with bloode
> 51. 16 for drede of hys wratthe
> 62. 37 by good meanys of the barownes

63. 32–34 than had the kynge and all the barownes . . . grete despite at him
64. 9–10 the beste frende that ye have
64. 3 God thanke youre Hyghnesse . . . Your bounte may no man prayse halff unto the valew
65. 5 God thanke youre good grace
68. 25–27 Peradventure . . . fallith on hymselff
70. 1 for sorow he myght no lenger beholde them
82. 11 he had good chere
99. 13–14 We fyght but for a symple mater
112. 28–29 that was a bettir knyght than he
129. 14–15 I shall honoure the whyle that I lyve
140. 12 In Grete perell of deth
143. 24–25 and seyde, "Hit is no tyme for me to suffir the to reste"
144. 9–11 For though I lak wepon . . . that shall be thy shame
146. 5–7 "Well," seyde kyng Arthure, &c.
150. 20 she alyght of hir horse
157. 6 Many knyghtes wysshed hir brent
158. 16–17 into a grete foreste
159. 32–33 of this dispyte of parte I am avenged
169. 4–5 that I may se your vysage
169. 11–12 that is grete pyte, for he was a passynge good knyght of his body.

Vinaver explains that the Huth version of the *Suite du Merlin* is in many ways more "advanced" than that in the Ribston manuscript; it has moved with the times, so to speak, in the direction toward sophistication apparent in other stories of Merlin. "Malory had no knowledge of this development," he says (Malory, *Works*, vol. 3, 1282), and thus his version of the story betrays an earlier, less polished aspect.

Yet Vinaver stops short of acknowledging the Ribston manuscript as Malory's direct source. For Malory wrote into his *Morte* a great deal of his own composing, which of course cannot be found elsewhere.

Scholars in their scholarly way always hope that some unknown manuscript may turn up that is an exact match for Malory's version. Vinaver himself deprecates this tendency among medieval textual critics when he is studying Eduard Wechssler, saying, "To show how the urge to discover what lies *behind* the extant texts can blind otherwise clear-sighted critics to simple facts it is enough to refer to the view, put forward by Wechssler in his treatise on the Boron Cycle, that some proper names in Malory, such as Margawse (the Queen of Orkney), Garnyssee (the 'sorrowful knight'), and others, which are found nowhere else, must belong to 'redaction A' [an imagined, as-yet-unknown manuscript]. That Malory might have invented these names never occurred to Wechssler or to any of his followers" (Malory, *Works*, vol. 3, 1268–1269n). And yet Vinaver was unable to resist that same scholarly tendency himself in considering whether the Ribston manuscript is Malory's direct source. There are things in the *Morte* not in the manuscript, presumably put there by Malory. Vinaver says, "This is especially true of the minor details of the narrative which are not at present traceable to any French source, but which a lucky discovery may yet show to be part of the French tradition" (Malory, *Works*, vol. 3, 1281). This tendency to brush Malory's own creative genius aside and posit as his source a phantom French manuscript, as yet unknown to mankind, must be very strong.

But there may be another reason, more historical than literary, why Vinaver, after detailing the many correspondences of the Ribston manuscript with the *Morte*, correspondences not found anywhere else, stops short of actually proposing that this manuscript is Malory's direct source. Vinaver had quite possibly never even heard of a Thomas Malory from Yorkshire. It was not until William Matthews unearthed this Thomas and advocated for him in 1966, when Vinaver's monumental edition was nearing completion, that Malory scholars became aware that there was a contender for authorship living in the neighborhood of Ribston, where the manuscript was housed. If Vinaver had been fully aware of the case for this Yorkshire Malory, his judgment may have been different.

Some scholars have differed with Vinaver, notably Michael Murrin, Jonathan Passaro, R.H. Wilson and Fanni Bogdanow. Murrin appears to hold that the Ribston/Cambridge manuscript is Malory's direct source.[46] Both Wilson and Bogdanow seem to hold that the manuscript could have been Malory's direct source, but that fact is not what interests them most; they are interested in finding the sources for that manuscript, especially Bogdanow. She says, "Since Malory and the Cambridge [that is, Ribston] MS. differ in certain details, Vinaver originally suggested that both go back to a common source which represents the original form of the *Suite du Merlin*. More recently R.H. Wilson has denied that there was anything in Malory's account of the rebellion which could not be derived from the [Ribston] Cambridge MS. But the mere fact that the text used by Malory may have been identical in this instance with the Cambridge MS. does not affect the main point at issue."[47] So, we ask, what is the main point at issue? And it turns out to be not the same as our own. Bogdanow and Wilson study the details of various manuscripts to learn how they influence one another. We are searching for the identity of the author of *Le Morte*. Therefore, we need not concern ourselves with the pre-Malory development of the *Suite du Merlin* as it is found in the Ribston/"Cambridge" manuscript. It was what it was, and what it still is now, when he used it.

Jonathan Passaro has argued that this manuscript is Malory's source text. He cites the evidence presented by Helen Cooper in her "extensive study of W's practice of abbreviating Merlin's name to a single red 'M' at various points, a common practice in Cam ['Cambridge']," and quotes her: "The initialization appears more telling still in light of the fact that such an abbreviation never

[46] Michael Murrin, *History and Warfare in Renaissance Epic* (Chicago: University of Chicago Press, 1994), 40.

[47] Fanni Bogdanow, *The Romance of the Grail* (Manchester: Manchester University Press; New York: Barnes and Noble, 1966), 31–32. Further citations of this work will be in parentheses in the text.

appears in W after the point in the text where Malory ceases to use the *Suite* as his source."[48] Then Passaro lists the handful of articles that have glanced at Malory's relationship to this manuscript since the 1950s, and goes on to his own study of the entire text of Ribston/"Cambridge." He concludes that his details of textual analysis, added to Cooper's evidence of the treatment of names, especially the name Merlin, in both the manuscript and in Malory, "offer compelling support for the claim that we have at last identified one of Malory's source manuscripts" (Passaro, 73)

Passaro's argument that the Ribston manuscript is Malory's source is convincing, and no one has presented an argument for any other source text. In fact, there is no other option available. Half a century has passed since Vinaver expressed his hope for a lucky discovery of another manuscript, one that will show Malory's alterations to be not really his own after all. Amazing things can happen, of course, like the finding of the Winchester manuscript of Malory's work in 1934; however, in this case, it seems perverse to insist that we wait for such a discovery to happen again before we say that we know at least one of Malory's direct sources, the Ribston/"Cambridge" *Suite du Merlin*, which declares for itself, in the margin, "Here begins the book which Sir Thomas Malory, Chevalier, reduced into English and caused to be printed by William Caxton." Remember Malory's own signature, in his book, as a Chevalier (chapter 3 above). The margin note in this manuscript builds on that claim of identity and is solid, non-circumstantial evidence concerning the identity of the author of *Le Morte Darthur*. It points squarely to Thomas Malory of Studley and Hutton, Yorkshire, because of his home so close to Ribston, whereas the only other current candidate for authorship, Malory of Newbold Revel, lived much farther away, in Warwickshire, and presumably had no

48 Helen Cooper, "Opening Up the Malory Manuscript," quoted in Jonathan Passaro, "Malory's Text of the *Suite du Merlin*," in *Arthurian Literature* 26, edited by Elizabeth Archibald and David F. Johnson (Cambridge: D. S. Brewer, 2009), 42. Further citations of this source (Passaro) will be in parentheses in the text.

access to an old trunk in a small house of monks in a distant part of England. If Malory of Yorkshire was a Knight Hospitaller, the evidence of the Ribston manuscript is even more compelling, because the house and the trunk and its contents, including the manuscript, belonged to the Chevaliers and they kept it stored at their commandery at Ribston.

There is additional evidence that connects this man with the Hospitaller house at Ribston. It helps to convince us that a Hospitaller knight of the name Thomas Malory, of the Studley and Hutton family of Malorys, after he had served out his years of fighting the Turk in the Holy Land, would have been placed by his superiors in that very house. Gregory O'Malley makes the point that seven of the order's twenty non-prioral commanderies, and some of the richest, were in Yorkshire or Lincolnshire; therefore it was probably not difficult to place a Yorkshire or Lincolnshire man close to his home. Moreover, explaining the order's practice in "collating to benefices," that is, in stationing the members in its various commanderies, O'Malley says that in case of competition for an assignment to a particular spot, "a vacant commandery would be adjudged to the brother who had been born nearest to its site."[49] As we saw above, Thomas Malory was born within walking distance of the Ribston commandery, about ten miles away.

Apparently even more important in the Middle Ages than neighborhood was family. The Malorys were one of the acknowledged "Hospitaller families," who contributed disproportionately of their goods and their sons to the order, and of course the order reciprocated their generosity. A Thomas Malory with a religious vocation would likely choose to be a Hospitaller. Helen Nicholson notes that "men and women might choose to enter the Hospital rather than another religious order because it was the geographically nearest house, or because their relatives had already joined the Order, or because their family had a tradition of donation to the Order (especially if their family had

[49] Gregory O'Malley, T*he Knights Hospitaller of the English Langue* 1460–1565 (Oxford: Oxford University Press, 2005), 42. Further citations of this work will appear in parentheses in the text.

founded the local house of the Order) or because the Hospital had done them services in the past."[50]

In the case of Ribston Commandery, there would certainly be ample cause for the superiors of Thomas Malory to associate his name with the house itself. *In 1217, that house and all of the property associated with it had been a gift from Malory's direct-line ancestor, specifically his fifth great-grandfather, the second Robert DeRos.* The Knights Templar were the recipients of his gift. In fact, that order was the recipient of gifts and treasure beyond counting, from the families of Christendom; Templars became the bankers of the crusading effort as well as the great band of warriors they were. But less than a century after Malory's ancestor donated the house and land at Ribston to the Templars, that order of monk-warriors was disbanded and dispersed. When the Templars were disbanded, what remained of their order melded with the Order of Hospitallers, which welcomed those Templars who wished to join them; all Templar real estate including Ribston Hall passed, by the command of the pope, to the Hospitallers.

The DeRos connection is interesting to Malory scholars for more than one reason. That family came over with the Normans who conquered England, and it became one of the most powerful families among the lords of the north. Peter DeRos, who lived during the reign of Henry I (1100–1135), married Adeline l'Espec, the sister of Walter l'Espec, who founded Cistercian abbeys at Rievaulx (1131) and Warden (1135). Thus the remote great-grandmother and uncle of our Thomas Malory had a strong attachment to the Cistercian Order, so influential in the *Morte,* as it became established in England in the twelfth century, a connection that continued until our Thomas's time, as we have seen. This Walter l'Espec, as it turns out, owned a copy of Geoffrey of Monmouth's *History*. He lent it to a friend, who lent it in turn to her friend Geoffrey Gaimar, who used it

50 Helen Nicholson, "The Knights of Christ? The Templars, Hospitallers and Other Military Orders in the Eyes of Their Contemporaries, 87," ORB: Online Reference Book for Medieval Studies, the-orb.net. Further citations of this work will be in parentheses in the text.

as a source as he composed the first known romance history in vernacular French, *L'Estoire des Engleis,* in the 1130s.[51] It is naturally of interest to Malory scholars to trace the connection between Cistercians and the first stories of King Arthur and his knights, particularly the Grail stories. Both Monmouth's book and Gaimar's book are early items in that history. Already, as the Cistercians got their first toehold in England, credited to Walter l'Espec as a builder of monasteries, we find the Cistercians affiliated not only with such romance-histories but also with Thomas Malory's family. By the time we come to 1217, the DeRos connection with our Thomas is even more obvious. In that year, Malory's fifth great-grandfather Lord Robert DeRos deeded his property at Ribston to the Knights Templar, whence it came within a century to the Knights of St. John, Hospitallers.

We have noted that the document that records DeRos's gift is one of those that were hidden away in the old hide trunk together with the Ribston manuscript of the *Suite du Merlin* for so many centuries and brought out at last by the Dent family in the 1940s, during the Second World War. The charter of bequest is a literary production in itself, in beautiful prose; here is part of it:

> I . . . have given, granted, and by this my present charter have
> confirmed to God and Blessed Mary and the Brethren and
> the Knighthood of the Temple, my manor at Ribston,
> with the advowson of the Church of the same township,
> and the vill of Walshford with the mills of the said vill,
> and with all other their appurtenances and franchises,
> and free customs and easements, to wit,
> with demesnes and homages,
> with free tenants and rents,

[51] Paul Dalton, "The Date of Geoffrey Gaimar's *Estoire des Engleis,* the Connections of His Patrons, and the Politics of Stephen's Reign," *The Chaucer Review* 42, no. 1 (2007): 23.

with assises and villenage,
with woods and plains,
with meadows and pastures,
with ways and paths,
with waters and mills,
with pools and fishponds,
with moors and marshes,
with turbaries and all commons,
with free entries and exits
in all things and places
within the vill and without,
to the aforesaid manor of Ribston appertaining,
without any withholding,
as wholly as I ever held the said manor, entirely....
And this gift I have made to God and St. Mary and the
aforesaid brethren of the Knighthood of the Temple
with my body and in aid of the Holy Land in the east.

The document reads like a medieval litany. It ends with DeRos's oath that "I the aforesaid Robert and my heirs the aforesaid gift ... against all men will warrant, acquit, and defend forever."[52] But forever is a long time. In 1312, only ninety-five years later, the Order of the Knights of the Temple was dissolved. Nevertheless, after a brief scuffle with the English king, who tried to claim it, the property went by papal order to the Knights of St. John, the Hospitallers. The document, which was stashed away with some other documents pertaining to the property and some old French romances, stayed in its trunk at Ribston. The DeRos family connection continued.

In the Middle Ages, from generation to generation there were few changes. There were wars of course, but then there are always wars. Most people lived where their ancestors had lived, if not in the same

52 Robert DeRos, in William Dugdale, *Monasticon Anglicanum* 7 (London: Sam Keble, 1692), 841.

house then in the same district. When the Knights of the Temple were disbanded, the transfer of their property and their members to the Hospitallers meant that their mission continued, and the communities that had formerly been home to a house of Templars became home to a house of Hospitallers, but the two orders of knight-monks were similar enough in their ways to make little difference to the neighbors. A case in point is that of the family of our Thomas Malory; the close connection between this family and the Templars became the close connection between them and the Hospitallers.

Besides the greater stability of lifestyles from generation to generation as compared with our own age, there is another significant aspect of culture in the Middle Ages that is different from our own: whereas there are many today who hardly know who their own grandparents were, medieval people knew their lines of descent. In our democratic age, when we are more or less expected to find our own way in life, it is hardly necessary for us to know our ancestors; consequently, as a rule, we do not. But in the older, hierarchical system, placement in every aspect of life was by heredity. Especially the higher levels of society demanded that their members know well who their people were. There is no question that in the fifteenth century, in Yorkshire, both the superiors in the Order of Knights Hospitallers and the

Sir Robert DeRos, Fursan, effigy

Malory family would have been aware of their history of association, and of the family pedigree.

Sometime around the beginning of the 1400s, Sir William Malory, the father of our Thomas, was born. William's mother, the grandmother of our Thomas, was Joan Plumpton, daughter of Sir William Plumpton. Sir William Plumpton was the son of Sir Robert Plumpton and Lucy DeRos. Lucy DeRos was the daughter of Sir William DeRos of Igmanthorpe, who was the son of William DeRos of Helmsley, who was the son of Lord Robert DeRos of Helmsley, the man who gave Ribston to the Templars in 1217.[53] He was the First Baron of Helmsley, and he held the castle at Helmsley, in ancient times called Hamelac, and also one at Warke. (It is notable for our purpose, because of the much-noticed fact of the preponderance of northerners in the membership of the Order of Hospitallers, that this family, as lords of the north, resided always either in Northumberland or in Yorkshire.) Lord Robert in ancient records is sometimes called *Fursan,* a word difficult to translate or define. It seems to be a nickname describing his role in the Order of the Knights Templar, connoting both respect and affection, possibly something akin to our word *boss*. His aunt, Hyllaria Trussebut, sister to Lord Robert's mother, speaks of him as "brother Robert DeRos, my nephew," so it seems likely that Lord Robert, late in life, became a secular brother of the Order of the Temple. "He married

53 Multiple genealogies online connect these generations. For example, the one found in http://www.southern-style.com/descendants-of-robert-de-ros.htm shows the connection between DeRos and Malory. Matthews gives us a brief pedigree of the Yorkshire Malorys (*Inquiry*, 161), which shows the Plumpton connection but does not notice that Lucy Plumpton, mother of Joan Plumpton Malory, who was the maternal grandmother of Thomas Malory, was born a DeRos. The pedigree chart found at geneologieonline.nl/en/genealogy-heynen/p6616.php shows that Sir Robert De Plumpton, Knight, was married to Lady Lucy DeRos, and that Sir William Plumpton, grandfather of our Thomas, was their son. I attribute the widespread failure to point out that Lucy Plumpton, who was the great-grandmother of Thomas Malory, was born Lucy DeRos, to the overemphasis on names in the male line, which often causes researchers to ignore mothers, who customarily use their husbands' surnames.

in 1191 Isabella, daughter of William the Lion, King of Scotland, and widow of Robert the Bruce, and was one of the 25 barons appointed to enforce the decrees of *Magna Charta*."[54] At any rate, a descendant of this man, named Thomas Malory, wishing to enter the Order of St. John, Hospitallers, would have had no trouble providing the requisite certification of his knightly pedigree; and that same Thomas Malory, if he was a fully proven knight who had served his years of fighting in the Holy Land, would have been a perfect fit for the commandery at Ribston. This is so clear that if a skeptic were to contend otherwise the burden of proof would be on the skeptic. Add that to the fact that the same house was home to the manuscript that Sir Thomas Malory used as his source, and we see that the one fact is evidence for the other: his use of the Hospitallers' manuscript shows that Malory was at Ribston; the fact that he was at Ribston shows that he used the manuscript and was a Knight Hospitaller. The two pieces fit together and verify each other like pieces in a machine or a jigsaw puzzle; there is no need to "file to fit"; there is no need to trim the edges — there is no need to alter the evidence in any way. And there is no discoverable connection whatsoever between Thomas Malory of Newbold Revel and this monastery or this manuscript. The Thomas Malory who fits the picture so comfortably is Thomas Malory of Studley and Hutton, Yorkshire.

[54] Speight, *Nidderdale*, 171. Speight's chapter on "Ribston and the Old Knight Monks" gives us the whole history of the DeRos family from the time they left France in the train of the Conqueror and became established in Yorkshire, until the late nineteenth century, including in detail their association with the knight-monks and the gift of Ribston Hall by Robert DeRos. Of course, it says nothing about the *Suite du Merlin* manuscript, which was not recognized until the twentieth century, nor does it mention the ancestral connection with the Malorys of Yorkshire. But Speight is like a "modern" Dugdale; his book is an encyclopedia of Yorkshire facts and families, reminiscent of *The Antiquities of Warwickshire*. One delightful entry is his drawing of the effigy of Sir Robert DeRos found in the Templars' church in London. Sir Robert appears, in the monument attached to his grave, like a friendly curly-headed boy, meaning that someone who remembered him at that stage of his life must have directed the sculptor of the effigy in his representation.

8

Problems Solved

THERE ARE SOME significant difficulties involved with seeing our author as the Newbold Revel Malory that identifying him as a Knight Hospitaller neatly solves. First, the latter identification summarily deals with the primary problem that readers have found with calling the Newbold Revel knight the author: the seemingly irreconcilable differences between the character of a brigand who had been in and out of jail on serious criminal charges, charges of a violent and terrifying nature, for upwards of ten years, and the gentle persona of the author and his civilized book. *Le Morte Darthur* is, after all, the very book that captures for all subsequent readers in English the whole glorious saga of Arthur and his knights, of the quest for the Holy Grail, of the tragic downfall of the Round Table because of human weakness and sin, of the code of chivalry and the honoring of ladies — in short, it is the very epitome and embodiment of Christian romance. We have had some trouble believing that a man like Sir Thomas Malory of Newbold Revel wrote it. On the other hand, positing a monk-knight as our author suddenly refocuses our view, and the perceived discordance between the writer and his book vanishes.

Second, identifying the author as a Hospitaller knight also gives us an avenue to follow in tracking down the sources that Malory used in his project of translation and adaptation. The author of *Le Morte* says he was a prisoner when he finished his book. Fifteenth-century prisons did not offer the niceties of research libraries for their inmates. In considering that problem, Matthews pointed out that the author could have been a prisoner of war, confined in some country house or castle.

But those places seldom had such a collection of valuable manuscripts either; Matthews tells us that "a library of this kind was never owned by any man less than a prince" (Matthews, 52). However, monasteries did have books. Indeed, it was that fact that led Edward Hicks into some confusion when he claimed that Malory of Newbold Revel, when he was imprisoned in Newgate, must have found the nearby Greyfriars monastery library quite convenient, suggesting that the felons of Newgate might just drop in at will and borrow a book or two from the monks. Monasteries guarded their treasured books; it was commonplace that the books were chained to the desks to foil theft. But monasteries did sometimes lend their books to other religious houses.[55] If Malory was a member of one of those houses, his chances of gaining access to the books he needed were a great deal better than those of an ordinary layperson.

Third, our new thesis belies the argument that only the man of Newbold Revel, of all the candidates for authorship, was a knight. Scholars have long searched for some sort of indication that a Thomas Malory other than the Newbold Revel man was indeed knighted, either in the field or elsewhere, and have found none. If our author was a knight of the Church, however, we can stop searching; the reason that his title is not found in the public records is that part of the ethos of the knightly order to which he belonged was humble retirement from public notice. Moreover, the records of the order in England were confiscated and destroyed at the time of the closing of the monasteries in the sixteenth century, so there exists today no comprehensive list of members.

Fourth, this identification also removes the problem of the author's age. There is clear documentation, found in Sir William Dugdale's encyclopedic work *The Antiquities of Warwickshire,* that Sir Thomas Malory of Newbold Revel was a soldier in the forces of Richard Beauchamp in 1414–1415. If that is so, then this man was almost certainly too old in 1469–1470 to be writing the *Morte*. However, if the author

[55] cistercians.shef.ac/uk/fountains/buildings/library.

of the *Morte* was not the same knight who went soldiering with Richard Beauchamp to Calais, then there is no reason to think he was an old man in his seventies when he wrote the book. If he was the son of William and Dionisia Malory of Hutton and Studley, then he was probably born in the 1430s or 1440s, and he was in the middle of life in 1469–1470 when the book was completed.

Fifth, identifying our author as a knight of the Church explains why there is no record of any wife or children of Thomas Malory of Studley and Hutton, making him almost invisible to researchers; it was not until Matthews discovered by intense search into all the branches of the Malory family that he found a Thomas in Yorkshire; up until then this man was unknown to scholarship. His vow of celibacy forbade him to marry, and his lack of wife and children meant that he was seldom mentioned in family documents. Field mentions this scarcity of records for the Yorkshire man in his argument for the Newbold Revel candidate; he contends that it means the Yorkshire Thomas Malory was of no importance and therefore could not be a knight (Field, 11–24). But the answer is actually in the very fact of his knighthood, since his vocation effectively removed him from public life and the occasions that ordinarily generate public records: marriage, baptism of children, inheritance of property, making of wills and other disposition of goods, service in government posts, record of death and burial, and so forth.

Sixth, it explains why there is confusion in the pedigrees of his family as to his proper place in the lineup of his parents' children; he is variously said to be the first, the third, the fourth, and the sixth son. It is easy for a man who does not marry or beget children to be forgotten in family trees; no one traces his own lineage back to such a man, and therefore the memory of a childless man is apt to be lost altogether. Gregory O'Malley mentions this problem in his history of the priors of the English Hospitallers; he says that it is difficult to track exact family relations for the knights because they are often missing from family pedigrees (O'Malley, 33). In our Sir Thomas's case, he is not missing, but his proper place among his brothers and sisters is uncertain.

Seventh, it removes the necessity of positing in the author repeated changes of allegiance from Yorkist to Lancastrian, and then back again to Yorkist. Peter Field had to face this problem when he was trying to make a certain medieval document, which we will examine in detail presently, refer to the Malory of Newbold Revel. That particular Sir Thomas is generally believed to have been Yorkist in his politics. However, the name appears on a list of men excepted from a general pardon issued by Edward IV in 1468, and scholars have agreed that those refused pardon must have been supporters of the Lancastrian claimant to the throne, the deposed king Henry VI; they must have committed some "treason" against Edward in order for him to deny them pardon. But why would the Yorkist knight Thomas Malory of Newbold Revel commit such an act against his Yorkist king? Faced with some difficulty as he tries to convince us that the man named on the list is the Newbold Revel man, Field proposes that this Sir Thomas turned his coat. But of course, the betrayal was only temporary, and afterwards Sir Thomas was filled with a most dreadful remorse and turned his coat back again in time to write *Le Morte Darthur* (Field, 30ff). All of this fluid allegiance is not necessary, of course, if the man on the list is the Knight Hospitaller Thomas Malory; in fact it is not even necessary to ask ourselves what his political convictions may have been. Whatever faction his superiors in the order told him to support, presumably he did so, by force of arms if directed: he was vowed to obedience.

Eighth, it offers us an answer to a question that also vexed Professor Field as he was studying another medieval document, a list of *milites* — one of them Thomas Malory — who traveled north with King Edward IV in 1462: Who were all these knights, twenty-three of the fifty-nine names on the list, who were otherwise unrecorded? Field, unable to answer that question, fell upon the expedient of accusing the compiler of the list of egregious fraud: "It is incredible," he declared, "that there should be so many entirely unrecorded knights in late fifteenth-century England" (Field, 28). Of course, Field was looking for secular knights; it apparently did not occur to him that some or all of those men may have been knights of Christ; and again, if so, their vocation would have largely kept them out of public records. More about this later.

Ninth, it offers a possible explanation for Caxton's reticence about the author of *Le Morte*. Maybe the author gave the printer no information about himself except that which shows up in his book, because he was conforming to his order's expectation of humble self-effacement in its members, the avoidance of vainglory. If the manuscript of Malory's book was delivered to Caxton by someone other than the author, perhaps the same reason holds; maybe the messenger knew little about the knight who wrote the book, because he was a monk as well as a knight, vowed to withdrawal from worldly acclaim.

Tenth — if we posit not only that our author was a Knight Hospitaller but also that he was the Thomas Malory of Yorkshire supported by William Matthews as the author of *Le Morte* — then we have solved the whole vexed question of dialect, for the dialect that bleeds through the standard English of *Le Morte Darthur* is not that of Warwickshire, the home of the Newbold Revel man; it is a dialect that encompasses the northerly part of England, including Yorkshire (a full discussion is found in the following chapter).

Finally, it gives us an answer to that most puzzling thing of all: Why would a Sir Thomas Malory of Newbold Revel write this book in the first place? Many people have pointed out the discrepancies between the persona of the author, as exemplified in *Le Morte*, and the rakehell character of Sir Thomas of Newbold Revel. Yet no one, to my knowledge, has pointed out that it simply defies common sense and all we know about human nature to think that a thug and a gang leader, a thief and a rapist, a man who does not hesitate to break into homes and abbeys and inflict grievous bodily harm, and a would-be murderer, who finds himself in jail with some time on his hands until he figures out how to get out, would turn to translating some old French manuscripts. That simply does not make sense. The students in my Malory class laughed when I proposed it to them; they know thugs and violent street gangs, both political and nonpolitical, from the news of the world. Suppose, I asked them, such a man were trying to think of something to do to while away the time. He can't visit his friends or invite them to visit him. He can't watch movies or play a computer game. He is bored out of his mind. Does he think, "Oh, I know! I'll translate some old French manuscripts, long ones; that ought to keep me busy for a long time, especially since some of them are written in poetry. And while I'm at it, I'll turn some of those old English poems, which are so hard to read, into prose, too." The idea defies belief. In fact, it is laughable. On the other hand, if the author of *Le Morte* was a religious, a knight-monk, he was perfectly comfortable doing such a thing. The very writing of *Le Morte Darthur*, the reducing into English of all those voluminous French manuscripts, was, after all, quite a monkish thing to do.

SECTION THREE

The Artist at Work

9

Dialect Matters

ONE IMPORTANT TASK in solving the mystery of who wrote *Le Morte Darthur* is to identify the dialect in which it was written and find a man named Thomas Malory who would have been likely to use that dialect. Scholars seem to agree that a published comprehensive study of the language of the *Morte* would be helpful, but so far, unless someone is at this moment planning the publication of such a tool, no one has taken on that daunting task. Critics have contented themselves with pointing out that no such comprehensive study is available and have gone on without it, making such comments as they choose to make about Malory's probable dialect.

But it is disingenuous to pretend that no work of any significance has been done on this subject. In fact, William Matthews, in arguing for the Yorkshire Thomas Malory as author of the *Morte,* produced a lengthy linguistic examination of the book, in which he identified and compared dialectal forms in grammar, spelling, vocabulary, and the alliteration typical of poetry composed in the north of England. Matthews introduced his linguistic analysis by devoting the first twenty-five pages of chapter 3, "The Locale of *Le Morte Darthur,*" to the task; after that he presented his findings in a series of five appendices, labeled D through H. Reading such material is not only time consuming; it can be tedious in the extreme to anyone not particularly fascinated by the variations in our language from one dialect area to another. Indeed, it seems likely that the very fact of its tediousness is what prompted William Matthews to put all this material in appendices, but that placement, added to the fact that the study is hard to read, may be the reason it is largely overlooked by scholars. Yet it is vital to our search for the identity of Sir Thomas Malory, and it cannot be left out of our serious consideration. For the convenience of readers, therefore, dialect analysis is here offered in two parts. We begin our study with a discussion of the implications of existing study to our search for Malory's identity; those readers who are interested in the specifics of dialectal variation may consult appendix A for a summary of the evidence of examples offered by Matthews. However, readers are strongly urged to read Matthews's book; what we have here is only a sample of his expansive and meticulous work.

The reader can readily see that Matthews has done a detailed study of the dialect in *Le Morte Darthur*; however, because of the way the material is crowded onto the page in his book, few could give this work the close attention it requires. It would seem that few have done so. Some major critics appear to be unaware of the extent of Matthews's work, or, if they are aware, decline to acknowledge it, even though they do admit the importance of dialect study in identifying the author of the *Morte*. P.J.C. Field, for example, says that if Matthews's "linguistic arguments that the *Morte* was written in Yorkshire English had been valid, they alone would have made his case almost irresistible." But then Field goes on to say that "the leading authority," by which he means Angus McIntosh, "decisively rejected his linguistic arguments" (Field, 11). No such thing.

First, a more attentive reading of Matthews's study would have shown Professor Field that Matthews, while he is convinced that Thomas Malory of Yorkshire is the author of the *Morte*, does not say that "Yorkshire English" is its language. Likewise, he does not say that "Northern English," meaning the recognized northern dialect, is its language. The term "Yorkshire English" in this context is Field's, not Matthews's. Rather, in a detailed and meticulous study that sets out hundreds of particular forms and usages, Matthews says repeatedly that various forms in Malory are classified in his sources as "north Midland and northern" (Matthews, 178–180), and he says that the language of *Le Morte* is "northernish" (Matthews, 85, 179, 192). Angus McIntosh says that it is "northerly" (McIntosh, *Aevum,* 346). Of course, the country is not divided by fences separating the speakers of one dialect from the speakers of the next. There will always be overlapping, English being the motley language that it is. As for vocabulary, for example: in setting out the variety of nonstandard words in *Le Morte Darthur,* and giving (in appendix D) their dialect sources, Matthews almost always names more than one dialect for each word. Consider the word *AWKE,* for example. The abbreviations that Matthews uses for his reference sources for this entry are OED = *Oxford English Dictionary*; MED = *Middle English Dictionary*; and EDD = *English Dialect Dictionary*:

> AWKE, crosswise; perverse, 415.7: OED, prob. from ON [Old Norse], rare and most examples Nthn; MED, same; EDD, Yks, eAng. SCys. (183)

Notice that the study is fulsome and appears to be complete, that respectable sources are used for the dialectal information, and that four different dialects are named for this one word. In this particular appendix, Matthews treats about **550** words in this way. I have counted the times he says that his sources designate a word as Yorkshire (Yks): **30** times. I have counted the times he says a word is designated NMid, or North Midland: **32** times. He says far more times that his sources call a word Sc, Scottish, **135** times, and, most prevalent, Nthn, northern: **171** times. In vocabulary, considering only those words not standard English, Matthews does not claim that Yorkshire forms predominate but that northern, plus North Midland, plus Yorkshire, plus Scottish — in other words (that is, using Matthews's term), "northernish" — forms definitely do, and he offers good evidence, the entries in three respectable Middle English dictionaries.

In fact, Angus McIntosh, although he is obviously irritated by Matthews, does not appear to disagree seriously with what Matthews actually means. A comparison of certain passages may be enlightening.

Compare Matthews: "The localisms scattered throughout those sections of the Winchester Text that Malory translated from French are distinctively Northern *and North Midland* [emphasis mine] characteristic of the area that flanks the River Humber in Yorkshire" (Matthews, 78).

And McIntosh: "It can be shown that almost all the dialectal forms which Prof. Matthews takes to be northern could well be no more than 'northerly,' i.e. characteristic of anywhere roughly speaking north of a line from Chester to the Wash" (McIntosh, 346–348).

Again, Matthews: "The only deductions to be drawn from the substantial array of northernisms in Winchester and the confirming and additional northernisms in Caxton are, first, that both texts are standardized and, second, that the text from which they both ultimately derive was considerably more northern than they" (Matthews, 88).

And McIntosh: "I believe that the original text behind *W* (and *C*) must have shown even clearer signs than the extant texts of a linguistic ingredient rather more northerly in flavour" (McIntosh, 346).

And again Matthews, this time in a key point in the rebuttal of the Newbold Revel Malory: "The conclusion must be that by far the greatest part of the forms and words which have been listed from *Le Morte Darthur* reflect an origin other than Warwickshire" (Matthews, 205).

And, again, McIntosh, agreeing with Matthews: "To put the matter simply, the *Le Morte Darthur* contained various forms which are too northerly for the everyday language of Newbold Revel" (McIntosh, 348).

The careful reader, as we see, will discern substantial agreement between Matthews and McIntosh, despite their being at loggerheads over terms.

The fact is, however — and there is no reason to deny it — these two scholars support different candidates for author of *Le Morte Darthur*. Matthews supports the Yorkshire Malory and McIntosh supports the Warwickshire Malory. Matthews wrote a whole book proposing and supporting his candidate with all the evidence he found. McIntosh is a little bit more subtle (although actually not all that much). He, the well-known expert on Middle English, offers a short comment on Matthews's case, saying, "The linguistic evidence does not support the hypothesis that the author of *Le Morte Darthur* was from the Ripon-Fountains area" (McIntosh, 347). Fair enough; that is clear-cut. But notice: he does not make any suggestions as to how supporters of a man from that area might figure out some way to show that the linguistic evidence is not conclusive, and thus bypass it. His approach to the other candidate, the one he himself supports, is different. Again, he makes the required clear-cut statement, even though as if reluctantly, and in his prolix fashion: "Yet, as has already been noted, it cannot be denied that the text of *W* as a whole (and ignoring any special features characteristic of the Roman War episode) has a linguistic flavour which hardly accords with everything one would expect to have been current in Newbold Revel in the fifteenth century. Nor can it be denied that there are features even in *C* which point the same way" (McIntosh, 348). But after acknowledging that the linguistic evidence does not support the hypothesis that the author of *Le Morte Darthur* was from Newbold Revel either, McIntosh then goes on to suggest ways in which a supporter of such a candidate might bypass the linguistic evidence. He says it would not be necessary to give up the "old" candidate — that is, the Warwickshire man — and posit a new Sir Thomas Malory. Oh, no. The "old" Sir Thomas may simply have read a great many northern romances, and all that reading of northern romances, suggests McIntosh, may have influenced him to copy their dialect when he wrote *Le Morte Darthur*. He does not mention that a man of the north, likewise, could have read many northern romances, and in his case his own dialect could be suitable for imitating them; then there need not be any effort to copy a dialect not his own, such as the Newbold Revel man would have had — an enterprise that is actually more difficult than it may seem at first glance.

And there is more. McIntosh judges the dialect of the source poem *Morte Arthure* to be not more northerly than Lincolnshire, the next county down from Yorkshire (McIntosh, 347). Then, two separate times in his short review of Matthews's book, he urges the backers of the Warwickshire candidate to look at Axholme (in northern Lincolnshire) for evidence to support their case. First, "the mysterious connection of Sir Thomas Malory of Newbold Revel with Axholme," says McIntosh on page 347, "may therefore be of considerable importance, and worthy of fuller investigation." Then again, on page 348, he suggests that because Sir Thomas of Newbold Revel may have had connections in Lincolnshire, "such a possibility should be looked into by historians, starting perhaps with the Axholme clue." The Axholme clue to which McIntosh alludes twice is the mention by Matthews of an order to arrest Sir Thomas Malory of Newbold Revel, when he was on his famous crime spree, and requiring him to provide guarantors that he would not harm the monastery at Axholme (Matthews, 21). Now, there is no reason why any seeker of the true identity of the author of *Le Morte* should not be urged to follow up on a connection with Lincolnshire. The interesting thing about McIntosh's insistence that the Newbold Revel man may have had some special connection with that county is that McIntosh nowhere suggests that a similar clue regarding Lincolnshire should be followed up by the supporters of the Yorkshire Malory. That clue is this: in listing the landed property of the Yorkshire Malorys, William Matthews names several manors and other holdings; then he says, "It is possible they had interests in Lincolnshire too" (Matthews, 120), and then, in a matter-of-fact way, goes on with his list. Surely the fact that the parents of the Yorkshire Thomas Malory may have held property in Lincolnshire is a clue just as well worth following as the fact that Thomas Malory of Newbold Revel was arrested on suspicion of intending to harm a Lincolnshire monastery, but McIntosh does not urge anyone to follow it. He favors Malory of Newbold Revel.[56]

McIntosh takes issue with Matthews's conclusion that "the residual northern dialect in both texts establishes almost as a certainty that the author must have lived in the north and probably in Yorkshire" (Matthews, 113). McIntosh says that almost all the forms

[56] The problem of bias in the study of dialect is a serious one; the example given here, of the renowned dialectician Angus McIntosh and the stumbling block of his own bias in favor of the Warwickshire Malory, demonstrates how human partiality can get in the way of objective study. There is now great promise of solving this problem with cutting-edge computer technology, dubbed artificial intelligence, or AI, which can eliminate the human factor in dialect analyses. The technology works not by examining scholarly analysis typed into charts but by mimicking the "deep neural networks" of the brain, with no preconceptions, forming conclusions based exclusively on labeled sample texts presented to it.

Recent AI studies of medieval dialects are pertinent to our search for Malory's identity. In 2021, two young women, Victoria Baker and Catriona Linton, who had learned the technique in their school data science club where J. R. Linton was their mentor, trained an AI system to consider dialects and presented their findings to the International Congress of Medieval Studies. An abstract says that the system is "a classifier program capable of identifying the correct dialect of a previously unseen Middle English document with greater than 94% accuracy, using a system of nine dialects. General language training used the University of Michigan Corpus of Middle English. The dialectal distinctions were based on those used in the University of Edinburgh LALME and LAEME projects; these were used to label sample texts with specific geographic origins from the University of Stavanger MELD and MEG-C CORPORA."

Ongoing work by J. R. Linton has increased the overall accuracy of the program to greater than 95 percent. Linton has applied the AI to the texts of *Le Morte Darthur*, with reference to two candidates for author, Malory of Newbold Revel and Malory of Hutton-Conyers: "The [initial] analysis shows a near-total lack of support for Malory of Newbold Revel (approximately 1% in both Caxton and Winchester) ... and consistent support for Malory of Hutton-Conyers (16% in both texts)." In both texts, there is significant "noise" in the data from several different dialect areas not corresponding to any known Malory candidate for author of *Le Morte*; this problem possibly can be explained by the fact that Caxton's typesetters and the scribes who worked on both texts may have come from various parts of England. If it were not for that possibility, and the fact that we have no information about their origins, the identification of dialect may have been even stronger. Linton concludes that "the residual dialectal character of both Caxton and Winchester lends strong support for Malory of Hutton-Conyers as the original author."

Matthews calls northern could be no more than northerly, and that Matthews's "case for the northern origin of the text is gravely weakened by his enthusiastic obfuscation of this matter" (McIntosh, 346). There is no doubt that Matthews enthusiastically supports the Yorkshire candidate, and although he does not claim a dialect called "Yorkshire English" for his man, in his discussion he does mention that county several times. The way he words his conclusion in this case, however, is unfortunate, putting so much weight as it seems to do on the dialect of the Caxton and Winchester versions of *Le Morte Darthur*. However, despite the unfortunate wording, what Matthews means is obvious to his readers. He makes this assertion as part of his summation of all sorts of evidence, not only textual, for the Yorkshire Thomas Malory, and his readers know by this point in his book that there was only one Thomas Malory to be found in the North Country — the one from Yorkshire. The fact of the residual dialect features comes as a final point in a long argument for this man. Some other points included in the argument and in the summation of evidence include local place names found in the book but not in its sources; the author's evident knowledge of legends of the north; familiarity with important northern poems; ability to understand and translate the difficult northern poetic language; and facility with the particularly northern poetic technique of alliteration, which comes easily and even insistently to Malory throughout his book. Matthews adds all this to the fact that there were Malorys in Yorkshire, and one of them was named Thomas. He asserts that the northern features found in the author's dialect cap the argument: he must have been from the north. And since there is only one candidate for authorship from the north, the author must have been, in fact, the Yorkshire Thomas Malory.

As to McIntosh's own assessment of the dialect of the *Morte*, he states it briefly by declaring that dialect to be not "northern" precisely but "northerly" (McIntosh, 346) — not much different, many readers will surely think, from Matthews's "northernish" (Matthews, *Inquiry*, 85, 179, 192).

McIntosh defines the area of this "northerly" language to be north of an imaginary line drawn "from Chester to the Wash." He has this to say about where the residual traces of nonstandard English forms in the *Morte* originate:

> A great deal of even professional discussion of such problems is often bedevilled by a confusion about the term "northern dialect." In the present instance it can be shown that almost all the dialectal forms which Prof. Matthews takes to be northern could well be no more than "northerly," i.e. characteristic of anywhere roughly speaking north of a line from Chester to the Wash. (McIntosh, 346)

Angus McIntosh is obviously annoyed by any sort of sloppiness in designating a form "northern." However, since he does not make clear how he himself would define that term, either in this review of Matthews's book or in his essay that touches upon the same annoyance, "The Textual Transmission of the Alliterative *Morte Arthure*," we are obliged to look elsewhere for a working definition of "northern" English dialect. Thomas Pyles, in his history of the English language, says that in Middle English, "the Northern dialect corresponds roughly to Old English Northumbrian, its southernmost eastern boundary being also the Humber."[57] So, because McIntosh has made it clear that he objects to calling Malory's dialect "northern," we infer that even though McIntosh says Malory's English sources were composed "anywhere roughly speaking" north of a line between Chester on the west and the Wash on the east, he actually means not exactly anywhere roughly speaking but anywhere roughly speaking except Northumberland, Durham, and most of Yorkshire. In fact, he specifies that he judges Malory's sources to have been "most at home" (McIntosh, 348) in Lincolnshire, which is the county immediately adjacent to Yorkshire, to the southeast, but still north of his invisible

[57] Thomas Pyles, *The Origin and Development of the English Language*, 2nd ed. (New York: Harcourt, Brace, Jovanovich, 1971), 55.

boundary of "northerly" English. Matthews judged the dialect to be "distinctively Northern and North Midland, characteristic of the area that flanks the River Humber in Yorkshire" (Matthews, 78). The Humber marks the dividing line between Yorkshire and Lincolnshire. Axholme, the location that McIntosh advises supporters of the Newbold Revel Malory to investigate, is about fifteen miles south of the Humber. Without knowing exactly how much area "flanks" the Humber in Matthews's estimation, if we follow his directions in looking for Malory's dialect, we might get pretty close to Axholme. We can see that these two scholars vary somewhat in their conclusions, but there is an underlying similarity in what they both judged to be the dialectal origins of Malory's work. Only a small area is under consideration: in the eastern part of England, the land between the northern bank of the Humber River and southward to the northern bank of the Wash; see map. Matthews is the more specific

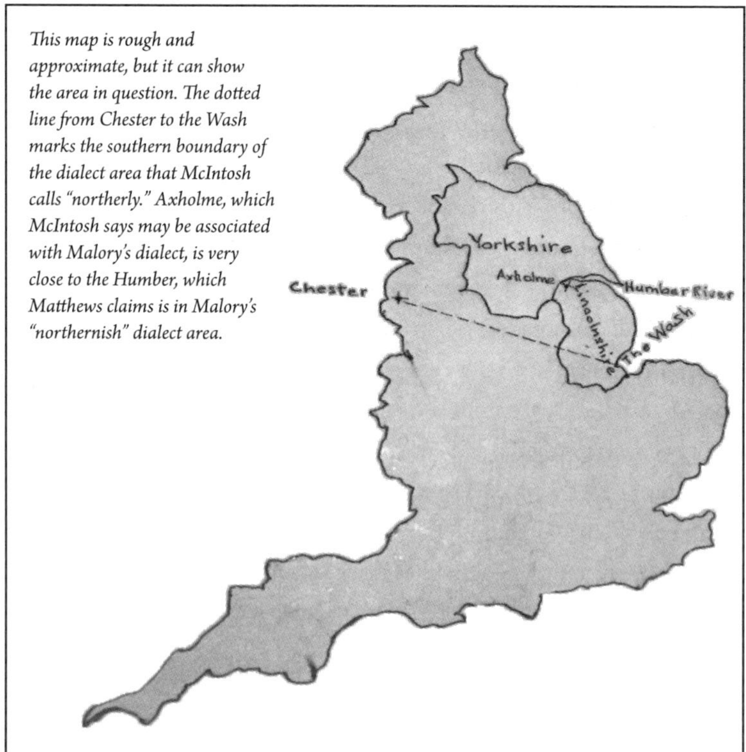

This map is rough and approximate, but it can show the area in question. The dotted line from Chester to the Wash marks the southern boundary of the dialect area that McIntosh calls "northerly." Axholme, which McIntosh says may be associated with Malory's dialect, is very close to the Humber, which Matthews claims is in Malory's "northernish" dialect area.

of the two — he specifies the area that flanks the Humber. McIntosh directs us toward Axholme, which is only about fifteen miles away from the Humber, and a good bit north of the Wash. And certainly they are agreed that the language of Newbold Revel, Warwickshire, is right out of consideration.[58]

McIntosh has more than this to say on what he thinks is the provenance of Malory's book. He discusses the Winchester manuscript, with its two "hands," and tells us he judges both to be from Northamptonshire (just south of Lincolnshire). However, hand A is "more northerly in flavour" than hand B; therefore, he believes that "the original text behind *W* (and *C*) must have shown even clearer signs than the extant texts of a linguistic ingredient rather more northerly in flavour than what one would associate with the everyday language of West Northants" (McIntosh, 346). To recapitulate, here are McIntosh's pronouncements:

First, the alliterative *Morte Arthure* and the stanzaic *Le Morte Arthure* were both probably written not in Yorkshire but in the next county down, Lincolnshire. Therefore, McIntosh declares the language in them to be not northern but northerly.

Second, although both *W* and *C* were probably copied in Northamptonshire, the original from which Malory's two scribes copied his work in *W* and *C* was written farther north than Northamptonshire. We can take note that north of Northamptonshire lie Lincolnshire, Yorkshire, Durham, and then, at the extreme north of England, Northumberland, and deduce that McIntosh believes the copies were made from an

58 Richard R. Griffith, "The Authorship Question Reconsidered: A Case for Thomas Malory of Papworth St Agnes, Cambridgeshire," in *Aspects of Malory*, ed. Toshiyuki Takamiya and Derek Brewer (Woodbridge: D. S. Brewer 1981), 165, reminds us that the elimination of Malory of Newbold Revel by this conclusion regarding dialect still leaves the field open for his candidate, Malory of Papworth St. Agnes. However, the difficulty regarding that candidate is not his dialect but the fact that he was not a knight, unless he was so dubbed at the very end of his life, and there is no evidence that he was ever a prisoner. We know he was not a monastic knight either, for he was a married man with ten children. Subsequent citations of this source will be in parentheses in the text.

original that was composed in either Lincolnshire, Yorkshire, Durham, or Northumberland; however, since, as we have seen, he is irritated by the designation of these forms as "northern," corresponding to Old Northumbrian, we may be correct to eliminate Northumberland from consideration, for the dialect of Northumberland is unquestionably northern. We are left with the vastness of Yorkshire right in the middle of the area "north of Northamptonshire." The interesting thing, of course, is that in spite of McIntosh's edginess over definitions and boundaries, Matthews says something quite similar to what McIntosh says. Matthews says there are many forms in *Le Morte* that are "northernish" (Matthews, 85, 179, 192); McIntosh says that the residual dialect forms in Malory are not northern but "northerly" (McIntosh, 346). Concerning the two texts of *Le Morte*, McIntosh says, "I believe that the original text behind *W* (and *C*) must have shown even clearer signs than the extant texts of a linguistic ingredient rather more northerly in flavour than what one would associate with the everyday language of West Northants." The reader may agree with me that the wordiness in McIntosh's review makes it difficult to follow his argument. However, if we take the trouble it requires, there is, behind the pettishness, not support but certainly not a resounding rebuttal of Matthews, who found that Malory's English sources are northernish, and that the *Morte* itself was probably written in the area flanking the Humber in Yorkshire, which we can see is in the middle of the area mentioned by McIntosh, that is, farther north than Northamptonshire (but not so far north as Northumberland, where the dialect is not northerly or northernish but decidedly northern).

But it can't be missed that McIntosh likes the Newbold Revel candidate. He ends his review of Matthews by telling us that when Malory turned to reading northern romances, "what he could have drawn on in this way was therefore almost certainly accessible to him, still in substantially northerly form, *in his own neighbourhood of Warwickshire, Leicestershire and Northants*" (McIntosh, 348, emphasis mine). Thus we see McIntosh simply assuming a priori that Malory of Newbold Revel is the author under discussion; he reveals his bias by his placid assumption that Malory's neighborhood was

Warwickshire, Leicestershire, and Northamptonshire. But we could, of course, logically make the same argument he makes in support of Malory of Newbold Revel about all the candidates for authorship; any one of them actually could have had special connections with Lincolnshire, and any one of them could have had access to northern romances. We could also add to his list of the author's neighbors all the corners of Yorkshire, and Papworth, and even Wales, since candidates have been proposed for each of those places at one time or another, if we were objective. But McIntosh is not objective. He believes in the Newbold Revel man. This sort of argument obviously makes hash out of any sort of logical inquiry into a person's dialect.

However, McIntosh does say, unambiguously, that the dialect of the *Morte* is "too northerly for the everyday language of Newbold Revel" (McIntosh, 348). Professor Field, that most ardent advocate of the Newbold Revel candidate, does not mention that pronouncement from McIntosh. He says, instead, that if Matthews's linguistic arguments had been valid, "they alone would have made his case almost irresistible. As we have seen, however, the leading authority decisively rejected his linguistic arguments" (Field, 1). I repeat: no such thing.

10

Of Manors and Manuscripts, Part II

THE DEROS CONNECTION with the Malorys of Yorkshire has gone unnoticed in Malory scholarship until now, but it is of utmost importance in our search for the author's source books. It may well be that the Ribston *Suite du Merlin* was part of the gift of Lord Robert DeRos to the Templars. Vinaver believed that this manuscript was an early fourteenth-century copy by an Anglo-Norman scribe from an original written in the French dialect of Picardy. Some of the deeds and documents pertaining to the Ribston property, stored in the same trunk as the Ribston *Suite,* date to the eleventh century. We have examined one record, the transfer of the DeRos property to the Templars, which is dated 1217. In trying to learn when the manuscript was stored away with these deeds, our first question must be, of course, *When were the two stories that are bound together written?* One of them, as mentioned above, is *L'Estoire del Saint Graal,* which is less important in our search because Malory did not use it; the other is the *Suite du Merlin,* which he did use. The *Estoire del Saint Graal* has been studied by Alison Stones, who tells us that "the *Estoire* branch of the Lancelot-Grail romance is based on a verse text composed c. 1200 by an author who names himself Robert de Boron."[59] Only one copy survives of

[59] Alison Stones, "The Lancelot-Grail Story: Summary of the Branches," University of Pittsburgh, https://www.lancelot-project.pitt.edu/LG-web/TheStory-Summary.htm. Further citations of this work will be in parentheses in the text.

Robert de Boron's verse *Estoire,* but prose adaptations, of which the Ribston copy is one, proliferated early in the thirteenth century. We can say, therefore, that the Ribston *Estoire* could not have been written before about 1200; possibly it was written within a few years after that date. Stones says that "the *terminus ante quem* ... for the composition of the prose *Estoire* is determined by its presence ... in Rennes, BM 255, which is datable c. 1220 or early in the 1230s." Let us assign to our copy of the *Estoire* a composition date of 1215; this date falls midway between the "not earlier than" date of 1200 and the "not later than" date of the Rennes BM manuscript, 1220 to early 1230s, and 1215 seems about right. So, by our reckoning, the *Estoire del Saint Graal* that is bound together with the *Suite du Merlin* (which proclaims itself the book used by Thomas Malory) could have been stored at Ribston around 1215, before the property was given to the Templars by Thomas Malory's ancestor in 1217. It could have belonged to Lord Robert DeRos and been part of his gift to the monks.

Now we consider the book bound with it, the *Suite du Merlin,* Thomas Malory's source for the beginning of the *Morte.* This manuscript, remember, is said by Eugene Vinaver to be a copy of a Picard original. The Merlin romance embodied in this manuscript is given the same *terminus ante quem* as the accompanying *Estoire,* by the fact that it also is found in the Rennes, BM 255 file, which is datable 1220. Alison Stones: "The Middle English prose *Merlin* offers a straight-forward and fairly accurate translation into English of a single source, the Merlin section of the Old French Vulgate Cycle, an interconnected set of Arthurian works composed during the first half of the thirteenth century.... The work is a treasure-trove of Arthurian characters, incidents, and motifs—many of which are found nowhere else in Arthurian literature" (Stones). We know that Malory used it; the margin note in the manuscript tells us so. And possibly its date of composition matches that of the *Estoire* that accompanies it in the Ribston trunk. Both of them are bound within the same binding. Both are included in the BM 255 file, datable 1220. We have posited a composition date of the *Estoire* as circa 1215. There seems to be no reason why the accompanying *Suite du Merlin* could not have been written around 1215 as well and deposited in the trunk, along with the *Estoire,* before Ribston was given to the monks. Paleographers, in dating a medieval manuscript, regularly allow a margin of at least seventy to eighty years. If we use a margin of about eighty-five years, it will not be necessary to dispute Vinaver's dating, for our date of 1215 is eighty-five years before the beginning of the 1300s; Vinaver says that the Ribston copy of the *Suite* is the work of an Anglo-Norman scribe, and he puts its date early in the 1300s. We see that both the *Estoire* and the *Suite* bound with it could possibly have been part of the original gift of Ribston and all its appurtenances to the Templars from Thomas Malory's ancestor Lord DeRos. The DeRos family was Anglo-Norman; it had a close affinity to the Order of Knights of the Temple, and the majority of the original Templars were from Picardy. Stored with the manuscripts in the same old hide trunk are the family's deeds and other documents relating to its Ribston property. Moreover, as we have seen, the family had a very early interest in romance history; its ancestor Walter l'Espec had owned a copy of Geoffrey of Monmouth's *History* by 1140.

If our chronology of these manuscripts and their provenance is roughly right, then the manuscript *Suite du Merlin,* Sir Thomas Malory's source for the beginning of *Le Morte Darthur,* from the date of its composition was owned by the family of Sir Thomas Malory of Studley and Hutton, Yorkshire.

And not only does the Malory-DeRos family connection lead us directly to the monastery at Ribston where the *Suite du Merlin* manuscript was housed; it also gives us a path to other manuscripts to which Malory almost certainly had access. The DeRos family's interest in Arthurian literature continued into our Thomas Malory's time. Thomas's distant cousin Sir Richard Ros was one of the few Englishmen to own medieval manuscripts of the Arthurian tales. William Matthews, in his meticulous listing of the medieval manuscripts known to have been in certain hands in the fifteenth century, tells us that Sir Richard Ros owned a "great book containing an *Estoire del Saint Graal,* a *Quest,* and a *Mort Artu*" (Matthews, 141). Matthews knew, and mentioned in another part of his book, that Sir

William and Dionisia Malory, our Thomas's parents, "near Rievaulx Abbey and not far from Newton" (the home of Robert Thornton, the scribe who copied the only extant copy of the alliterative *Morte Arthure*), "had a half share in the manor of Upper Helmsley" (Matthews, 120). Matthews said nothing about the fact that the castle at Helmsley was the ancestral home of the DeRos family, from whom our Thomas was descended, or that there is some interest to us in noting that Thomas's parents owned part of the Helmsley estate, but in fact there is. We see by the fact that William and Dionisia were still not only, of course, part of the DeRos kindred; they were also owners of part of the old DeRos property. And it is remarkable that Thomas's distant cousin Sir Richard Ros was also, like Thomas, a writer. Probably his most famous work is a poem called "La Belle Dame sanz Mercy"; apparently, also like his cousin, he was interested in translating French poems, for the earliest print of "La Belle Dame," in 1532, includes the notation that it was translated out of French.[60]

Another aspect of this DeRos connection that is of interest to us in our search is that Richard Ros the poet, who owned some of the books that our author needed for his project, was close kin, either brother or father's brother, to Thomas DeRos, Ninth Baron of Helmsley, who was comrade in arms to Sir Humphrey Neville. These DeRos family members were distant cousins, in different lines, of both Neville and Thomas Malory. As we have noted, Humphrey Neville and Thomas DeRos went with King Henry VI and Queen Margaret when they fled into Scotland after the Battle of Towton. After that, Thomas and Humphrey together went on private raids into the north of England and later also into battles, until DeRos was caught and beheaded in 1464. All of this, of course, is connected with Thomas Malory because of the kinship between him and Thomas DeRos, Humphrey's friend and kinsman, and because Malory's name is adjacent to the name Humphrey Neville in King Edward's list of those excepted from a general pardon in 1468.

[60] Harl. Manuscript 372, the poem, first printed in Thynne's Chaucer of 1532, is ascribed "Translatid out of Frenche by Sir Richard Ros." "Richard Ros," Wikiwand, https://www.wikiwand.com/en/Richard_Ros.

So, we have the Malory-DeRos familial connection. We have Thomas Malory's parents' ownership of a part of the ancestral DeRos property, about an hour away on horseback from either the Ribston commandery or the Malory home at Studley. We have the kinship between Sir Richard Ros and Thomas Malory, and their common interest in Arthurian literature and in translating French poems. And we have Thomas Malory connected with Humphrey Neville, comrade in arms of Richard Ros's brother or nephew, Baron Thomas DeRos; Malory and Neville are listed together in King Edward's 1468 list of unpardonables. Together, all of this amounts to a strong argument that Richard Ros knew his Malory kinsman well enough to make his manuscript collection available to him, especially if Thomas Malory resided in the very monastery that their common ancestor Lord Robert DeRos had donated to the monks.

If Ros did lend his books to Malory, and if our author did use the Thornton manuscript, then we have found Malory's sources of the *Queste* and the *Mort Artu,* and we can add them to the Thornton manuscript of the alliterative *Morte Arthure,* and the Ribston manuscript of the *Suite du Merlin*. It seems probable that all these books were to be found within a tight geographical compass; all of them except the Thornton at Newton where the scribe lived could be reached easily on horseback in about an hour from one location to another. The *Suite du Merlin* was at Ribston. The *Queste* and the *Mort Artu* were probably at Helmsley, the DeRos home. Even the Thornton was about two hours distant, at East Newton. Mary Hamel tells us that "Robert Thornton, lord of East Newton in Ryedale in the North Riding of Yorkshire, was a gentleman amateur who copied this variety of works for his own and his family's use and enjoyment.... MS T [*Morte Arthure*] itself shows marked signs of family use at least until the late sixteenth or early seventeenth century, and it probably left East Newton only in the late seventeenth century."[61] Only one

[61] Mary Hamel, ed. *Morte Arthure: A Critical Edition* (New York and London: Garland, 1984), 4. Further citations of this work will be in parentheses in the text.

manuscript copy of the alliterative *Morte Arthure* exists. Exactly where the poem was composed is not known. William Matthews, author of the only full, book-length critical analysis of the poem,[62] believed, possibly because it was written in the northern dialect and because Robert Thornton who copied it was a Yorkshireman, that it was written in Yorkshire. Matthews credited the dialect scholar Angus McIntosh with saying the original of the poem had been written "not many miles from York" (Matthews, 92), but McIntosh denied the attribution (McIntosh, 347).

Morte Arthure's northern dialect is difficult. Matthews makes the point that even modern scholars, with all their scholarly resources, find it hard to understand, and quotes this passage as illustration:

> Than gliftis the gud kynge and glopyns in herte,
> Gronys fulle grisely with gretande teris;
> Knelis downe to the cors and kaught it in armes,
> Kastys upe his vmbrere and kyssis hyme sone,
> Lokes one his eye-liddis, that lowkkide ware faire,
> His lippis like to the lede, and his lire falowede. (Matthews, 93)

Matthews believed it unlikely that anyone not a native of the northern part of England would have had the required expertise in that dialect to use the Thornton manuscript, transliterating it into standard English as Malory did.

Adding to our difficulties, Eugene Vinaver and E. V. Gordon in 1937 introduced the idea that the version of the poem found in Thornton is exceedingly corrupt,[63] and certain others since then have supported that view. Some scholars, notably those who endorse Thomas Malory of Newbold Revel, Warwickshire, so far away from

62 William Matthews, *The Tragedy of Arthur: A Study of the Alliterative "Morte Arthure"* (Berkeley and Los Angeles: University of California Press, 1960).

63 E. V. Gordon and E. Vinaver, "New Light on the Text of the Alliterative *Morte Arthure*," *Medium Aevum* 6, no. 2 (1937): 81–98.

the northern dialect area, believe that there must have been another copy of the poem somewhere, and Malory must have used that one. That one has vanished from the known world, but these scholars are ever hopeful that it will reappear someday. William Matthews was convinced that Malory himself introduced all the "corruptions" that are found in parts of the Winchester text of *Le Morte,* which has Thornton as its source; Malory seems to have been adept at changing the poem to suit himself. One of Matthews's points of support is Malory's aptitude with alliteration, which is scattered throughout *Le Morte,* even where Malory is translating from French or composing new material; there seems to be no real explanation for his insistent use of that technique except that he enjoyed it and was good at it. Alliteration, long associated with the poetry of the north, came easily to Malory. Matthews makes another point: the changes that Malory made in the narrative of the poem are so significant that they clearly demonstrate his skill in altering his source; he changed the tragic ending of Arthur's life to a triumphant one, and he did it so smoothly and well that it is, Matthews says, "straining at a gnat" to think Malory would not be capable of altering the alliterative poem himself and making it what it is today (Matthews, 98).

Terence McCarthy has entered the lists as another supporter of Malory himself rather than some unknown previous writer as the one who changed the alliterative poem. Concerning the "corruptions" that have caused scholars to posit a lost manuscript, McCarthy says, "It seems much more plausible to believe that Malory's working method brought about a vast number of changes to the alliterative poem," and goes on to say that the claim that "anything original to Malory and tainted with alliteration is a remnant of some Ur-Morte Arthure [*sic*] is unacceptable" (McCarthy, "Alliterative Tradition," 63). He asks, *Why do we need to posit a lost version of the poem, when Malory himself was making his own version of it?* "Minor repair work on the Thornton text can well be undertaken by using the Winchester manuscript, but we should go no further." The evidence of Malory's text in syntax, vocabulary, alliteration, rhythm, and phraseology is that if Malory was not responsible for the changes, then the lost poem would have had to be radically different from the Thornton (63). "But I fail to see," says McCarthy, "why we must postulate a lost reviser of the poem when we have Malory. If Malory offers evidence that the poem has been tampered with, the evidence that he offers is that, more often than not, he is to blame" (64). And, to continue, "the fact that Malory did not apparently notice that he had barely standardized the language of the poem suggests a familiarity with the alliterative tradition that very few of his contemporaries would have shared. It is hard to believe that such a familiarity could be merely accidental and that having been idiosyncratic enough to integrate a poem from his native tradition into a series of French-based romances he should then merely forget that native tradition altogether" (94n). Indeed.

Then McCarthy suggests that Malory's own version of the story found in the poem may have been composed by memory (McCarthy, 64). That suggestion is intriguing. We know that the alliterative tradition, characteristic of the ancient Germanic poems of the great north, is believed to have been sung or recited by a *scop,* from memory, for passing ages before those poems were ever written down. The presence of Danes in *Beowulf,* the best known of them, reminds us that we are talking about the *far north.* It is not surprising that, as the alliterative tradition moved into England, it came first and was preserved longest in the northern counties, meaning that if Malory was accustomed enough to oral presentation and memorization to be able to work within that milieu himself, then he probably was a northerner. McCarthy closes his article by saying, "By the fifteenth century the alliterative movement was in decline or travelling north. In the south there was one last major moment of rejuvenation when Malory took up the *Morte Arthure* and fitted it in to his own anthology" (McCarthy, 80), thus showing us that he believes in the southern candidate, the man from Warwickshire, as author of *Le Morte Darthur.* But he does not explain why he believes in that man, or why the northern poem would have been so far south in the first place.

We do have one piece of evidence that Malory heard, rather than read, the name of a major character in his romance, *The Wedding of Sir Gawain and Dame Ragnell.* That one example of obviously oral transmission of the Norse word *grome,* man, places Malory in the ancient oral tradition associated with the north of England (see chapter 11, "A Tale of a Loathly Lady"). It is not difficult to believe, possibly with Terence McCarthy, that Malory was able when he so chose to write out old alliterative stories, or at least parts of them, from memory.

Meanwhile, the discussion continues as to whether Malory used the Thornton copy of *Morte Arthure* or some long-vanished other copy. In 1935, J. L. N. O'Loughlin brought attention to one line near the end of the Thornton manuscript, as the story of Arthur's death comes to a close: "And many men say that there ys wrytten upon the tumbe thys: hic iacet Arthurus, rexquondam rexque futurus." O'Loughlin observed, "There is no foundation for saying that this remark is the work of the poet. The line has been added in a much later hand.... It is the inscription on Arthur's tomb.... put there in 1278, and the line is also quoted in *Arthur* (ed. Furnivall, 1864), line 624."[64] Mary Hamel, in notes to her 1984 edition of *Morte Arthure,* agrees that the line was certainly not part of the poem and lists three other places where it appears: in *Arthur,* in Malory's *Le Morte Darthur,* and in Fordun-Bower's *Scotichronicon* (397). That line is a key element in Matthews's argument, one that is hard to dispute. His dialect study includes a full consideration of Malory's use of the Thornton manuscript, showing that Malory certainly could and did understand its dialect. But even those who have read Matthews's dialect study may have overlooked his analysis (Matthews, 89–100) of Malory's relationship to the Thornton. Among other things, for example, Matthews discusses Malory's use of that famous epitaph, placed just after the burial of Arthur in *Le Morte Darthur* (Matthews, 98). Of course, it is the source of T. H. White's title, *The Once and Future King.* But it is not by any means the only ancient epitaph of Arthur that was available. Matthews gives us these:

[64] J. L. N. O'Loughlin, "The Middle English Alliterative *Morte Arthure,*" *Medium Aevum* 4 (1935): 159.

> *Mort Artu*: "Ci gist li rois Artus qui par sa valeur mist en sa subjection xii. roiaumes."
>
> Gerald of Wales: "Hic iacet sepultus inclytus rex Arthurus cum Wenneveria uxore sua secunda in insula Avallonia."
>
> Gerald of Wales: "hic iacet sepultus inclytus rex Arthurus in insula Avallonia cum uxore sua secunda Wenneveria."
>
> Ralph of Coggeshall: "hic iacet inclitus rex Arturius, in insula Avallonis sepultus."
>
> Camden's Brittania, citing a first copy in Glastonbury Abbey: "Hic iacet sepultus inclitus rex Arturius in insula Avalonia."
>
> Bishop Usher, crediting Simon of Abingdon: "Hic iacet gloriosissimus rex Britonum Arturus."

Malory used none of the above epitaphs; he used the one in the Thornton copy of *Morte Arthure*. Then things get interesting. Matthews goes on:

> But an important detail concerning it has escaped recent notice. In the Thornton manuscript, the epitaph appears between the last line of the poem and the copyist's colophon, "Here endes Morte Arthure, writene by Robert of Thorntone." The most significant facts however are these: the epitaph is written in a different hand from that of the poem and that of the colophon; it is also written with a thinner and now browner ink. The deduction can only be that the epitaph was not part of the original poem or of the copy that Thornton used: someone unknown had added it to Thornton's manuscript. If that is so, it is peculiar to this copy. (Matthews, 99)

The inescapable deduction is that Thomas Malory used this very copy of the alliterative poem. It overstrains credulity to propose that a vanished manuscript of *Morte Arthure*, wherever it may be, also has this epitaph added in. Obviously, Malory *saw* the words *rexquondam rexque futurus* that had been added to the Thornton copy, and he added them to *Le Morte Darthur*. Matthews continues, "The manuscript is now in the Lincoln Cathedral library.... Names scribbled in the margins indicate the manuscript was still in Thornton possession in the seventeenth century. If Malory did use this manuscript, therefore, he probably used it in Yorkshire" (Matthews, 99). Where else?

Professor Field says, "Matthews argued that Malory worked up the Roman War story from the only known manuscript of the Alliterative *Morte Arthure*, but to my knowledge no other scholar has been persuaded to share that view."[65] I share that view.

There is still the mystery to be considered of who wrote the famous inscription in the margin of the Ribston/"Cambridge" manuscript, informing us that this is the beginning of the book that Sir Thomas Malory reduced into English and caused to be printed by William Caxton. It could have been anybody, say the scholars; most do not even speculate as to who it was. If pressed, they may emphasize that the note could have been written long after *Le Morte* was finished, by anyone who took an interest in it. All that is true, of course. But now that we have noticed that the manuscript was owned by the Hospitallers, that it was housed in a Hospitaller monastery, and that it was signed with a Hospitaller cross, we can see that whoever wrote the margin note in the late fifteenth or early sixteenth century was almost certainly a Hospitaller himself, who lived in that same house. It might have been someone who knew the author well. But scholars have avoided mentioning the elephant in the room: it could have been Sir Thomas Malory himself.

[65] P. J. C. Field, "Caxton's Roman War," in *The Malory Debate*, ed. P. J. C. Field (Cambridge, MA: D. S. Brewer, 1998), 143.

11

A Tale of a Loathly Lady

The Wedding of Sir Gawain and Dame Ragnell is a fifteenth-century romance in English verse, which tells the story of King Arthur's entrapment while he is out hunting, by a knight with a peculiar name, Sir Gromer Somer Joure, who accuses Arthur of having stolen his lands and given them to Sir Gawain. Sir Gromer gives Arthur a year to answer the question "What do women want?" or lose his head. Sir Gromer's sister, who is the cause of the entrapment, and is truly a loathly lady, wants to marry Sir Gawain. The plot is as familiar as the characters, and nobody is surprised when the story proceeds in time-honored fashion to the happy ending. However, there are some surprises. One is that the name of the knight who accuses Arthur, Sir Gromer Somer Joure, appears in only one other medieval story, *Le Morte Darthur*.[66] Another is the author's announcement, at the end of the story, that he is a prisoner, "be-sett withe gaylours many / That kepen hym fulle sewerly / Withe wyles wrong and wraste" (ll. 844–846).[67] And a third is that the author ends his poem, just as the author of the *Morte* ends his book, with an earnest prayer for God's help.

66 Insert on page 94, from N. R. Ker, ed., *The Winchester Malory: A Facsimile* (London: Early English Text Society, 1976), pages not numbered.

67 Laura Sumner, ed. "The Weddynge of Sir Gawen and Dame Ragnell," *Smith College Studies in Modern Languages* 5, no. 4 (July 1924) (Northampton, MA: Smith College, 1924), ll. 844–846. Further citations of this work will be in parentheses in the text.

These striking elements strongly suggest Sir Thomas Malory as the author of the poem.

However, even though Professor Field and I are in agreement concerning who wrote *Ragnell*, I find something in Professor Field's assessment of Malory's relation to the poem with which I must take issue. Field has stated that, although he has no objection to believing that Malory wrote the poem, he considers the point unimportant because Malory's authorship of it tells us nothing about Malory that we cannot learn from *Le Morte Darthur* (Field, 2). I assume that he has Sir Thomas Malory of Newbold Revel, Warwickshire, in mind when he sees nothing new in the poem related to Malory, because he always has that Malory in mind, and I assume he is right; the poem tells us nothing in particular about that Malory. But I see a great deal of importance in studying *Ragnell* precisely because it does tell us much about the identity of its author. There is much in the poem that points due north, so to speak. It strongly indicates that the author was a northerner.

First, the action in the poem takes place in the north of England, in Inglewood Forest and Carlisle. William Matthews, who did not notice Malory's probable authorship of *Ragnell*, but did notice the poem as a northern composition, comments that "the single surviving text of this romance is in East-Midland dialect of about 1450. But that there was a northern original is made probable by the locale of the action and by some close resemblances to other northern poems that Malory seems to have known. The locale is Carlisle, Inglewood Forest, and Tarn Wadling" (Matthews, 102). The extant medieval copy of the poem is in East Midland dialect; it would be expected that an East Midlander who composed a tale himself would place it in his home region, among the sights and customs that he knew well, rather than at a distance. This romance takes place near the very border of Scotland. Moreover, its locale, distant from the East Midlands of the copyist, is only the first of the northern elements that critics have noticed in the poem.

Second, the author seems to have known other northern poems, as Matthews and others have pointed out. Ralph Norris studied possible sources for *Ragnell*, particularly *The Tale of Florent, The Awntyrs off*

Arthur at the Terne Wathelyn, and *The Marriage of Sir Gawain*; he pays particular attention to *The Marriage* as possibly a direct source.[68] At least two of these romances are northern compositions. Thomas Hahn, as editor of *Sir Gawain: Eleven Romances and Tales*, has this to say: "*Ragnelle* never stipulates the location of his [Gromer's] estates. It does, however, identify the mysterious woods where he makes his appearance: he and his bewitched sister inhabit Inglewood Forest (lines 16, 152, 764, 835), the Cumberland setting for *Avowyng*, *Awntyrs*, and, by implication, for *Marriage*. In addition, the Round Table resides at Carlisle (lines 127, 132, 325), a center for Arthurian adventures in *Carlisle, Avowyng, Awntyrs, Greene Knight, Marriage*, and *Carle*. These allusions connect *Ragnelle* with other Gawain romances, and confer on the whole group a remarkable regional coherence."[69] The region in question is, of course, the north of England.

Third, Laura Sumner, in the introduction to her edition of the poem, observes in *Ragnell* the motif of Ragnell's extraordinary appetite at the wedding feast and tells us that it is common in northern folklore. Sumner points out that Francis Child, in his edition of popular ballads of England and Scotland, "gives a brief discussion of this feature. Since all the instances that he cites are found in Scandinavian stories, we infer that the motif of the bride's appetite indicates that a northern influence has been brought to bear on the loathly lady story" (Sumner, xvii).

Fourth, another northern folklore theme found in *Ragnell* is that of the wicked stepmother. Ragnell is under the spell of her stepmother; that is why she is so ugly. Says Sumner: "If we may accept the statement of Mr. Joseph W. Beach to the effect that the stepmother is very common on Germanic soil, and so common and so well defined in Icelandic tales of magic that the whole class is commonly called stepmother's

68 Ralph Norris, "Sir Gawain and Dame Ragnell Reconsidered," *Arthuriana* 19, no. 2 (Summer 2009): 82–102. Further citations of this work will be in parentheses in the text.

69 Thomas Hahn, ed., *Sir Gawain: Eleven Romances and Tales* (Kalamazoo, MI: Medieval Institute, 1995), introduction, 44.

tales," then we can see that the story of Gawain and Ragnell the loathly lady contains a further northern element (Sumner, xviii).

Fifth, in arguing for a northern author of *Le Morte Darthur,* William Matthews followed several lines of thought, summing up by listing eleven "criteria by which the candidates must be judged" (Matthews, 150), based upon some known facts concerning *Le Morte.* Certain of those criteria have particular interest in our study of *Ragnell* in connection with Malory. Here they are.

To begin with, says Matthews, Malory's *Le Morte Darthur* "draws heavily from two English poems that were written in Yorkshire, one of which is very difficult in its language" (Matthews, 150). (Certain other scholars contend that the poems were not actually written in Yorkshire; however, the acknowledged scribe was Robert Thornton, a Yorkshireman.) Matthews here is referring to the two poems usually tagged the alliterative *Morte Arthure* and the stanzaic *Morte Arthur.* The northern poems in English that were used by the author of *Ragnell,* according to Ralph Norris, are particularly *The Tale of Florent, The Wife of Bath's Tale, The Marriage of Sir Gawain,* and *The Awntyrs of Arthure at the Terne Wathlyng,* but allusions to certain places indicate a familiarity with northern locations featured in some other poems, showing that the author had reference to them as well; Matthews, still speaking of Malory's *Le Morte Darthur,* says, "It also shows the author's knowledge of other northern English romances" (Matthews, 150).

Then, "local English references that Malory adds to his story indicate he ... was certainly familiar with some places, institutions, and legends of the north of England" (Matthews, 150). The setting of *Ragnell* is Inglewood Forest and Carlisle, as it is, Hahn reminds us, in *Carlisle, Avowyng, Awntyrs, Greene Knight,* and *Carle,* all located in the north of England.

And finally, Matthews turns to the dialect of the *Morte,* applying many dialect tests to that work, and here I have followed his lead, examining *Ragnell* to learn whether the same northern dialect features that Matthews detects in *Le Morte* may be found in *Ragnell* as well. Matthews tells us of *Le Morte Darthur*, "Its language is mainly standard English, but northern dialect words and forms are scattered throughout the two surviving texts, and they were almost certainly present in the original form of the book" (Matthews, 150). Here is what I have found in the poem, as compared with Matthews's findings in *Le Morte*.

Matthews: "There is a light powder of variants from the standard spellings, which taken together form a combination rarely found south of Lincoln. Thus, a great many words that are normally spelt with *i* are here spelt with *e*: *preson, velony, rever, drevyn, gresly* and so on. This was a practice that may be found in texts from many parts of the country; but it seems to have begun in the North, and it was always more frequent there than elsewhere" (Matthews, 78).

Likewise, in the poem, we find *geve, gevyn, pety*.

Matthews: "The ... device of representing 'long *e*' as *ei* or *ey*, which Malory used frequently in such words as *teithe* 'teeth,' *treys* 'trees' ... is most typically northern" (Matthews, 79).

Likewise, we find in the poem *freynd, theym*.

Matthews: "Although his use of *y* as the vowel in unaccented syllables was not absolutely northern, his marked preference for it over the standard *e* was similar to the preference of northern writers: his *gyfftys* for 'gifts,' *longyth* 'longeth,' *castyste* 'castest,' *sendis* 'sends,' *bettir* 'better,' *sadyll* 'saddle,' and *bakyn* 'baken' are a pinch from the myriad examples that give a northern tinge to the Winchester text" (Matthews, 79).

The poem likewise has a marked preference for this form; we find *flowyr, grathyd* "prepared," *nothyng, promyse, promysed, sekyr* "secure," *servyce, opynyd, virgyn, wepyns, worshypp, worshyppt*.

Matthews: "In *W* [Winchester], the characteristic vowel in inflections is *i/y*.... This spelling practice is not regional in any absolute sense, but it is more prevalent in northern documents" (Matthews, 180).

In the poem, the inflections in *i/y* include *askyng, agrevyd, answeryd, berythe, bleryd, brasyd, brynnyng, chargyd, cloteryd, clothyd, comyn, comyng, comyst, defoylyd, disformyd, dyssevyr, enqyeryd, gegylyd, gevyn, glosyng, grevyd, helpyng, herys, justyng, lesyng, listenythe, lokyd, lovyd, lumpryd, lykyng, lykys, mannys, meanyng, mornyng, myddys, offendyd, passyd, savyd, savyng, sholdyst, slepyst, sorowyst, stalkyng, stowpyd, sygnyd, talkyng, thankyd, tumblyd, turnyd, tydynges, wakyd, warrauntyng, weddyd, weddynge, wenyst, woldyst, ynchys.*

Matthews: "Another practice characteristic of the North which appears very frequently in *Le Morte Darthur* is the representation of the final consonant in 'five,' 'live,' 'grieve,' 'cleave,' 'prove,' and similar words, not with standard *v* but with *f* or *ff*; among Malory's many examples are *gyff, lyff, gryff, olyff, roff*" (Matthews, 79). In the poem an example of such usage is *stryfe* as the verb "strive."

Matthews: "A further consonantal variant, which was commoner in the North than elsewhere, is what is known technically as metathesis of *r*; Malory has several examples of this ... such as *gerte* 'great,' *thirste* 'thrust,' *shirly* 'shrilly,' *postern* 'postern,' and *honderd* 'hundred' " (Matthews *Inquiry* 79).

Examples of this variant found in *Ragnell* are *bren* "burn" and *brynnyng* "burning."

Matthews: "*Them, their,* and *scho* are personal pronouns that were seldom used far south of the Humber in Malory's time, and they contrast with the *hem, hir, she* in standard use. It is significant, therefore, that samples of the Winchester text use *them* as often as *hem*, and *their* twice as often as *hir.* Its regular feminine pronoun is *she*" (Matthews, 79–80).

In the poem, the *th* forms are standard; two exceptions occur, one *her* for "their," and one *hem* for "them." The feminine singular is *she* throughout the text.

Matthews: "While standard English used *-est, -yth,* and *-e, -ent, -eth* when the subject was '*thou*,' '*he*,' or a plural, northern English used *-ys* in all cases ... scattered throughout [the Winchester text] are some seventy examples of such northernisms as *she sendis, he dredis*" (Matthews, 80).

There are in the poem three instances of this usage, *nedys*, appearing twice, and *lykys*. All three occur in impersonal constructions.

Matthews: "In words like 'clerk,' Malory very often used *ar*. This too was a practice that began in the North; and although it gradually affected standard spelling in the fifteenth century, in certain words it is rarely found in any documents except northern ones. It is therefore highly significant that a good proportion of these typical northernisms were used frequently in the Winchester manuscript: *warse* 'worse,' *warste, warke, warre* 'worse,' and *warwolf* are the most frequent" (Matthews, 78).

Examples in the poem include *ware* "were," *wore* "were," *art, starke, yard.*

Matthews: "The present participial inflection in both texts is the standard *-ing* (in its various spellings). W, however, once uses the characteristic northern *-ande*: *dryvande,* and this is confirmed by C's *dryuend*" (Matthews, 179).

In the poem, the predominating present participle ending is *-yng*. These exceptions occur: *comyn* (twice), *tydand, sembland, helpand.*

Miscellaneous other northernisms pointed out by Matthews in *Le Morte Darthur* and occurring also in *The Wedding of Sir Gawain and Dame Ragnell* include *tyll* "to," *or* "ere," *ylle* "evil," *untille* "to," *gate* "way," and *itt* rather than *hit* as neuter pronoun.

Le Morte Darthur contains many thousands of words; *Ragnell* has only about one thousand. It is therefore not surprising that several dialect tests for northern usages that Matthews successfully applies to *Le Morte,* when applied to the poem yield nothing. What is perhaps more interesting is that the poem contains some words peculiar to the north or originating and predominating there, which do not appear in the *Morte*. Some examples are *grome,* from Old Norse "man"; *grathyd* "prepared," from Old Norse *greiðr; stound,* "time, while," from Old Norse *stund; brayd* "deed," from Old Norse *bragða,* "to move or stir"; *frende* "kinsman," from Old Norse *frændi.*

All of the points above strongly support the conclusion that the author of *The Wedding of Sir Gawain and Dame Ragnell* was a northerner, and of course that information points to Thomas Malory of

Yorkshire, William Matthews's candidate for authorship, and away from the man from Newbold Revel in Warwickshire.

The three outstanding features that *Ragnell* shares with *Le Morte Darthur* and no other medieval work, which have led to the conclusion that the poem is the work of Thomas Malory, are, one, the name of the knight who accosts Arthur in the woods and accuses him of having stolen his land, Sir Gromer Somer Joure; two, the information that the author is a prisoner; and three, the intrusion of the narrator at the end to beg God to deliver him from his captivity. Malory disperses his declarations that he is a servant of Jesus, and his petitions for prayers, throughout *Le Morte Darthur*. There are few things relevant to the identity of this author upon which everyone agrees, but maybe one of them is that he must have been a man of sincere religion; it is virtually impossible to doubt the sincerity of these petitions in the *Morte*. Likewise the similar petition at the end of *Ragnell*. After we hear that the adventure in the story is ended and all is well with Arthur and Ragnell and Gawain, we get this:

Nowe God as thou were in Bethleme boren
Suffer nevere her soules be forlorne
In the brinning fire of helle!
And, Jhesu, as thou were borne of a virgin,
Help him oute of sorrowe that this tale did devine,
And that nowe in alle hast,
For he is beset withe gailours many,
That kepen him fulle sewerly,
With wiles wrong and wraste.
Nowe God, as thou art veray king royalle,
Help him oute of daunger that made this tale,
For therin he hathe bene long.
And of great pety help thy servaunt,
For paines he hathe strong.
Here endithe the wedding of
Sir Gawen and Dame Ragnelle
For helping of King Arthoure. (ll. 838–855)

There is plenty of evidence in the *Morte* that its author was a northerner, and a religious man; however, because all of that evidence is diluted in a thousand-page book, it shows up more clearly in a thousand-word poem. If Malory wrote both works, then whatever we learn about his character from the poem applies equally well to the character of the author of *Le Morte Darthur*, for it is the same man. What we have verified, from the poem, is that Malory was a northerner and a man of sincere religion. So was the author of the *Morte*.

There are two more things in *Ragnell* that are pertinent to our identification of the author. One of them has to do with his attitude toward marriage. That attitude is another point of evidence in *Ragnell* that is pertinent to our search for the identity of Thomas Malory. Professor Field noticed it, and noticed that the author of the poem reflects the same attitude as that of the author of the *Morte*, in his argument that these two authors are one and the same man. But I draw your attention to what that attitude is. This is Field's comment: "Gawain and Ragnell have a son Gingalin who eventually becomes a Knight of the Round Table, but Ragnell dies after five years of marriage, and Gawain, although he marries again 'oft,' never loves so deeply again. The logic of the story does not demand any of this either, and there is no hint of it in the other analogues." He continues: the author "added Gawain's remarriages in an effort to harmonise his story, his moral sense, and Gawain's reputation as a lover."[70] Exactly. Malory had a strong moral sense, a deep respect for loyalty and particularly the kind of loyalty called marriage, and an aversion to promiscuity, easy to discern in the *Morte Darthur*. He was, as we have seen above in his sincere prayers at the end of both his poem and his book, a religious man; possibly his obvious respect for marriage is a product of his religion. If Professor Field had in mind Sir Thomas Malory of Newbold Revel as the author of *The Wedding of Sir Gawain and Dame Ragnell*, and he almost surely did, then he was right

[70] P. J. C. Field, "Malory and *The Wedding of Sir Gawain and Dame Ragnell*." *Archiv für das Studium der neueren Sprachen und Literaturen* 218 (1982): 374–381. Further citations of this work will be in parentheses in the text as "Field, *Archiv*."

in thinking that a study of the poem will not teach us about its author; it has nothing to say about that Malory. However, what it has to teach us about the real author is significant: he introduced the notion of faithful love and marriage into his handling of the old loathly lady story. The poem thus takes us that much closer to the character of the writer whose identity we are seeking.

Finally, there is the most pointed way in which *Ragnell* helps to identify our author as a man of the North Country. One of the most interesting things about the poem is that peculiar name of the knight who challenges Arthur, Sir Gromer Somer Joure. Remember that only Malory uses this name, once in the *Morte Darthur*, and again in this poem. Much speculation has been spent on its meaning. Gromer Somer Joure has been called most often Summer Day Man, and it has been proposed that he is a sort of leftover from some woodland myth, possibly somewhat on the order of Gawain's Green Knight. Vinaver offered a gloss on the name in his edition of the *Morte* (which he called *The Works of Sir Thomas Malory*):

> Gromersom Erioure [Gromore somyr Ioure], possibly a combination of O. F. Helynas de Gromoret and Eliors, paralleled in the Weddyng of Sir Gawen and Dame Ragnell (ed. Sumner), l. 62; companion of Agravain and Mordred, 1164. Caxton's variant, if authentic, would make this character identical with Grummor, q.v. (Malory, *Works*, vol. 3, 1682)

That was not very helpful. Professor Field gave it a better shot. He said that "its origin and meaning are unknown, and the gloss sometimes offered of 'summer's day man' is as despairing a guess as the consequential derivation from Hafgan King of Annfawn in the Mabinogian. There is no reason to suppose that fifteenth-century scribes found the name any more comprehensible than do twentieth-century philologists" (Field, *Archiv*, 375). Yet Field reminded us, "a name as long, as unusual, and as difficult as Gromer Somer Joure suggests a very close relationship between the two works." We read: it cannot be a coincidence. There must be one author here.

Finally, help came, from Karen Trimnell. Ralph Norris comments that she "persuasively argued that the mysterious name Gromer Somer Joure derives from the French verse romance *L'Atre perilleux*. Trimnell rejects earlier attempts to identify this character with supernatural figures such as Hafgan from *The Mabingion* [*sic*] and suggests that the unusual name is a corruption, more likely to be a mishearing than a misreading, of Goumeres sans Mesur, a hostile knight from *L'Atre perilleux*. This theory is clearly the best offered so far in explanation of this bizarre name, and therefore, must be accepted as the only currently viable theory" (Norris, 89; note 43 referring to Trimnell's article *The Disenchanting of Sir Gromer Somer Joure* in *Medium Aevum* 71, no. 2, 2002: 294–301). Norris is right; clearly this is the best explanation offered so far for the name. And here is where things get interesting for the searcher after Thomas Malory's identity. Notice that the misinterpretation by the author of "Goumeres sans Mesure" for "Gromer Somer Joure" had to be based on a mishearing, not a misreading of a text; Malory was listening to the story, or some part of it, when he failed to catch the name properly. And his mind provided him with what he thought he heard, Gromer Somer Joure, which combines the French *somer jour*, summer day, with the Old Norse word *gromr*, meaning "man." The French is easy to explain, but why *gromr*, why Old Norse "man"? Here is a piece of good evidence that Malory was a man of the north, for that is the part of the country where Old Norse forms were still a noticeable part of English in his time. It is not likely that a listener in any other section of England would mishear "Goumeres sans Mesure" and then have his mind interpret for him by providing the word *gromr*. Moreover, the word *grome* appears in the text of the poem referring to the strange woodland knight: "Streighte wher cam to him a quaint grome / Armid welle and sure" (ll. 550–51). Obviously, Malory must have been fluent and comfortable with northern speech, and, of course, the obvious way to acquire that fluency is to be a native of the North Country.

12

MALORY THE WRITER

IN THE FAMOUS colophon at the end of "The Tale of King Arthur" in the Winchester manuscript, the author tells us this: "This was drawyn by a knyght presoner sir Thomas Malleorre, that God sende him good recover. Amen, etc. EXPLICIT" (Malory, *Works*, 133). But after all is said and done, it is not Malory's knighthood, nor is it his prison record, that touches our own lives. It is his writing. We do not know about Malory's exploits on the field of battle, or why he was a prisoner. We do know his writing. And, knowing that most writers reveal themselves in their writing, we searchers for Malory's identity will do well to look closely at what he has written. It has been a long time since any scholar has seen it as merely a translation and abridgement of the French sources.

There are, of course, flaws in the *Morte*. E. K. Chambers lists some of them:

> It is full of beginnings which have no end and of ends which never had a beginning. It does not perhaps matter much that knights who have been killed in one book live to fight and be killed again in another. But Merlin comes and goes, and we are never told who or what Merlin is. First Pellinore and then Palomydes pursues the questing beast, but the nature of the quest remains dark. The adventures of Balin bear many suggestions of their significance in relation to the Grail, but when the book of the Grail comes, they are found not to have

> been significant. Malory has in his hands two of the world's dozen great love stories, and does not succeed in telling either of them completely.

The beginning of the Tristram story is confused and the end is missing, says Chambers:

> When the end comes, it is not the pathetic and imaginative story of the black sail, with which we are familiar from the old poems, but only a treacherous stabbing in the back by Mark. Moreover, if Malory robs us of the end of Tristram, he robs us of the beginning of Lancelot. There is nothing of the changeling boyhood, nothing of the coming to court and of Lancelot's trembling at the sight of Guenevere, not even that episode of that first kiss, of which Dante makes such unforgettable use in the *Divine Comedy*.[71]

And, for a last point, says Chambers, the noble Gawain gets pretty shabby treatment.

All true. And yet the *Morte Darthur* is a magnificent production. As William Matthews said in speaking of critics who have complained that the book is full of vice, surely to denigrate it that way is "to make molehills outtop the shining mountains" (Matthews, 48). There is simply nothing like *Le Morte Darthur*. It is a big book, but probably no more than 10 percent of the size of the material that Malory used as his sources. He "reduced into English" all that vast body of stories of Britain's ancient mythical king Arthur and his knights, his Round Table, their chivalry, their loves, their adventures, their wars, which up until Malory's time, except for a couple of poems written in an English dialect difficult for most Englishmen to understand, had been written in

[71] E. K. Chambers, "Sir Thomas Malory," *The English Association Pamphlet* 51 (January 1922), pages unnumbered. Further citations of this work will be in parentheses in the text.

French, and most of them in poetry. Ever since Malory produced his book, that body of lore has belonged to the English-speaking people of the world. It may be that in pre-Malory days, the old French books were widely enjoyed among those Englishmen who could read French. However, once Malory wrote the *Morte*, there was simply no contest, and there is none today. With the exception of some highly specialized medieval scholars, very few English speakers read Malory's French sources. Everybody reads Malory, or some derivative of Malory. No other English writer comes to mind who has made such a mighty book, with such widespread influence, not only in literature but in our culture generally.

So, what kind of man would write such a book? It is a commonplace of modern criticism that all writers, whether what they write purports to be fiction or fact, have a rhetorical purpose: they all have something to "sell." What Thomas Malory sells most ardently in the *Morte Darthur* is religion, and, more specifically, monasticism. Of course, in the fifteenth century, England was a Catholic country, and as it was in medieval life generally, religion is ubiquitous in the *Morte Darthur*. It is not surprising that time was measured by the annual recurrence of feast days of the Catholic liturgical calendar (when the kingship of Arthur cannot be ratified by Christmas, the nobles try again on Candlemas; when they still have no decision, another attempt to reach agreement is held at Easter, until finally Arthur is crowned on Pentecost), or that everyday conversation was sprinkled with references to God: "And than he was ware of sir Gawayne and salewed hym, and prayde to God to sende hym muche worshyp. 'As for that,' seyde sir Gawayne, 'gramercy. Also I pray to God sende you honoure and worshyp'" (Malory, *Works*, 119). But things are different today. It may not be impossible, but it is not easy, for the ordinary reader five hundred years after Malory, who lives in a largely God-free culture, to comprehend how pervasive, how all-encompassing, their religion was to Englishmen of the Middle Ages. The difficulty manifests itself in various ways in the study of literature. For example, Kip Wheeler points out that "occasionally a student discovers an unusual passage in literature that is difficult to interpret.... A medieval jokebook might refer to a cord of scarlet tied in a window. Chaucer might make a pointed reference to the Wife of Bath's deafness. To make sense of these passages, the student creates all sorts of elaborate allegories or symbolic interpretations. Frequently, however, the answer is much simpler; it's an allusion to something in the Bible."[72] But who reads the Bible? Clearly, we are at a disadvantage.

The disadvantage may be even more noticeable in Britain than in America. A poll conducted by ABC News reported that "eighty-three percent of Americans identify themselves as Christians," while 4 percent combine other non-Christian religions—Jews, Muslims, Buddhists, and so forth—and 13 percent reported "no religion."[73] In a similar 2016 poll by the *Daily Mail* in Britain, only 30 percent of the British population claimed to be religious, and 13 percent claimed to be "convinced atheists."[74] In our modern quest to discover the identity of the author of the *Morte*, atheism, or, at the very least, "post-Christianity," which is gaining ground in the United States and already widespread in Britain, has negatively influenced the search. Scholars can know and even teach that in the fifteenth century the Catholic Church was powerful, without ever having a clear idea of what that power was; in fact, although the influence of Catholicism extended into the secular sphere, the greatest power of the Church was, as it always has been, spiritual. It is easy to see the spirituality in *Le Morte Darthur*, but most do not see it. And as for the temporal role played by the Church in the lives of ordinary medieval Englishmen, it is widely misunderstood, and this lack of clear understanding has had noticeable effects in Malory studies. Scholars have failed to see

[72] Kip Wheeler, "Common Religious Texts: The *Pater Noster, Credo,* and *Ave Maria* in the Late Medieval Period (1281 AD–1400 AD)," Dr. L. Kip Wheeler, Carson-Newman University, https://web.cn.edu/kwheeler/lords_prayer_1400.html.

[73] Garry Langer, "Poll: Most Americans Say They're Christian," ABC News, July 18, 2001, accessed July 18, 2016, abcnews.go.com/US/story?id=90356.

[74] *Daily Mail*, January 17, 2016, www.dailymail.co.uk.

how unusual it was for an Englishman, a layman, a knight, to involve himself in translating and copying out old manuscripts, the traditional job of a monk, if he was not himself a monk. But it was very unusual indeed. In fact, there is only one layman that we know of who ever did such a thing, to the extent of producing a major standalone piece of literature. That person is Sir Thomas Malory. That is, unless he himself was not a layman at all but a monk.

The modern person not living in a Catholic country but instead native to a secular and even widely atheistic culture, may know that in the Middle Ages England was a Catholic country but still not notice that there is a great deal of difference between an ordinary member of the Catholic laity and a monk. To that modern person, it may be that all medieval Catholics look pretty much alike, but they are not all alike. A monk is, and has always been, a man who abjures the world, withdraws into the privacy of communal life among other monks, other men with similar devotion to their religion, and takes sacred vows to ensure his lifelong separation from the world, vows of poverty, chastity, and obedience. Moderns often sneer at men who do such things, thinking they cannot possibly be sincere; they are at best naïve and at worst hypocritical. But monks are, and were, neither. And in the Middle Ages, even into Malory's time, although the monastic life separated a man from the life of the world going on around him, still the monk made a powerful cultural contribution to that world. We tend to forget the great legacy of these men; it is no secret, although it is often forgotten, that we owe our wealth of literature, both religious and nonreligious, largely to the monk in his monastery, with its scriptorium and its library. By the time of Thomas Malory, the career of scribe was no longer the exclusive province of the monk; there were, as well as monks in their scriptoria, secular scribes in England, men who made their living by copying documents. However, Sir Thomas Malory was not such a man.

And that means that it was a very strange thing he did, when he was in prison somewhere where there were some old French manuscripts. Why would he even consider doing such a thing? This task would be perfectly suited and natural to a monk, most unusual to one who was not a monk, and unthinkable for a thug and gang leader who had spent years in and out of London jails for every sort of violent crime. If Malory of Newbold Revel did such a thing, it was peculiar indeed. On the other hand, maybe Thomas Malory the author of the *Morte* was not that thug at all but a member of the class of men for whom such esoteric activities as copying manuscripts were second nature, in fact, a monk. In that case, he was a man of devout religion, and it is not surprising that religion is so ubiquitous in the *Morte*. Moreover, if Malory was a monk, we have found the obvious explanation of why his identity has always been unknown.

It is by no means only the everyday-Christian manifestations such as the liturgical calendar, and greetings such as "God sende you honoure and worshype," that are so noticeable in Malory's book; religion is everywhere. Dying knights and ladies ask for the rites of the Church: "Now wille ye sende for a preest that we may receyve our sacrament and receyve the blessid body of oure Lord, Jesu Christ?" (Malory, *Works*, 69). "'My fayr lordes,' sayd sir Launcelot, 'wyt you wel my careful body wyll into th'erthe, I have warnyng more than now I wyl say. Therfore gyve me my ryghtes.' So … he was howselyd and enelyd and had al that a Crysten man ought to have" (Malory, *Works*, 880). And of course Catholic ritual is not only for the dying. We never know when the story will pause for someone to go to Mass: "So on the morne sir Arthure was armed and well horsed, and asked sir Damas, 'Whan shall we to the felde?' 'Sir,' seyde sir Damus, 'ye shall hyre masse.' And so Arthure herde a masse" (Malory, *Works*, 103).

Consulting the will of God is a recurring topos. When the nobles and commons are trying to discern whether Arthur is their true king, they decide to put the question to God, and trust what He tells them:

> Thenne stood the reame in grete jeopardy long whyle, for every lord that was myghty of men maade hym stronge, and many wende to have ben kyng. Thenne Merlyn wente to the Archebisshop of Caunterbury and counceilled hym for to sende for all the lordes of the reame and alle the gentilmen of armes that they

> shold to London come by Cristmas upon payne of cursynge, and for this cause, that Jesu, that was borne on that nyghte, that He wold of His grete mercy shewe some myracle, as He was come to be Kynge of mankynde, for to shewe somme myracle who shold be rightwys kynge of this reame. (Malory, *Works*, 7)

God cooperates fully with their plan; after the first Mass of Christmas, He miraculously sets up in the churchyard a great stone with a steel anvil in the middle of it, "and theryn stack a fayre swerd naked by the poynt, and letters there were wryten in gold aboute the sword that saiden thus: WHOSO PULLETH OUTE THIS SWERD OF THIS STONE AND ANVYLD IS RIGHTWYS KYNGE BORNE OF ALL ENGLOND" (Malory, *Works*, 7). The rest of the story is well known. Subsequently, God, apparently pleased with the success of this technique of communicating His plan, writes messages in gold more than once in *Le Morte*.

The theme of putting the question to God, and the related one of accepting His will, continue in great and small ways throughout the *Morte*. Balyne tells his brother Balan the unfortunate ending of the story of his encounter with the Lady of the Lake, and that "the dethe of thys damesell grevith me sore." "'So doth it me,' seyde Balan. 'But ye must take the adventure that God woll ordayne you'" (Malory, *Works*, 52). This acceptance of God's action in human life blends almost imperceptibly with giving God the glory; a small example among many: when Arthur has overcome Accolon and Accolon surrenders, he says to Arthur, "Ye ar the beste knyght that ever I found, and I se well that God is with you" (Malory, *Works*, 105). Of course this theme is best served by Sir Lancelot's deeply moving prayer before he attempts to heal Sir Urry: "I beseche The of Thy mercy … Thou Blyssed Trynyte, Thou mayste yeff me power to hele thys syke knyght by the grete vertu and grace of The, but, Good Lorde, never of myselff'" (Malory, *Works*, 814).

Nor is it only Arthur's stalwart knights who acknowledge the power of God. Merlin warns Arthur early in the book that God's vengeance will come upon him for having lain with King Lot's wife and begotten Mordred, who will be Arthur's undoing (Malory, *Works*, 35).

Mellyagaunt, the dastardly kidnapper of Guenevere, administers a severe warning to Lancelot when Lancelot offers to prove with his hands that Guenevere is true to Arthur: "'My lorde sir Launcelot,' seyde sir Mellyagaunce, 'I rede you beware what ye do; for thoughe ye ar never so good a knyght, as I wote well ye are renowned the beste knyght of the worlde, yet shulde ye be avysed to do batayle in a wronge quarell, for God woll have a stroke in every batayle'" (Malory, *Works*, 803).

Any list of the religious elements in the *Morte Darthur* would be a long list; religion is the warp and woof of this book. It seems sometimes that there is an abbey, a church, a hermitage, or some other establishment of religion at every crossing. Sue Ellen Holbrook, in her study of Guenevere as a nun, is primarily interested in religious houses for women; yet in her study of the *Morte* she turns up all of this:

> Apart from numerous places designated as chapels and hermitages, such as those at Glastonbury, my survey uncovers the following religious establishments: two different nunneries (counting Amesbury); ten different priories, including one with women; and sixteen different abbeys, including two with nuns. In three of the priories, the sole occupant is a man of religion; at the others, no one is mentioned as being in charge. Just one of the men's abbeys has an abbot.... The second "abbey of nunnys" appears at the beginning of the Grail quest; it is the setting for Lancelot's first meeting with his son, who has been "norysshed" [fostered] by the nuns there (2.853.30, 854.15). Although no governor for the first abbey is mentioned, this second one has an abbess. It is Malory who adds that information.[75]

Religious houses are everywhere, as Holbrook notes: "some modest, others rich, that provide knights, ladies, and their companions with

[75] Sue Ellen Holbrook, "Guenevere: The Abbess of Amesbury and the Mark of Reparation," *Arthuriana* 20, no. 1 (Spring 2010): 30. Further citations of this work will be in parentheses in the text.

good counsel, confession, last rites, interment, even adventures, and above all both medical care and ... lodging" (Holbrook, 30). Clergymen, likewise, are always showing up in the *Morte,* performing their proper functions, from the archbishop of Canterbury, who presides over the sacred enterprise of choosing and crowning Arthur, to the "gostly fadir" of the Fayre Maydyn of Astolat, who counsels her to give up her inappropriate thoughts of Lancelot, and is probably surprised at the insouciance of her answer: "Why should I give up such thoughts?" she says. "Am I not an earthly woman?" (Malory, *Works,* 779). Then there is the bishop who, "as he laye in his bedde aslepe, he fyl upon a grete laughter" because of a dream. " 'Truly,' sayd the Bysshop, 'here was syr Launcelot with me, with mo angellis than ever I sawe men in one day. And I sawe the angellys heve up syr Launcelot unto heven, and the yates of heven opened ayenst hym' " (Malory, *Works,* 881). It turns out that Lancelot has just died and the bishop has witnessed his death in a dream-revelation.

Probably the references to religion that have drawn the most attention from scholars are the prayers that Malory inserts in the form of colophons at various places throughout *Le Morte Darthur.* The most famous is the one that comes after "The Tale of King Arthur" in Vinaver's edition, the one that caused such a stir among scholars who had speculated that the author was a prisoner; it confirms their supposition with the words "This was drawyn by a knyght presoner, sir Thomas Malleorre." But it goes on into Mallory's prayer for deliverance from his prison, "God sende hym good recover. Amen" (Malory, *Works,* 133). There are several more prayers and requests for prayers, inserted into the text. There is, for example, Malory's own direct prayer, in which he refers to himself as the Lord's knight: "Therefore on all synfull, blyssed Lorde, have on thy knyght mercy. Amen" (Malory, *Works,* 623). And at the end of the book there is this:

> Here is the ende of the hoole book of kyng Arthur and of his noble knyghtes of the Rounde Table, that whan they were hole togyders there was ever an hondred and forty. And here

> is the ende of The Deth of Arthur. I praye you all jentylmen and jentylwymmen that redeth this book of Arthur and his knyghtes from the begynnyng to the endynge, praye for me whyle I am on lyve that God sende me good delyveraunce. And whan I am deed, I praye you all praye for my soule. For this book was ended the ninth yere of the reygne of King Edward the Fourth, by Syr Thomas Maleore, knyght, as Jesu helpe hym for hys grete myght, as he is the servaunt of Jesu bothe day and nyght. (Malory, *Works*, 883)

Malory thus ends his great work; the last thing he says is that he serves Jesus day and night. Today, we are living not only in the post-Reformation, the post-Christian, and the (suspicious!) post-Freudian world but in the deconstructionist world as well. All of this makes it not only possible but almost required, if a man says he is the servant of Jesus, to argue with him. Critics have difficulty simply accepting his word. D. Thomas Hanks and Janet Jesmok, in the introduction to their critical anthology *Malory and Christianity*, list some of those critics and comment briefly on their various takes on whether Malory really was a Christian: Eugene Vinaver argued that Malory was "uninterested in Christianity," but C. S. Lewis "argued seriously that Malory's text deals seriously with Christian themes and motifs," and E. K. Chambers subtly associated Malory with the Lollards's strong feeling against religious houses. P. J. C. Field discussed Malory's family connection with the Knights Hospitallers and thereby suggested his conventional piety; but Alec Ryrie among others has pointed out that Protestantism was on the horizon in Malory's time, and its rebellious spirit may have touched him. Catherine Bates saw problems with using Malory's class to deduce his religious perspective, while Colin Richmond "argues for gentry religion," and Eamon Duffy saw a clue as to Malory's religion in the fact that the laity of his time were "active and publicly pious."[76] And

[76] D. Thomas Hanks ["Tom Hanks the Elder"] and Janet Jesmok, *Malory and Christianity: Essays on Sir Thomas Malory's Morte Darthur* (Kalamazoo, MI: Medieval Institute, 2013), 1–2. Further citations of this work will be in parentheses in the text.

so on. We might imagine that all of this would leave Thomas Malory himself scratching his head in bewilderment. And it must be acknowledged that without the distorting spectacles of our devoutly cynical era, it probably would not occur to us to doubt that our author was a religious man, any more than it would occur to us to doubt that he was a knight or a prisoner — for he told us those three identifying things about himself in his book. Not only is his book full of Christian themes and practices, but he prays for himself and asks his readers to pray for him throughout the *Morte,* and he flatly states in his final words that he is a servant of Jesus. It is always to be expected in our contentious times that certain readers will "deconstruct" what a writer actually says about himself, but Field deserves the last word here. He says, "For identification purposes, the most important part of the evidence that the *Morte* provides is that of its closing words, whose patent sincerity, confirmed by their request for prayers, makes it unthinkable that the man who wrote them should not be what he there said he was" (Field, 5) — that is, a knight, a prisoner, and a servant of Jesus both day and night. That characterization of himself, together with the fact that he took on such monkish employment as the translation and compilation of a large body of medieval French romances, is one of the greatest clues, if we will but acknowledge it, to the identity of Sir Thomas Malory: possibly Malory's obviously sincere religion and his monkish predilection mean that he was, in fact, a monk.

Yet we are arguing here that Malory was not only a monk but a certain kind of monk, a member of the monk-knights of St. John of Jerusalem, the Knights Hospitallers. If that is true, what clues to that identity might we reasonably expect to find in *Le Morte*? Concerning knighthood itself, we could expect our author to consider it sacred. We could look for hints about what we might call Hospitaller protocol, their rules and attitudes. We could certainly expect to find war, with Muslims portrayed as the enemy of our protagonists, or at least as negative characters. We might look for references to naval battles against the Turk, because the Hospitallers had a mighty navy for that purpose. Possibly we would see allusions to pilgrimages to the Holy Land or references to the recovery of the True Cross. Regarding courtly love, we could expect to find the viewpoint of a man who has vowed himself to lifelong chastity. We could expect references to St. Bernard of Clairvaux and the Cistercians. And, of course, because if Malory was a Knight Hospitaller he was a monk as well as a warrior, we could expect to find strong, devout, pervasive religion. Some close reading of *Le Morte Darthur* is in order.

First of all, we would not be surprised to find, in a book written by a member of the Order of St. John, Knights Hospitallers, the view that knighthood is a high calling, a sacred order, the next thing to a religious vocation, because it comprises a band of men dedicated and sworn to high ideals and purposes, and that is, of course, the viewpoint that we do find in Malory. Of all the many references in the *Morte* to knighthood as a high order, none is found in a French source. Vinaver comments on the first such reference: "Than com Grifflet that was but a squyre, and he was but yonge, of the ayge of the king Arthur. So he besought the kynge for all hys servyse that he had done to gyff hym the Order of Knighthoode" (Malory, *Works,* 37). Vinaver's note: "F: *que vous me faichies chevalier.*" After translating the phrase as "that you will make me a knight," Vinaver continues, "In F Arthur says that Gryfflet (Gifflet) is too young to undertake such a difficult adventure"[77] (Malory, *Works,* vol. 3, 1299), and he goes on to say, "The 'high order' in the sense of 'knighthood,' is M's own phrase" (Malory, *Works,* vol. 3, 1300). The next time Malory refers to knighthood as a high order — "Ye ar a passyng good juster as ever y mette withall, and onys for the hyghe Order of Knyththode lette us jouste agayne" (Malory, *Works,* 39) — Vinaver's comment is simply "*for the highe Order of Knyghthode.* Not in F" (Malory, *Works,* vol. 3, 1301). After that, Vinaver offers no further comment on the multiple uses of the phrase. He has established that it is not taken from any French source; it is Malory's own. Not before Malory, indeed, were the knights of the old French romances seen as

[77] Sir Thomas Malory, *The Works of Sir Thomas Malory,* ed. Eugene Vinaver, 3 vols., 2nd ed. (Oxford: Oxford University Press, 1967), 3:1299. Further citations of this work will be in parentheses in the text, by volume, as distinct from the one-volume Works (which is simply cited as *Works*).

any sort of band of brothers, united in lofty endeavors. They were, instead, individualistic adventurers, facing on their own, or possibly with a sidekick, whatever befell them.

That phrase, "the high Order of Knighthood," and the attitude it reflects in the author of *Le Morte*, is one of the remarkable aspects of Malory's book. It changes the coloring, one might say, of the Arthurian legends. It takes the chivalric stories out of the category of picaresque adventure tales and raises them to a level that asks to be taken seriously. Historically, knighthood in England began as a simple bargain made between a chieftain (a *cyning*) or warlord and a young man: You fight for me in this raid and I'll give you a share of the loot. The derivation of the word *knight* itself from Anglo-Saxon *cniht*, meaning "boy," or "servant," suggests that knights were young and probably strong but also possibly in need of an income. The role of knights gradually became something else — more stable, more organized, more respected. Eventually knighthood became little more than a sinecure, and by the fifteenth century, it did not necessarily require any military service at all; we might find Sir This and Sir That who never took up arms, and certainly did not consider their knighthood as any sort of holy calling. It was the orders of military monks founded in the 1090s, in service of the Crusades, that gave knighthood the idealistic, almost religious, image of itself that Sir Thomas Malory used in the *Morte Darthur*. That image of knighthood was supported by an increasingly prominent and complex organization of monk-knights, over the span of several centuries. The Order of St. John, Hospitallers, was the first such knightly order established, and it was the only one still left standing in England by Malory's time, when the Order of Templars had long been disbanded and any remnant of it blended into the Hospitallers' order. The Hospitallers were still a prominent part of English society and, indeed, a prominent part of the Malory family; remember that the Hospitallers' prior of the English language during the years 1433–1440 was Sir Robert Malory.

Terence McCarthy, who considers Malory's interest in the bond among warriors a legacy from the strong masculine element of the alliterative poetic tradition (a tradition that, it is worth noting, has its provenance in the far north), points out that it becomes the basis of the whole of *Le Morte Darthur,* even including the love affair between Lancelot and Guenevere; he says that Malory

> creates a world in which women have a reduced role, a world of soldiers, the military world of uniforms, rank, and duty, where a man has a proper role to play more than an individual identity . . . a masculine world of military campaign and honor. The importance of the bond of loyalty between Arthur and his men . . . is one of the key themes of Malory's book. The passage where Arthur grieves more over the disbanding of the Round Table than over the loss of his wife is often, and rightly, quoted. Even when Malory writes a tender love scene — the final meeting of Lancelot and the Queen — the lovers regret the havoc that their love has caused in terms of the breakdown of a whole society in which unity and faithfulness had been so important (McCarthy, 76).

This emphasis on knightly bonding, on the high calling and brotherhood of knights, is Malory's own.

In chivalric literature, moreover, not only was Thomas Malory the author who introduced the idea of knighthood as a sacred order; he was also the author who introduced the oath that King Arthur requires his knights to take, and to renew each year at Pentecost; the knights pledge "never to do outerage nothir morthir, and allwayes to fle treson, and to gyff mercy unto hym that askith mercy, uppon payne of forfiture [of their] worship and lordship of kynge Arthure for evirmore; and allwayes to do ladyes, damesels, and jantilwomen and wydowes [socour:] strengthe hem in hir ryghtes, and never to enforce them, uppon payne of dethe. Also, that no man take no batayles in a wrongefull quarell for no love ne for no worldis goodis" (Malory, *Works,* 91). The taking of the Pentecostal oath itself is a reminder that the Hospitallers, as a religious order of knights, took the customary monastic vows as they were admitted to the order. In Malory, the brotherhood of the Round Table under King Arthur, seen as an order in itself, demands all devotion from its adherents. Percival's recluse aunt tells him,

> For all the worlde, crystenyd and hethyn, repayryth unto the Rounde Tale, and whan they ar chosyn to be of the feloshyp of the Rounde Table they thynke hemselff more blessed and more in worship than they had gotyn halff the worlde. And ye have sene that they have loste hir fadirs and hir modirs and all hir kynne, and hir wyves and hir chyldren, for to be of youre feloship. (Malory, *Works*, 659)

James W. Spisak gives us an interesting light on Malory's use of the word *lose* to mean "let go" or "give up" in several places in the *Morte*;[78] the usage by Percival's aunt in the sentence here — "they have lost hir fadirs and hir modirs and all hir kynne, and hir wyves and hir chyldren, for to be of youre feloship" — is such an instance. Giving up fathers, mothers, wives, children, and all their kin is not normal for ordinary secular soldiers volunteering for service to a particular king or country, but it is normal for persons entering a religious order. All of this suggests strongly that Malory was himself not just a randomly dubbed, individual, secular knight, who ran for Parliament and collected his rents, but a member of a high order of knighthood. Supposing that was the case, then there can be no doubt that the order in question was the Order of St. John, the Knights Hospitallers.

There are other hints, scattered throughout the *Morte*, that its author was a Hospitaller. It is a commonplace in Malory studies, for example, that just as he shies away from courtly love, he is rather particular about noble birth. No matter how poor a newcomer to Arthur's court might be, or how humble — Malory's own creation, Gareth of Orkney, is the perfect example — we are sure to learn, if he turns out to be a knight of noble exploits, that he is of noble, not to say royal, birth as well. That is the general way of literature of the

78 James W. Spisak, "Malory's 'Lost' Source," in *Studies in Malory*, 227–230.

Middle Ages, of course; churls do not count for much, and anyone of low rank will be a villain indeed. But in the *Morte,* things are even more particular than that. Knights must be of gentle strain on both their "fadir syde and modir syde"; anyone lacking that qualification need not apply. Arthur has this requirement explained to him early in his reign. When the damsel sent from the great Lady Lyle of Avilion comes to Arthur's court, she announces to Arthur that she seeks a passing good knight to pull out the sword from its sheath that is hanging by her side. However, only a certain kind of knight will do, as the damsel explains: " 'But beware ye be nat defoyled with shame, trechory, nother gyle, for than hit woll nat avayle,' seyde the

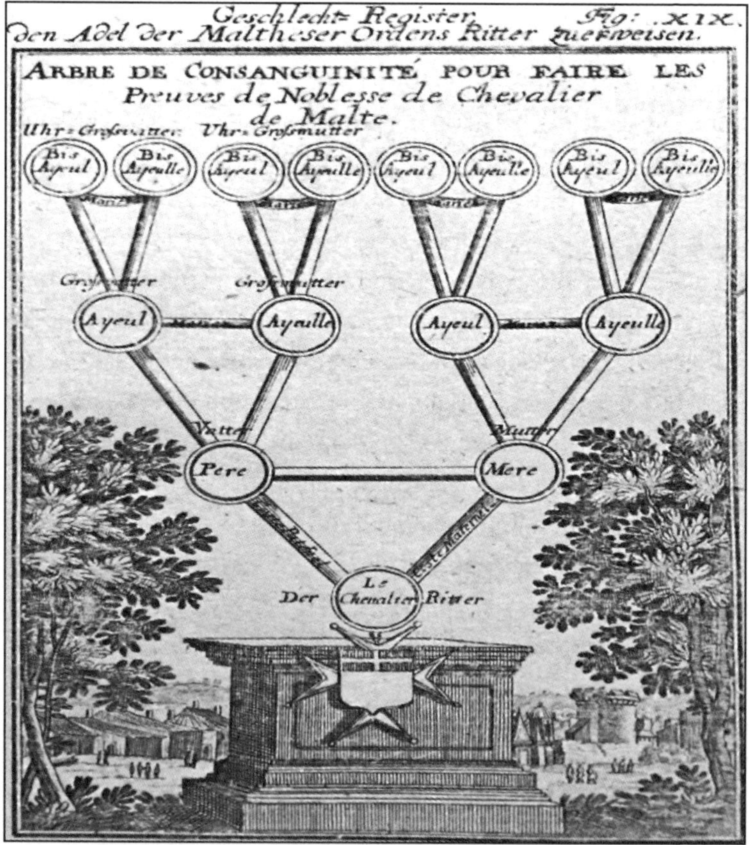

Hospitaller application proving nobility four generations, father's side and mother's side

damesel, 'for he must be a clene knyght withoute vylony and of jantill strene of fadir syde and of modir syde'" (Malory, *Works*, 46). When Sir Trystram applies to King Mark for permission to do battle with the challenger Marhalte, he tells Mark, "Lat hym wete that I am commyn of fadir syde and modir syde of as noble blood as he is" (Malory, *Works*, 283). When Gareth, who is called Beaumains, asks Lancelot to give him the order of knighthood, Lancelot asks him for his true name, but he shrinks from giving it. "Sir," says Lancelot, "you must tell me your name of ryght, and of what kyn ye be borne." So Beaumains yields: "Than he seyde, 'My name is Garethe, and brothir unto sir Gawayne of fadir syde and modir syde'" (Malory, *Works*, 217), that is, the son of King Lot and Queen Morgawse, whereupon Lancelot gives him the order of knighthood. When Agglovale and Percival go to visit their mother, "whyche was a quene in tho dayes," she implores them to abide at home with her, but they decline. "'A, my swete modir,' seyde sir Percyvale, 'we may nat, for we be comyn of kynges bloode of bothe partis. And therefore, modir, hit ys oure kynde to haunte armys and noble dedys'" (Malory, *Works*, 597). This requirement for knighthood, contributed by Malory, is more specific than in English law or common knightly practice outside of *Le Morte Darthur*. It comes straight out of the rule book of the Order of St. John, Knights Hospitaller; no man was eligible to be admitted as a knight of the order unless he submitted proof of noble birth on his father's side and his mother's side. According to Gregory O'Malley, "Just as secular knighthood was increasingly conferred only on candidates of gentle family and legitimate birth, in 1262 the Hospital established that no brother was to be knighted unless he was of knightly family, a stipulation followed eight years later by the requirement that knights should be born of legitimately married parents, unless they were the sons of counts or of greater nobility. In the fifteenth century these regulations were interpreted to mean that both parents of brother knights were to be 'gentlemanly' in name and arms" (O'Malley, 26–27). Charles Browne gives the further information that "the Knights were obliged to prove sixteen of nobility in their arms; or in other words, to show that they came of eight ancestors on each side, paternal and maternal, of noble rank, and entitled to bear arms."[79] (The Hospitaller form shown above is an original Mallet print of 1719, Lindisfarne Antique Prints, Shrewsbury, showing the applicant's four generations of knightly birth on both sides.) The candidate for authorship who is being considered here, Thomas Malory of Studley and Hutton, Yorkshire, easily fulfilled the lineage requirement, and the author's use of this standard for knighthood in his book gives us one more piece of evidence that he was a knight of the Order of Hospitallers, and therefore well accustomed to their strict pedigree requirement for knighthood. Professor Field, in arguing for Sir Thomas Malory of Newbold Revel as our author, suggests that this man could have shown knightly lineage for both of his parents (Field, 51). That is interesting, but in fact, Sir Thomas of Newbold Revel, being a secular knight, would not have been required to do so. However, a Thomas Malory who was a Knight Hospitaller would.

The Order of Hospitallers was instituted in service to the Crusades; its two functions were to provide hospital care for those in need of it and to kill Muslims who violated the Holy Land. That being the case, of course we would expect to find war and disdain for the "Sarazens" in a book by a Hospitaller, and so we do. Some of Malory's sources, notably the English alliterative *Morte Arthure,* mention Saracens, but there are additional such Malorean episodes and comments scattered through *Le Morte,* some of which may make us wonder whether Malory could be speaking from his own experience in fighting in the wars against Islam. Sir Lancelot du Lake is Malory's favorite character and his *alter ego*. It seems sometimes, in encounters with the Muslims, that Lancelot is acting or speaking from Malory's memory. For example, an episode, which Vinaver tells us is doubtless Malory's

[79] Charles Browne, *Transactions of the St. Paul's Ecclesiastical Society* 2, February 1884 (London: Alabaster, Passmore, and Sons), 13.

invention, is interjected into the midst of the battle taken from the alliterative *Morte Arthure*:

> Than sir Launcelot lepe forth with his stede evyn streyght unto sir Lucyus, and in his wey he smote thorow a kynge that stoode althernexte hym, and his name was Jacounde, a Sarazen full noble. And than he russhed forth unto sir Lucyus, and smote hym on the helme with hys swerde, than he felle to the erthe; and syth he rode thryse over hym on a rowe, and so toke the baner of Rome and rode with hyt away unto Arthur hymself. And all seyde that hit sawe there was never knyght dud more worshyp in hys dayes. (Malory, *Works*, 159)

Vinaver says, "This feat of gallantry is not recorded in *MA*. The episode is doubtless *M*'s invention designed to enhance the reputation of his favorite character" (Malory, *Works*, vol. 3, 1390). It does enhance Lancelot's reputation, of course. More interesting is the fact that this is the only mention of Jacounde the "full noble" Saracen in the *Morte* and probably anywhere, suggesting that Malory did not invent the episode, as Vinaver believed, but remembered it.

This is only one of many passages in the book that enhance Lancelot's reputation as a fighter, the greatest knight in the world. At the end of the battle with Lucius and his partly Roman, partly Saracen army, we find that Arthur's enemies have been slaughtered in huge numbers by his greatly outnumbered forces. Arthur praises his men for their courage against great odds. Then he weeps and wipes his eyes with a kerchief, and tells them that their courage and hardiness could well have destroyed them, and if they had turned back from the battle they would have lost no honor, for it is foolish for knights to stay and fight when they are so greatly outnumbered. "'Not so,' seyde sir Launcelot, 'the shame sholde ever have been oures.' 'That is trouthe,' seyde sir Clegis and sir Bors, 'for knyghtes ons shamed recoverys hit never'" (Malory, *Works*, 157). Vinaver offers his comments on this passage. First, he says that "with a keuercheff wyped his iyen" is not in *Morte Arthure*; then, concerning the discussion of knights leaving the field if they are "overmacched," he says, "*MA* (1925–6) [that is, Malory's source] does not generalize to this extent, and the controversy about 'useless' fighting is only vaguely suggested. In *M* [Malory], on the other hand, it is carefully elaborated. The argument is that honor comes before strategy, and that no knight should avoid a battle no matter what the odds against him might be" (Malory, *Works*, vol. 3, 1388). All this is a vivid reminder of the letter of St. Bernard of Clairvaux praising the new knighthood of warrior monks fighting for the Holy Land:

> These men charge the enemy, regarding the foe as sheep, never — no matter how outnumbered they are — as ruthless barbarians or as awesome hordes. Nor do they presume on their own strength, but trust for victory in the Lord of Sabaoth. They are mindful of the words of Maccabees, "*It is simple enough for a multitude to be vanquished by a handful. It makes no difference in the sight of the God of heaven whether he grants deliverance by the hands of few or many; for victory in war does not depend on a big army, but bravery is the gift from heaven.*" As they have on numerous occasions experienced, one man may pursue a thousand, and two put ten thousand to flight. (St. Bernard, 47–48)

Naturally a knight of the Hospital would have heard these words many times, especially, we imagine, as he headed out to engage the mighty armies of the infidel. Doubtless it was this same religiously inspired determination to wipe out the violators of the holy places that inspired another of Malory's additions to his source. Lucius, as we have seen, uses Saracen troops alongside his Romans. In Malory, though not in his source, Arthur instructs his men not to try to save the Christians in the enemy army; "save none for golde nothir for sylver: for they that woll accompany them with Sarezens, the man that wolde save them were lytyll to prayse. And therefore sle doune and save nother hethyn nothir Crystyn" (Malory, *Works*, 224).

It is not surprising that Muslims were held in low regard in the Christian world during the centuries of the Crusades. It is particularly plausible that any knight who had been to the Holy Land himself and engaged in those great battles would hold Saracens in disrespect. We see another piece of evidence of Malory's standing as such a warrior in a few episodes and descriptions found in the *Morte Darthur*. For example, this one: Corsabryne and Palomydes are both Muslims who are friendly with Arthur's knights; Palomydes is the "good" one because he has made up his mind to be baptized as soon as he has achieved a certain chivalric status. The two are engaged in a duel over a damsel. "And then they pulled oute their swerdis and dressed their shyldis and layshed togydirs mythtyly as myghty knyghtes, that there was no pyse of harneyse wolde holde them, for this Corsabryne was a passynge felownse knyght." Palomydes gets the better of his opponent, then, "'Fye on the,' seyde sir Corsabryne, 'and do thy warste!'" So Palomydes does his worst: "Than he smote of his hede. And therewithall cam a stynke of his body, whan the soule departed that there myght nobody abyde the savoure. So was the corpus had away and buryed in a wood, bycause he was a paynym" (Malory, *Works*, 496). Malory's source for this episode was probably the prose *Tristan*, says Vinaver. He tells us that it says nothing about the stench of Corsabryne's dead body; in the French, Corsabryne commits suicide and the devil carries off his soul (Malory, *Works*, vol. 3, 1507). Malory makes the more emphatic point that even the body of a dead Saracen is repulsive, because he is unbaptized. This attitude would seem credible in a warrior for Christ against the Muslims. It balances, in fact, the sweet smell mentioned in the story of the death of Lancelot, who dies in the state of God's grace, as Malory tells it: "So whan syr Bors and his felowes came to his bedde they found hym starke dede; and he laye as he had smyled, and the swettest savour aboute hym that ever they felte" (Malory, *Works*, 881).

The Order of St. John of Jerusalem, Knights Hospitaller, was the only monastic fighting order left still fighting the Muslims during Malory's lifetime, the Templars having long been blended with the Hospitallers after the Order of the Temple was dissolved in 1312. As we have seen, St. Bernard of Clairvaux was the guiding spirit behind these orders, and the family of Thomas Malory of Yorkshire was closely connected with them for generations; in our Malory's time, the Malorys were known as one of the "Hospitaller families." They were also deeply influenced by Bernard's other order, the Cistercians, to whom their ancestors as far back as the beginnings of these orders had made tremendous contributions; moreover, these Yorkshire Malorys lived adjacent to the great Cistercian monastery of Fountains Abbey, and our Thomas grew up there. Therefore, if our author was the Yorkshire man, of Studley and Hutton, we can expect to find Cistercian influence in *Le Morte Darthur*, and we do. The fact that Thomas Malory chose to use the version of the *Quest of the Holy Grail* that was written by a Cistercian monk results in a Cistercian coloring to the whole *Morte*. To be more specific, for example, Malory has his Lancelot accused several times of being "not stable," meaning that he will likely not keep his promise to avoid Guenevere's company after the quest for the Grail is ended, even though he "hath takyn upon hym to forsake synne" (Malory, *Works*, 685). Dhira Mahoney gives us a full discussion of the word *stable* as used in this context, pointing out that it means more than simply "constant"; it has a strong religious connotation. She tells us that a novice in the Benedictine Order makes a promise of stability, signifying his intention to persevere in the order. Mahoney quotes Timothy Fry, O.S.B., in a note, to the effect that the new Benedictine actually promises stability twice, once as he enters the order and then again after a year; the early promise "simply means that the candidate ... has decided to stay and wants to persevere through the novitiate to profession. The second promise, at the end of the year, means that he wants to make profession and bind himself permanently to all the obligations of the monastic life."[80] What is more significant still for our purpose is the fact that Cistercians also make a vow of stability. Recall that the first Cistercians were initially Benedictines, who had

[80] Dhira B. Mahoney, "The Truest and Holiest Tale: Malory's Transformation of *La Queste del Sainte Graal*," in *Studies in Malory*, 127, n. 27. Further citations of this work will be in parentheses in the text.

become disaffected because the old Rule of St. Benedict, written in 533, was being widely ignored in worldly monasteries; these men left their Benedictine houses and eventually became a new order under the guidance of Bernard of Clairvaux, but they still cherished the Benedictine Rule. Our Malory of Studley and Hutton, Yorkshire, was intimately connected with the Cistercians at Fountains Abbey. He adds to his source the accusation against Lancelot that he is not stable, an accusation that would be meaningful to Cistercians. Interestingly, in adding the several accusations of instability against Lancelot, Malory out-Cistercians his Cistercian source, the *Queste del Saint Graal*, which does not use that word.

One of the most striking small pieces of evidence found in *Le Morte* that the author was a Hospitaller is the clear demonstration of his interest in naval battles against the infidel. The Hospitallers in the fourteenth and fifteenth centuries operated a mighty navy in seagoing combat with Muslims. The order was particularly engaged against Barbary pirates, who were the affliction of commerce of all sorts around the Mediterranean, but the overarching purpose of the Hospitaller navy, as with their dry-land military operations, was to recapture parts of the Holy Land already taken by the Muslims and to guard against further incursions. The evidence in *Le Morte* that Malory took an interest in this naval combat is found in the "Tale of Alexander the Orphan." Here is the story.

> So hit befelle on a tyme that the myscreauntys Sarezynes londid in the contrey of Cornwayle sone aftir the Sessoynes were departed. And whan the good prynce sir Bodwyne was ware of them when they were londed, than at the londynge he areysed the peple pryvayly and hastyly.
>
> And or hit were day he let put wylde fyre in three of his owne shyppis, and suddeynly he pulled up the sayle, and wyth the wynde he made tho shyppis to be drevyn amonge the navy of the Sarezynes. And to make a short tale, tho three shyppis sett on fyre all the shyppis, that none were saved. And at the poynte of the day the good prynce Bodwyne with all his felyship set on the myscreauntys with showtys and cryes,

> and slew the numbir of forty thousand and lefft none on lyve. (Malory, *Works,* 472)

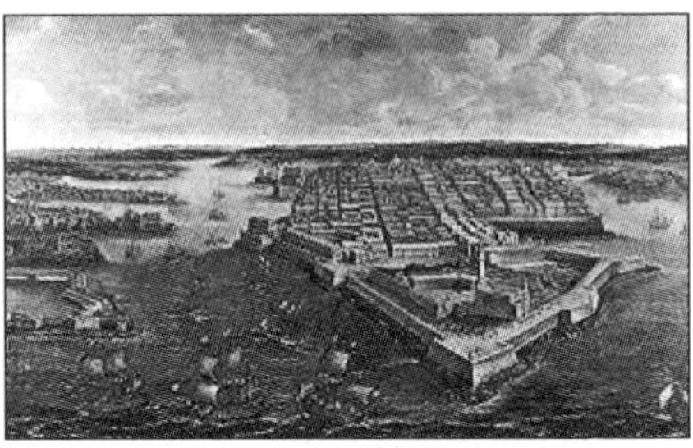

Hospitaller ships at Malta's harbor, by unknown artist

This story, inserted at the beginning of the "Tale of Alexander the Orphan," nephew of King Mark, is entirely Malory's own contribution, as is the name Bodwyne for Mark's brother and victim. It is interesting that the name Baldwin, so similar, was the name of a succession of kings of Christian Jerusalem, and Baldwin I was the monarch who, in 1104, recognized and confirmed the Hospitallers as an order of monk-knights. This Baldwin had some involvement himself with seagoing warfare against the Muslims; in 1097, he "took Tarsus from Tancred ... with help from a fleet of pirates under Guynemer of Boulogne"; in 1101, he "captured Arsuf and Caesarea with assistance from a Genoese fleet"; and in 1110, he captured Sidon "with aid from Ordelafo Faliero (who brought a Venetian fleet)."[81] Malory's story of seagoing enterprise against the Saracens has the ring of truth, as does so much of his work. Perhaps the Hospitaller knight Sir Thomas Malory, as part of his required service in the Holy Land, either participated in the naval triumph he describes or heard of it from other knights who did seagoing duty, giving us one more piece to fit into our puzzle for identifying Thomas Malory, the writer of *Le Morte Darthur.*

[81] wikipedia.org/wiki/Baldwin_I_of_Jerusalem.

13

Lancelot: Malory's Favorite Knight-Monk

E. K. CHAMBERS once observed that Sir Thomas Malory came late to his high theme, meaning that the *Morte Darthur* was written at the very end of the Middle Ages, long after the old chivalric tales had lost their initial freshness and charm (Chambers). But Chambers might just as well have been referring to the fact that the book is half over before Malory finds his way out of the shallowness and sometimes even silliness characteristic of the old romances and finds his own strong narrative. There are, as Chambers says, "stirring and amusing tales enough in the earlier books," but they have a flat quality, almost like a cartoon, or, in Chambers's analogy, a tapestry; he suggests that you can

> half close your eyes and watch a pleasant landscape, full of running waters, and moated castles, and hermitages, and green lawns, and "plumps" of wood, amongst which move bright little figures in blue and white and red armour, every now and again stopping to lay spears in rest and upset one another, and then swearing eternal friendship and riding away again. Here is a ford perilous, and at the door of a pavilion a dwarf watches a shield, hung there for the challenge of any knight who has a mind to end an ill custom. There a tired knight sleeps under a great apple-tree that stands by a hedge, and presently his horse grimly neighs, and by sweep four

queens on white mules under a canopy of green silk, and cast an enchantment upon him.

But along about the middle of *Le Morte Darthur,* Malory seems to realize what he really wants to say. As Chambers says, "Light breaks over the story. We no longer see men walking as trees darkly. They begin to arrange themselves in definite patterns, and to move through real conflicts of character and passion to a deliberate end. Henceforward everything centres round Lancelot." Malory has come, albeit late, to his high theme, and even though Chambers does not say so, Malory's high theme turns out to be the maturing of Lancelot and the salvation of his soul. In all of this we can clearly see the Novel in its wobbly infancy.

William Caxton called Malory's book *The Death of Arthur,* when in fact the death of Arthur comes and goes, and the book goes on much longer. But when Lancelot dies, the story ends. Lancelot is in Malory's telling the greatest knight in the world, far overshadowing Arthur, Gawain, Tristram, Galahad, and all the others. Lancelot is the knight Malory loves, the knight who speaks for Malory, Malory's *alter ego*. Malory scholars have tacitly acknowledged Lancelot's status as Malory's mouthpiece: when they wish to comment upon what seems to be Malory's view of an issue, they frequently quote Lancelot. Therefore it behooves us as inquirers into the identity of Sir Thomas Malory to look closely at Sir Lancelot du Lake.

Here is a vital point in Malory studies, which scholars have tended to forget or ignore, as they wander in the morass of manuscripts and textual emendations and influences, and claims of now-vanished sources: Thomas Malory wrote *Le Morte Darthur*. He took a great deal from his French sources, but he also rejected a great deal, probably upwards of 90 percent of the French material available to him. And he composed for himself a great deal as well. This way of composition means that, in spite of the patchwork nature of his labor, the *Morte Darthur* remains Malory's own. It was he who decided what to retain, what to reject, what to compose, however modestly he refers to his project as merely reducing into English the old French tales. Therefore, we can expect that Malory, like other authors who reveal themselves in their books, will reveal himself in *Le Morte Darthur*. Moreover, in a more particular way, we can expect that he will reveal himself in his portrait of Lancelot, for he makes Lancelot the focal point of his book.

Scholars have long noticed Malory's apparent dislike of courtly love,[82] which manifests itself in shying away from scenes of intimacy between Lancelot and Guenevere. Although he obviously knew that in the French tales those two were adulterous lovers, Malory never says that they are. He adroitly leaves his readers the option of considering Lancelot and Guenevere innocent of adultery however much they love each other, and however much the members of the court suspect them. Our author is not interested in writing a tale of lasciviousness and court intrigue. When he tells the story of Lancelot, what he is writing is the story of a human soul, following his favorite through tests and humiliations and temptations, sin and repentance and resolution and then again sin, from his entry into Arthur's court as a callow young man who falls in love with a queen, to his death many years later in the odor of sanctity with a sweet smile on his face. Malory is far more interested in Lancelot's spiritual development than in his love for Guenevere, his service to Arthur, or his position as the best knight in the world. That spiritual development takes over in the later tales until Lancelot's standing with God becomes the main focus of the book. And in writing the story of Lancelot, Malory proves his mettle as a writer. There is nothing superficial or facile about this story; it is the story of a man in conflict with himself, and it grapples with the realities of that conflict in almost a modern fashion.

Lancelot is guilty of pride, and no wonder; he is the greatest knight in the world, and the queen loves him. Early in the book, we are given to understand that those two facts are inextricably linked in Lancelot: he does knightly deeds to please Guenevere; and Guenevere loves him because of his knightly deeds. Lancelot first enters the story of Arthur and

[82] For an example, see P. E. Tucker, "Chivalry in the *Morte*," in *Essays on Malory*, 64–103.

his knights when Arthur tells Merlin that he has decided to take a wife, and he asks for Merlin's advice. Merlin asks him, "Now is there any that you love more than another?" and Arthur unhesitatingly says yes, he loves Guenevere. Merlin replies that Guenevere will do; if Arthur's heart were not set on her, Merlin would find another damsel, but where a man's heart is set, there is no changing him. "But Merlyon warned the kyng covertly that Gwenyver was nat holsom for hym to take to wyff. For he warned hym that Launcelot scholde love hir, and sche hym agayne" (Malory, *Works*, 71). Thus we have the love predicted already, before Lancelot even comes to court, and the technique is established for telling the story of the queen and the knight who loves her: it is to be told, in Malory, by members of Arthur's court, gossiping. It is not long before Lancelot shows up. He is young—probably about sixteen, to judge from the age of other newly made knights in the book. Arthur is gathering an army to go after five rebellious kings, and we are told, "Than leepe in yong sir Launcelot de Laake with a lyght herte and seyde unto kynge Arthur, 'Thoughe my londis marche nyghe thyne enemyes, yet shall I make myne avow aftir my power that of good men of armys aftir my bloode thus many I shall brynge with me: twenty thousand helmys in haubirkes attyred that shall never fayle you whyles oure lyves lastyth" (Malory, *Works*, 138). At this point, we have seen already introduced one of the major themes of the book: Lancelot pledges his undying fealty to Arthur, but he is destined to love Guenevere, and she him again.

Some fifty pages or so later, we find the eager young knight with the light heart being talked about in the court for his derring-do, and we learn that he and Guenevere have fallen in love. Lancelot is acclaimed already, from the beginning of his life at court, as the best, the "fyrste knyght." This accolade is repeated throughout the book, in multiple situations, and we are told and told again that he is never beaten except by treachery or sorcery. At this point in the story, there have been many grand tournaments to celebrate Arthur's success in Rome against the five kings who have rebelled against him, and his return to England, and many knights have proven that they can do noble deeds of chivalry.

> But in especiall hit was prevyd on sir Launcelot de Lake, for in all turnementes, justys, and dedys of armys, both for lyff and deth, he passed all other knyghtes, and at no tyme was he ovircom but yf hit were by treson other inchauntement. So this sir Launcelot encresed so mervaylously in worship and honoure.... Wherefore quene Gwenyvere had hym in grete favoure aboven all other knyghtis, and so he loved the quene agayne aboven all other ladyes dayes of his lyff, and for hir he dud many dedys of armys. (Malory, *Works*, 180)

Thus early in the book we are given to understand that Lancelot has attracted Guenevere by his strength at arms; he does manly deeds for her, and she accordingly rewards him with her love. All of this is standard behavior for boys, of course, not much different from Tom Sawyer's attempt to impress Becky Thatcher by doing handsprings and jumping over fences. However, we notice that already the idea has been planted in Lancelot that, first, he is the greatest knight of all, and, second, that as long as he can outperform all other knights, Guenevere will love him. Thus, the two weaknesses of Lancelot mentioned several times throughout the book, his "pryde and bobbaunce of the world," and his love for the queen, take root in him from his youth; he has already been acknowledged as the greatest knight and Guenevere's special favorite.

Lancelot's pride in his skill at arms and in the queen's love does not surprise us, of course. But what comes after this does. Readers who are familiar with the old story, either from the early French versions or from the modern retellings, may expect scenes of scarlet passion between Lancelot and Guenevere; if so, they will be disappointed. There is simply nothing like that between these two to be found in *Le Morte Darthur*. Malory reduces the famous love affair to gossip in the court. Chambers, listing the flaws he detects in the *Morte*, complains that Malory botches up the love story; there is "nothing of Lancelot's trembling at the sight of Guenevere, not even that episode of that first kiss, of which Dante makes such unforgettable use in the *Divine Comedy*" (Chambers). But Malory leaves out the famous kiss because that kiss is not part of the story that he wishes to tell. We have seen that the first mention of Lancelot in the book is the prophecy of Merlin that there will be trouble if Arthur marries Guenevere, because she will love Lancelot and he will love her. The whole story of their love is told like that, by other characters who think they detect suspicious doings. As Terence McCarthy says, Malory "reduces Lancelot's role as lover to a mere rumour … to nothing more than the amorous reputation which courtiers give him and which he rejects outright. The mere idea goes against everything he stands for as a knight, he protests."[83] Notice that Malory's distancing of Lancelot from the old French role of adulterous lover, ubiquitous in the French romances, is a clue to Malory's own attitude concerning such matters.

Rather early in the book, Malory, in episodes of his own composing, not in his sources, gives Lancelot several chances to tell us whether the rumors are true. Once, four queens are out riding together and come upon Lancelot sleeping under an apple tree. Immediately they "began to stryve for that knyght, and every of hem seyde they wolde have hym to her love" (Malory, *Works*, 183). Morgan le Fay, who is one of the four, proposes a plan: she will put a spell on the knight so that he will remain asleep while the queens carry him on his shield to her castle, where she will awaken him, and they will make him choose which of the women he wants as paramour. They try it. When Lancelot awakes, he is told that he must either choose one of them or die in their prison; for they "know well there can no lady have thy love but one, and that is quene Gwenyvere, and now thou shalt hir love lose for ever, and she thyne" (Malory, *Works*, 183). However, Lancelot is appalled at the offer and answers immediately, "Yet had I lever dye in this preson with worship than to have one of you to my peramour, magre myne hede. And therefore ye be answeryd: I woll none of you." Moreover, he tells them, "And as for my lady, dame Gwenyvere … she is the treweste lady unto hir lorde

[83] Terence McCarthy, "Malory and His Sources," in *A Companion to Malory*, ed. D. S. Brewer (Cambridge, MA: D. S. Brewer, 1996), 86.

lyvynge" (Malory, *Works,* 184). This is Lancelot's usual answer; every time he is accused of an affair with Guenevere, he stoutly defends her innocence. And we have no evidence to the contrary; we have never seen these two in any sort of compromising situation.

Another time, he is charged by a damsel with being a womanless knight; he is courteous and meek with the ladies, she says:

> But one thyng, sir knyght, methynkes ye lak, ye that ar a knyght wyveles, that ye woll nat love some mayden other jantylwoman. For I cowde never here sey that ever ye loved ony of no maner degre, and that is grete pyte. But hit is noysed that ye love quene Gwenyvere, and that she hath ordeyned by enchauntemente that ye shall never love none other but hir, nother none other damesell ne lady shall rejoyce you; wherfore there be many in this londe, of hyghe estate and lowe, that make grete sorow. (Malory, *Works,* 194)

He answers that he can't help what people say, but he has no plans either to marry or to take a paramour; first of all, if he were married, he would have to stay beside his wife and end his knight-errantry — no more arms and tournaments, battles and adventures. And as for taking paramours, that would offend God. Moreover, knights who have paramours are weakened for chivalric activities:

> I may nat warne peple to speke of me what hit pleasyth hem. But for to be a weddyd man, I thynke hit nat, for than I muste couche with hir and leve armys and turnamentis, batellys and adventures. And as for tho sey to take my pleasaunce with peramours, that woll I refuse; in prencipall for drede of God, for knyghtes that bene adventures shold nat be advoutrers nothir lecherous, for than they be nat happy nother fortunate unto werrys; for other they shall be overcom with a sympler knyght than they be hemself, other ellys they shall sle by unhappe and hir cursednesse bettir men than they be hemself.

> And so who that usyth peramours shall be unhappy, and all thynge unhappy that is aboute them. (Malory, *Works*, 195)

Stephen Atkinson points out that unless we accept Lancelot's words here at face value and assume that Lancelot has no paramour, then we must consider him a rank hypocrite.[84] But there is no reason to suspect young Lancelot of any misrepresentation of himself and his motives. We can assume that he is simply telling the truth; after all, he has just turned down the offer of choosing from among four queens. Of course, every time some lady, maiden, or gentlewoman makes an attempt on Lancelot and charges him with loving the queen, the unspoken question is always *Does she or doesn't she?* But even though the question goes unasked, Lancelot never allows it to go unanswered; his answer is always emphatic: She doesn't. Guenevere, he says, is the truest lady living to her lord. But note well the manifesto that Lancelot has pronounced above, concerning what happens to a knight who takes his pleasaunce with paramours, for our author will return to that theme. Malory has told us that Lancelot loves Guenevere, and she him, and he has told us that Lancelot is the greatest knight of the world. He has not told us that the lovers are adulterers. In the working out of his story, he will allow us to judge whether in fact they are, and he will tell us that Lancelot is, whether adulterous or not, guilty of sin — and that his sin is the direct result of his love for Guenevere, and, even more particularly, of her love for him. Malory shifts the focus away from adultery and toward a sin even more dangerous, the sin against which St. Bernard so emphatically cautioned his monks.

Lancelot is guilty of pride, and his pride must be rebuked.

Let us step back for a moment from our story in order to study its background, and especially to consider Bernard of Clairvaux. He is the saint, we remember, who was so tremendously influential in the founding and propagating of the two religious orders to which the

[84] Stephen B. Atkinson, "Malory's Lancelot and the Quest of the Grail," in *Studies in Malory*, 131.

Malorys of Yorkshire were closely attached, the Order of St. John, Hospitallers, and the Cistercians. Along with being a statesman, a diplomat, a theologian, a founder of monasteries, and a saint, he was one of the most prolific writers of the Middle Ages. He wrote many sorts of things, most importantly for us a series of homiletic treatises to guide his monks in their striving for holiness. We have already looked at one of Bernard's famous pieces, "In Praise of the New Knighthood." Another treatise that is of use to us in our search for Thomas Malory's identity is the one concerned with humility, *De Gradibus Humilitatis,* or "The Twelve Degrees of Humility and Pride." This is probably the first such homiletic piece he wrote and certainly the first he recorded in his own list of his writings, made in 1127. This work is the remote ancestor of Alcoholics Anonymous "Twelve Steps to Sobriety." It lays out twelve seemingly small steps by which a man can gradually exalt himself into the vice of pride, and, conversely, twelve steps by which he can lower himself out of that sin and acquire humility. It shows the deep importance that St. Bernard assigned to humility and the serious threat that he believed pride poses for the human soul. Any follower of St. Bernard, particularly any member of the Cistercian or the Hospitallers' order, would be well acquainted with this treatise, and with the necessity of rooting out pride and embracing humility in the quest for sanctity. If Sir Thomas Malory who wrote *Le Morte Darthur* was a knight of the Hospitallers' order, it is not surprising that his favorite character and *alter ego*, Lancelot du Lake, must be subjected to a rigorous therapy of rebuke and humiliation for his pride as the greatest knight of the world. This despite the fact that Lancelot never boasts, is always courteous, always deflects public tributes to himself. His pride is not that of a braggart; it is more subtle. He believes in his heart that he cannot be defeated except by treason or sorcery. He believes that Guenevere's love, which has always upheld him, always will. But Thomas Malory humbles him, and he does so in a thoroughly Bernardian manner. Paralleling the life of Bernard himself, who was born into the riches and aristocratic mores of his family castle, and left that world as a very young man to embrace the monastic life of the Cistercians and thus the pursuit of closer union with God, Malory juxtaposes in his book two worlds, the secular world of Arthur's court and Round Table, and the spiritual world of the Holy Grail. He had several versions of the Grail story from which to choose, and he chose the version written by a Cistercian monk, more spiritual and less secular than that which was more convenient to his hand because it was bound together with another work that he was using, as his model for the Grail world. Thus Malory has the character of Lancelot as the greatest worldly knight, and he sets about transforming him into a pilgrim in pursuit of union with God, symbolized by the Holy Grail. Lancelot gets along without much trouble in the secular world of the Round Table as long as the Grail world leaves him alone. He never fails in any competition. He is lauded universally and pursued by ladies who are passing fair everywhere he goes. He is loved faithfully by Queen Guenevere. He has everything he needs. Or so he thinks. But Lancelot does not initially know that his name has been mentioned in a certain prophecy, and he is a marked man. Eventually the world of the Grail claims him and thus begins his long humiliation — and his conversion.

In the lore of the Middle Ages, the story grew up that the Holy Grail was the vessel of the Blood of Christ, shed when He was crucified, and caught by Joseph of Arimathea, who is mentioned in the Gospels as having provided a tomb in which to bury Jesus. According to this legend, Joseph and his descendants have thus become the caretakers of the Grail, and they have brought it to England. They wait in hope for the prophesied Galahad to be born; only when a sinless descendant of the original Joseph goes on a quest for the Grail, and finds it, can the second-generation member of that line, who is now over four hundred years old, die at last. At least, that is one way in which the story is told; there are various versions. In Malory, not much in the way of background is provided. He simply tells us that one day, when Lancelot is out riding, he comes to "the fayryste towre that ever he saw, and thereundir was a fayre lytyll towne full of people. And all the people men and women, cryed at onys, 'Wellcom, sir Launcelot, the floure of knyghthode! For by the we shall be holpyn oute of daungere!'" (Malory, *Works,* 582). Lancelot's first task in helping them out of danger is to take the hand of a beautiful lady who has been boiling hot for five years because of a spell cast upon her by Morgan le Fay. She seems to be caught in a sort of permanent hot flash; apparently she is so hot that she has thrown off all her clothes, for she appears before Lancelot "as nakid as a nedle" (Malory, *Works,* 582). The poor fair lady will suffer until the best knight of the world has taken her by the hand. Lancelot, of course, does not hesitate to take her hand, and the lady, of course, is healed, whereupon the people bring her some clothes and they all go together to the church to thank God. Lancelot's next task is to slay "a fyendely dragon spyttynge wylde fyre oute of hys mowthe" (Malory, *Works,* 583), which also has been troubling the people of the town. Again, the chore presents no difficulty; Lancelot's prowess is easily up to the job of slaying the dragon. The significant thing to notice in these exploits is that Lancelot readily responds to the petitions of the people who need the help of the best knight of the world and consider him to be that knight; he assumes that they are right, and apparently they are, because he succeeds with both lady and dragon.

But the next thing that happens is portentous. The boiling hot lady and the fiendly dragon are merely preliminary to the main business of Lancelot in the fair little town. This, although he does not know it, is the begetting of Galahad. The good and noble king comes to greet Lancelot, and tells him, "My name ys kynge Pelles, kynge of the forayne contre and cousyn nyghe unto Joseph of Aramathy" (Malory, *Works,* 583). When Pelles says that he is the king of the foreign country, he appears to be referring to the alien country, the "Other" side, the supernatural country. He is, in fact, the caretaker of the Holy Grail. It turns out that Pelles has been given the prophecy that his own daughter, Elaine, will be the mother of Lancelot's peerless son, Galahad, and King Pelles needs to get Lancelot into her bed in order to bring all this about. Elaine's servant is Brusen, a sorceress. Brusen comes to the aid of the prophecy by sending messengers to Lancelot ostensibly from Guenevere, offering as token a ring like one that Guenevere wears, directing Lancelot to come to her.

We are told of his eagerness: "And whan sir Launcelot saw that tokyn, wyte you well he was never so fayne" (Malory, *Works,* 584). The deception continues. When Lancelot arrives at the meeting place, he is given wine laced with something that makes him "asoted and madde." In this stupor brought about by drugs and sorcery, Lancelot, believing that Elaine is Guenevere, spends the night in her bed and there begets the new flower of knighthood, Galahad.

Now, what Lancelot thinks about all this does not matter to the others, and nobody asks him; he is simply used as a sperm donor. All the same, Malory, in his continuing characterization of Lancelot, allows the reader to know how Lancelot feels. All the windows of Elaine's chamber have been shuttered so that no slightest daylight can be admitted — apparently Brusen's spell cannot withstand the light of day. When Lancelot rises late in the morning and opens the shutter, immediately the enchantment is over. "Then he knew hymselff that he had done amysse. 'Alas!' he seyde, 'that I have lyved so longe, for now I am shamed,' And anone he gate his swerde in honde and seyde, "Thou traytoures! What are thou that I have layne bye all this nyght? Thou shalt dye ryght here of myne hondys!'" (Malory, *Works,* 585). But Elaine skips out of bed and falls on her knees before him, begging for mercy and telling him that she has conceived in her womb his child, who is destined to be the most noble knight of the world. Malory is specific; Elaine is young and fair and lusty, he says, and wise (the reader may wonder whether her wisdom is likely to appeal to Lancelot at the moment), and naked, warm from her bed, and kneeling before Lancelot. She seems to be hoping that he will just forget about Guenevere and come on back to bed. But he does not. Lancelot is not pleased. He has drawn his sword on Elaine, the medieval equivalent of pulling a gun on her, and he is holding it in his hand. However, he has taken an oath to give mercy to anyone who begs mercy. He takes her up and kisses her once and forgives her, but he says that he will never forgive Brusen; in fact, if he ever finds her he will cut off her head: "But her that made thys enchauntement uppon me and betwene you and me, and I may fynde her, that same lady dame Brusen shall lose her hede for her wycchecrauftys, for there was never knyght desceyved as I am this nyght." There is no tarrying; he gets dressed and leaves: "And so sir Launcelot arrayed hym and armed hym and took hys leave" (Malory, *Works,* 586). This story constitutes the beginning of Lancelot's long-continuing humiliation. He has been deceived and violated by Elaine and her servant, with her father's consent, this knight who gave his heart to Guenevere when he was only a boy and has been faithful to her ever since, in spite of all the many attempts on his virtue by other women. Elaine is the predestined mother of Lancelot's only child, but she is not Guenevere. When Guenevere hears the news that Lancelot has begotten a child with Elaine, she rebukes him seriously, calling him false knight, but when she learns how he has been deceived, she forgives him. This time.

The next time, Malory draws on the power that Guenevere herself possesses over Lancelot and has the queen participate in his humiliation. Elaine decides that she wants more of Lancelot's company, and so she comes to a ball at Arthur's court, looking more beautiful than any other lady in the world. Dame Brusen pulls out her bag of tricks again and deceives Lancelot into Elaine's bed. However, Guenevere hears Lancelot talking in his sleep, in his drugged and deceived condition, in Elaine's room, and this time there is no forgiving him: "A, thou false traytoure knyght! Loke thou never abyde in my courte, and lyghtly that thou voyde my chambir! And nat so hardy, thou false traytoure knyght, that evermore thou com in my syght!" (Malory, *Works,* 594). Lancelot faints, and when he comes to himself, he leaps out a window, "and there with thornys he was all to-cracched of his vysage and hys body, and so he ran furth he knew nat whothir, and was as wylde ... as ever was man" (Malory, *Works,* 594). And so the humbling of Lancelot continues. During the long time of his running mad in the wilderness, he is subjected to cold, hunger, and thirst; dogs chase him; boys run after him throwing excrement; he is treated as a fool by everyone who encounters him. For a year and a half he is bound hand and foot by a kindly lord who gives him food and shelter but is afraid of him. He is gored by a boar and then carried on a cart alongside the boar to the home of a hermit, who doctors his wound. Finally, in an episode that serves as our introduction to the Grail, someone kindly gives Lancelot some clothing and straw for a bed under the gate of a castle. The castle happens to be in Corbyn, the fair little town that we remember as the home of King Pelles and his daughter Elaine. Elaine recognizes Lancelot; she and Pelles and Dame Brusen the sorceress take him to the chapel where the Grail is kept, and, at long last, Lancelot is healed of his madness by the Grail. Thus we see its great healing power; when Lancelot has been broken and shamed utterly, there is only one cure — the Grail of the Blood of Christ. Malory has established his high theme, and he pursues it through the remainder of Lancelot's story.

When Lancelot is well, he is abjectly apologetic to Elaine for drawing his sword against her after spending the night in her bed. He is ashamed. But he has not forgotten the wrong she and her servant did to him; he tells her that his threatening action happened because they had made him lie with Elaine in spite of his own wishes: "'Ye and dame Brusen made me for to lye be you magry myne hede.' 'That ys trouthe,'" says Elaine (Malory, *Works,* 611). In this way, Malory reminds us that even though Lancelot has fathered a child, he is still a pure knight; Malory is not ready to accuse him of unchastity. Lancelot is homeless, since Guenevere has expelled him from his home at Arthur's court. He must beg a home from Pelles, who allows Lancelot to live in one of his castles, with twenty ladies and twenty knights, including Pelles himself and Elaine, who promises not to leave him. The false name that Lancelot takes, Le Shyvalere Ill Mafeete, "the knyght that hath trespassed" (Malory, *Works,* 611), shows us that he is realizing his own faults, but we get no further elucidation of that point at this stage of the story. There is, however, no mention of any romance between Lancelot and Elaine even though they are living so close to each other. Lancelot has a shield made picturing a queen with a knight kneeling before her, and "for ony myrthis that all the ladyes myght make hym, he wolde onys every day loke towarde the realme of Logrys, where kynge Arthure and quene Gwenyver was, and than wolde he falle uppon a wepyng as hys harte shulde tobraste" (Malory, *Works,* 612).

Well might Lancelot weep, for he has suffered a great deal. He has been bereft of his lady, his knightly honor, his long-preserved celibacy, his pledge to Guenevere to belong always to her alone, his home in King Arthur's court, even his sanity. When finally Percival and Ector de Marys find Lancelot and persuade him to go with them back to the court, and when Guenevere hears the story of his long and patient suffering, she "wepte as she shulde have dyed" (Malory, *Works*, 617). Malory has taken seriously the teachings of St. Bernard that the way to Christian perfection is humility and the rebuking of pride; his treatment of Lancelot before "The Tale of the Sankgreal" thus has prepared us for what comes next, as Lancelot finds his way through the "forayne country" of the Grail, in the story written by Bernard's Cistercians, *The Quest of the Holy Grail.* What comes next is more and more humiliation. In the Grail world, Lancelot must learn the uselessness of the everyday ideals of Arthur's court.

Of great significance to our inquiry is the fact that Malory chose to use the Cistercian version of *The Quest of the Holy Grail,* preferring it to the other, more secular, versions he could have used. It is hard to explain why any knight living an ordinary worldly life, such as Sir Thomas Malory of Newbold Revel, would put aside the Grail story as told in the prose *Tristan* for example, his source for the tale of Tristram, and turn instead to the Cistercian work, which is so obviously a product of intensely devout religion. Yet that is exactly what our author did, and in fact he changed this source less than any other of his sources; Malory's retelling, except for some long, high-flown passages of preaching that are omitted, and the serious examination of Lancelot's love for Guenevere that is added, is almost a duplicate of the Cistercian work. In that tale, even though Galahad is the only knight destined to "encheve" the Holy Grail, Lancelot takes over as the main character, and Malory keeps him so. In *Le Morte,* the *Quest* is an essential part, but still only one part, of the story of Lancelot's spiritual development; the quest of the Grail serves in the purification of his soul.

Before the quest even begins, we have been notified that Lancelot is going to have some difficulty with it; an old man has come to

Bors in a vision and given him a message for Lancelot: Go and tell him that "had nat bene hys synne, he had paste all the knyghtes that ever were in hys dayes. And telle thou sir Launcelot, of all worldly adventures he passyth in manhode and proues all othir, but in this spyrytuall maters he shall have many hys bettyrs" (Malory, *Works,* 590). Lancelot is certainly not accustomed to having many his betters; however, as we have seen, his humiliation and initiation into the knowledge that he is vulnerable to defeat has already begun. Little has been said among the scholars about that first stage of Lancelot's education in humility before he enters the world of the Holy Grail, but a great deal has been said about its continuation as he pursues and fails to achieve the Grail. The rules of the Round Table world do not apply in the Grail world, and the skills that bring Lancelot so much renown in the Round Table world do nothing for him in the world of the Holy Grail. Says Dhira Mahoney: "Throughout the narrative a constant dichotomy is built up between the worldly, chivalric values of the Arthurian knights and the spiritual values by which their actions must now be interpreted. What each knight has to learn is that this is a totally new order of adventure: to succeed in this quest … he must learn to think in a new way, to abandon his traditional values and adopt a new ethic" (Mahoney, 113–114). That ethic is no less than the repudiation of the values of the secular world and a movement toward those of the monastic world.

The humbling of Lancelot continues: he is robbed of his horse, his helmet, and his sword, the symbols of his knighthood; he gets them back, and then he has them stolen again. Once he joins in a war between the holders of a castle and the invaders of it; not knowing who the contenders are, he decides to help the losing side, for "incresyng of his shevalry" (Malory, *Works,* 677); that choice turns out to be wrong. He is soundly berated by various hermits who know what a sinner he is; he is told by one that he may pursue the Holy Grail, "but thoughe hit were here ye shall have no power to se hit, no more than a blynde man that sholde se a bryght swerde. And that ys longe on youre synne, and ellys ye were more abeler than ony man lyvynge" (Malory, *Works,*

672). Once, in a chapel, he falls into a sort of waking sleep; he can hear the voices of those around him but cannot move. He hears a mysterious voice telling him that he is not fit to be there, and to withdraw from that holy place. Lancelot is devastated by all of this affliction. He "was passing hevy and wyst nat what to do. And so departed sore wepynge and cursed the tyme that he was borne, for than he demed never to have worship more" (Malory, *Works,* 54).

However, Lancelot is ever courteous; he never blames anyone but himself. He laments, "My synne and my wyckednes hath brought me unto grete dishonoure! for whan I sought worldly adventures for worldely desyres I ever encheved them and had the bettir in every place, and never was I discomfite in no quarell, were hit ryght were hit wronge. And now I take uppon me the adventures to seke of holy thynges, now I se and undirstonde that myne olde synne hyndryth me and shamyth me" (Malory, *Works,* 654). He seeks out a hermit priest to hear his sins. The hermit tells him that he has been presumptuous to take upon himself to be in the presence of God, in a church, when he is in deadly sin. "And there is no knyght now lyvynge that ought to yelde God so grete thanke os ye, for He hath yevyn you beaute, bownte, semelynes, and grete strengthe over all other knyghtes" (Malory, *Works,* 655). Sir Lancelot weeps "with hevy hart" (we are reminded of the first description we ever had of him, when he first came to Arthur's court; he was "yong sir Launcelot de Laake with a lyght herte" Malory, *Works,* 138). And then, in a passage composed by Malory in an alteration of his source, Lancelot confesses the sin that he has been withholding for so many years:

> He tolde there the good man all hys lyff, and how he had loved a quene unmesurabely and oute of mesure longe. "And all my grete dedis of armys that I have done for the moste party was for the quenys sake, and for hir sake wolde I do batayle were hit ryght other wronge. And never dud I batayle all only [for] Goddis sake, but for to wynne worship and to cause me the bettir to be beloved, and litill or nought I thanked never God of hit." (Malory, *Works,* 656)

Lancelot does not confess adultery, and we have no reason to think he is guilty of adultery; certainly Malory has not accused him. It is as Dhira Mahoney says, "the fault is not so much that the love is adulterous, as that it exists at all" (Mahoney, 120–121). But Lancelot has enshrined Guenevere in his soul, as the courtly lover is enjoined to do in the chivalric tradition, and that won't do for the knight who pursues holiness. Lancelot has done all his brave deeds to make Guenevere love him more, and he has accepted all the glory, never giving the credit to God. As Pauline Matarasso concludes, cited by Mahoney, Lancelot's sin is not adultery but idolatry;[85] he has put the queen in God's place.

The reader will notice how monkish all of this is, rather surprisingly if our author was that scapegrace Sir Thomas Malory of Newbold Revel, but not surprising at all if our author was himself a monk as well as a knight, and a monk steeped in Cistercianism at that. After his confession, the hermit tells Lancelot to stay away from that woman as much as possible when he gets back to court, and then he absolves him. But privately he tells Ector that, although Lancelot has repented, "leffte hys pryde and takyn to humilite," the hermit does not believe Lancelot will be able to keep his good resolutions, for "he ys nat stable ... God knowith hys thought and hys unstablenesse" (Malory, *Works*, 685). As we have seen, "stableness" is an important ideal among the Cistercians, so much so that they, like their spiritual ancestors the Benedictines, take a vow of stability when they are accepted into the order. To these monks, stability means not simply faithfulness. It means determination in the pursuit of their religious calling; it is obvious that Malory, in having Lancelot's hermit-confessor use the term in talking about Lancelot, is linking Lancelot not only with the pursuit of religious perfection but with the particularly Cistercian view of that perfection.

Eventually, after pleading with God to "show me somthynge of that I seke" (Malory, *Works*, 726), Lancelot falls into a deep sleep for

85 Pauline Matarasso, *The Redemption of Chivalry: A Study of the "Queste del Saint Graal,"* 145–149; quoted in Mahoney, "The Truest and Holiest Tale," in *Studies in Malory*, 127, n. 28.

twenty-four days, representing, we are told, the twenty-four years that he has loved Guenevere, and dreams "grete mervayles that no tunge may telle, and more than ony herte can thynke," and he is satisfied: " 'Now I thanke God,' seyde sir Launcelot, 'for Hys grete mercy of that I have sene, for hit suffisith me' " (Malory, *Works*, 728). Lancelot has been humbled and has reconciled himself to his new humble position; it suffices him. He is ready to go home.

But Malory is not through with Lancelot yet. Lancelot is not yet a monk.

Because Malory never accuses Lancelot of improper behavior with Guenevere, critics have sometimes considered him squeamish about such matters. Yet Malory is not really squeamish. He apparently has no difficulty telling stories of women who are killed by means of brutal rape; or the story of Arthur's castration of the giant of St. Michael's who is one perpetrator of that abomination. Likewise, Malory has no problem with telling us about the maid of Astolat, who wants Lancelot however she can get him, either as husband or as paramour, and defends herself to her confessor when he chastises her for impure thoughts: "Why sholde I leve such thoughtes? Am I nat an erthely woman?" (Malory, *Works*, 779). Not particularly squeamish but focused on his theme, Malory writes about normal and abnormal carnality whenever it properly belongs in his story. However, that Malory hates adultery becomes evident in the way he deals with it in his book. Very early in *Le Morte*, he has Merlin tell Arthur that Mordred, the child of his adultery, will be his undoing; and he emphasizes the point, by telling the readers twice, that Arthur did not know Mordred's mother was his own half-sister, thereby letting us know that the sin to which Merlin is referring, which brings down the Table, is not the fact that the union was incestuous but the fact that it was adulterous, and therefore quite serious enough to serve. In another episode, Malory has a mother murdered in her bed by her own sons, because she has committed adultery against their father. In dealing with the traditional love story of Tristram and Isolde, Malory changes the order of things and thus effectively bypasses the adultery. His lovers have already fallen in love without the aid of any magic potion, plighted their troth to each other, and exchanged rings, before King Mark decides to marry Isolde, and sends Tristram to fetch her, with the ensuing famous episode of their drinking the love potion that makes them love each other forever. Thus Malory steals a march on Mark; it is Tristram who is seen as the real husband and Mark who is effectively made the adulterous suitor in this triangle; he becomes the sneaking villain in Malory's telling. Tristram and Isolde eventually set up housekeeping in one of Lancelot's castles, which he renames Joyous Garde in their honor, and become indistinguishable from a settled married couple, until Mark kills Tristram by stabbing him in the back.

Malory brings home even more forcefully his point concerning adultery by making his "Tale of Sir Gareth of Orkney That Was Called Bewmaynes" a crucial part of his main story, the spiritual development of Sir Lancelot. "Gareth" is Malory's own composition. Vinaver pointed out that there are many details in the story that appear here and there in various French romances, but there is no particular French tale that can be considered Malory's source. As of 1967, when Vinaver published his second edition of Malory's *Works,* he was still hoping for such a source to turn up (Malory, *Works*, vol. 3, 1427–1434). Instead, since then, almost all scholars have accepted "The Tale of Sir Gareth of Orkney" as Malory's original work. The other tale of Malory's own composition is "The Healing of Sir Urry," which also powerfully serves the story of Lancelot, as we shall see. In "Sir Gareth," Malory uses the conventions of courtly chivalry—the Round Table, the errant knights looking for adventures, the sorcery in service of love, the tournaments, and so forth, but he leaves out altogether the theme of adultery, devising instead the character of a knight who is not interested in another man's wife. Gareth is like Lancelot but better. Both come to Arthur's court very young, ready and eager to do knightly deeds and win worship, in approved courtly fashion. However, Lancelot's success at arms is immediate, and he is proud of it. He is acclaimed as the best knight of all almost as soon as he arrives. Moreover, almost as soon as he arrives, he falls in love with Queen Guenevere, and she with him, and she, of course, is the wife of another man. Thus the pattern of Lancelot's life — his prowess, his pride, his love for the queen — is set. Gareth, on the other hand, comes humbly to Arthur's court, asks for nothing but food and drink for a year, and spends the first year of his life there in the kitchen, working for Kay the Seneschal among the pots and pans. He is derided for being lowly born, tagged with a scornful nickname, Handsome Hands (Beaumains), and accepts the derision with uncomplaining humility. At the end of Gareth's year in the kitchen, the damsel Lyonet comes to court one day asking for a knight to take an adventure on her behalf, to rescue her sister from a tyrant. Gareth takes on the task, but his journey with Lyonet means simply more mockery and humiliation at her hands. He never quits. He never complains. He obeys.

In military prowess, as well as in his humility, Gareth shows himself superior at least once even to the great Lancelot. Gareth challenges Lancelot to joust one day:

> Eyther bare other downe to the erthe and sore were they brused.... Than Beawmaynes threw his shylde frome hym and profyred to fyght wyth sir Launcelot on foote. So they russhed togydyrs lyke two borys, trasyng and traversyin and foynyng the mountenaunce of an houre. And sir Launcelot felte hym so bygge that he mervayled of his strengthe, for he fought more lyker a gyaunte than a knyght, and his fyghtyng was so passyng durable and passyng perelous. For sir Launcelot had so much ado with hym that he dred hymself to be shamed, and seyde, "Beawmaynes, feyght nat so sore! Your quarell and myne is nat grete but we may sone leve of."

They leave off. Gareth says he was not even doing his "utterance." " 'In Goddys name,' seyde sir Launcelot, 'for I promyse you be the fayth of my body I had as muche to do as I myght have to save myself fro you unshamed' " (Malory, *Works*, 217).

Eventually, after Gareth has proved his skill in numerous contests of arms, he sees and falls in love with Lyonet's sister Lyonesse, and she with him. Their love story is told with a large portion of sorcery administered by Lyonet, who has turned out to be skilled in such magic. However, Malory reverses the standard narrative of an aphrodisiacal potion given secretly or accidentally to lovers: although Gareth and Lyonesse are ardent for each other and continuously making secret plans to be alone, Lyonet's spells are all focused on preventing unchastity between them, rather than making them want each other all the more. In fact, this part of the tale turns into a rollicking slapstick comedy about the contrivances of young love and the way they are foiled. At last everyone ends up back at Arthur's court, where Gareth and Lyonesse are joined in matrimony with enormous joy and pomp and circumstance:

> So than the kynges, quenys, pryncis, erlys, barouns, and many bolde knyghtes went to mete; and well may ye wete that there was all maner of plente and all maner revels and game, with all maner of mystralsy that was used tho dayes. Also there was grete justys three dayes, but the kynge wolde nat suffir sir Gareth to juste, because of his new bryde; for . . . dame Lyonesse desyred of the kynge that none that were wedded sholde juste at that feste. . . . And so they helde the courte fourty dayes with grete solempnyte. (Malory, *Works,* 272)

This wedding celebration is in vivid contrast to the ending of "La Cote Male Tayle," a tale somewhat similar to "Gareth" that Malory took from the French prose *Tristan* and translated for the *Morte Darthur*. That ending, the wedding of the hero and his lady-love, simply says, "sir Breune le Noyre wedded that damesell Maledysaunt, and aftir she was called the lady Byeaue-Vyvante" (Malory, *Works,* 355–356). Malory's tale of Gareth amounts to his tribute to marriage in *Le Morte,* using and yet spiting the conventions of courtly love. The ending of "Gareth" reminds us of Malory's other romance, *The Wedding of Sir Gawain and Dame Ragnell,* which ends in not only a wedding but true love and a happy marriage for Gawain and his erstwhile loathly lady Ragnell. In that story, as we have seen, Malory tames the well-known ladies' man Gawain, turning him into a loving husband. We recall P. J. C. Field's comment that when Ragnell is dead, Gawain "never loves so deeply again. The logic of the story does not demand any of this either, and there is no hint of it in the other analogues" (Field, *Archiv*, 380). Malory distinguishes himself as a writer of romances by using romance conventions but sidestepping the adultery usually found in stories of courtly love. All of this, of course, offers us more hints that our author was not the felonious knight of Newbold Revel who was sent to prison for raping Joan Smyth, the wife of Hugh Smyth, twice.

Nevertheless, if Malory is to finish the story of Lancelot, if the cataclysm resulting from adultery between Lancelot and the queen, together with Arthur's adultery that begot Mordred, his son by another man's wife, is to come about, Malory must deal with adultery. When Lancelot returns to Arthur's court after the quest of the Holy Grail, the story is moving toward its conclusion, and yet the love between Lancelot and Guenevere is still merely the subject of unsupported gossip in the court. We have never seen these two in any scene of intimacy. Malory has not yet brought himself to accuse them of adultery. Indeed, even later in the story, when the jig is truly up, when Aggravayne and Mordred and their gang are pounding on the door of Guenevere's room, knowing that Lancelot is in there with the queen, still our author shies away from an outright accusation: "As the Freynshhe booke seyth, the quene and sir Launcelot were togydirs. And whether they were abed other at other maner of disportis, me lyste nat thereof make no mencion, for love that tyme was nat as love ys nowadayes" (Malory, *Works*, 821). Yet Malory has chosen to tell the ancient story, at least as old as the fall of Troy, of how adultery can bring worlds crashing down, and if he is to tell that story, he must allow Lancelot to sin with Guenevere. He handles the necessity in a somewhat oblique fashion.

Let us go back to the time when Lancelot is newly come home from the Grail quest. He is still aglow with the wonders he has seen; nevertheless, Lancelot's hermit-confessor was right in believing that Lancelot would not be able to keep his resolution to stay away from the queen. Back in familiar surroundings, his love for Guenevere, and hers for him, flares up "more hotter" than before. Lancelot tries to deflect suspicion and avoid scandal by spending more time with other ladies of the court: "In all such maters of ryght sir Launcelot applyed hym dayly to do for the plesure of oure Lorde Jesu Cryst, and ever as much as he myght he withdrew hym fro the company of quene Gwenyvere for to eschew the sclawndir and noyse." Whereupon we are not surprised to learn that "the quene waxed wrothe with sir Launcelot" (Malory, *Works*, 744). He tells her, "I was but late in the quest of the Sankgreall.... And if that I had nat had my prevy thoughtis to returne to youre love agayne as I do, I had sene as grete mysteries as ever saw my sonne sir Galahad, Percival, other sir Bors.... Hit may nat be yet lyghtely forgotyn, the highe servyse in whom I dud my dyligente labour" (Malory, *Works*, 745). Guenevere bursts into tears, calls Lancelot a false knight and a common lecher, says she will never again love him, and tells him to be gone and never darken her doorway again. We have seen this behavior in Guenevere before. The first time she was jealous and afraid of losing Lancelot to Elaine. This time she has more reason to be afraid—she may be losing him to the Holy Grail. He is definitely showing his longing in that direction. Guenevere, unable to take on directly this new threat, focuses her wrath on Elaine (as John Michael Walsh notes, "It is easier to compete with Elaine than with God").[86] In any case, ever obedient to his lady's commands, Lancelot sadly leaves the court.

For a long section of the story now, the lovers are reunited and then separated, then reunited and separated again. The worldly life closes around Lancelot, and the glow of the Grail grows dimmer and dimmer. Lancelot's pride keeps surfacing and yet goes on being soundly rebuked. By jousting in disguise against the knights of the Round Table, just to prove he is still the greatest and can beat them all, he almost brings about his own death. A lady hunter (Malory is responsible for adding the detail that the hunter who shoots Lancelot is a woman, apparently for no

[86] John Michael Walsh, "Malory's 'Very Mater of La Chevaler du Charyot': Characterization and Structure," in *Studies in Malory*, 226, n. 38. Further citations of this work will be in parentheses in the text.

reason except to add to his humiliation) shoots him in the buttock when he is sleeping by a well, and he is so badly injured that for a long while he can't sit in a saddle. In a later humiliating episode, he has his horse shot out from under him and ends up riding in a cart, like a felon to the scaffold, and being mocked by the passersby. But that ride in the cart affords Malory his chance to bring our lovers together, with the calamitous results so familiar in the tale of Lancelot and Guenevere.

Authorship of the tale of the knight of the cart is attributed to Chrétien de Troyes, and Chrétien is probably Malory's direct source, but Malory changes the story in many ways. In *Le Morte,* Guenevere is kidnapped by a would-be rapist, Mellyagaunt, when she is enjoying a picnic with ten of her special knights and ten ladies; the knights are dressed for an outdoor party and wear no armor, so they are easily bested by the abductor's men. Guenevere, seeing her men suffering significant injuries in defending her, agrees to go with Mellyagaunt if she may keep her knights with her, and she covertly sends a message to Lancelot to come to her rescue. The villain locks Guenevere up in a high room in his castle, with bars on the windows, and the wounded knights in the adjacent room. Lancelot, of course, comes hotfoot, but Mellyagaunt's men are guarding the road, and they shoot Lancelot's horse, so he ends up compelling a carter to take him in his cart to the castle of Mellyagaunt. And thereby we come to the crux of *Le Morte Darthur*.

After some shuffling around and some misunderstandings about what Guenevere actually wants him to do, Lancelot waits until night and then gets a ladder, props it outside her barred window, and goes up. They whisper in the darkness, for the wounded knights are very near, in the next room. After they speak together for a while, Lancelot says that he wishes he might come into her room. And then, to our surprise, Guenevere invites him in: "'Wyte you well,' seyde the quene, 'I wolde as fayne as ye that ye myght com in to me.'" Lancelot can hardly believe his ears. "'Wolde ye so, madame,' seyde sir Launcelot, 'wyth youre harte that I were with you?' 'Ye, truly,' seyde the quene. 'Than shall I prove my myght,' seyde sir Launcelot" (Malory, *Works,* 801). And he proves his might. He "sette hys hondis uppon the barrys of iron and pulled at them with suche a myght that he braste hem clene oute of the stone wallys." But in doing so he cuts his hand on one of the bars, so that it bleeds significantly and causes trouble in the morning. Lancelot hardly notices it tonight: "So, to passe uppon thys tale, sir Launcelot wente to bedde with the quene and toke no force of hys hurte honde, but toke hys pleasaunce and hys lykynge untyll hit was the dawnyng of the day; for wyte you well he slept nat, but wacched. And whan he saw hys tyme that he myght tary no lenger, he toke hys leve and departed at the wyndowe, and put hit togydir as well as he myght agayne, and so he departed" (Malory, *Works*, 801).

Readers may be left asking themselves at this point, *What just happened?* Was this the famous adultery, at last? Chrétien, in his telling of the story, makes no bones about it:

> And the Queen extends her arms to him and, embracing him, presses him tightly against her bosom, drawing him into the bed beside her and showing him every possible satisfaction.... Now Lancelot possesses all he wants, when the Queen voluntarily seeks his company and love, and when he holds her in his arms, and she holds him in hers. Their sport is so agreeable and sweet, as they kiss and fondle each other, that in truth such a marvellous joy comes over them as was never heard or known. But their joy will not be revealed by me, for in a story, it has no place. Yet, the most choice and delightful satisfaction was precisely that of which our story must not speak. That night Lancelot's joy and pleasure were very great. But, to his sorrow, day comes, when he must leave his mistress' side.[87]

Malory rejects the leering lewdness of Chrétien, but what does he mean when he tells us that Lancelot went to bed with the queen and took his pleasaunce and liking until morning, for he watched all night? Could it be

[87] Chretien de Troyes, *Lancelot: The Knight of the Cart*, trans. William W. Comfort (readaclassic.com, 2016), 69. Further citations of this work will be in parentheses in the text.

that all his pleasure and liking were simply to guard her against the intended attack by Mellyagaunt? Certainly it would be reasonable for Guenevere to say she wants him to be in the room with her to protect her from her abductor and would-be rapist, rather than standing on a ladder outside the barred window. And certainly Mellyagaunt does really plan to attack the queen, as evidenced by the fact that he enters her bedroom in the morning and actually parts her bed curtains.

However, the story itself, the way Malory unfolds it, shows us that this night, the night of the knight of the cart, the broken window bars, and the bloody hand causing the bloody sheets, is the very night that brings down the Round Table and the whole world of chivalry associated with it. Recall that Lancelot himself, long ago, answering the fair damsel who wanted to know why he does not have a woman, has told her that knights who take their pleasaunce with paramours are unfortunate in war, for either they are overcome by lesser knights, or they slay by accident better knights, because of their sin:

> As for to sey to take my pleasaunce with peramours, that woll I refuse: in prencipall for drede of God, for knyghtes that bene adventures sholde nat be advoutrers nothir lecherous, for than they be nat happy nother fortunate unto the werrys; for other they shall be overcom with a sympler knyght than they be hemself, other ellys they shall sle by unhappe and hir cursednesse bettir men than they be hemself. And so who that usyth peramours shall be unhappy, and all thynge unhappy that is aboute them. (Malory, *Works*, 195)

Helen Cooper, in her gloss of the significant word *unhappy*, tells us that "'unhappy' is a strong word in Malory, meaning 'doomed' or 'doom-bearing,' almost 'accursed.'"[88] Another highly significant word in this

[88] Helen Cooper, ed., *Sir Thomas Malory*: Le Morte Darthur: *The Winchester Manuscript* (New York: Oxford University Press, 1998), 535. Further citations of this work will be in parentheses in the text.

passage is *pleasaunce*; Malory uses it in Lancelot's answer to the curious damsel, and then uses it again in the episode of the broken bars and bloody sheets. Lancelot, speaking to the damsel, has declared that a knight who takes his pleasaunce with paramours is doomed, and then has foretold exactly how his own story will go after this night, when he takes his "pleasaunce and lyking" with Guenevere. He is defeated by knights who are beneath him — Mordred, Aggravayne, and the others who trap him in the queen's chamber — and he slays by mishap, because of his sin, his "cursednesse," the knight who is better than himself.

But how can this be — is there actually any knight who is better than Lancelot? And there is: remember Gareth, the knight of Malory's own composition. Our author has introduced into the story of Lancelot the knight who fulfills precisely Lancelot's own manifesto, the knight who is better than Lancelot; Gareth is humble, and chaste, and better at deeds of arms. And Lancelot kills Gareth by "unhappe," as a direct result of his sin: in the battle to rescue Guenevere from death by burning for adultery, Lancelot does not recognize Gareth in the melee, kills him, and by so doing brings about his own prophecy upon himself, because he causes Gareth's brother Gawain to force Arthur to exact revenge. Although Lancelot is Malory's favorite, he cuts no slack for Lancelot; he is like the Lord who chastiseth whom He loveth.

And he is still not through with Lancelot, for Lancelot is still not yet a monk.

Malory was undoubtedly influenced by Chrétien to postpone the consummation of Lancelot and Guenevere's long love affair until the episode of the "Knight of the Cart." In Chrétien's story, Guenevere, before she is taken captive by Mellyagaunt, hears a false rumor that Lancelot is dead, and in her grieving she laments that she has always refused his wooing: "Alas! How much better I should feel, and how much comfort I should take, if only once before he died I had held him in my arms!" (de Troyes, 63). It seems apparent that Chrétien's purpose in portraying Guenevere as the standard "cruel" object of the knight's love, who scornfully refuses his suit until the very moment when she doesn't, is simply to give to their eventual consummation the titillation of delay. However, Malory's long postponement of the moment of adultery between Lancelot and Guenevere, and his making of it a sole act, never repeated, is different. It is a way of giving importance to their adultery, by emphasizing the calamitous power of a single transgression; it can bring down the Round Table, and—what is just as interesting to Malory—it can bring Lancelot's soul to the edge of perdition.[89]

The morning after Lancelot has broken the window bars to come into Guenevere's room, when Mellyagaunt himself comes in, apparently to pursue his plan of taking Guenevere by force, and discovers blood on her sheets and accuses her of having had one of the wounded knights in bed with her, Guenevere is innocent, but only on a technicality. Lancelot, knowing that Mellyagaunt is unaware of his overnight visit to Guenevere, takes up Mellyagaunt's challenge to prove in a duel that the queen is innocent. As Walsh points out in his discussion of that duel, what comes next "is a powerful dramatization of the destructive potential of guilt and of the way in which the adultery is mining their characters" (Walsh, 213). That destructive power manifests itself immediately. By the time Lancelot has met and killed Mellyagaunt on the field of honor, he has violated every tenet of his knightly oath, which Arthur requires his knights to renew every Pentecost: "Never to do outerage nothir morthir, and allwayes to fle treson, and to gyff mercy unto hym that askith mercy, uppon payne of forfiture [of their] worship and lordship of kynge Arthure for evirmore; and allwayes to do ladyes, damesels, and jantilwomen

[89] This is not the only example in *Le Morte* of the terrible consequences of even a single sin against chastity. In the quest of the Holy Grail, three knights are serious contenders for its "enchevement." Only the sinless Galahad succeeds in the Grail quest. Lancelot fails because his desire for the Grail is weakened by his desire for Guenevere. Perceval is disqualified for having committed one sin against chastity in his life: once when a mysterious gentlewoman of great beauty appeared and demanded that he submit to her, he was smitten with desire and promised to be hers alone. But, just in the nick of time, as they lay down together, he noticed his sword on the ground with an image of the cross on its pommel and, remembering his knighthood, he blessed himself with the Sign of the Cross. The lady vanished in a cloud of black smoke. Perceval never actually touched her, but he enjoyed the idea.

and wydowes [socour:] strengthe hem in hir ryghtes, and never to enforce them, uppon payne of dethe. Also, that no man take no batayles in a wrongefull quarell for no love ne for no worldis goodis" (Malory, *Works*, 91). Lancelot, along with Guenevere of course, has, by the very act of adultery with the queen, committed treason. He has done murder, in obedience to Guenevere, who has given him the equivalent of a "thumbs down" signal over the abject and pleading Mellyagaunt:

> And then he cryed uppon hym lowde and seyde, "Most noble knyght, sir Launcelot, save my lyff! For I yelde me unto you, and I requyre you, as ye be a knyght and felow of the Table Rounde, sle me nat, for I yeld me as overcomyn."… Than sir Lancelot wyst nat what to do, for he had lever than all the good in the worlde that he myght be revenged uppon hym. So sir Launcelot loked uppon the quene, gyff he myght aspye by ony sygne or countenaunce what she wold have done. And anone the quene wagged hir hede uppon sir Launcelot, as ho[90] seyth "sle hym." (Malory, *Works*, 662)

In addition, Lancelot has done battle in a wrongful cause, knowing that, although Guenevere did not have one of her wounded knights in her bed, she did have Lancelot himself there. He has been cruel to Mellyagaunt, teasing him with hope of victory, in a ploy added by Malory, by offering to fight with no armor on one side of his body and with one hand tied behind his back, and then summarily splitting Mellyagaunt's head in two, denying his pleas for mercy. The one element of the knightly oath that Lancelot keeps to the letter, always to do ladies, gentlewomen, and damsels succor, has become the very occasion of sin, and not only the sin of adultery but also the sin of murder, because Lancelot has put his mission to rescue Guenevere above all other considerations, even the life of an innocent underling. The murder of Mellyagaunt is not the only murder Lancelot

90 "She," from Old English "heo." Malory, *Works*, vol. 3, 1139, line 1, as here, "as ho seyth 'sle hym.'… C[axton] 'as though she wold saye slee hym.'"

commits in this story. In his desperate haste to rescue the queen, he kills a carter who refuses to drive him to Mellyagaunt's castle, and after that, the terrified second carter consents to Lancelot's demand. Nor does Lancelot's famous physical prowess, the source of his pride, benefit him in this tale; instead, it is shown to be dangerous to Lancelot's soul. First, that very prowess is the thing that enables him to break the iron bars of the queen's window and enter her bedroom and commit adultery. Then Lancelot's great might enables him to lure Mellyagaunt with the promise of handicapping himself for further fighting by immobilizing one side of his body, knowing well that he can still easily kill the luckless Mellyagaunt. Thus, as Walsh points out,

> It was the first time he had knowingly put his prowess in the service of a wrong quarrel, and he had been driven by a vengeful thirst for his opponent's blood. With the ruse of handicapping himself he lured the already defeated plaintiff to his death. It was the ultimate display of the kind of spectacular skill for which people had long regarded him as the greatest of knights, only it has spoiled his taste for the title. (Walsh, 218)

All of this is the direct result of the adultery. When Mellyagaunt dies, Lancelot's knightly honor is in shreds. And what is even more important to Malory, the death of Mellyagaunt marks the nadir of Lancelot's soul.

14

The Healing

LANCELOT KNOWS IT, of course. All the humiliations that have rained down on his head since his meeting with Elaine and Brusen have not had such an effect on his pride as do these violations of his knighthood committed by Lancelot himself. Never again, after the killing of Mellyagaunt at Guenevere's behest, does Lancelot exhibit his former pride. He knows that he is no longer the greatest knight, nor even a good knight, nor even a good man. As Walsh says, the greatest knight would not have done what Lancelot did to Mellyagaunt (Walsh, 219). Malory has brought Lancelot very low indeed. So now, where can Malory take his story? His sources, which do not emphasize Lancelot's humiliation and loss of honor as Malory does, offer no help. Lancelot has begun as the greatest knight of the world, and now he is at the bottom of the heap. It will be necessary for Malory to resurrect him somehow. And here again he displays his skill as a writer, if there were any doubt of it after the subtle and skillful fitting together of his composition, "The Tale of Sir Gareth of Orkney," into the story of Lancelot. Again he composes a tale of his own to serve the story of his favorite knight, and he places it immediately after the Mellyagaunt episode. This time, Malory's tale demonstrates more forcefully than all the others the hand of God reaching out to lift Lancelot: "The Tale of the Healing of Sir Urry."

Scholars have suggested that Malory took the germ of his story of the healing of Urry from a tale in the French prose *Lancelot*. Vinaver is skeptical. He says this:

> Mr. P. E. Tucker has suggested that the source of this episode was a passage in the Agravain section of the Prose Lancelot describing how an anonymous knight was pursued by an assailant as far as a fountain in which two damsels were bathing. One of the damsels promptly took a bow and arrow and shot the unfortunate knight in the thigh. A passing damsel then told him that he would languish until the best knight in the world had removed the arrow.... At this point—and at this point only—there is a distinct similarity between the two incidents. (Malory, *Works*, vol. 3, 1611)

Robert Kelly, however, points out that there are three elements that Malory uses in "Urry" that could have been suggested by the *Lancelot* tale: one, a wounded knight is brought to court as the only place he can be healed; two, Lancelot heals him; and three, "Lancelot embodies a religious conception of knighthood."[91] But Malory's development of these elements into a story of his own constitutes some of the strongest evidence in *Le Morte Darthur* that our author was a Hospitaller knight. He builds the tale around three interlocking themes: first, the perfection of knighthood and its manifestation; second, the Bernardian virtue of humility; and third, healing of the sick.

Urry is brought to the court by his mother. He has been wounded in battle, and although his opponent was a villain and Urry has killed him, Urry is desperately ill because the dead opponent's mother is a sorceress and she has put a spell on Urry, specifying that he can never be whole again unless the greatest knight in the world "searches" his wounds. We remember that Lancelot has been called upon, by virtue of his standing as the greatest knight, to perform a similar office for the boiling hot lady in the little town of Corbin; in that instance Lancelot does not hesitate; he knows that he is the greatest knight,

[91] Robert L. Kelly, "Wounds, Healing and Knighthood in Malory's 'Tale of Launcelot and Guenevere,'" in *Studies in Malory*, 175. Further citations of this work will be in parentheses in the text.

and he takes the hot lady by the hand, and she is immediately healed. This time is different.

Lancelot is absent from court when the sick man arrives. One by one, going on through the catalog—"kynge Claryaunce of Northumbirlonde serched, and hit wolde nat be. And than sir Barraunte le Apres, that was called the Kyng with the Hundred Knyghtes, he assayed and fayled. So ded kynge Uryence of the londe of Gore. So ded kynge Angwyshe of Irelonde, and so ded Kynge Newtrys of Garloth" (Malory, *Works*, 810). All the knights in court that day, listed each one thus in loving detail to the total of 110, examine Urry's wounds, but he does not get better. Malory parades all the brave knights of the Round Table before us, demonstrating that the full embodiment of chivalry itself has no force to meet this challenge. Then Lancelot arrives in court. Arthur directs him to try to help the sick man. At first, Lancelot shrinks from the job, protesting that he surely cannot do what so many good knights have failed to do: "'Jesu defende me,' seyde sir Launcelot, 'whyle so many noble kyngis and knyghtes have fayled, that I shulde presume uppon me to enchyve that all ye, my lordis, myght not enchyve'" (Malory, *Works*, 813). Arthur says, "You have no choice. I command you to try." Again Lancelot protests: "'My most renowmed lorde,' seyde sir Launcelot, 'I know well I dare nat, nor may not, disobey you. But and I myght or durste, wyte you well I wolde nat take uppon me to towche that wounded knyght in that entent that I shulde passe all othir knyghtes. Jesu deffende me frome that shame!'" (Malory, *Works*, 814). Arthur assures Lancelot that he will not be trying to heal Urry from presumption but for fellowship with the other knights who have tried.

Notice two things: one, it is not now with Lancelot as it was when he quite readily took the boiling hot lady by the hand to heal her, confident that he was indeed the greatest knight and therefore could handle the job; and, two, this is the first time that Lancelot has ever shrunk from immediate obedience to King Arthur. He is excruciatingly aware of his decline. Finally, Lancelot humbly obeys, saying to Arthur, "I must do youre commaundemente, whych ys sore ayenste my harte" (Malory, *Works*, 814). He speaks to the wounded knight, addressing him as his lord, and thus reminding us of the ancient fourth vow of the Hospitallers, to be always "serfs and slaves to their lords the sick":[92] "'A, my fayre lorde,' seyde sir Launcelot, 'Jesu wolde that I myght help you! For I shame sore with myselff that I shulde be thus requyred, for never was I able in worthynes to do so hyhe a thynge'" (Malory, *Works*, 814). After speaking thus to Urry, he kneels beside the wounded knight and humbly prays, "saiynge secretely unto hymselff, 'Now, Blyssed Fadir and Son and Holy Goste, I beseche The of Thy mercy that my symmple worshyp and honeste be saved, and Thou Blyssed Trynyte, Thou mayste yeff me power to hele thys syke knyght by the grete vertu and grace of The, but, Good Lorde, never of myselff.'" When Lancelot, "devoutly knelyng," handles Urry's wounds, they are immediately healed. "Than kynge Arthyr and all the kynges and knyghtes kneled downe and gave thankynges and lovynge unto God and unto Hys Blyssed Modir. And ever sir Launcelote wepte, as he had bene a chylde that had bene beatyn!" (Malory, *Works*, 815). Lancelot weeps because he has a guilty conscience, of course, but there is more to it than that. Lancelot is overwhelmed by the miraculous power of God, not only to heal Urry but to forgive and heal Lancelot. The simile Malory chooses evokes the image of a father who has chastised his child but still loves and forgives him — and gives him what he asks to reward his humility.[93] At the close of the tale, Malory — and only Malory — tells us that Lancelot never rode on a horse for a full year after this; instead he always rode in a cart, the implement and the symbol of his humiliation and his voluntary penance.

92 David Nicoll, *Knight Hospitaller*, vol. 2 (Oxford: Osprey, 2002), 10. Further citations of this work will be in parentheses in the text.

93 Robert L. Kelly says that "unquestionably the intent of the Urry story is, as Vinaver has observed, to show Lancelot at 'the height of his glory' on the eve of 'the catastrophe that was to put an end to Arthurian knighthood'" (*Works*, 1591; Kelly, 173). But obviously the height of Lancelot's glory is the depth of his humility. When Lancelot at last acknowledges that his own power is nothing and God is all, he is glorious: God allows him to perform a miracle. And Lancelot, overpowered with emotion, weeps like a beaten child.

In writing this tale, Malory shows clearly that ideal knighthood involves healing the sick, and it involves humility. Healing had been the primary function of the Knights Hospitallers since the earliest beginnings of their order. Whitworth Porter remarks that, during the era of its greatest growth, in members and in wealth, in Palestine, the wealth of their order brought the Hospitallers many enemies, ready enough with their slander; "still we never hear, amongst the many crimes laid to their charge, even by the most rancorous of their foes, that of negligence in this the fundamental obligation of their profession" (Porter, vol. 2, 234). Later, after the Knights of St. John were expelled from Palestine and Cyprus and had taken up their new headquarters at Rhodes, there were no longer sick and weary pilgrims needing attention as they made their perilous way to the holy sites, but the Hospitallers' care of the sick continued: "Strangers of every description could still, when sick, procure every needful assistance from the hospital of the Order." Later still, when the Knights of St. John had been driven from Rhodes to their final outpost on Malta, "one of their earliest measures, when establishing their convent upon the rocky inlets of their new home, was to found a hospital" (Porter, vol. 2, 234). Porter quotes a passage from the Hospitallers' statutes: "Physicians shall be employed for the cure of the sick, experienced and talented, who shall be bound to take a vow, before the eight brethren of the languages, that they will watch over the sick with great care, and according to the prescribed rules of medical science, and they will visit them twice a day, that they will order such things as are necessary for their cure, and will carry them out without delay in spite of every obstacle" (Porter, vol. 2, 235). In "The Tale of the Healing of Sir Urry," Malory dramatically reminds us of this ancient and never abrogated commitment.

And, tellingly, Malory uses this tale to heal not only Urry but also Lancelot. Lancelot here acknowledges that he is not greater than all the other knights, although he has thought so in the past. He pleads, in his new humility, that he has no power in himself to heal Urry. He prays that Urry will be healed by the miraculous power of God, and he is.

Malory incorporates humility into the tale of Lancelot and the healing of Urry because he knows that a worthy knight in the tradition of St. Bernard of Clairvaux is humble. The first of Bernard's famous moral treatises was his "Steps to Humility," laying out the way a monk must try to abjure pride and strive to be humble, acknowledging always that every gift, every ability, is from God, never from man himself. Throughout Malory's telling of Lancelot's story, Lancelot's chief sin has been his pride; his love for Guenevere has been inextricably connected with that sin. Malory continually shies away from accusing Lancelot of lust, all the while making us understand that he loves the queen because of his pride: he does great knightly deeds because he hopes they will gain for him the love of Guenevere, and they do. He is the greatest knight of them all, and the greatest lady loves him.

In comparing Malory's tale with the "germ" tale in the prose *Lancelot,* Robert Kelly notes that Malory moves away from the emphasis on compassion, extolled in the older story as the virtue of a worthy knight, and emphasizes instead the virtue of humility. In his argument that Malory was strongly influenced by that prototype story, Kelly says that "evidently, for Malory healing, humility, and supremacy as a knight are all associated. The prose *Lancelot* explains everything but Malory's emphasis upon humility, rather than compassion, as the chief virtue of the knight. Malory would have found a strong recommendation of humility, in [Ramon] Lull's treatise, assuming that he knew it." Or, he continues, possibly Malory based his emphasis on humility on St. Augustine's *Christus medicus* (Kelly, 179). Maybe Malory knew Lull, or maybe he did not, but there can be very little doubt that a Knight Hospitaller, particularly a Malory whose family had a generations-long intimate connection not only with that order but also with the Cistercians, would know St. Bernard's love of humility and would know *De Gradibus Humilitatis.* Kelly's observation that "healing, humility, and supremacy as a knight are all associated" (Kelly, 179) in Malory's tale is exactly the position appropriate to the Order of St. John, Hospitallers, who were healers, who were monks, who were intrepid knights. Porter: "The Knight returned from his brilliant career on the battlefield, and oblivious of the renown which he and his brotherhood had there gained for themselves, doffed his harness, laid aside his trusty falchion, and, assuming the black mantle of his Order, proceeded to assist in those peaceful acts of charity which were ever being performed within his convent walls" (Porter, vol. 2, 233). Yet neither Kelly nor any other critic has considered this fact, possibly because most do not consider the author of the *Morte* as associated with that order, having in mind Sir Thomas Malory of Newbold Revel. This a priori identification of that candidate as our author obscures the fact that Malory's "Tale of the Healing of Sir Urry" is strong evidence that Sir Thomas Malory who wrote *Le Morte Darthur* was actually a member of the Hospital, a knight of St. John.

There is some evidence that Malory himself was a self-effacing man, in the very difficulty there has always been in identifying him. In the *Morte,* he tells us his name, his rank, the fact that he was a prisoner, and the date when he finished his book, but he certainly does not crow about his magnificent achievement. Caxton, as we have seen, adds nothing to these bare facts, and it is likely that he did not know any more. John Bale, the first man recorded as having

Lifting of the Siege of Malta, by Charles Philippe Lariviere; Hospitallers doing battle and caring for wounded

searched for the identity of our author, was born in 1495, just ten years after *Le Morte Darthur* was first printed, and lived until 1563. The *Morte* was enormously popular from the start and, as we have seen, was reprinted in five editions over the next century and a half, four times during Bale's lifetime. Bale's great interest was the literature of Britain, his major work being *Illustrium Majoris Britanniae Scriptoru,* a summary of the major British writers, published in 1548 and revised and reprinted in 1559. By that time, Malory's work had been printed in 1485, 1498, 1529, and 1559. Those editions were followed in 1582 and 1634. But even though Bale's active interest in British literature occurred at the same time Malory's book was so popular and was being reprinted time after time, Bale did not succeed in finding our author. He eventually came up with the theory that Malory may have been a Welshman. His failure to find out much about Malory's identity was largely caused by Malory's own reticence. This reticence goes ill with the flamboyant and aggressive personality of Sir Thomas Malory of Newbold Revel; however, it is entirely to be expected of a member of the Hospital, one of St. Bernard's spiritual sons. Self-effacement was — is — a particular desideratum of any monk, and notably of Bernard's followers.

15

Home at Last

THE BARE OUTLINE of the end of the story of Lancelot is taken from Malory's sources: when Mordred and Arthur have killed each other on the battlefield and Arthur's body has been buried, Guenevere joins a nunnery; Lancelot visits her there and asks her to go with him to live in his own realm, and she refuses; after that, Lancelot goes into a monastery. But Malory has a great deal more to say about Lancelot and Guenevere than he found in his sources. In his telling are added the great pathos of the lovers' final farewell, the tragedy of the destruction of the whole social order because of their love, and the deep sincerity of Lancelot's call to the religious life. When Lancelot first arrives at Guenevere's abbey and she sees him as she is walking in the cloister, she faints. Thus begins the highly emotional scene that shows her sending him away even though she still loves him, because their love has been the cause of so much destruction and death. She tells him, in Malory's words, "For as well as I have loved the heretofore, myne harte woll nat serve now to se the; for thorow the and me ys the floure of kyngis and knyghtes destroyed" (Malory, *Works*, 876). Then she tells him to go to his own realm and take a wife, but he says that there is no chance he would ever do such a thing, and thus break all his promises to her; on the contrary, he will take the same destiny that she has taken.

And then Guenevere says a peculiar thing: "'A, sir Launcelot, if ye woll do so and holde thy promyse! But I may never beleve you,' seyde the quene, 'but that ye woll turne to the worlde agayne.'" This is not the first time in the book that Lancelot has been accused of instability, of course—recall the hermit-confessor's words back in the realm of the

Holy Grail. But Lancelot has always been absolutely rock-steady in his love for only Guenevere, and these words come as a surprise from her. They do not appear in the poem *Le Morte Arthure,* Malory's source. However, it is not difficult to figure out why the distraught Guenevere first tells Lancelot to go and find a wife, and then accuses him of fickleness. When she says he will surely fail to keep a resolution not to marry, she is speaking out of her great pain, for she still loves him. Only in Malory, Lancelot answers her thus, making particular reference to his experience in seeking and failing to achieve the Holy Grail:

> "Well, madame," seyde he, "ye say as hit pleasith you, for yet wyste ye me never false of my promyse. And God deffende but that I shulde forsake the worlde as ye have don! For in the quest of the Sankgreall I had that tyme forsakyn the vanytees of the worlde, had nat youre love bene. And if I had done so at that tyme with my harte, wylle, and thought, I had passed all the knyghtes that ever were in the Sankgreall excepte syr Galahad, my sone. And therfore, lady, sythen ye have taken you to perfeccion, I must nedys take me to perfection, of ryght. For I take recorde of God, in you I have had myn erthly joye, and yf I had founden you now so dysposed, I had cast me to have had you into myn owne royame. But sythen I fynde you thus desposed, I ensure you faythfully, I wyl ever take me to penaunce and praye whyle my lyf lasteth, yf that I may fynde ony heremyte, other graye or whyte, that wyl receyve me. Wherfore, madame, I praye you kysse me, and never no more."
>
> "Nay," sayd the quene, "that shal I never do, but absteyne you from suche werkes."
>
> And they departed; but there was never so harde an herted man but he wold have wepte to see the dolour that they made, for there was lamentacyon as they had be stungyn wyth sperys, and many tymes they swouned. And the ladyes bare the quene to hir chambre. (Malory, *Works,* 877)

This is the heart of *Le Morte Darthur,* quintessential Malory. Here Malory brings to its close the struggle between Lancelot's desire for Guenevere and his desire for God. There is nothing in the old romances to match the skill with which Malory has woven together their various threads concerning Lancelot, sometimes translating indeed, but sometimes composing tales of his own to add clarity of circumstance to his theme, which is the conflict in the depths of the human heart. And, as to Malory's prose style, there is nothing in English prose of the Middle Ages, and possibly even until the advent of the true novel, to exceed — or even to match, come to that — the strength and poignancy of such passages as "I take recorde of God, in you I have had myn erthly joye," or "I praye you kysse me, and never no more," or, most haunting of all, "And the ladyes bare the quene to hir chambre."

Guenevere tells Lancelot to marry and then tells him she doubts his resolution not to do so, because that is the sort of thing Malory's Queen Guenevere does; she is highly volatile, and sometimes in an emotional state she says things she does not mean. More than once she has told Lancelot to go away and never come back. But, in addition to those things, her accusation that Lancelot is unstable gives Malory a chance to allow Lancelot to tell us his own feelings. We remember that he was accused by the hermit-confessor of being not stable in the pursuit of holiness, because of his love for Guenevere, and the hermit was right; Lancelot did return to her love. His first loyalty, above all others, even God, was to Guenevere. Yet he is not unstable; on the contrary. He has longed for what Galahad achieved, union with God represented by the Grail. He has said as much to the queen before now, when she accused him of withdrawing his love from her, soon after his return from the Grail quest. "'A, madame,' seyde sir Launcelot, 'in thys ye must holde me excused for dyvers causis: one ys, I was but late in the quest of the Sankgreall.... And wyte you well, madam, hit may nat be yet lyghtly forgotyn, the hyghe servyse in whom I dud my dyligente laboure'" (Malory, *Works,* 745). If he had not loved Guenevere so much, he tells her, he would have pursued holiness. But now that Guenevere is sending him away from her, he is free to "take him to perfection." We believe him when he says to Guenevere, "Sythen I fynde you thus desposed, I ensure you faythfully, I wyl ever take me to penaunce and praye whyle my lyf lasteth" (Malory, *Works*, 877).

And so he does. For the rest of his life, Lancelot grows in sanctity. When he rides away from Guenevere, weeping, he comes to a chapel and stops to hear Mass, which is sung by someone he knows, the bishop of Canterbury. Lancelot asks the bishop "that he myght be hys brother. Than the Bysshop sayd, 'I wyll gladly,' and there he put an habyte upon syr Launcelot. And there he servyd God day and nyght with prayers and fastynges" (Malory, *Works*, 878). Lancelot's renewed search for holiness is inspiring to his old friends from Round Table days. Like the brothers and friends of Bernard of Clairvaux, who flocked around him and accompanied him to Citeaux to join the Cistercians, Lancelot's friends search for him, and within six months seven of them have found and joined him, for "whan they sawe syr Launcelot had taken hym to suche perfeccion they had no lust to departe but toke such an habyte as he had" (Malory, *Works*, 878). After six years, Lancelot becomes a priest. The other knights remain with him. Malory tells us that "their horses wente where they wolde, for they toke no regarde of no worldly rychesses; for whan they sawe syr Launcelot endure suche penaunce in prayers and fastynges they toke no force what payne they endured, for to see the nobleste knyght of the world take such abstynaunce that he waxed full lene" (Malory, *Works*, 878).

Malory continues his departure from his sources through the death and the elaborate burial of Guenevere, directed and presided over by Lancelot himself, and then Lancelot's rapid decline. He spends his time weeping on the grave that is shared by Guenevere and Arthur. A hermit reproaches him, saying that such sorrowing is displeasing to God:

> "Truly," sayd syr Launcelot, "I trust I do not dysplese God, for He knoweth myn entente: for my sorow was not, nor is not, for

> ony rejoysyng of synne, but my sorow may never have ende … whan I remembere me how by my defaute and myn orgule and my pryde that they were bothe layed ful lowe, that were pereles that ever was lyvyng of Cristen people, wyt you wel," sayd syr Launcelot, "this remembred, of their kyndenes and my unkyndenes, sanke so to myn herte that I myght not susteyne myself." (Malory, *Works*, 880)

We notice that Lancelot, in his killing grief, accuses himself of "myn orgule and my pryde," the sin for which Malory has so intently rebuked Lancelot throughout the *Morte*. Lancelot's adultery has been subsumed in this more serious matter. Dhira B. Mahoney offers some light on this complex subject, crediting Pauline Matarasso: "The desire for possession is linked with the desire for self-aggrandizement: both are forms of concupiscence in which the main object is self-gratification instead of the service of God. Lancelot's love for Guenievre [*sic*] is indeed idolatrous; he has seen her as the source of his prowess and must learn that the true source is God" (Mahoney, 119).

Now, as Lancelot comes to the end of his own life, he has learned. We have witnessed the moment when the love of Guenevere and the accoutrements of chivalry fail him, and he must turn to God, his only hope. That moment has come after the tale of the healing of Sir Urry. At the close of that story, in its only mention of Guenevere, we are told that "every nyght and day sir Aggravayne, sir Gawaynes brother, awayted quene Gwenyver and sir Launcelot to put hem bothe to a rebuke and a shame" (Malory, *Works*, 815). This comment introduces the climax of the love story, for which Malory chose to use but modify material from his source books. The tradition was that Arthur's men trapped the lovers by having them told that Arthur would be away all night, and then caught them *in flagrante delicto*. Malory uses the ambush story. However, when fourteen of Arthur's warriors are pounding on the door of Guenevere's room and demanding that Lancelot come out and meet his punishment at their hands, Malory tells us that even though Lancelot and Guenevere were together, he cannot accuse them of having been in bed together (Malory, *Works,* 821). This subtle suggestion of course makes us wonder, *If Lancelot and Guenevere were not in bed, then why were they there and what were they doing?* And here, if we read carefully, we may be led to believe that Lancelot has come to say goodbye. This passage, coming as it does so soon after Lancelot's deep conversion in the tale of Sir Urry, is a continuation of that conversion. When Guenevere sends for Lancelot, Bors strongly advises him not to visit her while Arthur is away, because Aggravayne and his cronies have planned a trap. Lancelot tells Bors that he must see the queen but promises that he won't stay the night; his visit will take only a few minutes and he'll be right back: "'Have ye no drede,' seyde sir Launcelot, 'for I shall go and com agayne and make no tarynge'" (Malory, *Works,* 821). He does not expect a confrontation and does not arm himself. But this decision puts him in deadly peril when the knights come pounding on the queen's door. Lancelot has always taken his strength from Guenevere's love, and now in desperation he turns to Guenevere: "'Madame,' seyde sir Launcelot, 'ys there here ony armour within you that myght cover my body wythall?'" But Guenevere must let him down: "I have none armour nother helme, shylde, swerde, nother speare." There is only one course that Lancelot can take, and he takes it: he says a tender farewell to Guenevere, prays "Jesu Cryste, be Thou my shylde and myne armoure!" and opens the door (Malory, *Works,* 822). This whole passage is Malory's original work. As Vinaver tells us, "There is nothing in the extant texts that can be regarded as a counterpart to this" (Malory, *Works,* vol. 3, 1630). Malory has shown us Lancelot putting on the armor of God.

Now his death, sad as it is for his friends, is apparently happy for Lancelot: "He laye as he had smyled, and the swettest savour aboute hym that ever they felte" (Malory, *Works,* 881). And they bury him in the choir of the church at Joyous Garde, that is to say, in the sanctuary, because he is a holy man, even, according to Ector in his eulogy, "the godelyest persone that ever cam emonge prees of knyghtes" (Malory, *Works,* 882).

Most of the elements of the story of Lancelot were available for Malory to use, in what he called his "Frensshe book," which of course is not actually a single book and not actually all French. But, in the way of medieval authors in general, he was free to alter the existing material as he saw fit. In relating Lancelot's story, Malory altered it by reducing to the very minimum any reference to adultery with the queen; by changing Lancelot's sin from unchastity to pride; by punishing the pride in Lancelot in multitudinous ways throughout the book; and by expanding and emphasizing Lancelot's quest for holiness, so that his saintly end is absolutely right for Malory's story. All of these changes are hard to explain if the author was a thief, a rapist, a raider of monasteries and churches, and a failed murderer, such as Sir Thomas Malory of Newbold Revel. They are, however, easy to understand if the author was a monk-knight vowed to chastity and, specifically, a follower of St. Bernard, that advocate of humility as the path to God. Moreover, the seven other knights who follow Lancelot into the monastery, inspired by his sanctity, constitute a little band of knight-monks themselves. Their primary wish is prayer and fasting in pursuit of salvation, and Malory adds the information that four of them — Sir Bors, Sir Ector, Sir Blamour, and Sir Bleoberis — "wente into the Holy Lande, thereas Jesu Cryst was quycke and deed," and "these foure knyghtes dyd many bataylles upon the myscreantes, or Turkes" (Malory, *Works*, 883).

16

FLASHBACK: THE CRUSADES

SCHOLARS HAVE COMBED *Le Morte* for clues as to Malory's political allegiance in the Wars of the Roses that raged around him, but they have found precious little, and, of course, they interpret what they find in accordance with their own opinions, since Malory is so silent about his. Amy S. Kaufman remarks that "Malory's sympathies in the Wars of the Roses are a matter of constant debate," and she gives some examples: Sarah L. Peverly believes that Malory "very subtly supports York"; however, says Kaufman, Robert L. Kelly, Raluca L. Radulescu, and Colin Richmond argue for Lancastrian sentiments.[94] P. J. C. Field is unable to detect conclusive evidence on either side, and so he claims that Malory was mostly Yorkist but turned his coat at least once, after which he was so sorry for betraying his king that he wrote his book as a sort of penitential offering (Field, 30ff). Field is not the first to make that sort of proposal. William Matthews answered it long ago: "The thesis that *Le Morte Darthur* is an act of contrition, interesting as it is, is an idea only. Nothing in the book refers to Malory's own penitence for either sins or crimes. In his several prayers he does ask for Jesu's mercy, of course; but so must any man, even a saint" (Matthews, 48). There is one much-quoted passage in *Le Morte* commenting on the abandonment of Arthur by his people, in which Malory

[94] Amy S. Kaufman, "'For This Was Drawyn by a Knyght-Presoner': Sir Thomas Malory and *Le Morte Darthur*," in *Prison Narratives from Boethius to Zana*, ed. P. Phillips (New York: Palgrave Macmillan, 2014), 35–55.

inveighs against his fellow Englishmen for their discontentedness in the matter of kings:

> Lo, ye all Englysshemen, se ye not what a myschyff here was? For he that was the most kynge and nobelyst knytht of the worlde, and moste loved the felyshyp of noble knyghtes, and by hym they all were upholdyn, and yet myght not thes Englyshemen holde them contente with hym. Lo thus was the olde custom and usayges of thys londe, and men say that we of thys londe have nat yet loste that custom. Alas, thys ys a greate defaughte of us Englysshemen, for there may no thynge us please no term. (Malory, *Works*, 861–862)

This passage probably refers to the deposing of the crowned and chrismed king Henry VI, Lancastrian, which took place during Malory's lifetime. However, Malory names no names. (The fact that he names no names is one more small clue to his identity: if our author was a Knight Hospitaller, in naming no names he was simply obeying the ancient rule of his order, which forbade the knights to take sides in the disputes of Christian princes.) All that this passage tells us is that Malory deplores disloyalty. In any case, any scholar who hopes to find more evidence than that concerning Malory's political stance, whether Yorkist or Lancastrian, is doomed to dig deep and yet be disappointed. The word *Lancastrian*, like the word *Yorkist*, never appears in *Le Morte Darthur*. Neither does the name *Henry*. The name *Edward* referring to King Edward IV appears only in Malory's final colophon, where he tells us that he finished writing the book in the ninth year of that king's reign. On the other hand, the word *Saracens* in its various spellings appears many times. The fact is, Malory seems to have no particular interest in the Wars of the Roses. The wars that interest him are the Crusades. Most of us moderns have only the haziest notion of what the Crusades were, and if we are to have even enough understanding of those mighty struggles, so far from us in time and in philosophy, as to enable us to read Malory, we will require a little background.

Scripture tells us that Jesus wept over Jerusalem, and well He might. Jerusalem, the ancient city of David the king of Israel, has had a sad and perilous history for the last three or four thousand years, most of that time afflicted by invasion and threats of invasion, as indeed it is today. To Christians, it is the sacred city where Jesus died the horrible death of crucifixion and then rose alive from His grave, demonstrating that death, even death on a cross, has no lasting power. Jerusalem is also the place where, on the night before He was crucified, He instituted the Holy Eucharist, whereby He instructed His followers to eat His Flesh — in the form of bread — and drink His Blood — in the form of wine — and thus have Him present with them always. Constantine, the first of the Roman emperors to embrace Christianity, built, on the site of the ancient city of Byzantium, a new Eastern capital for the Church. The new Christian city, which the emperor named after himself, Constantinople, was dedicated in 330. From there, his mother Helena went to Jerusalem looking for the True Cross, that is, the very Cross upon which Jesus died, and she found it, as well as the rock tomb within which His dead body had lain. The story goes that she was led by a man who lived in the neighborhood to the place traditionally named as the location of the Crucifixion, and there, after some excavation in a long-dry cistern more or less under a pagan temple, were found three fragmentary crosses. Helen believed that one of them must be the Cross of Christ, but which one? Here, the story diverges into two versions: one version has it that a miracle identified the True Cross; it was placed on the body of a newly dead person, and the dead person came back to life; or possibly, it was brought to a dying woman to touch, and she was instantly healed. The other version is more prosaic. In 395, Bishop Ambrose of Milan, in a funerary oration for Emperor Theodosius, said that Helen identified the True Cross by the tablet still attached to it, on which Pontius Pilate had ordered the reason for Christ's Crucifixion to be written, in three languages — "Jesus of Nazareth, the King of the Jews." In 335, the Church of the Holy Sepulchre, where the Cross was held for veneration, was built over the site, and from that time, Christian pilgrims began to make their way from their homelands across the eastern desert to Jerusalem, to pray.

That story the Christians of the Middle Ages knew. Here is the sequel to it:

After upwards of three centuries of more or less peaceful pilgrimages of Christians to the holy city, there came, like a hot wind out of the desert, Mohammed, determined to conquer the world for his god, Allah. There was to be no mere reliance on teaching, on simply spreading the word; any refusal to accept Allah made one vulnerable to the sword. The very name of the new religion, Islam, meant "submission." There were to be only two "houses," or nations: Dar al Islam, the Abode of Islam, and Dar al Harb, the Abode of War. Mohammed began preaching in Mecca, and then, in 622, moved to Medina and eventually became not only the religious but also the secular ruler there, early establishing his new religion as a theocracy. He waged war, first against other Arab towns, then against Mecca, thus also establishing early the practice of jihad, holy war, war for the purpose of gaining territory for Allah. Mohammed died in 632, leaving his followers with the final directive to "fight all men until they say, 'There is no god but Allah.'"[95] Accordingly, Islam proceeded with its conquering of the peoples of the desert: In 635 Syria fell to Muslim armies, in 637 Antioch, in 637 Persia, in 638 Jerusalem, in 642 Egypt. From the desert places, the marauding Muslims went on, into Africa and Europe. "By the eighth century," Thomas Madden tells us, "Muslim expeditionary forces were crossing the Pyrenees and marching into the heart of Catholic Europe. In 732, at the famous Battle of Tours, Frankish leader Charles Martel defeated the Muslims, driving them back into Spain."[96] Yet the conquest by Islam continued, in small stages and great, but

95 Muhammed ibn Umar al-Waqidi, *Kitab al-Maghazi*, vol. 3 (London: Oxford University Press, 1966), 1113; quoted in Steve Weidenkopf, *The Glory of the Crusades* (El Cajon, CA: Catholic Answers Press, 2014), 33.

96 Thomas F. Madden, *The New Concise History of the Crusades* (New York: Barnes and Noble, 2007), 4. Further citations of this work will be in parentheses in the text.

never with any real abatement, for three more centuries. In 1071, the Turks defeated the Byzantine army and captured the Byzantine emperor. After this, says Madden, "the citizens of Constantinople could look across the Bosporus and see the land of the Turks" (Madden, 5).

In 1081, a new emperor, Alexius I Commenus, came to power, and he decided to turn to the West for help. Today, that seems like a rather obvious move, considering that the Eastern Christian Church, with its capital at Constantinople, and the Western Christian Church, with its capital at Rome, were both Christian. However, some theological differences had caused a rift between the two, and it was in fact a major decision on the part of Alexius to approach the pope in Rome, a decision that led to the Crusades. But the stage had been set for the Crusades four centuries before 1081, in the taking of Jerusalem by Muslims, back in 638. Jerusalem was the city that called to the Christian world with the strong emotional appeal necessary for the gathering of thousands upon thousands of Christians for the long trek over the sands to war; it was the seat of the death and rising of Christ, and, as well, the place where the Sacrament of His Body and Blood was instituted, on the night before He was crucified. Eventually, the crusading knights who went East took a sacred vow, binding in canon law, to go to Jerusalem and fight for its rescue from the nonbelievers.

To satisfy the curiosity of the patient reader who has followed the story this far: yes, the First Crusade did succeed in recapturing Jerusalem, but the Christians were not able to keep it for very long. For the next ninety years or so, after the initial crusading armies had disbanded and gone home, the city was the target of a constant struggle, sometimes conquered by Muslims, sometimes by Christians, until, in 1187, al-Malik al-Nasir Salah ed-Din Yusuf, better known simply as Saladin, captured the city, and it stayed captured. Madden tells us: "On the afternoon of July 3, 1187, at the waterless plateau near Hattin, the crusaders met the first parts of Saladin's army.... It was a hellish night. The soldiers were parched, yet there was no water. In the darkness, the Muslims surrounded the campsite, tormenting the Christians with taunts and threats. They also lit large brushfires, filling the crusader camp with horrible heat and choking smoke" (Madden, 76). In the morning came the hopeless battle. The Christians held out as long as they could, but their defeat was total. Thousands of common soldiers were sold into slavery, and Saladin ordered the execution of all Hospitallers and Templars who had been part of the Christian forces. His secretary, Imad ed-Din, recorded the story, and his record survives:

> He [Saladin] ordered that they should be beheaded, choosing to have them dead rather than in prison. With him was a whole band of scholars and sufis and a certain number of devout men and ascetics; each begged to be allowed to kill one of them, and drew his sword and rolled back his sleeve. Saladin, his face joyful, was sitting on his dais; the unbelievers showed black despair.[97]

And that was not the end of the day's triumph for Saladin; he also won a great symbolic prize, the True Cross. The grand preceptor of the Temple at Jerusalem wrote a letter (Porter, vol. 1, appendix 9, 500) to Henry II of England, reporting on the day's terrible losses: "Know that Jerusalem, with the citadel of David, has been given up to Saladin." And then this: "Saladin has removed the Cross from the Temple of our Lord, and has had it dragged about the streets for two days, and publicly defiled" (Porter, vol. 1, 500). That is a thing to break the Christian heart.

After that, Saladin turned the Church of the Holy Sepulchre into a mosque.

This is the situation to which Thomas Malory alludes when he tells us a certain detail concerning Arthur's death, that "men say that he shall com agayne, and he shall wynne the Holy Cross"; and, after Lancelot's death, that his last four faithful friends "wente into the Holy Lande, thereas Jesu Cryst was quycke and deed," and there "these foure

[97] Imad-ed-Din, in trans. and ed. by Francesco Gabrieli (Berkeley: University of California Press, 1984), 100; quoted in Madden, *The New Concise History of the Crusades*, 76.

knyghtes dyd many bataylles upon the myscreantes, or Turkes." These details do not appear in any of Malory's French sources; he added them himself. The addition is one more piece of good evidence that Malory's point of view is just what we would expect of a consecrated knight of one of the orders founded to fight in the Crusades, in fact, one of the two orders whose men were beheaded en masse by the order of Saladin after his capture of Jerusalem.

In Malory, history and literature come together. But history and literature were coming together already in the eleventh and twelfth centuries, in the inception of the whole chivalric preoccupation, in France — in Troyes, in Champagne, in Burgundy. Who can explain the sweep of great cultural movements, which sometimes seem to come out of nowhere and powerfully attract peoples of many nations? For example, when we tell the story of the beginning of the Crusades, it is easy enough to say that a wild-eyed and ragtag revolutionary called Peter the Hermit came out of Picardy preaching the First Crusade in the 1090s, rode a donkey across France and then into Germany and Bulgaria and Hungary, and that thousands of people dropped their everyday lives and followed him, with the intention of taking back Jerusalem. Peter the Hermit inspired the masses, but then what inspired Peter? After all, Jerusalem had been in the hands of nonbelievers for centuries, yet suddenly the time had arrived. And consider the towering coincidence — if coincidence is indeed what it was — that dictated that at the same time the Western world decided to take up arms against Islam in a quest to rescue the True Cross and take back the holy city of Jerusalem, the world of literature virtually exploded into a new theme — the knightly contest of arms, chivalry, courtly love, and the quest for the Holy Grail, the vessel that held the sacred Blood of Christ. We probably will never know what inspired Peter the Hermit, but in the case of that other coalescence of impulse and circumstance, one is irresistibly tempted to say that all this is not coincidental at all. Rather, the historical fact of the whole drama of the Crusades was actually the most important cause of the flowering of what we have come to call the chivalric tradition in literature. In that mysterious, half-conscious and half-unconscious place in the mind where human experience is turned into Story, and where literature begins, it seems almost inevitable that the Crusades would lead to the story of the Grail. Consider: Jerusalem was the target of an enormous quest involving Western Christendom in an attempt to recover the True Cross, the very Cross on which Jesus had died. The questing armies knew that their cause was deeply concerned with the death of Christ. They also knew that on the night before Jesus was put to death, during the Passover meal that He was sharing with His followers, He had offered them His Body and Blood as food and drink. What could be more natural than that the quest for the Cross should be metamorphosed in Story into the quest for the vessel that held the sacred Blood, both in the form of wine at the last meal Jesus shared with His apostles, and in the blood that issued from His wounds as he hung on the Cross? The quest for the Cross and the quest for the Grail are, in essence, the same quest, both the Cross and the Grail being receptacles of the blood of Christ. The Grail was a newcomer to literature in the twelfth century, but the Cross had been seen in just this symbolic way, as vessel of the holy blood, at least since Anglo-Saxon times — witness the Old English poem "The Dream of the Rood." The Eucharist, the instituting of which was such an integral part of the Crucifixion story, was intended to be an intimate union with Jesus and therefore with God; likewise, in the stories of the quest for the Grail, its achievement was to become symbolically the achievement of transformative union with God. It seems almost inevitable that this story should come out of the Crusades and develop in just this way. But of course, hindsight does teach us a great deal, and of course the story did develop in just this way. The two phenomena, both martial (the Crusades) and literary (the chivalric preoccupation with quest, with its ultimate apotheosis the quest of the Grail), were at their height at the same time. Moreover, one of the guiding lights of the literary phenomenon was closely connected with the quest for the Holy Land, in particular Jerusalem.

That was Bernard of Clairvaux, often called the Man of the Twelfth Century. He was a small child when his father died in the First Crusade, and a very young man when he became a Cistercian monk and began his career of spreading Cistercian mysticism across Europe. In the middle of his life, he wrote the monastic rule upon which the new order of the Knights of the Temple was founded, one of the two great orders of fighting monks who were the mainstay of the crusading armies. As we have seen, after the Order of the Templars was suppressed in 1312, the remnant of that order was fused with the Hospital of St. John, the pope having decreed that all temporal property of the dissolved order was thenceforth the property of the Hospital, and many surviving Templar knights becoming Hospitallers. These two orders of fighting monks had always had a close association. Many times they fought side by side in the same battles, like the battle for Jerusalem after which Saladin ordered the wholesale beheading of Templars and Hospitallers.

Bernard's connection both with the fighting monks — he played a great role in the founding of the Order of the Temple, which included writing their rule — and with the contemplative Cistercians, of which he was not only a member but the greatest and most influential member, is inextricable. Because of this connection, these orders were closely linked with each other, sharing his vision and his mission, and dividing the monks' calling between them. The Templars and Hospitallers were the fighters for Christ; born in response to the Crusades, the Order of Hospitallers were the cohorts, and in time the heirs, of the Templars, founded on the rule written by Bernard. The Cistercians were their cloistered, contemplative counterparts, who pondered the mysteries of the Faith and supported the crusading effort with their prayers — and wrote the *Queste del Saint Graal,* Thomas Malory's source for his "Tale of the Sankgreal."

Both the monk-warriors and their cloistered brothers had the greatest possible influence on the knightly literature and, eventually, on Malory. Karen Ralls draws our attention to the fact that "remarkably … the first Grail romance, like many of the first Templar knights, came from the area around Troyes, Champagne. With both subjects — the Templars and the Grail legends — Troyes seems to figure prominently" (Ralls, 124–125). That fact seems less remarkable when we consider that Bernard of Clairvaux, a generation earlier, was born in that same district of France, so that he was in his full maturity and association with the Templars and Cistercians at the same time and place that the chivalric tales began to flourish. In 1136, he wrote his famous treatise "In Praise of the New Knighthood," defining the chivalrous virtues of the new orders of monk-knights.

Sometime between 1135 and 1190, Chrétien de Troyes wrote the first recorded Grail story, *Le Conte del Graal.* It is incomplete, breaking off in the middle of a sentence. It is also embedded in a larger story of Joseph of Arimathea. Chrétien does not give us the background of the Grail, nor does he associate it with the Blood of Christ; nor does he call it holy. It is simply a dish of some sort and, along with a mysterious lance, it appears and disappears without explanation. Maybe Chrétien intended to say more about the Grail, but he died before finishing his work. The next redactor of interest to us as students of Malory is Robert de Boron, who, writing his version in 1190, contributed greatly to the information about the Grail itself. He tells us that "the Grail was the Vessel of the Last Supper and was after the crucifixion given by Pilate to Joseph of Arimathea who used it to catch the last drops of Christ's blood" (Bogdanow, 3). Then comes *L'Estoire del Saint Graal,* which tells us how the vessel came to Britain; it was brought by Joseph: "After converting many Saracens, Joseph and his people come in a miraculous way to Britain where they establish the Christian faith" (Bogdanow, 5). *L'Estoire* leaves a four-hundred-year gap in the story, between the time of Joseph of Arimathea and the time of King Arthur, which is covered in a subsequent version by having Joseph's son live for hundreds of years so that he can be available to greet Galahad when he comes. *L'Estoire del Saint Graal* constitutes vital evidence in our search for the author of *Le Morte Darthur,* not because Malory used it, but because he did not. He chose instead to use the Cistercian version of the tale, the *Queste del Saint Graal.*

In our study of the Ribston manuscript, used by Malory in his translation project, we noted that the boards binding this manuscript enclosed both the *Suite du Merlin,* which is recast by Malory into his "Tale of King Arthur," and another book, which Malory chose not to use. The rejected book is *L'Estoire del Graal.* Malory, in writing his "Tale of the Sankgreal," chose to use, rather than the convenient book, the one in his hand, the one in the same binding with the *Suite du Merlin* that he was using, the Cistercian version of the Grail story: the *Queste del Saint Graal.* Scholars have noticed this choice. It is made obvious not only in Malory's abjuring *L'Estoire,* so convenient to his hand, but also in his rejecting the version of the Grail story found with the prose *Tristan.* For example, Mary Hynes-Berry says,

> It is clear that Malory made a deliberate choice: the colophon testifies that he knew and rejected the prose *Tristan* version of the *Queste del Saint Graal.* The manuscript Malory used for his *Book of Sir Tristram* had the Grail interpolation in its third book, but Malory says: "Here ys no rehersall of the thirde booke. But here folowyth the noble tale of the Sankegreall" (*Works,* 845.27–31). "The *Tale of the Sankgreall,*" in conjunction with this colophon, establishes that Malory was definitely interested in a spiritual centre for his Grail romances, rather than in simply recording chivalric adventures.[98]

Dhira Mahoney agrees: "Given such chivalric predilections, it would not be surprising to find Malory secularizing the Grail story when he came to translate what is, after all, primarily a theological treatise on

98 Mary Hynes-Berry, "A Tale Breffly Drawyne oute of Freynsche," in *Aspects of Malory,* 106. Further citations of this work will be in the text in parentheses.

salvation, in which innumerable hermits and recluses explicate the visions and adventures 'in [the] bitterest detail,' as E. K. Chambers puts it. Yet Malory's colophon shows that he held the story in great reverence, and he seems to have chosen the Vulgate version in preference to the more secular version that he is likely to have known from the prose *Tristan*, his source for the Tale of Tristram" (Mahoney, 112). Neither Hynes-Berry nor Mahoney mentions Malory's rejection of the *L'Estoire del Graal* that was bound within the same boards as the *Suite du Merlin* in the Ribston ("Cambridge") manuscript, but that rejection, also deliberate, would have strengthened their argument. *L'Estoire* is bound with the *Suite*, which Malory chose to use, in the manuscript housed for so many centuries, including of course Malory's century, in the Ribston monastery of the Knights Hospitallers.

The reason that Malory's choice of the particular version of the Grail story that he did choose is significant to our inquiry is that this version was almost certainly written by a Cistercian monk; in fact, the *Queste* is itself a long disquisition on the Cistercian theology and way of life. For the last century or so — at least since 1921, when Albert Pauphilet published his analysis of the Cistercianism embedded in the *Queste* — most scholars have acknowledged that unmistakable bent in this version of the Grail story. As long ago as 1934, Edmund McCorkell re-presented Pauphilet's arguments and added some examples of his own to the evidence that the *Queste* was written by a Cistercian monk, "or at least a writer who came under the influence of the Cistercian movement" (McCorkell, 6). As recently as 2003, Karen Ralls flatly stated that the *Queste del Saint Graal* was "written by a Cistercian monk in 1215 for another crusader patron, Jean de Nesle" (Ralls, 138). Mary Hynes-Berry has declared, "Written about 1225 by a Cistercian monk, the work allegorizes a specific mystical doctrine of the Eucharist" (Hynes-Berry, 94).

Of course, there have been some dissenters through the years. Jill Mann, for example, believes that the evidence offered by Pauphilet is weak and unconvincing; she favors an argument brought forth by Jean Frappier that the Cistercians would not write such a frivolous piece of literature as a romance; they were not only cloistered but seriously austere, and such literature would have struck them as altogether too worldly.[99] But there is always a place in the human heart for a good story. Pauline Matarasso, in the introduction to her translation of the *Quest*, tells us about "the pleasant story cited in 1220 by the Cistercian monk, Cesarius of Heisterbach, telling of how the abbot Gevardus, faced with a chapter full of dozing monks, exclaimed: 'Listen, brethren, listen! I have something new and wonderful to tell you: There once was a king, whose name was Arthur…' Here he broke off to point the obvious moral to rows of upturned and, one fears, crestfallen faces. The author of the *Quest* resorted to much the same means, but refrained from turning the carrot into a stick" (Matarasso, 10).

Karen Pratt disagrees with Matarasso; she does not believe the *Queste* was written by a Cistercian. Her conclusion: "Despite the moral and religious didacticism of the *Queste*, the romance presents us with the mystical glorification of an elite group of fighting men, bound together by lineage and the conventions of the 'ordre de chevalerie.' Its hero is a knight with a Messianic mission, not a monk."[100] But Pratt is ignoring the fact that in the Cistercian world, *knight* and *monk* blur together. Bernard of Clairvaux, the most renowned of the Cistercians, was intimately connected with the knightly orders — the Templars for whom he wrote the community rule, and the Hospitallers by their close association with the Templars — as well as with his own cloistered order of Cistercians. Members of both fighting orders were monks *and* knights. If Thomas Malory was a Hospitaller, then he was a monk and a knight, and the blurring of roles in the *Queste* would be more or less expected in his work. In fact, it would be hard to compose a more elegant statement of the Bernardian ethos than

99 Jill Mann, "Malory and the Grail Legend, " in *A Companion to Malory*, ed. Elizabeth Archibald and A. S. G. Edwards (Cambridge: D. S. Brewer, 1996), 207.

100 Karen Pratt, "The Cistercians and the *Queste del Saint Graal*," *Reading Medieval Studies* 21 (1995): 69–96.

Pratt's own words. The Templars and Hospitallers were indeed "an elite group of fighting men bound together by lineage and the conventions of the 'ordre de chevalerie' "; the "mystical glorification" of these knight-monks, which gripped the imagination of the world to the extent that it continues even today, was instigated by the great saint of the Cistercians, St. Bernard. An item of great interest in the ongoing discussion of the Cistercian interest in the glories of knighthood is Bernard's letter to the master of the Templars, "In Praise of the New Knighthood":

> This, I repeat, is a new kind of knighthood and one unknown in ages past. It indefatigably wages a twofold combat, against flesh and blood and against a spiritual host of evil in the heavens. When someone bravely resists a physical foe, relying solely on physical strength, I find this hardly astonishing, since this is not uncommon. And when war is waged by spiritual [strength] against vices or demons, this, too, is nothing remarkable, though I consider it praiseworthy, for the world is full of monks. But for a man powerfully to gird himself with both swords and nobly mark his belt [with the cross] — who would not consider this worthy of great admiration? . . . Truly a fearless knight and secure on every side is he whose soul is protected by the armor of faith just as his body is protected by armor of steel. (St. Bernard, 33–34)

And further, "I do not know if it would be more appropriate to refer to them as monks or as soldiers, or whether it would perhaps be better to recognize them as being both" (St. Bernard, 48). His "cavaliers of Christ," he says, "lack neither monastic meekness nor military might."

There is demonstrably no reason to think that Cistercians in their cloister would decry the virtues and the glories of knighthood. Karen Cherewatuk considers an analysis by Kenneth Hodges of Malory's handling of these matters: Hodges, and Cherewatuk with him, holds that Malory, in shifting the burden of moral interpretation to his readers, "simply will not allow a separation of ideals into sacred and secular categories."[101] They are not separate in real life, and they cannot be separated in great fiction. Moreover, Fanni Bogdanow, in her long and painstakingly detailed "An Interpretation of the Meaning and Purpose of the Vulgate *Queste del Saint Graal* in the Light of the Mystical Theology of St Bernard," shows virtually line by line how the *Queste* emerges from the writings of Bernard.[102] In founding his many monasteries of Cistercian monks, Bernard sometimes called those monks *soldiers* or *warriors*, and their houses *forts* or *castles*, to be defended against incursions of the devil, but he did not confine his sponsorship of knighthood to metaphor. And never to be forgotten when we talk about the eleventh, the twelfth, the thirteenth centuries, is that ubiquitous fact of medieval life, the Crusades. Any story of a knightly quest for a religious object must be considered in the light of recruitment of warriors in that religious cause, the call to take back the Holy Land and especially Jerusalem, home of the True Cross, the Crucifixion of Jesus, and the Holy Eucharist.

In view of all this, and since Thomas Malory wrote his "Tale of the Sankgreal" in adaptation of the Cistercian *Queste*, we see more evidence that Malory was not the secular knight that he has been considered but one of Bernard's knights of Christ. The Cistercians were inextricably connected with the Hospitallers because both orders were strongly influenced by the ethos of Bernard of Clairvaux, and both orders had immeasurable influence in the life of the Malorys of Yorkshire. Recall that the Malorys were one of the acknowledged "Hospitaller families," and that those of Yorkshire were closely connected with Cistercians as well; they made their home within yards, not miles, of the great Cistercian abbey of Fountains. Moreover, strong connections

101 Karen Cherewatuk, "Christian Rituals in Malory: The Evidence of Funerals," in *Malory and Christianity*, 88.

102 Fanni Bogdanow, "An Interpretation of the Meaning and Purpose of the Vulgate *Queste del Saint Graal* in the Light of the Mystical Theology of St. Bernard," in *The Changing Face of Arthurian Romance: Essays on Arthurian Prose Romances in Memory of Cedric E. Pickford*, ed. Alison Adams et al. (Cambridge: Boydell Press, 1986), 23–46.

between these Malorys and the Cistercian Order are found in their family history. We have seen that Lord Robert DeRos, the ancestor of Thomas Malory and himself probably a lay brother in the Order of the Temple, donated his manor at Ribston to the Templars, from whom it was inherited by the Hospitallers. As to the Cistercian connection, Rievaulx Abbey and Warden Abbey were founded by this same family; Everard DeRos gave land in Helmsley for their foundation. The DeRos family was patron of Rievaulx over the next 250 years, with several of them buried there, beginning with Peter DeRos, about 1155. So, too, did others of Thomas Malory's ancestors grant land to the Cistercians. Remember the recorded deed of 1347, by which Sir Roger Conyers and Sir Christopher Mallore, Lord of Hutton, two of Thomas's great-grandfathers, granted lands at Lynton to the Cistercian Fountains Abbey. So, when Thomas Malory was choosing a Grail story to incorporate into his *Morte Darthur*, he had every reason to prefer the Cistercian telling, considering the long-enduring connection of his family with the order, and considering that he himself was steeped in Cistercian thought, as Vinaver said long ago the author of the *Morte* must have been, by having grown up within the shadow of the great Fountains Abbey. Quite likely Thomas and his brothers were educated at a Cistercian abbey school at Fountains.

Likewise, our Thomas Malory had every reason to be a Hospitaller knight. We can tell by his book that his was not a contemplative nature; he loved martial doings, and there was an ideal outlet for both his religious feelings and his military leanings ready to hand. His family's connection with the Order of St. John of Jerusalem, Knights Hospitallers, warriors to the Holy Land, was as long-enduring as their connection with the Cistercians, dating at least from 1217. That was the year that their DeRos ancestor gave his manor at Ribston, about ten miles away from the Malory home at Studley, which adjoins the grounds of the Cistercian Fountains Abbey, to the Templars, "in aid of the Holy Land in the east," swearing that the aforesaid gift he and his heirs would "warrant, acquit, and defend forever." Within a century, as we have seen, the Templars' order was dissolved, and their property, including this same monastery at Ribston, passed to the Order of Hospitallers by papal decree. That house, first a DeRos holding, then a Templar preceptory, and then a Hospitaller commandery, until it passed into private hands at the dissolution of the monasteries of England in the sixteenth century, is the same house where during passing centuries the Ribston (today dubbed "Cambridge") manuscript of the *Suite du Merlin* lay still stored in the same ancient hide trunk that held also the old DeRos deed of gift. This manuscript, the note in the margin tells us, was the very same one that Malory used as the source of his "Tale of King Arthur."

It is generally supposed that by the time of Thomas Malory, interest in the Crusades and in the quest to rescue Jerusalem, and even in the chivalric literature, had significantly abated, and that may be so. After 1291, when Aker, the last Christian stronghold in the East, fell to the Muslims, the Christian fervor for crusading no longer had the high hopes to feed it that the initial impulse had had. However, there was still, in Malory's day, one band of knights who had not lost interest. Even after that time, even until the time of Napoleon, the Order of St. John, the Knights Hospitaller, still held their intrepid stand, isolated on the great rock fortress of Malta, where they had been driven by the superior strength of the Muslim forces, first out of Palestine and then out of Cyprus and then out of Rhodes, and still continued to do battle for the Holy Land, with high hearts. Every knight of the Hospital, as soon as he was initiated into the order, went straight to the east to fight the Turk, for up to five years. If our Malory was indeed such a knight, he had spent a significant part of his life doing battle against Islam, the "miscreaunts," misbelievers, as he calls them in the *Morte*. His preoccupation with crusading comes as no surprise.

P. J. C. Field has the best commentary I have seen on this aspect of Malory. He points out that the major components of the story of Arthur existed already, in accepted forms that Malory was not free to change, but there was always some leeway in the telling: "Malory considerably altered the proportions, tone, and interpretation of his story, so that it suggested ideals of man and society more in accord with the ideals of the military orders than is usual in his sources or in romance in general — in, for instance, his apparent indifference to ceremony and conspicuous consumption, his dislike of courtly love, and his presentation of knighthood itself as an 'order' with a moral purpose and a religious justification." Field goes on with his remarks, so beautifully that I cannot resist quoting a rather long passage:

> Malory's changes suggest not only chivalric ideals but also specific political aims in accord with and perhaps inspired by those of military Orders. It is natural in a romance for real political aims to remain in the background; but crusades and the defence of Christendom against Islam are more conspicuous in the *Morte Darthur* than in Malory's sources or in most other English Arthurian romances. While reducing other things in his sources, he tends to preserve or add to their sporadic references to Islam as a hostile power on the edge of the Arthurian world, so that such references become proportionately more conspicuous. Sometimes they provide an interpretive yardstick, as when, at the beginning of the *Morte,* the wrongness of the rebellion against Arthur is shown by its result, a Saracen invasion. That invasion becomes a campaign of devastation and indiscriminate slaughter, as natural a consequence of the enemy's "mysbylevyng" as the chivalric virtues were of Christianity. In the second section of the *Morte,* it appears that Malory felt that such behaviour deserved retaliation in kind, for he gives King Arthur an exhortation not in his source: "Therefore save none for golde nothir for sylver: for they that woll accompany them with Sarezens, the man that wolde save them were lytyll to prayse. And therefore sle doune and save nother hethyn nothir Crystyn." Alterations elsewhere also present crusades in a more conspicuous and more favourable light. In the long fifth section of the *Morte,* Malory untangles an episode in the French prose Tristan so that his admired Sir Tristram no longer refuses a

> genuine papal summons to go on crusade to Jerusalem. The climax of the section is the conversion of the Saracen knight Sir Palomides, an episode not in Malory's source. In the last section of the *Morte,* he adds to the famous legend that King Arthur would one day return to Britain the notion that, if he did, it would be to recapture the Holy Cross. The close of the *Morte Darthur* was also altered to introduce the idea of a crusade. In both Malory's sources, when Sir Lancelot is dead his kinsmen retire to a monastery for the rest of their lives, but Malory says instead that they went crusading to the Holy Land, where they "dyd many bataylles upon the myscreantes or Turkes," and there, in the last words of his book, "dyed upon a Good Fryday for Goddes sake." (Field, 81–82)

Those are not quite the last words of Malory's book. After this statement concerning Lancelot's friends, Malory dates his completion of the work, asks us to pray for him, and tells us, in his final words, that he is the servant of Jesus both day and night.[103]

[103] Field (81) proposes that the obvious bias toward the "military orders" in Malory's work means that Sir Robert Malory, prior of the Hospitallers in England, somehow influenced Sir Thomas Malory of Newbold Revel to write his book to reflect the Hospitaller point of view. However, he does not explain how the prior managed to achieve such influence on the Warwickshire man.

SECTION FOUR

But What about Newbold Revel?

17

Dugdale Defended

WE HAVE SEEN plentiful circumstantial evidence, and some apparently irrefutable direct evidence as well, to support Thomas Malory of Studley Royal and Hutton Conyers as the author of *Le Morte,* and we shall see more. However, in order to avoid the injustice of special pleading, or even the appearance of it, it is vital that we acknowledge the evidence that has been offered against this Malory and in support of Thomas Malory of Newbold Revel. A number of scholars during the late twentieth and the early twenty-first centuries have come to take it for granted that the Newbold Revel man has been somehow shown to be our author, and therefore they do not question his position. However, if we wish to discover the truth without being overawed by apparent consensus, we must look carefully at the evidence that has been offered for this man and evaluate it for ourselves. Besides Malory's own work, there are a few coeval and almost-coeval documents that mention a Thomas Malory and therefore touch on our argument. We shall look carefully at each of them to discover what they can teach us about the author of *Le Morte Darthur.*

Sir William Dugdale's *Antiquities of Warwickshire,* 1656, is the last-published of the historical documents of interest in the search for Thomas Malory's identity, but it deserves first place in our consideration because it is the book that caught Kittredge's attention in 1894 and convinced him that the author was the Warwickshire man from Newbold Revel, and therefore it has influenced all modern searches. However, a challenge has arisen to a key part of Dugdale's sketch of this Malory's life, the part that leads us to put his birthdate at about

1393. That date would make this Malory about seventy-seven in 1469–1470, when *Le Morte* was finished, too old to be writing such a book. The disagreement is pertinent to our search, so the question of Dugdale and his sketch of Thomas Malory requires close study.

We begin by asking why Dugdale did not ascribe the authorship of *Le Morte Darthur* to Malory of Newbold Revel if he was the author. Between 1485 and 1635, the first century and a half of the *Morte*'s history in print, its popularity is attested by the fact of its six separate printings: Caxton's own in 1485, Wynken de Worde's including his woodcuts in 1498, de Worde's second printing with additional woodcuts in 1529, William Copland's in 1559, Thomas East's of 1583, and William Stansby's in 1634. A. S. G. Edwards, discussing these reprintings, the reception of Malory's book, and its tremendous influence for five hundred years, says that

> it is clear that Caxton's edition and its early reprints by de Worde were widely read. Paradoxically, the chief evidence of this is negative: very few copies survive of Caxton's 1485 edition and de Worde's of 1498 and 1529, and those that do are usually imperfect. For such a large work the virtual disappearance of editions is striking. It suggests the degree to which Malory's work, like other early editions of romances, was literally read to destruction.[104]

In 1634, the year that Stansby's edition was printed, Sir William Dugdale was twenty-nine, a member of a scholarly circle that led to his collaboration with Roger Dodsworth in producing the *Monasticon Anglicanum*, and eventually to his own production of that encyclopedic history of his home county, *The Antiquities of Warwickshire*. It is hard to believe that Dugdale was not aware of *Le Morte Darthur*,

[104] A. S. G. Edwards, "The Reception of Malory's *Morte Darthur*," in *A Companion to Malory*, ed. Elizabeth Archibald and A. S. G. Edwards (Cambridge: D. S. Brewer, 1996), 243.

and that he was not aware that it was written by a man of his own county, if it was. Certainly Dugdale knew of Thomas Malory of Newbold Revel and his family; he wrote the brief genealogy and biography of this Thomas that has formed the basis of all modern searches into his life. It is unusual to find a quarrel with Dugdale, who has been respected for his accurate reporting. *Britannica Online* calls him "preeminent among the medievalist scholars in his time. An authority on genealogy and charters, he displayed accurate scholarship and insight unusual for his period."[105] My favorite comment on Dugdale is the Duchess of Cleveland's; her three-volume catalog of those families who really did come over with the Conqueror, *The Battle Abbey Roll, with Some Account of the Norman Lineages,* is itself an astonishing achievement. In the preface, she has this to say about her difficulties in compiling her catalog: "Chartularies and public records appear to be the only reliable guides in the study of genealogies, and I own to having been lost in amazement at some of the pedigrees furnished by the heralds." But she adds, "This does not apply to Dugdale, who evolves no fictions from his inner consciousness, but is invariably and scrupulously honest."[106]

Dugdale's sketch of the life of Sir Thomas Malory of Newbold Revel is simple. It says that a man of this name and habitation went soldiering at Calais with Richard Beauchamp, Earl of Warwick, during the reign of Henry V (that is, during the years 1413–1422), that he brought with him in his own retinue "one lance and two archers, receiving for his lance and 1 archer xx li. per an., and their dyet; and for the other archer, x marks and no dyet." Later in his life, Dugdale tells us, this Thomas Malory served in Parliament, and when he died, he was buried in the great church attached to Greyfriars Abbey in

105 *Encyclopaedia Bitannica Online,* s.v. "Sir William Dugdale," https://www.britannica.com/biography/William-Dugdale.

106 Catherine Lucy Wilhelmina Powlett, Duchess of Cleveland, *The Battle Abbey Roll with Some Account of the Norman Lineages,* 3 vols. (London: John Murray, 1889), iii–iv.

London. There, his gravestone, which was destroyed along with Greyfriars Abbey by Henry VIII, read (in Latin):

HERE LIES SIR THOMAS MALORY
VALIANT SOLDIER
DIED 14 MAR 1470
OF THE PARISH OF MONKS KIRBY
WARWICKSHIRE

Now, current scholarship is perfectly satisfied with Dugdale's research skills, care for details, and probity, as far as his reporting that this Malory was from Warwickshire, in the parish of Monks Kirby; that he was the son of John Malory of Newbold Revel; that he died in 1470 and was buried in a splendid church with a splendid stone to mark his resting place. However, when Dugdale says that Malory served under Beauchamp during the reign of Henry V, P. J. C. Field, who firmly believes that Malory of Newbold Revel wrote *Le Morte Darthur*, says that Dugdale must have had this Malory mixed up with somebody else. The reason this part of Dugdale's report must be denied is the supposition that a man who was old enough to be a soldier and a leader of other soldiers during the reign of Henry V would have been too old in 1469–1470 to be writing such a book. William Matthews by his meticulous research (detailed on pages 67–73 in *The Ill-Framed Knight*) has demonstrated that the time of Malory's service with Beauchamp was the deployment to Calais in 1414–1415. Edward Hicks says, "The young man who in 1415 was accompanied by a lance and two archers when he joined the Earl of Warwick's retinue must have been something like 21 years of age. Hence when Sir Thomas Malory died in March ,1471, he must have been somewhere about 77 years old" (Hicks, 13). That means that when the book was being finished in 1469 or 1470, this man was old. He was a very old man by medieval reckoning, and he was close to death. Of course, there are many septuagenarians today who are vigorous and hard-working, but today everyone knows that seventy is the new forty. In the Middle Ages, there were no miracle drugs for high blood pressure and high cholesterol, no bypass surgery for clogged arteries, no anti-inflammatories either nonsteroidal or otherwise, no bifocals for aging eyesight (and, as anyone knows who has ever tried to read a medieval manuscript, in French no less, that alone could have stopped the project), no painkillers for stiff joints, not even so much as an aspirin. According to Neil Cummins, average adult life expectancy in the fifteenth-century English peerage was fifty-four, independent of the fall in violent battle deaths from the previous century.[107] As William Matthews says so vividly, "There is considerable evidence that the medieval view was that by sixty a man was bean fodder and forage, ready for nothing but death's pit" (Matthews, 68). Moreover, the actual writing of manuscripts was backbreaking work. In scriptoria, the youngest members of a house would ordinarily be favored for the work of scribe, because of their stamina and good eyesight. Germaine Greer quotes the complaint of a tenth-century scribe: "Only try to do it y'self & you wille learn how arduous is the writer's task. It dims your eyes, makes your back ache, and knits your back & chest together. It is a terrible ordeal for the whole body."[108] And Thomas Malory was not doing the simple work of a scribe; he was handling great heavy manuscript books, organizing the material in them, translating, and composing *Le Morte Darthur*, while confined in some sort of prison.

Therefore Dugdale, no matter how well respected and trusted he is, must be refuted if we are to be persuaded that Malory of Newbold Revel was a much younger man than Dugdale's sketch leads us to believe. It will be necessary to convince us that this Malory was not born until 1414 or 1415. P.J.C. Field claims that Dugdale's source of information concerning Malory of Newbold Revel, a 1415 retinue roll of men who served with Beauchamp at Calais, is not actually a list of men who served under Beauchamp at Calais at all. Field proposes that it is only a list of recruits indicating their willingness to serve, and therefore

[107] Neil Cummins, "Lifespans of the European Elite, 800–1800," *The Journal of Economic History* 77, no. 2 (June 2017): 406, http://neilcummins.com/Cummins2017.pdf

[108] Germaine Greer, quoting unnamed scribe, in *The Obstacle Race: The Fortunes of Women Painters and Their Work* (New York: Tauris Parke, 2001), 155.

the Newbold Revel Thomas Malory may never have seen any actual service; in fact, if he had even been born yet, he was only a new baby when the list was compiled (Field, 55). Therefore, Dugdale must have been confused; the Malory he described was not the man of Newbold Revel. He must have been somebody else.

The problem is that nobody else was available. Professor Field certainly tried to find someone else who would do. He spent pages in *Life and Times* (56–62) detailing his meticulous search of the records of nine of the ten Thomas Malorys he found in Warwickshire in the fifteenth century, numbered 1–10. We get the details of all the records, including their dates of birth, pedigrees, wills, wills of their parents, their wives' pedigrees, children, places of abode, witnessing of contracts, military service, social rank, death dates, inquisitions post mortem, and so on, skipping the records of only one Thomas Malory, the one he tags Number 3. That one gets very short shrift; concerning him, Field says only that "Thomas Malory esquire is recorded in Beauchamp's retinue roll in the summer of 1415, as above," meaning, of course, the retinue roll quoted by Dugdale as part of his biography of Malory of Newbold Revel. Yet in spite of all his research, Field failed to find any replacement for the Newbold Revel Malory, written up by Dugdale so long ago, and does not offer us one. We must infer, therefore, that Dugdale was right. His Warwickshire man, Thomas Malory Esquire, who rode with Beauchamp during the reign of Henry V, will have been at least sixteen when his name appeared on the retinue roll, the standard minimum age for men called to present themselves for military duty. Common sense tells us, however, that a lad of sixteen would not likely be the commander of other soldiers — in this case, a retinue of one lance, usually comprising three or four men — and two archers. And common sense is not all we have to draw on here. Matthews tells us, "The few esquires in Dugdale's list about whom we have exact dates were mostly in their later twenties" (73). But Malory could have been a good bit younger than that and still have been an old man when *Le Morte* was finished in 1469–1470. If he was older than sixteen but still young — say twenty-one for a guess — he was about seventy-six when the book was finished; if twenty-five, then about eighty. Shortly after *Le Morte Darthur* was finished, he died.

The attempt to undermine the trustworthiness of Dugdale may cause scholars some uneasiness, since of course we know that once part of the Dugdale biography of Malory is doubted, the whole thing thus becomes suspect. If Dugdale got his man mixed up with some other, why should we believe that this Warwickshire man of Newbold Revel died in 1470? Why should we believe that he was buried in the Greyfriars church under a fine monument? We cannot simply go and look at Malory's grave and read the inscription that Dugdale copied for us, because the thing itself was destroyed, along with many other cultural treasures, by the angry hands of reformationists, a long time ago. Moreover, there are other important pieces of information about Malory in *The Antiquities of Warwickshire*, which are not part of Dugdale's synopsis of Malory's life. One is the armorial window in the parlor at Newbold Revel, showing the arms of the Malorys. P.J.C. Field considers that window solid evidence of pedigree; he says of Thomas Malory of Newbold Revel, "We cannot know how much he himself knew of his ancestry. We can only say that ... it must have been more than we can prove from the only solid evidence, the armorial window" (Field, 37). And yet the only way we know there was such an armorial window is that Dugdale sketched it; it no longer exists. Another piece of evidence from Dugdale is the picture he made of a stained glass church window depicting a John and Philippa Malory, believed by many to be the parents of the Newbold Revel knight. Another is the information on that knight's gravestone, quoted above, which was destroyed by Henry VIII, meaning that we first learned about the gravestone, and thus the information on it concerning Malory, from Dugdale. Proponents of the Newbold Revel Malory as author often accept Dugdale's sketches and his biographical comments about this man, with the sole exception being the information that Malory fought with Beauchamp during the reign of Henry V, simply because this information means he was too old in the late 1460s to write *Le Morte*.

Those who contend that Malory of Newbold Revel, contra Dugdale, was born around 1415 thereby strip him of his achievement as a "valiant soldier," which was recorded on his tombstone. They seem to forget altogether the fact that Dugdale is not the person who ordered Malory's gravestone and directed that it record the high achievement of his life, that he valiantly served his king and country. Dugdale, writing his *Antiquities of Warwickshire* almost two hundred years later, merely copied what he read on the stone. It was someone who knew Malory well, probably someone in his own family, very likely one of the people who stood around his grave as he was lowered into it, who ordered the inscription. They knew that this man was a valiant soldier. That was his claim to be remembered. It seems somehow unfair to strip him of it in order to make him the author of a book that he probably never even heard of because he died fifteen years or so before it was printed and disseminated.

As for the other contribution that Dugdale made to what we know about this Malory, his sketch of a window at Newbold Revel, the very fact that Dugdale made the picture means that he saw the window. That means of course that he visited the Newbold Revel manor house, which had been the home of Sir Thomas Malory and of his descendants for some generations after him. The owners of the house at the time of Dugdale's visit obviously knew that the reason he wanted to sketch their window was that the house had been the Malorys's home. If any relatives or acquaintances of the Malorys were still in the house or the neighborhood, then they certainly were a source of information for Dugdale. They may have been able to confirm that their ancestor served with Beauchamp; that is just the kind of story that comes down through families. And if he had been the author of *Le Morte Darthur*, the famous book that had already gone through six separate printings at the time of Dugdale's visit, there can be little doubt that they would have known, and they surely would have told Dugdale, and he surely would have put that information into his outline of Sir Thomas Malory's life. He didn't.

The fact that Dugdale never mentioned any connection between Thomas Malory of Warwickshire and *Le Morte Darthur* is highly significant. He tells us the man's name and the brief sketch of his life and death mentioned above, and that is all. His book, published in 1656, is an encyclopedia; in fact, its full title is *The Antiquities of Warwickshire Illustrated: From Records, Leiger-Books, Manuscripts, Charters, Evidences, Tombes, and Armes, Beautified with Maps, Prospects, and Portraitures*. His method of collecting information was to travel around the county and look at everything and question everybody. He noted everything pertinent to the history of Warwickshire, copying or commenting on legal records, church records, gravestones, church windows, chronicles, and deeds. He interviewed families and their friends and recorded family stories and pedigrees. He sketched artworks that represented the people of Warwickshire, including the church window that depicted Malory's family members, and the parlor window that depicted their coats of arms. In all this collecting of records and facts, Dugdale never associated Malory of Newbold Revel, Warwickshire, with *Le Morte*, although the book was very well known in Dugdale's time. He would undoubtedly have claimed credit for his fellow Warwickshire man Sir Thomas Malory if that person had been known to be the author of *Le Morte Darthur*. Surely this omission is a piece of evidence in itself that this Malory had never been connected with the authorship, even in his own lifetime. If he had been, no matter when or where he might have been in prison, someone near him would have known what he was doing. Someone had to supply the books he used. Someone would have asked him conversationally about his project. We know of no particular reason why that project should have been a secret, but even if all witnesses had been asked to keep silent, someone would have talked about it. Especially after the book was popular and the man was dead, someone who remembered this man would have mentioned his authorship, maybe even recorded it somewhere. Yet nobody did, at least not in his home county. If someone had, Dugdale would have noted something so notable in his biographical sketch of this Malory.

He did not. Thus, what we have is analogous to a biographical sketch of, say, Dante Alighieri, written in the 1500s or thereabouts, which notes his birth and death dates and the location of his grave; notes that he was once mayor of Florence, and, getting into political hot water, got himself banished; but does not say a word about *The Divine Comedy*. Those who believe that such a thing could happen must surely be few. It seems almost impossible to believe that anyone could think such a thing happened in the case of Thomas Malory. And apparently nobody did; it seems not to have struck anyone, for upwards of 450 years, that Dugdale's brief biography of Malory left out a key piece of information, for no one connected this man with the *Morte*. Then, in 1894, George Lyman Kittredge declared his belief that the Sir Thomas Malory who was written up in *The Antiquities of Warwickshire* was the author of *Le Morte Darthur*. However, as we can see, Dugdale's piece on Malory does not really support Kittredge's belief in the Newbold Revel man as author.

But for those readers who still believe in Kittredge's candidate and are still looking for some hint that Dugdale may have been mistaken, there is the study of the mother of the Newbold Revel Malory, also done by Professor Field. He discovered that in 1434, Sir Thomas's mother Philippa, who was a widow by that time, was making arrangements for her daughter's marriage. Moreover, this same Philippa in 1436 is found in a tax assessment to be the holder of some land in Warwickshire. Again, in 1437, she is shown to have been the executrix of her husband's will (Field, 64). From these three pieces of information Field concludes that Philippa's son Thomas was not off in Calais doing military service; he was a minor in 1434, 1436, and 1437—otherwise he, rather than his mother, would have been named in all such family matters. But Philippa presumably held the land as part of her widow's jointure; and of course her husband could have appointed her as his executor (and it certainly would have been reasonable for him to do so if his only son was a soldier in France); and doubtless, like most mothers, she had a proper role to play in planning her daughter's wedding. As for her holding land in Warwickshire, that land was apparently the manor of Newbold Revel, and apparently it was still part of her legacy, not her son's, many years later, after her son Thomas had died as an old man; his inquisition post mortem indicates that at the time of his death he owned no such property. His grandson (and, of course, Philippa's great-grandson) had inherited the holding of Newbold Revel. It appears that Sir Thomas never held the manor, nor did his son Robert. It seems to have passed from his mother Philippa to his wife Elizabeth, and then to Nicholas Malory, Elizabeth and Thomas's grandson. So much for the argument that the reason Philippa Malory held Newbold Revel in her own name in 1436 was that her son Thomas was a minor, too young to hold property. It is interesting as well that Edward Hicks, in his biography of Malory of Newbold Revel, notes that Malory's wife Elizabeth sometimes handled the business of collecting rents on Malory property (Hicks, 56n). Hicks does not imply any sort of incapacity in the husband, but the interested can speculate. Maybe Sir Thomas Malory, being the man of action we know he was, simply hated that sort of work. Maybe he found it boring or difficult. Maybe he chose to let his wife, as he had let his mother, handle family business, rather than go home and do it himself. Maybe he was illiterate; that would not have been surprising of a man of his social position in the fifteenth century; there were still those who considered writing too menial a skill to be appropriate for gentlemen. According to Christopher Hibbert, "among the upper classes there was a common feeling that learning was for clerks and not for noblemen,… an opinion violently expressed at a dinner party," where a certain gentleman, "roused with sudden anger," shouted, "I swear by God's body I'd rather my sons should hang than study letters. For it becomes the sons of gentlemen to blow the horn nicely, to hunt skillfully and elegantly carry and train a hawk. But the study of letters should be left to the sons of rustics!"[109]

To conclude on this evidence alone — that because Sir Thomas's mother Philippa arranged her daughter's wedding, held some land to which she had jointure rights as John Malory's widow, and acted as

[109] Christopher Hibbert, *The English: A Social History 1066–1945* (New York and London: Norton, 1987), 120–121.

executor to her husband's will in the 1430s—that her son could not have been old enough to handle family business for her, and therefore was young enough to write the *Morte* in the late 1460s, is thin. And, of course, there is the always-present tacit understanding, evidenced by the determined attempts to deny Malory's age, that critics know Matthews was right when he said that the mid-seventies is no age at all to be writing *Le Morte Darthur* (*Inquiry*, 73).

There is another telling point. The first public record of Sir Thomas Malory of Newbold Revel appears on May 23 of 1439, when he is seen witnessing a land settlement. Malory's old captain of the Calais action in 1414, Richard Beauchamp, died in Normandy on April 30, 1439, and three weeks later we find Malory in England for the first time, witnessing a transaction. It looks as though Malory was, after all, the valiant soldier that the people who knew him claimed on his gravestone. The records dovetail perfectly; he served for twenty-five years under the gallant Beauchamp, and then, when Beauchamp died, Malory came home. If that is true, of course Sir Thomas was not a child in the 1430s, but a man away on his own adventures. P.J.C. Field knows all this; he acknowledges that "the gap in the records until 1439 could be plausibly explained by Malory's having taken part in the wars in France under Richard Beauchamp, who died in 1439" (55). Nevertheless, he insists that Malory's first recorded legal action, in 1439, shows not that he had been away in France but that he had recently come of age and begun his adult life. Our scholar compares two competing sources of evidence concerning the whereabouts of Thomas Malory before 1439: the English public records, which show nothing at all about Sir Thomas Malory, just a completely blank space; and Dugdale's history of Warwickshire, which gives us a brief coherent biography. Then he awards the citation for best evidence to the blank space.

Field guesses that Malory was in his early fifties when he died in 1470, and he asserts that "this is entirely consistent with both the literary and the historical record" (64). By "historical" he means the silent public record; he chooses to deny the historical record contributed by the historian of Warwickshire, Sir William Dugdale. In spite of all this spinning of evidence, it is truly surprising how many fans of the Warwickshire candidate for author assume it has been proven that Sir Thomas Malory of Newbold Revel did not go soldiering with Beauchamp as Dugdale says, because he was too young, possibly not even born yet, and therefore he was not too old to write the *Morte* in the 1460s. It appears that those people either have not read the argument or have given it only a quick once-over, so they do not realize how flimsy the attempt to discredit Dugdale really is.

18

MYSTERIOUS *MILITES*

"THES BE THE namys of dewkes, erlys, barons, and knytes beying with owre soveryn lord Kyng Edward in his jorney in to Scotland at the fest of Seynt Andrew in the month of December, Anno Domini 1462."[110] Thus begins the next old document, first noticed by a Mr. T. Williams who reported it in a letter to the *Athenaeum* in July 1896. The document names a Thomas Malory in a list of knights who rode with Edward IV to the far north in the winter of 1462, to besiege and regain from the Lancastrians three castles — Bamburgh, Alnwick, and Dunstanburgh — along the Scottish border. This list has caused a long-standing brouhaha among the scholars because, although it mentions a Thomas Malory and does not specify to which Thomas Malory it refers, it may hint at the identity of the author of the *Morte*. Both William Matthews, the advocate of the Yorkshireman Thomas Malory as author of *Le Morte*, and P.J.C. Field, who supports the Warwickshire man, have closely studied the document and given us their conclusions, but both of them failed to notice a certain highly significant feature of the names on the list.

Of course, we would expect the two scholars' conclusions to differ, since they back different candidates for author, but it is also interesting

[110] James Gairdner, ed., *Three Fifteenth-Century Chronicles with Historical Memoranda by John Stowe, the Antiquary, and Contemporary Notes of Occurrences Written by Him in the Reign of Queen Elizabeth* (Westminster: J.B. Nichols and Sons, 1845, 1880), preface, xviii; 157–158. London: Forgotten Books, 2013, https://www.forgottenbooks.com/fr/books/ThreeFifteenthCenturyChronicles_10315053. Further citations of this work will be in parentheses in the text.

to observe the differing approaches to the argument taken by the two of them. William Matthews provides the context of the list, alphabetizes the names of knights, and attempts to attach additional information to each name (Matthews, 171–174). He offers a few ancillary observations, gleaned from his study of the document, which support his conclusion that the Thomas Malory listed was a northerner: the date of the list at a time when the king was in Yorkshire recruiting; its "intimate knowledge of northern affairs"; the northern provenance of the list, at Ely; northern spellings and names; kinship of several men listed with the Malorys of Yorkshire; preponderance of northerners on the list; and so forth (Matthews, 127–130). Matthews concludes, "One thing taken with another, it is likely that the man in the list was Thomas Malory of Studley and Hutton [Yorkshire]" (Matthews, 130).

Professor Field simply states, without offering any supporting evidence, that number 43 on the list is "Sir Thomas Malory of Newbold Revel, Warwicks., Yorkist, d. 1471" (Field, 200).

In dealing with other names on the list, Field also uses some surprising techniques. He states that he has failed to find twenty-three of the fifty-nine men on the list in any public records. He proposes that the list is a fraud. And he changes the list.

He changes John Gryffon to John Griffith.
He changes Thomas Nocston to Thomas Kingston.
He changes John Apylton to Roger Appleton.
He changes Pers Glyfton to Robert Clifton.
He changes Roger Coneres to Robert Conyers.
He changes Peers of Grethorne to Ralph Crathorne.
He changes Roger Danby to Robert Danby.
He changes George St. George to William St. George.

Field then attaches an identifier to each name on the list, thus giving us what looks like a complete listing of identities. However, because he tells us that twenty-three of the knights are "entirely unrecorded" (28) and does not give us a list of those that are unrecorded, or explain why he has changed some of the names, other than saying that in some cases he finds a new name "preferable" (Field, 197–198), we can only wonder. Field tags only one, Piers Padolyse, as unidentifiable.

However, there is good reason to trust that the names are accurate as listed. James Gairdner, who edited the list of Edward's men, pointed out that such phrases as "Thes tythinges hath my lord of lyncolne," and "The king is holding Christmas at Durham" show that the information was obtained orally (Gairdner, preface, xviii). That very oral transmission is a key element in our study of this document. In fact, it is hard to imagine how the information could have been obtained otherwise than orally, on the march to battle or on the battlefield, presumably by a chronicler hurrying along with the troops, possibly standing or squatting beside each one in turn, writing down names as the men prepared their bivouac for the night. There are things in the document that convey the breathlessness of the situation: the spelling is erratic; some of the names are given the title *Sir*, while others omit it; the document itself is jumbled together with others of its kind, not in any obvious order, somewhat like notes intended to be edited and transcribed later. Immediately before the list of warriors who accompanied King Edward to Northumberland, for example, is an account, dated 1464, of the Battle of Hedgeley Moor, which did not take place until two years after Edward's foray into the north. That account was obviously hot off the press, except that there was no press, and the chronicler included wrong information about who was killed in the day's work: "An ther is slayn the lord Hungyrford, Sir Raf Percy, Sir Raf Gray, the Duk of Somershed, the lord Roos takyn and Taylboos the erl of Kym and many odyr gentylys and comons slayn on that party" (Gairdner, 156). The news apparently came in by rumor, and the reporter wrote it down, but the rumor was false and the report was wrong; Hungerford, Percy, Grey, Somerset, Ros, and Tailboys actually survived the battle that day. And then, a sure sign of oral transmission of information, the chronicler concluded his report by saying, "How many be slayn on Kyng Edwardes party is not spoke of as yt" (MS Lambeth Palace, 448, fol. 146r; Gairdner, 156). However, the report has value, in spite of its errors, in its immediacy. Gairdner says that it is an "exceedingly rough and careless, but still contemporary, register of current events." Concerning the account we are considering of King Edward's ride into the north to retake the three castles, he notes that "the sieges in Northumberland in 1462 are described in the present tense, as if they were still going on, and the account of them is concluded by the statement, 'Rex tenet Natale suum apud Dorham' the King *is keeping* his Christmas at Durham. Even the errors as to matters of fact in some cases are such as could only have been made at the time" (Gairdner, preface, xviii).

This obviously oral transmission of information is integral to our list of soldiers, and it has much significance in any serious study of the list. It means that the names as listed are *correct,* because they were undoubtedly given to the reporter by the men themselves. Every man knows his own name. Thomas Kingston will not say his name is Thomas Nocston, nor will John Griffith call himself John Gryffon. A man named Roger Appleton will not give his name as John Apylton; nor will Robert Clifton say his name is Piers Glyfton; Robert Conyers will not name himself Roger Conyers; Ralph Crathorne will not say he is called Piers of Grethorne; Robert Danby will not say he is Roger Danby; and William St. George will not give his name as George St. George. There may be a suggestion of a claim that the chronicler could have misheard in some cases; possibly he thought both of the men called "Roger" said "Robert" when asked their names. But there is no chance that he thought one Piers was actually Robert and the other Piers was Ralph, and certainly no chance that, when George said his name was George, the reporter thought he said William. Therefore, there is no justification from a claim of error for changing these names.

Field says that the names are wrong, and that if they are not mistakes, then they are lies (Field, 27–29). But we know, of course, that names on a list cannot be judged right or wrong except as they serve or fail to serve some predetermined purpose. His predetermined purpose is to prove that the Thomas Malory listed among the knights riding with King Edward is the man from Newbold Revel, the only man of that name, as he believes, who was a knight, and thus the author of *Le Morte Darthur*. The names on this list frustrate him because they do not support that assumption. Sometimes, when Field changes a man's name, he does so with no explanation. Sometimes, on the other hand, he explains the change by saying that he finds the new name "preferable." It may be that the new name is preferable to his argument that Sir Thomas Malory of Newbold Revel wrote *Le Morte*.

At any rate, we are not surprised when we see that Field's conclusions differ from those of Matthews, who was, the reader will remember, looking for evidence to support his own candidate from Yorkshire. Matthews, after supplying what additional information he can for each knight on the list, concludes that "one came from each of these counties: Northumberland, Warwick, Gloucester, Leicester, Derby, Cambridge, Oxford, Northampton, Berkshire, and Staffordshire. Two came from Nottingham, Kent, Essex, Lancashire, and Westmoreland. Eight came from Cumberland. And sixteen came from Yorkshire, most of them from the North Riding. In short, two-thirds of the soldiers who can be identified were northerners, and half of them were Yorkshiremen" (Matthews, 129).

Field says that Matthews failed to look beyond the north for evidence (Field, 196), an assertion belied by Matthews's assigning so many knights to counties not in the north, and he claims that this failure resulted in a distortion of the list in favor of northerners. After disputing the presence of many of the men listed, after repeated accusations of either ignorance or fraud on the part of the compiler (Field, 27–29, 196), after an elaborate mathematical study of the list — that is, the list he himself has produced by changing names at will (Field, 201–202) — he concludes that "of the 54 possibly present [remember that he believes that the list is full of lies], 22 were from the 6 northern counties, 11 of them from Yorkshire: 40.1% and 20.0% respectively" (Field, 202).

Thus do the two scholars see the same document.

But it is easy to see that out of the seventeen counties that according to Matthews contributed knights to the list, if 40.1 percent of those knights were from the northern counties, as Professor Field reckons, then there is a heavy preponderance of northerners in the list. If Professor Matthews, who did not change the list but examined it as he found it, is right in saying that two-thirds were from the north, then there is an even heavier preponderance of northerners in the list. However, both William Matthews and P.J.C. Field fail to mention something that is of key importance in identifying the Thomas Malory listed and thus the author of the *Morte,* although Field comes closer, when he states that twenty-three of the knights listed are absolutely missing from public records.

It is time to look at the contingent of knights who have not been considered up until now but who were almost certainly present at Edward's siege of the northern castles — the Knights of St. John, the Hospitallers. England had no standing army in those days; the recruitment of fighting men was directed toward each particular battle as it was being planned, and the call for men went out from the king to his lords, directing them to gather what forces they could and present them ready and equipped to fight for their sovereign. The process would be repeated any time the king needed an armed force; that force would disband when the battle was over. The closest thing to an exception was the order of fighting religious, the Hospitallers. Both monks and warriors, they lived together in their various communal houses, which they called commanderies, caring for the sick and poor, living according to their monastic rule and the vows they had taken — and standing by, prepared for war. It is simply not believable that Edward IV would not have needed and expected these men to aid him in his siege. He had sent out a call for men from sixteen to sixty, and that call was meant to be obeyed. He would have required the fighting service of the Hospitallers in England. Make no mistake: these were trained and experienced warriors, and they had weapons, and they had horses. Each one of them, upon his admission to the order, had been required to bring his own horses and to spend years — five years on average — fighting the infidel in the Holy Land, before he was assigned to a commandery in his homeland, where he would be always standing by, ready for the next call to battle. Simon Phillips makes the point that "the reason for the initial five-year service on Rhodes was military training"; he also tells us that there were 113 brethren in the English priory in 1338.[111] The number probably would have changed somewhat by 1462, but whether increased or decreased we do not know. They were few, but they were renowned fighters—like the U.S. Marines, a few good men. Gregory O'Malley, discussing the slacking off of English participation in Crusades to the East in the later Middle Ages, says that "crusading energies were increasingly directed elsewhere, into royal service. From the thirteenth century onwards, but particularly during the Hundred Years War and later, kings claimed an enhanced authority over their leading subjects, forcing them to advantage patriotic over confessional military activity. Although lesser lights made their way to the east in small numbers well into the fifteenth century, magnates and knights were more or less compelled to organize their crusading activities during lulls in the fighting [at home]" (O'Malley, 89). Even so, the great service of Prior Robert Botyl (who was prior during the siege of the three northern castles) to Edward's struggle to take the throne was recognized as particularly useful; O'Malley calls it "without parallel among his predecessors" (O'Malley, 126). Although the Order of Hospitallers had been begun solely to nurse pilgrims in the Holy Land, after its mission was officially changed to include fighting in defense of the holy places, the knights began gradually to involve themselves with worldly enterprises. In compromise after compromise of the order's injunction to stay out of wars between princes, eventually the Knights Hospitallers began to fight even in civil wars when called upon by their secular rulers. O'Malley: "By the late thirteenth century regular military service was expected of the order's brethren in Ireland, similar requirements being occasionally imposed on English and Scottish Hospitallers in the fourteenth, fifteenth, and sixteenth centuries" (O'Malley, 17). He continues to make the point: "Monarchs clearly expected the order to actively pursue its

[111] Simon Phillips, "Walking a Thin Line: Hospitaller Priors, Politics, and Power in Late Medieval England," in *The Military Orders*, vol. 5: *Politics and Power*, ed. Peter W. Edbury (Hampshire, England, and Burlington, VT: Ashgate, 2009), 6. Further citations of this work will be in parentheses in the text.

defence of Christendom.... Lay persons ... had a similarly high regard for its military worth and took a similarly utilitarian view of its activities, evidently seeing the defense of Christendom and of the realm as comparably worthy objectives" (335). We know that both of the two English priors who governed the Hospitallers during the time that interests us led their contingent in the Wars of the Roses. Prior Botyl marched for Edward in the assault of London in 1461; and Botyl's successor, Prior John Langstrother, was beheaded by Edward at Tewkesbury in 1471 for taking up arms against him in support of Henry VI.

Just as it is not believable that Edward would not have required the military service of the Hospitallers, so it is not believable that they would have refused his call to arms. For one thing, the question of political allegiance would not arise in the case of the religious warriors. It is not necessary to ask whether each of them was a Yorkist or a Lancastrian. Their allegiance was to their order. In 1118, the second master of the Order of Hospitallers, Raymond du Puy, laying out the form for the ceremony of vows to be made by each new knight, commanded that the person appointed to perform the ceremony "shall point out the engagement he will have to enter into of perfect obedience; the severity of the rules, which will no longer permit him to act for himself, but, on the contrary, oblige him absolutely to renounce his own will and pleasure, and implicitly to comply with that of his superiors" (Porter, vol. 1, 33). The admission ceremony would not go forward until the candidate for knighthood in the order gave his assent. Hospitallers were vowed, each one of them, to obey, in every situation, their superiors in the order. And in 1462, the prior of England was Robert Botyl, who was by now a "noted Yorkist,"[112] although he had for a long time supported Henry VI.

True, when the Order of Hospitallers, which dates to the late eleventh century, was begun, it was formed strictly to care for the sick

[112] John A. Wagner, *Encyclopedia of the Wars of the Roses* (Santa Barbara, CA: ABC-CLIO, 2001), 144. Further citations of this work will be in parentheses in the text.

and injured in the Holy Land, particularly for those on Crusade or on pilgrimage. However, after the First Crusade, it was not very long before the mission of the order was expanded. Under Raymond du Puy, the knights were enjoined actually to take up arms against the Mohammedan and all enemies of Christianity. In time, the princes of Christendom began gradually to take advantage of whatever opportunity presented itself to make use of these monastic warriors. Helen Nicholson says that "from the first, the brothers of the military orders had been expected to serve the kings of the country in which they were based. This could involve acting as ambassadors, lending money, or holding offices close to the king, for example porters, chamberlains or almoners. They also came under pressure to commit their military resources to European Christian monarchs in their wars against each other" (Nicholson, 1128–1291). Simon Phillips agrees; he points out that the prior of the Hospital in England had the duty of not only diplomatic and governmental service but also military service to the crown (Phillips, 56).

We have seen that one acknowledged characteristic of the Order of St. John, Hospitallers, was that there were a certain few families that apparently had a particular loyalty toward the order, supporting it disproportionately, not only with their prayers but also with their money, with donations of their land and other property, and with their sons. This connection lasted with some of the "Hospitaller families" for generations, and even sometimes for centuries. Several scholars have commented upon it, including Gregory O'Malley, Simon Phillips, P. J. C. Field, and Helen Nicholson. O'Malley tells us:

> Incidental references in the order's internal documents, heralds' visitations, and family pedigrees prove a large number of family relationships between members of the order and hint at many more. Among at least 185 knight-brethren active in the priory of England between 1460 and 1559 no less than seventy-nine shared a surname with one or other of their fellows, while a fair proportion of others came from families that had

> provided the Hospital with brethren in the relatively recent past, such as the Malorys, Multons, and Wests. Additionally, several more knights appear to have been related to a sister or professed chaplain of the order and close ties of kinship existed between a number of "Hospitaller families." When the order's chief tenants and officers are thrown into the equation sympathy for Field's statement that "the late medieval English Hospitallers always arouse suspicions of nepotism" threatens to become overwhelming. (O'Malley, 33)

Notice the name *Malory* in O'Malley's list of known Hospitaller families.

And we have seen that the list of *milites* who accompanied King Edward in 1462 shows that there was a preponderance of northerners among English Knights Hospitaller. Again, Gregory O'Malley:

> What is immediately striking about these [Hospitaller] families is their geographical origin. Of the forty-seven ... English family seats listed for knight-brethren in Appendix VII, twelve were in Yorkshire or Lincolnshire, with a further six in Durham, Cumberland, or Westmorland. If one considers the almost certainly Yorkshire origins of the Tonges and Multons, the domination of northerners and north-east midlanders in the order's hierarchy is apparent. Moreover, several of those families which appear to be from the south such as the Rawsons and the southern branches of the Docwras and Westons had migrated from Yorkshire or Lincolnshire only one or two generations before they produced knights of St. John. (O'Malley, 38)

All of this has great relevance to the study of the list of knights accompanying Edward in 1462. In his study of the list, P. J. C. Field makes a telling point when, after placing as many of the knights as he can with any degree of confidence, he says: "The remaining 23 cases present the main problem by their sheer number; it is incredible that there should be so many, entirely unrecorded knights in late-fifteenth-century England" (Field, 28). This failure to find so many of the men may be the reason that Field suspected fraud and simply changed the list. But it is not incredible at all, in fact it is not even surprising, to find so many unrecorded knights if those knights were Knights Hospitallers. First of all, as Simon Phillips reminds us, the English Hospitaller archives are no longer extant (Phillips, 18) — they fell victim to Henry VIII when he dissolved the monasteries of England. As for the Hospitallers' absence from public records, these men chose not to be in the public records when they chose not to marry, not to beget children, not to inherit or otherwise acquire property, not to sell, not to pay taxes — in short, not to live an ordinary public life. By their vow of celibacy, they eschewed any mention of themselves in marriage records, baptism records of children, or provision for wives or offspring. By their vow of poverty, they took an oath not to own anything privately and agreed that anything they held at the time of their death would revert to the order automatically, so they made no wills. They were specifically forbidden, in the strongest terms, to make wills; the rule of Raymond du Puy, written circa 1118, and recapitulated in 1300 by Pope Boniface, read, "And if any brother shall have made a disposition of his property after his death, and shall have concealed it from his superior, and it shall afterwards have been found upon him, let the money be tied round his neck, and let him be severely beaten by one of the brothers in the presence of the rest, and let him do penance for forty days, fasting every fourth and sixth day on bread and water" (Porter, 496). And by their vow of obedience, the knights removed themselves from individual participation in public life — and consequently from ordinary commerce, contests in the law, and virtually anything else that would result in a public record that scholars could examine today. Moreover, besides their formal vows of poverty, chastity, and obedience, the Knights Hospitaller had a policy of humble self-effacement, of eschewing personal notice. The knight was expected to look as much as possible like all other knights, not to put himself forward. This policy was served by restrictions concerning adornment of clothing, horse harness, heraldry, and the like. The individual knight became so much simply one of the brethren that many of them were even missing from their family pedigrees. O'Malley makes the point that "the exact nature of the family relationships between members of the order is often unclear. Being celibate and ideally leaving no offspring, professed Hospitallers seem frequently to have been omitted from the family pedigrees given to Heralds" (O'Malley, 33). Thomas Malory of Studley and Hutton, similarly, was not omitted from his family pedigrees, but there seems to have been some difficulty in remembering where he fitted in among his parents' children; he is variously reported as being the first son, the third, the fourth, and the sixth.

All of this may have the reader mentally protesting that surely there were great names in the order, men of substance and even secular power and fame. And that is true, but they were relatively few. By and large, the knights' policy of low-key, humble service worked well; we have very few public records of their lives. Moreover, at the time of the dissolution of the monasteries, the Hospital suffered the same rough treatment as other monastic orders, and most of its internal records were confiscated and destroyed. It is not surprising that Professor Field failed to find any records concerning certain knights in the public archives of England, if they were Hospitaller knights. That failure is no evidence that they did not exist, or that they were not there fighting alongside Edward IV in his siege of the northern castles in 1462. Their identity as Hospitallers is, in fact, an obvious explanation of why, as Field says, "there should be so many, entirely unrecorded knights" (Field, 28).

And we have solid evidence that the Hospitallers were there, not only in common sense; not only in the facts that Edward called for all able-bodied men from sixteen to sixty and these men were renowned warriors always prepared for war; not only in the preponderance of northerners both in the list of knights in the siege and in the membership of the Hospital; not only in the facts that they had vowed obedience to their prior — and their prior in 1462 was the Yorkist Robert Botyl who had already fought in one siege for King Edward, the siege of London in the previous year — but also in another interesting fact. A substantial number — thirteen out of the fifty-nine knights, or 22 percent — shared a last name with at least one, and some with more than one, knight of St. John of Jerusalem — in other words, these thirteen belonged to recognized Hospitaller families. Here are their names and connections, followed by the sources of this information:

John Acheton and Thomas Acheton share a surname with Hospitaller Knights Edmund Asheton (Porter, 298; O'Malley 239, 240) and Nicholas de Assheton (Broun, 57).

John Boteler shares a surname with Hospitaller Knights Thomas Bouteler (Porter, 297) and James Butler (O'Malley, 97).

Thomas Malory shares a surname with Hospitaller Knights Robert Malory (Porter and O'Malley on various pages; Robert Malory was prior of England and therefore his name is mentioned frequently), John Malory Knight (O'Malley, 352), and John Malory Hospitaller Serving Brother (Field, 77).

William Bothe shares a surname with Hospitaller Knights John Bothe (O'Malley, 37) and John Bouth (Porter, 290).

Ralph Grey shares a surname with Hospitaller Knights Henry Grey (O'Malley, 243) and Bryan Grey (Porter, 288, 293).

Christopher of Carowen shares the family name Curwen, which is discussed at length as a Hospitaller family by O'Malley, 36, n. 80.

Roger Danby shares a surname with Hospitaller Knight Robert Danby (O'Malley, 296).

Thomas Feryr shares a surname with Hospitaller Knight William Ferrers (Broun, 52); moreover, a William Ferrers, Earl of Ferrers, granted land to the order in the twelfth century (Porter, 311).

Thomas Garard shares a surname with the founding Hospitaller knight, Peter Gerard, and Hospitaller Knights Gerard of Sidon (Porter, vol. 2, 516) and Henry Garard (O'Malley, 302)

Robert Harcourte shares the surname of the Harcourts, who are on the British Library list of sculptured arms of families serving as Knights Hospitaller on Rhodes.

John Howard shares the name of the Howard family, which is discussed as a Hospitaller family by O'Malley, 97, n. 58.

John Stanley shares a name with Hospitaller Knight John Stanley (O'Malley, 172) and a surname with Hospitaller Knight Edward Stanley (Porter, 117).

Moreover, of course, not every cousin or uncle or nephew or even half-brother shares one's surname; all of us have relatives with names other than our own. O'Malley, continuing his remarks on the difficulty of placing any knight of the Hospital in his own family with any certainty, notes that when Hospitallers do appear in family pedigrees, "the evidence is sometimes in conflict with the order's internal documents, in which *nepos* appears to have been used to denote any younger relative" (O'Malley, 34), presumably, we suppose, because of the difficulty in untangling the thread of kinship. The matter is complicated by the fact that several acknowledged Hospitaller families are closely related to others. The Westons, for example, produced at least four Hospitallers in the fifteenth century — Thomas, John, William Senior and William Junior. "Additionally," O'Malley continues, "the family was related to at least three other Hospitaller families," and he lists Dawney, Dalison, and Green, "which produced six or seven Hospitallers between them after 1450, and through them to the Docwras. Moreover, in 1475 William Weston senior was described by the order's chancery as the 'germanus' of John Botill . . . and thus was also presumably a relative of Robert Botill, the prior of England between 1440 and 1468. Finally, the son of William Weston junior's sister . . . became a brother knight in 1526" (O'Malley, 35). Thomas Malory of Yorkshire himself, as well as being a member of the recognized Hospitaller family Malory, was close kin to the Plumptons. His grandmother was Joan Plumpton, meaning that Plumptons of his own generation were his first cousins; the Hospitaller knight Thomas Plumpton of Yorkshire was granted the commandery of Carbrooke in May of 1481 (O'Malley, appendix, vii). Our Malorys were related as well to the Conyers family, which is also represented in our list of *milites*. Given the known tight web of kinship among the Hospitaller families, and the fact that the Malorys were part of that web, it may be that the Conyers, who were kin to the Malorys, have sons on this list because those sons also were part of the contingent of Hospitallers among King Edward's troops. And, of course, Sir Thomas Malory rode with them; his name is right there on the list.

It well may be that some or all of the names that were changed by Professor Field, because of his frustration, were not recorded anywhere else, not because the compiler of the list was lying but because those men were Hospitallers, listed by their real names. Maybe George St. George, for example, was actually not William St. George, as Field claims, but William's brother or cousin or uncle George. There is a *caveat*, of course: We cannot deduce that all of those whose names were changed by Professor Field were Knights Hospitallers; nor can we make a blanket pronouncement that all the knights on the list who were related to Hospitallers were themselves members of the order. Additionally, the researcher must deal with the obvious fact that families used the same first name again and again,[113] so it is hard sometimes to figure out which Ralph or John or

[113] A possible example of this practice may have been one of the names that caught the attention of Professor Field (28). The name Ralph Grey appears on the list of those accompanying King Edward on his journey north to besiege the northern castles, at the same time that Ralph Grey was defending

Robert is under consideration. But we can infer from all this new evidence that the men whose names Professor Field could not identify, and those who are linked by their surnames with recognized Hospitaller families, are likely to have been Hospitallers themselves. This list turns out to be strong circumstantial evidence that the Knights Hospitaller rode north with King Edward in 1462, and that Thomas Malory was one of them.

Bamburgh Castle. Field, mindful that the same man cannot attack and defend the same castle at the same time, accused the compiler of the list of obvious fraud. But it was a common practice for a family to use the same Christian name for more than one family member. Moreover, as mentioned above, Ralph Grey shares a surname with two other members of an acknowledged Hospitaller family.

19

The Kevin Bacon Connection

THERE HAS BEEN no satisfaction for scholars in looking for Malory of Newbold Revel in the Marshalsea, Ludgate, Tower, and Newgate prisons in 1469–1470, when *Le Morte* was finished, where he was apt to be found a decade or two earlier; there is no record of any incarceration after the pardon naming him in 1461. Consequently, much of the literary world has come to hold that he must have been a prisoner of war or a political prisoner. This idea has proved satisfactory because it solves the book problem. If we posit that Thomas Malory was held not in a jail for criminals but instead in a castle home, or possibly a monastery, there he could have been given access to the owner's collection of books. So far, so good. However, the proponents of this view, in arguing that Sir Thomas Malory of Newbold Revel wrote *Le Morte,* seem not to have noticed that in claiming house arrest for the author in some reasonably comfortable place well supplied with books, *they render completely irrelevant the undeniable fact that Thomas Malory of Newbold Revel went to prison on criminal charges, again and again, throughout the 1440s and '50s. That* imprisonment does not in any way increase the probability that he was a political prisoner later, above the probability that anyone else in the general population was such a prisoner. Logically, in the discussion of authorship, this man has lost any edge that he may have had for being a known jailbird. *Any* man called Thomas Malory, designated a knight, could have been imprisoned for political reasons, while the *Morte* was being written, and thereby have a claim on the authorship equal to that of Thomas Malory of Newbold Revel.

There is, however, one Thomas Malory who has a stronger statistical probability than the population in general of having been imprisoned for political reasons at that time. That is the Thomas Malory whose name appears on a general pardon issued by King Edward in 1468, specifying that he is excepted from the pardon. Because Malory's name is one of several listed on this document as excepted from the pardon, and others are known to have been Lancastrians who supported Henry VI in opposition to Edward, this Malory is assumed to have been a Lancastrian rebel also. Therefore, one task to be done in the search for our author is to determine which Thomas Malory is the one named on the list of unpardonables, and therefore more likely to have been imprisoned during the late 1460s.

This 1468 decree of general pardon, with its list of exceptions, was reissued several times. Pardons and exceptions from pardon proliferated in the time of Edward IV, but this is the one that interests us because it establishes the connection between Sir Thomas Malory and Sir Humphrey Neville of Yorkshire. Scholars assume that the crime considered unpardonable by Edward was simply the crime of taking up the Lancastrian cause against him, most of those listed, including Humphrey Neville, having been known to be strongly Lancastrian. If Malory of Newbold Revel, Warwickshire, served as a young soldier in 1415, and therefore was too old in 1469 to write *Le Morte*, it is all the less likely that he is the man listed as exempt from the pardon, and not only because of his age at the time. Sir Thomas of Newbold Revel was apparently a lifelong Yorkist, and therefore some additional difficulties arise in claiming that the Malory on this list of Lancastrian unpardonables is the Newbold Revel Malory. In 1468, this Sir Thomas was somewhere between seventy and eighty years old, an age when it seems unlikely in the extreme that a man would change his lifelong political allegiance. Additionally, claiming that he is one of those unpardonables suggests strongly that this elderly turncoat then may have traveled to the cold and harsh far north to cause trouble, unpardonable trouble, alongside the group of Lancastrian troublemakers also listed, and the trouble was against Edward, previously this Malory's man, but now betrayed by Malory. It matters which Thomas Malory is one of the listed unpardonables, because that man is clearly designated a knight in the document. In fact, P.J.C. Field concludes that "the Sir Thomas Malory who was exempted from pardon must have been the author of the *Morte*. No other conclusion is possible" (Field, 33). He thinks no other conclusion is possible because he always assumes that any mention of a knight called Thomas Malory must necessarily refer to Malory of Newbold Revel, who is, in Field's opinion, the only knight available, and therefore he is the author of the *Morte*. There is no unanimous consent to Field's conclusion, however; we can agree that the knight on the list wrote the *Morte* without necessarily believing that he was the man of Newbold Revel, for it is not proven that that man was the only knight. Remember, the strongest evidence so far offered that he was, is that the other contender, Thomas Malory of Studley and Hutton in Yorkshire, was omitted from his parents' will (see preface; see also Field, 4–20).

The particular nature of the unpardonable offenses against Edward IV is not specified, but both Field and Matthews have supposed that each of those listed was involved with one of these two causes:

> first, the then-current "treasonous conspiracy" in London;
> and
> second, the guerilla activities of Lancastrians in Northumberland.

The conspiracy was this: from her exile in France, Queen Margaret, wife of the anointed and crowned but subsequently deposed king Henry VI, and mother of his son, in her long effort to get her husband reinstated as king and her child recognized as heir to the throne, had sent letters to various people in London, trying to recruit their help in her cause. The letters were discovered in the possession of a certain John Cornelius who, under torture, confessed and accused others. They were charged with "being in treasonable correspondence with

Queen Margaret" (Matthews, 132). This "London conspiracy" is sometimes called the Cornelius plot.

There is no mention of a Malory in the government documents detailing the London conspiracy, and that fact can be taken as some evidence that the Malory listed was associated with the northern guerillas rather than the Londoners. Matthews points out that of the four men on the list who are labeled "lately of London," three are known to have been involved in the "London conspiracy," which took place in the summer of 1468, and others on the list are not known to have been associated with it. Matthews, arguing that the Thomas Malory mentioned as excluded from pardon is not the Warwickshire man but the Yorkshire Malory, simply presents us with the list of those not pardoned and asks us to consider the obviously deliberate pattern in which they are listed; he points out that the names are kept in this very order in all copies, except that the royal family is omitted from one extant copy.

Here is the list of those excepted from pardon. Without stating any of their offenses, it simply gives their names. I have added blank lines to help the reader understand the argument of William Matthews concerning the list as a whole, but I have made no other changes.

Humphrey Neville, knight
Thomas Malarie, knight

Robert Marchal, late of Culneham, Oxon, armiger

Hugh Mulle, late of London, gentleman
Gervase Clyfton, late of London, knight
William Verdon, late of London, scrivener
Peter House, late of London, esquire

Morgan ap Thomas ap Gruffuth of Carmathen, gentleman
Henry ap Thomas ap Gruffuth ap Nicholas, late of Carmathen, armiger

Maurice ap Owen ap Gruffuth, late of Carmathen, gentleman

Thomas Phillips, late of Rea, Gloucestershire, yeoman

Henry VI
Margaret his wife
Edward his son
those with them beyond the realm

the rebels keeping the castle or town of Harlech in North Wales

Matthews simply points out that the ordering of the names suggests that the two knights, Humphrey Neville and Thomas Malarie, are a group to themselves, and "this suggestion is negatively reinforced by the fact that none of the several other records of the London troubles, the Welsh revolts, and the Lancastrian court-in-exile mentions either Sir Humphrey Neville or Sir Thomas Malory" (Matthews, 132–133).

However, I notice something additional about the ordering of these names. They are organized geographically, gathered according to residence. It is easy for anyone, at a glance, to see certain deliberate groupings here: two knights, whose residence is not given; then one armiger of Culneham, Oxon; then four men lately of London; then three Welshmen lately of Carmathen; then one yeoman from Gloucester; then the royal family and their retinue "beyond the realm" (in fact, they were living in France); and finally, unnamed, the rebels holding Harlech in North Wales. This obviously deliberate arrangement requires no figuring out; anybody can see it. The plan is to group together those who lived in the same place. Humphrey Neville and Thomas Malory, the two knights, make a distinct, conjoined unit. The pattern of the rest of the names, grouped according to their last known residence, strongly suggests that the two knights as well are grouped that way, and in fact it is known to history that Neville was a Yorkshireman and that there was also a Yorkshireman named Thomas Malory. The overall pattern of the document shows us that the chronicler intended to designate, alongside Humphrey Neville, the other Yorkshireman Thomas Malory. Neville, the son of Richard Neville of Slingsby, was born at Slingsby Manor, while Thomas Malory was born at Hutton Conyers. They are divided from the four men of London, from the three Welshmen of Carmathen, from the armiger from Culneham, from the yeoman from Gloucester, from the royal family beyond the realm in France, and from the rebels in Harlech. The Thomas Malory of Warwickshire does not fit this pattern but the one from Yorkshire does, and that is good evidence that the Thomas Malory of Yorkshire is the man to whom the chronicler refers, the one he groups with the Yorkshireman Humphrey Neville.

It would take a pretty violent wrenching to detach the knight Thomas Malory of Yorkshire from company with the other knight Humphrey Neville of Yorkshire and put him into the London group. However, P. J. C. Field tries it, because it is so important to his efforts on behalf of the Warwickshire candidate that he should be the man on this list, since the Thomas Malory listed is clearly designated a knight, and Field's whole argument in favor of him is based on the insistence that the author of *Le Morte* was the only knight of that name in England at the right time.

However, the Newbold Revel Malory was a faithful Yorkist supporter of Edward IV. In 1468, he was an old man in his seventies. How could he ally himself in some unpardonable way against his king at this late moment of his own life and of the king's struggle to keep his power? And how could he, at age seventy-five or so, travel to the far north of England, in wintertime, and engage in some sort of guerilla activity with men half his age? Field succumbs to the necessity of accusing his Malory of betraying his king by siding with the Lancastrians, because he has no choice if he is to convince us that the Malory on the list is Malory of Newbold Revel. But he finds a way to spare his candidate the company of young warriors and the necessity of a northern sojourn in the dead of winter. The task that Professor Field sets himself is to try to connect Sir Thomas of Newbold Revel not with the rebels of the north but with the London conspirators, and it is truly a daunting one.

There is in the list as found no evidence of any such connection. Field's technique is to add a few names and then suggest that Malory was connected to the people he has added. Those are the following: the widow of John Hampden, now married to John House; Thomas Danvers of Waterstock, Oxfordshire; Richard Danvers of Prescott, Oxfordshire; John, Lord Wenlock; and Sir John Plummer. Field justifies these additions by telling us that the Hampdens were irreconcilable Lancastrians, and the others named, while they were not on the list of those excepted from the king's mercy, were involved in the conspiracy. Field concludes that, in addition to those designated "late of London" on the list of unpardonables, Marshall and Phillips also were associated with the London plot. He reasons from the locations where all these people, including those whose names he himself has added, lived and were active, and he says that they lived close together; therefore they all must have been involved in the London conspiracy. So that covers everybody except Neville, Malory, the Welshmen from Carmathen, the royal family, and the rebels in Harlech.

Then Field says this (notice that even though he mentions many names here, he never mentions any name actually found on the list of unpardonables except the name Malory):

In Malory's case, geography is unhelpful, but there are other and better clues. Richard Danvers of Prescott had a brother, Sir Robert Danvers of Culworth in Northamptonshire. When Sir Robert died in 1467, his executors were his brother Richard, his sister Agnes, Lady Wenlock, and his son-in-law George Burnaby of Watford, Northamptonshire. George Burnaby's father Eustace Burnaby of Watford (died December 1463) was the husband of Malory's sister Philippa, his partner in his earliest alleged crime in 1443, and one of that first set of feoffees who later transferred Malory's Leicestershire lands to Wolseley and the others. Malory, therefore, had in his nephew a strong link with the Danvers family and Wenlock, who were involved in the Cornelius plot. He had a second link with Wenlock through Warwick.

Surprisingly for someone involved in the Cornelius plot, Wenlock was one of Warwick's closest associates. (Field, 141)

On the next page, after two long paragraphs of speculation on various other topics, not particularly connected with the list of exceptions from pardon, Field gives us his conclusion:

> Since Malory had these connections with the Cornelius plot, and no discoverable ones with anyone else actively disaffected in 1468, we must assume that he was in some way involved in the plot, and that that was why he was excluded from pardon. (Field, 142)

That is all. Field offers nothing more in the way of evidence that Malory was involved in the London conspiracy. If we feel that we must have missed something and need to read it again, we read it again. We still have that feeling.

In plainer English, this is what Field has said:

> Richard Danvers of Prescott was involved in the London conspiracy.
> Richard Danvers was the brother of Robert Danvers.
> Robert Danvers had a daughter.
> The daughter of Robert Danvers was married to George Burnaby.
> George Burnaby was the son of Eustace Burnaby.
> Eustace Burnaby was married to Phillipa Malory.
> Phillipa Malory was Sir Thomas Malory's sister.
> Therefore, Sir Thomas Malory was involved in the London conspiracy.
> That is why Malory was excluded from the king's pardon.

To those who like to play Six Degrees of Kevin Bacon, this argument begins to look like a parlor game. Professor Field does, indeed, connect Malory with Richard Danvers (whose name is not on the list at all; Field himself has added it to his consideration), although not quite in six steps. However, unfortunately for his argument, he apparently does not know the basic premise of the game: anybody can make a six-step connection with Kevin Bacon, in just this kind of chain of acquaintance. In fact, *anybody* can make such a connection with *anybody*. Readers who do the work of deciphering Field's argument by digging his evidence out of this paragraph may not be impressed very much by this chain as a reason why King Edward excluded Thomas Malory from his general pardon.

There are two things to be pointed out in Field's conclusion. After making geographic connections among several men known to have been involved in the London conspiracy, and then claiming that others who lived in the same district must have been similarly involved, he says that "in Malory's case, geography is unhelpful" (Field, 141). Geography is unhelpful to Field in Malory's case because he is focusing on the wrong Malory and the wrong geographic location; in the actual list, geography is the very organizing template, and it puts Sir Thomas Malory firmly outside of London and firmly in the company of the other man from Yorkshire, Humphrey Neville. Field goes on to say, referring to his chain of acquaintance, "Since Malory had these connections with the Cornelius plot, and no discoverable ones with anyone else actively disaffected in 1468, we must assume that he was in some way involved in the plot, and that that was why he was excluded from pardon" (Field, 142). Notice that he is referring to the Thomas Malory of Newbold Revel in Warwickshire—he is always referring to that Sir Thomas unless he specifies otherwise, because he believes so firmly that that one is the only one that counts—and we trust that he is right when he says that that Sir Thomas has no known connection with others on this list. However, there are multiple connections, some of them pointed out by William Matthews, between the Thomas Malory of Yorkshire and Humphrey Neville, also of Yorkshire, whose name is paired with Malory's in the list. They both belonged to a web of kinship and neighborhood and social and political relationships almost impossible to untangle.

Critics have generally accepted without demur Sir Thomas Malory of Newbold Revel as the man named on the 1468 general pardon with its included list of those exempted from pardon, but it appears that they have done so without studying the claims of Thomas Malory of Yorkshire. To the best of my knowledge, the best argument so far offered for Sir Thomas of Newbold Revel is Field's hypothetical chain of acquaintance among certain London Lancastrians who are not named on the list of unpardonables, but who may have known the Newbold Revel Malory. But the case is thin at best, and it ignores the known, not hypothetical, connections between Humphrey Neville and the other candidate for authorship, Thomas Malory of Yorkshire. Probably the reason scholars have ignored that Malory is simply that the exceptions from pardon give Malory the title *Sir,* and Thomas Malory of Yorkshire has not been seen as a knight. However, this book argues that he was a knight and that his claims by right must be considered.

As we see, the argument for Sir Thomas of Newbold Revel is weak; it has nothing to offer except a theoretical acquaintance with some persons who are not listed but who are known to have been Lancastrian traitors to King Edward. So we turn for evidence to those whose names are actually on the list, and to the technique of the compiler in ordering them. The list of those not pardoned is arranged according to residence, and it lists the two knights, Sir Humphrey Neville and Sir Thomas Malory, together; they make a group unto themselves. Our task in discovering who the listed Malory is consists of discovering why the herald put these two men together in a separate unit. What do they have in common?

Neither Humphrey Neville nor Thomas Malory is mentioned in any of the official documents concerned with the London conspiracy; that in itself is some evidence that they were not involved in it. However, we don't need to search very far to find connections between Humphrey Neville and Thomas Malory of Studley and Hutton. In view of the fact that the list is organized by residence, it is greatly significant that both of these men were Yorkshiremen. They were members of a web of kinship and neighborhood and social and political relationships almost impossible to untangle, of which the few connections mentioned here are only a sample. These two may well have known each other since childhood; in fact, it is not too much to say that they probably did. They were country neighbors, members of the same social world; "both owned property in Ripon, and Sir Humphrey's manor and lands at Gillyng were only two miles from the Malory's [*sic*] manor at Helmsley" (Matthews, 136). Their two families shared Lancastrian political views, so even if Sir Thomas were not a monk, vowed to obedience to his prior, there would be no need to accuse this Malory of being a turncoat in riding with the Lancastrians. There are links of kinship as well. Both men had been connected with the DeRos family since the previous century. Malory's great-great grandmother in the paternal line was Lucy DeRos, and there had been two marriages in the fourteenth century between DeRos and Neville: Walter de Fauconberg the younger, son of Isabel DeRos and Walter Fauconberg the elder, had married Anastasia Neville; and William DeRos of Lincolnshire had married Margaret Neville of Raby. Anastasia Neville was Humphrey's great-aunt, the sister of his grandfather, Ralph, the First Earl of Westmorland and Fourth Baron Neville de Raby. Thomas DeRos, Ninth Baron DeRos, was a distant cousin of Thomas Malory and, in another line, distant cousin as well as companion in arms of Humphrey Neville during the 1460s; DeRos was the son of Eleanor Beauchamp, who was half-sister to Anne Neville, Countess of Warwick and a cousin of Humphrey. Thomas Malory and Humphrey Neville would have been aware of these family connections, but in Sir Humphrey's case, the connection with DeRos that was most important was his friendship with his and Malory's common distant cousin Thomas, Ninth Baron DeRos. Humphrey and this DeRos were both in the train of Henry VI and Queen Margaret when the royals fled into Scotland after Towton; and Neville and DeRos were comrades thereafter, going on private raids from Scotland down into northern England, and into pitched battles as well, until DeRos was captured and beheaded in the spring of 1464. This Thomas

DeRos was either the brother or the nephew of Sir Richard Ros the poet, whose kinship and connection with Thomas Malory of Yorkshire is discussed in chapter 10.

Another family connection between Thomas Malory and Humphrey Neville was their common kinship with the Conyers family. Malory's great-great grandmother was Joan Conyers, who married Sir Christopher Malory, thus bringing into the Malory family the manor of Hutton Conyers, where Thomas was born and spent a good part of his childhood (the Malorys resided both at Hutton Conyers and at Studley during those years). The names Conyers and Malory are linked in a number of records. One notable example is the deed of 1347, by which Sir Roger Conyers and Sir Christopher Mallore, as Lord of Hutton, granted lands to Fountains Abbey (Matthews, 162; 1480 ST 51/51). Similarly, the Conyers name is linked by family and otherwise with that of Neville. William Neville, the First Earl of Kent, was the father of Alice Neville, who married John Conyers, generally believed to be the "Robin of Redesdale" who gathered an army and marched against Edward IV in 1469. Thomas Malory's brother William was killed in this skirmish; his father, Sir William, fought as well, but survived. Robert Malory, who was possibly the brother of our Thomas and the son of William Senior, likewise fought and survived. Alice Neville Conyers, the wife of Sir John, and our Humphrey were first cousins once removed, she being the granddaughter and he being the great-grandson of Ralph Neville, First Earl of Westmorland; moreover, Alice and Humphrey were only two years apart in age, suggesting a common social group between the cousins. The home of Sir John Conyers was Hornby, North Riding, Yorkshire; Humphrey's birthplace at Slingsby was also in the North Riding. His sister Eleanor Markenfield was married to Thomas Markenfield, and a Christopher Conyers married Anne Markenfield (ca. 1404–ca. 1465). Markenfield Hall, still standing today looking very much as it always has, is walking distance from both Studley Royal and Hutton Conyers, the two homes of the Malorys.

Moreover, we have the evidence of a royal commission to prove that Humphrey Neville was acquainted with at least one kinsman of Thomas Malory, a Robert Malory. As we have seen above in chapter 6, in 1463, when Neville was engaged in helping Lancastrians who had seized the three northern castles Alnwick, Dunstanburgh, and Bamburgh for King Henry, Edward IV commissioned Sir John Langstrother, Sir James Strangways, Geoffrey Middleton, Thomas Scawsby the mayor of York, and Robert Malory to go and fetch Humphrey Neville from Northumberland and bring him to the king in court. They did so. There is good evidence that this Robert Malory was the brother of our Thomas Malory of Yorkshire, but whether he was the brother of Thomas or not, he was certainly a relative.

Notice again that the organizing technique in the list of those not pardoned is to give the last known residence of each person named. Those who live or have recently lived in the same place are grouped together: the four Londoners, Mulle, Clyfton, Verdon, and House, are gathered into one group; the three Welshmen from Carmathen into another group; the royal family and their retainers who are living "beyond the realm" into another; and the rebels stationed in Harlech into another. Even though no common residence is given for the two knights Neville and Malory, the pattern as a whole strongly suggests that the two knights also are associated with one place; as Professor Field says in another context, "Probabilities adducible from the pattern as a whole can be applied to any one doubtful case" (Field, 28). If this is true, it reminds us of two other aspects of this case. The first one is that Humphrey Neville was in hiding in 1468 and nobody knew where he was living, or where he had been living, since the summer of 1464 (for a full discussion of this point, see chapter 21, "Who Put Sir Thomas Malory in Jail?"). The other aspect is the strong suggestion that, wherever Neville was, the compiler assumed that Malory was probably nearby. Remember that the residence of Sir Thomas Malory of Newbold Revel was well known, and if the herald had meant to refer to him, it would have been easy to place him at Newbold Revel, but instead he left the Malory he listed without a habitation, presumably because he didn't know it. Like the whereabouts of the fugitive Humphrey Neville, the residence of a monk from Yorkshire quite reasonably could have been unknown to the herald. In fact, it is obvious that his information was incomplete; he made the reasonable mistake of placing Henry VI with his family and retinue "beyond the realm," at a time when Henry was actually being held in the Tower.

The resolute refusal to acknowledge that there is a Thomas Malory other than the man from Warwickshire, who could have written the *Morte,* has caused certain scholars to be blind to evidence that is not hard to find. Professor Field seems to have been a victim of that blindness as he tried to prove that the mention of a Thomas Malory in this pardon refers to his candidate. Because of the difficulties involved in claiming that his elderly Warwickshire knight belongs in the list with the northern guerillas, Field tried, by adding names chosen by himself to the list, to put his Malory into the London group. He failed, simply because there is no evidence that Malory belongs there. We may as well associate him with Kevin Bacon.

20

Objections to Malory of Newbold Revel

REMARKABLY, EVER SINCE Kittredge proclaimed that there was simply no other candidate for authorship of *Le Morte* than the Warwickshire Malory, even after William Matthews's book-length study of another Thomas Malory, from Yorkshire, critics tend to bend all of the evidence, of whatever kind, to support Kittredge's man. They seem to be unable to look past him. That is not universally true, of course, but it almost is. Nevertheless, there are several problems associated with accepting the knight from Newbold Revel as the author. Most of them were studied by Professor Matthews more than fifty years ago and have never been solved since. Some of those problems are these:

First, this Thomas Malory's age at the time *Le Morte* was written points to a very old man, one who would ordinarily be too old to handle the job. The document upon which all subsequent studies of Thomas Malory are based, William Dugdale's *The Antiquities of Warwickshire,* 1656, allows us to establish his birth date at about 1393. Dugdale has his Malory fighting with Beauchamp during the reign of Henry V, 1413–1422, and the usual age for soldiers was at least sixteen, but the average age of other men on that retinue roll was over twenty-one. That birth date means that when the *Morte* was completed sometime during the ninth year of King Edward's reign, that is, between March 4, 1469, and March 4, 1470, Malory was about seventy-seven years old, a very old man indeed in the

Middle Ages, and weakening down to death; just ten days after the close of that regnal year, Malory of Newbold Revel was dead. He died on the fourteenth day of March in 1470 (Dugdale, 55–56).

Second, the scarcity of references to Warwickshire locations in Malory's book has raised some scholarly eyebrows, for we are accustomed to find an author writing about places that are familiar to him. However, that absence in *Le Morte* is less disappointing to fans of the Newbold Revel Malory than is the inability of scholars to find a hint of Warwickshire dialect in Malory's work. In fact, the underlying dialect that "bleeds through" the dialect of copyists of the *Morte* shows evidence of originating in the northerly parts of England rather than in Warwickshire (see chapter 9, "Dialect Matters").

Third, there is no satisfactory explanation of how this man would have had access to the large library of French manuscripts that the author used in his project. In fact, it has proved difficult to explain how any one of the candidates for authorship acquired the needed books, but it is considerably more difficult in the case of the Newbold Revel Malory than in that of Malory of Yorkshire, since some of Malory's sources were known to be found in and near Yorkshire. In the early twentieth century, when scholars were so excited about learning that Malory of Newbold Revel spent time in Newgate Prison, Edward Hicks went so far as to claim that he used books from the nearby monastery, Greyfriars Abbey (Hicks, 68), but that claim has not held up, because if Malory was one of the notorious felons in Newgate, imprisoned for all sorts of villainy including theft and assaults upon monasteries, he certainly would not have been allowed to borrow valuable books in monastic ownership. The notion that Greyfriars was a sort of lending library, and that the friars would lend its precious manuscripts to such a man, is wholly untenable. Newgate Prison, moreover, did not have any facilities for using books. It was crowded, dirty, dangerous to life itself, the foulest possible place. Kelly Grovier, in *The Gaol: The Story of Newgate, London's Most Notorious Prison,* quotes "an unfortunate resident of Newgate Prison" as saying, "Hell itself, in comparison, cannot be such a place."[114] And that was said in 1662, after considerable effort had been spent on reforming the medieval London prisons.

Fourth, the author of *Le Morte* was a prisoner in 1469–1470, he tells us in his book. However, even though Malory of Warwickshire was in and out of various prisons between 1443 and 1461 on various felony charges, the prison records show that a general pardon was issued by the king on October 24, 1461, which specifically named Malory, and after that date he was never again either charged or jailed. Matthews gives us an intriguing picture of the end of Malory's criminal record, as announced in the pardon: "As a reader unrolls this great vellum, he may notice among its seemingly endless names a few that are familiar.... And then, after many an unwinding: 'Thomas Mallory miles alias dominus Thomas Mallory de Newbold Ryvell in Com Warw. Miles'" (Matthews, 31–32). Malory was at that time about sixty-eight, and apparently ready to give up his life of crime.

Fifth, this man was a Yorkist supporter of King Edward IV in the Wars of the Roses that raged around him, and yet scholars have not been able to find any real evidence that the author of *Le Morte Darthur* had any such allegiance. Although the book is intensely concerned with a king and his subjects and their loyalty to or betrayal of him, *Le Morte*'s only mention of King Edward comes in Malory's statement that he finished writing his book in the ninth year of that king's reign. In fact, the only hint we have of Malory's view of the wars is his nonspecific lament over the fickleness of the English people in the matter of kings: "Alas! thys ys a greate defaughte of us Englysshemen, for there may no thynge us please no terme" (Malory, *Works*, 862).

And finally, by far the most troublesome of all is his character. Malory of Newbold Revel was the man whose prison record caused so much elation among scholars when it was first found in the 1920s.

[114] Kelly Grovier, *The Gaol: The Story of Newgate, London's Most Notorious Prison* (London: John Murray, 2009), 7.

However, the record turned out to be more hindrance than help with the identification, for two reasons: first, because it shows Malory in prison at the wrong time to write the book, and second, because it shows a thoroughgoing blackguard — a thief, the leader of a violent gang, a livestock rustler, an extortionist, a vandal on a monumental scale, a rapist, and a would-be murderer. How can the reader reconcile this man's character with the even-tempered and gentle narrator of the *Morte*? How can we believe for a moment that a man like the Newbold Revel knight could have written the very "classic of chivalry" (Matthews, 49)? It seems that everyone who has written on the subject of Malory's identity recognizes the problem. Matthews quotes E. K. Chambers's mild comment that "it is difficult to resist the feeling that there is a marked spiritual cleavage between the Malory of romance and the Malory whom recent biographical research has revealed" (Matthews, 43). Helen Cooper, who apparently believes in spite of all that this Malory wrote the book, says, "The career of Thomas Malory of Newbold Revel, in Warwickshire, reads more like an account of exemplary thuggery than chivalry" (Cooper, x) Today, to all appearances, this Malory has won the field. But of course, the thuggery record does not go away, and the discussion goes on. The discordance between the man from Newbold Revel and the *Morte*, to one not already his firm advocate, is quite enough of an obstacle to push him right out of contention; however, there are certain scholars who so insistently believe in this candidate that they brush away any objection. And this is not a new thing; it began when his prison records began to surface. G. L. Kittredge, for example, in his preface to Edward Hicks's biography of Malory[115] written shortly thereafter, had this to say: "Let us not be over-much concerned by the charges brought against Sir Thomas Malory in 1451, serious as they may be in the light of modern manners ["manners"?

[115] George Lyman Kittredge, preface to Edward Hicks, *Sir Thomas Malory, His Turbulent Career*, 55. Further citations of this work will be in parentheses in the text.

"manners"?].... The statute against forcible entry was not passed until the fifth year of Richard II" (Kittredge, viii). Kittredge is apparently suggesting that until the statute against forcible entry was passed, it was perfectly acceptable for Malory to break and enter and take what he wanted of another person's property. Kittredge goes on: "A logical corollary to this rough-and-ready method of asserting title was the practice of seizing for one's self money or other personal property to which one laid claim." This is going pretty far to exonerate the Warwickshire knight just in order that Kittredge could keep him as the author of the *Morte*. He goes even further: "The double charge of rape was manifestly absurd — a mere legal formula if the woman of the house was present and had been forcibly removed from her dwelling while it was ransacked" (Kittredge, viii). Thus Kittredge dismisses larceny and rape.

But those rape charges do not support Kittredge's conclusion. The first time, "in company with William Weston of Newbold, gentleman, Thomas Potter of Bernangle in Warwickshire, husbandman, and Adam Broun of Coventry, weaver, the records charge that he, Thomas Malory of Newbold Revel, knight, feloniously had broken into the house of Hugh Smyth at Monks Kirby and there raped Mistress Joan Smyth" (Matthews, 17). The charge is in Latin, but there is no doubt about what it means; it does not say that Mistress Smyth was manhandled and thrown out of her house. It says *cum ea carnaliter concubuit,* that he had carnal intercourse with her. This was a married woman, in her home when it was invaded, and she was attacked. However much Kittredge et al. try to claim that these men merely wrestled her out of the house so that they could ransack it (in fact, no ransacking is mentioned in the charge), the charge sounds very much like some sort of gang rape, with Malory attacking while his buddies stand by, and the victim's husband unable to defend his wife against her assailants. If that is not what it was, one wonders what Malory's three cronies were doing there. The rest of the story reinforces that impression. A few weeks later, after charges were brought against Malory and his friends, Malory came back alone and raped Joan Smyth again, and this time he stole from Hugh Smyth property worth forty pounds, roughly the equivalent today of 33,390 pounds; Matthews makes the point that forty pounds was twice the annual value of Malory's three estates (Matthews, 17). This second attack sounds irresistibly like revenge.

As to the attempted murder charge, the charge that Malory and his gang had waited for Humphrey Stafford, Duke of Buckingham, in the park attached to his home near Coombe Abbey, and tried to kill him, this is how Kittredge views it: "Nor is there any likelihood that Malory had lain in wait to kill Buckingham, though he may have been in Coombe woods while the duke was a guest at the Abbey" (Kittredge, viii). Kittredge apparently pictured our knight enjoying a stroll through the Coombe Abbey woods; possibly he was trespassing but that is about the worst he could have been doing. The charge, remember, "declares that Thomas Malory, knight, together with twenty-six other persons, had lain in ambush in the woods of Combe Abbey, armed with staves, bows and arrows, glaives, jacks, sallets, and crossbows, intending to murder Humphrey Stafford, Duke of Buckingham" (Matthews, 16). The only man named in the charge is Malory, showing us that he led the ambush. And the thought of even one crossbow in such a context is seriously disturbing.

Edward Hicks went Kittredge one better in exculpating this Malory. In an impressive violation of logic, he considered the rape charge against his man, in the light of certain passages in the book where Lancelot inveighs against violence to women, particularly this one: "'What?' seyde sir Launcelot, 'is he a theff and knyght? and a ravyssher of women? He doth shame unto the order of Knyghthode, and contrary unto his oth. Hit is pyte that he lyvyth'" (Malory, *Works*, 193). Citing Oskar Sommer's point that the words *ravyssher of women* do not occur in the prose *Lancelot*, Malory's source book for this particular section of his work, Hicks deduced that "it seems incredible that the knight of Newbold Revel would have gone out of his way to mention this crime if he had himself been guilty of it" (Hicks, 55). That seems reasonable. However, Hicks's conclusion seems so unreasonable that it leaves the reader breathless. He does not conclude that, ergo, the rapist

Malory of Newbold Revel must not be the author of the *Morte*. No. He concludes that the rapes never took place!

Now, this sort of a priori argument may, unfortunately, be convincing to certain men in studies and library carrels five hundred years after the fact, but it is hardly just to Joan Smyth. It is, in fact, an egregious variation on the defense against rape charges that has kept violated women silent so often. First, such a woman must endure the outrage of the rape; then she must endure the outrage of the defense: "She asked for it." Hicks even goes so far as to suggest exactly that of Joan Smyth. He says that whether she "played the part of Potiphar's wife it is impossible to say" (Hicks, 57). However, the fact that it is impossible to say obviously does not stop him from saying it, by such blatant innuendo.

Sometimes we see a method of ameliorating Malory's guilt more subtle than that of Kittredge or Hicks. One plan is to try to connect a crime with some particular situation or happening in the world of politics, in order to argue that Malory's crimes were actually just political acts. The critic states the charge, then immediately skips to discussing politics. An example is the treatment of Lady Katherine Peyto, who was holding things together at home as best she could alone, because her husband was a prisoner in France. She wrote an almost despairing letter to the archbishop of Canterbury. The letter says she doesn't know where else to turn for help since the Earl of Warwick is away and begs the archbishop for protection against Malory. "Her complaint," says Matthews, telling the story, "still raw with her distress, is that Sir Thomas Malory, 'wyth force and armes and grate pepel arraied en fere of werre,' had burst into her estate,... assaulted her bailiff, a farmer named John Dercet, and driven away four rotherbestes [oxen]" (Matthews, 20). And now, pleads Lady Katherine, Malory is threatening John Dercet that if Dercet comes home he will maim or murder him. Lady Peyto was keeping a farm, and an ox was as essential to that enterprise as a tractor is to a modern farmer. Her loss of four oxen was a serious loss. Professor Field, having reported Lady Katherine's complaint to the archbishop, immediately switches to discussing the death dates of other officials to whom she could have complained, and who was retainer to what duke, and so forth. He considers Lady Peyto's letter to the archbishop, pleading for protection against Malory, and comments eventually that "the importance of this document lies not who [*sic*] was in the right in the theft (or pledge-taking or forcible repossession) of sheep at Camden. It is … that both sides were associated with Duke Henry" (Field, 92). Now, whatever this critic may judge to be the most important thing suggested by Lady Katherine's letter, it is highly unlikely that she herself would consider the most important thing to be that both sides were associated with Duke Henry. It was her desperate need for help against Malory. And there was no suggestion recorded, until it was made here, in 1993, that Malory's thieving was "pledge-taking or forcible repossession." It was plain and simple thieving.

Often the technique of whitewashing Malory's crimes is simply obfuscation. One sentence will make that method clear. Malory and his cohort Eustace Burnaby were accused in October of 1443 of "having insulted, wounded, and imprisoned" one Thomas Smythe, and stolen goods from him worth forty pounds (the 2020 equivalent value is 33,390 pounds). We are told not to worry; people were always making such accusations in the fifteenth century, so there is no need to take this one seriously. "However," continues the commentator, "this accusation provides a context for later accusations against Malory, making it less easy to believe that the first of them were wholly invented by his enemies, and the others simply the product of despair at being outmaneuvered earlier on" (Field, 87). The kernel of this sentence, of course, is that Malory was likely guilty as charged, but the obfuscation is obvious. Nobody had suggested, until it was suggested in this very sentence, that the accusations against Malory "were wholly invented by his enemies"; and nobody had suggested, either, until it was suggested in this sentence, that his crimes were "simply the product of despair at being out-maneuvered." What enemies? The critic does not say. Out-maneuvered how and where and why? He does not explain. He merely leaves the hint at nefarious moves against Malory hanging in the air.

In a court of law we make the assumption that a person charged with a crime is innocent until proven guilty. That is a good assumption to make in literary investigations as well, and so I shall make it here. However, while certain others have assumed the innocence of Thomas Malory of Newbold Revel, I assume the innocence of his victims; I assume that they are not guilty of that other crime, the one hitherto unnamed but always part of the judgment of the accused. I assume that they are innocent of bringing false charges, or in older words, bearing false witness. I assume here that in every case, Thomas Malory of Newbold Revel was guilty of the crime of which he was accused. If a charge says he stole four oxen, I hold that he stole four oxen. If another charge says that he and his gang broke down eighteen doors in a monastery close, rifled three iron chests, insulted the monks, and stole "forty-odd pounds in coin, three gold rings, two silver signets, two silver zones (belts presumably), three rosaries (one of them coral, one amber, the third jet), two bows and three sheaves of arrows" (Matthews, 22) — in fact, goods in today's money worth about 95,310 pounds, plus damage to the monastery building itself, to the modern value of about 414,800 pounds — I believe that that is exactly what happened. I see no reason why these crimes and the victims of them should be brushed aside as unimportant.

The various scholars who believe that Sir Thomas Malory of Newbold Revel, Warwickshire, wrote *Le Morte Darthur* find their own techniques of ameliorating this knight's guilt for crimes against his neighbors, because readers of the *Morte* have had trouble believing that such a villain could have written such a book. Apparently because of legal technicalities, his victims never had their day in court. They never saw their assailant convicted of his crimes. They never had restitution for the huge amounts of money and property he stole, or for the damage he inflicted on their buildings and their persons. That was in their own time. During the last century and more since the 1890s, they have been ignored or insulted by Malory scholars, who have even suggested at times that these people were to blame for their own persecution by this man. The following list may not be complete, but here are some names we know, and the crimes that were committed against them by Sir Thomas Malory of Newbold Revel:

Thomas Smythe: by force and arms insulted, wounded, imprisoned, and robbed of forty pounds in goods (2020 equivalent "relative value" 33,190 pounds).

Joan Smyth: home broken into; raped, on two separate occasions.

Hugh Smyth: husband of Joan Smyth; home broken into on two occasions; robbed of forty pounds in goods (2020 equivalent "relative value" 33,190 pounds); wife raped, on two separate occasions.

Margaret King: extortion with threats, one hundred shillings (2020 equivalent "relative value" 4,148 pounds).

William Hales: extortion with threats, one hundred shillings (2016 equivalent "relative value" 4,148 pounds).

John Mylner: extortion with threats, twenty shillings (2016 equivalent "relative value" 829.60 pounds).

John Dercet: Lady Katherine Peyto's bailiff, who tried to defend her from Malory's invasion; assaulted, driven away from home; threatened with maiming or murder if he returned.

Lady Katherine Peyto: invasion of home; theft of four oxen; threats and menaces.

John Grene: home invasion; theft of unspecified amount.

Duke of Norfolk, Archbishop of Canterbury, Humphrey Stafford Duke of Buckingham: these three men jointly owned the park at Caludon that Malory and his gang invaded, doing 500 pounds' worth of damage (in today's money, approximately 414,800 pounds). In addition, Buckingham was the target of the Malory gang's attempted murder.

Combe Abbey, monastery: Malory's gang attacked twice, fully armed. They broke down doors; forced open and rifled three iron chests, and stole "forty-odd pounds in coin, three gold rings, two silver signets, two silver zones,... three rosaries (one of them coral, one amber, the third jet), two bows and three sheaves of arrows" (Matthews, *Inquiry*, 22). The 1450 total value of coins and goods stolen is not

> known; it is estimated. In today's money, it is estimated at 95,310 pounds.[116] Total cost of damage to the monastery itself, at a "relative value" estimate, is 414,800 pounds.

These cost equivalency numbers may seem high to a modern reader, until we learn that the great keep of Bamburgh Castle was raised circa 1120 at the cost of four pounds — somewhat less than eight dollars.[117] Inflation we have always with us.

Obviously, the reason why Malory scholars have devoted such effort to exonerating the Newbold Revel candidate is that they have believed, and some still believe, that his jail record is pertinent to his candidacy for authorship. But that jail record ends in 1461, with his pardon from the king. The *Morte* was finished when its author was in prison in 1469–1470. Critics who assume that since he was in prison during most of the 1450s, he must have been in prison in 1469, seem to be assuming once a jailbird always a jailbird. But that is not true, and it has no value as either evidence or logical premise. Moreover, in this particular case, these critics are possibly also assuming that what a man will do in his fifties he will do also in his seventies — even though what he did in his fifties was breaking and entering, thieving, livestock rustling, attacking great monasteries, leading a gang of upwards of thirty brigands through the countryside, raping, and causing general havoc. A little common sense would certainly seem to be in order here. This man's jail record cannot tell us where the *Morte* was written or anything else about it; the only thing his prison record during the 1440s and 1450s teaches us is the man's character. And it shows us that his character was unsuitable for the job under consideration, translating old French manuscripts and writing *Le Morte Darthur*. It seems unlikely in the extreme that he is our author.

[116] Value is obtained by "a simple Purchasing Power Calculator … by multiplying [1450 value] by the percentage increase in the RPI from 1450 to 2020." RPI is British Retail Price Index; American equivalent is called Consumer Price Index (measuringworth.com).

[117] www.castlesfortsbattles.co.uk/bamburgh_castle-html.

Comparison of Two Candidates

Attribute	Sir Thomas Malory of Warwickshire	Sir Thomas Malory of Yorkshire
Birth date	ca. 1393, deduced from Dugdale's *Antiquities of Warwickshire*	ca. 1432–1442, deduced from mother's age
Birthplace	Newbold Revel, Warwickshire	Studley or Hutton Conyers, Yorkshire
Age when *Morte* was finished 1469–1470?	about seventy-seven	about thirty to forty
In prison when *Morte* was finished?	no	yes; see ch. 21, "Who Put Sir Thomas Malory in Jail?"
Dialect a match for the "northerly" in *Le Morte*?	no; West Midland dialect	yes; "northerly" dialect of Yorkshire and surrounding counties
Access to particular MS. labeled as the book Malory used?	no	yes; MS. located in Ribston Priory, where the Hospitaller Malory would have been stationed
Death date	March 14, 1470, from gravestone copied by Dugdale	no evidence
Knight?	yes	yes
Named on 1462 list of *milites*?	no evidence	yes; deduced from northern connections and known Hospitaller family
Named on 1468 pardon as excluded?	no evidence	yes; listed with Humphrey Neville, a Yorkshire neighbor with common kin, friends, and Lancastrian convictions
Access to source manuscripts	no evidence	four MSS. found in Yorks., Thornton alliterative all within easy reach of Yorkshire Malory

Attribute	Sir Thomas Malory of Warwickshire	Sir Thomas Malory of Yorkshire
Character consistent with the tone of *Le Morte*?	no; renegade, thug, rapist, violent gang leader, failed murderer	yes; devout religion pervades *Le Morte,* appropriate for a monk-knight
Reason for being in prison in 1469 when *Le Morte* was finished?	not applicable; not in prison in 1469	treason, deduced from association with Humphrey Neville in exemption from pardon in 1468
"Steeped in Cistercianism"?	no	yes; Cistercian abbey adjacent to Malory home; also likely educated at abbey school
Strong interest in Crusades?	no evidence	yes; as a Hospitaller, Malory was required to fight in the Crusades for five years, acquiring knowledge of warfare with Muslims
Explains why author's ID has gone unknown?	no	yes; Hospitallers give up identity when they join the order

SECTION FIVE

Wrap-Up

~21~

Who Put Sir Thomas Malory in Jail? A Perfectly Plausible Guess

IT IS MANIFEST that whoever imprisoned Thomas Malory was not his enemy and did not wish him any harm. In fact, despite the author's complaint against jailers "That kepen him fulle sewerly, / With wiles wrong and wrast" (*Ragnell*, ll. 844–845), Malory's jailers provided for our author a safe home for a number of years, at least comfortable enough to allow him to pursue his avocation of writing. And, after the first book Malory wrote, the romance in the northern style about Sir Gawain's involvement with a certain loathly lady, when he turned to writing *Le Morte Darthur*, he needed a significant number of big books on his desk as well, and his jailer provided them for him, or at least allowed the prisoner to have them.

Then there is that peculiar identification of Malory as a "knight prisoner," sometimes printed as a phrase and sometimes as a single hyphenated word: knight-prisoner. This is the tag that excited scholars in 1934, when it was found in the newly discovered Winchester manuscript of Malory's work, because it confirmed what they had guessed — that the author wrote his book in prison. It is not the fact of his knighthood that was new information; scholars had already deduced that, from the fact that the author called himself *Sir*. However, in their excitement over the fact that the author revealed himself to have been a prisoner, scholars missed another piece of information. The word or words *knight-prisoner* are just different enough from ordinary English usage to call attention to themselves. If a man, for example, wishes to convey the information that he is a baseball player and also a prisoner, he probably will not say, "I am a baseball player-prisoner." Conversely, if we hear someone say, for instance, "That man was an Israeli prisoner," we probably will not immediately take the statement to mean that he was an Israeli and also a prisoner. English is capacious, and there is certainly wide enough semantic space for that meaning, but it is not the most immediately obvious one. We will almost surely take the statement to mean that the man was a prisoner of the Israelis. Likewise, I think Thomas Malory intended to tell us that he was a prisoner of the Knights.

Of course, that reading immediately raises the question, *Did the Knights Hospitallers keep prisons?* And the answer is yes, they did, although not by any means in all of their commanderies. The Irish Hospitaller monastery Bree at Ballyhogue is one example. In 1375, the commander, John Fitzgerald, was ordered by the crown to "preserve the state of the king's faithful people, and to conquer rebels"; and also "to maintain a prison" for the "Irish who are not continually at peace.' "[118] Nor is the Order of St. John the only religious order that maintained prisons for transgressors, both members and nonmembers. Fountains Abbey, as excavations have discovered, had a prison with chains attached to the floor; excavators have found an inscription scratched on the wall by some long-dead prisoner, "Vale libertas," leading them to think that his sentence may have been lifelong imprisonment. However, it is unlikely that Thomas Malory was held in this kind of prison; the work he did during his confinement belies any such setting. Some form of house arrest is the only type of incarceration that could apply, given the requisite constant access to priceless books. Moreover, the Hospitallers had an elaborate system of courts, trials, and

[118] Caesar Falknier, "Hospital of St. John of Jerusalem in Ireland," *Proceedings of the Royal Irish Academy, Section C: Archeology, Celtic Studies, History, Linguistics, Literature* 26 (1906/1907): 301. https://breeheritage.com/2015/07/13/ballyhogue-and-the-knights-hospitallers/.

prescribed punishments for those who broke the rules of the order, and one of the possible punishments was house arrest. Alan Forey, in discussing judicial process and punishments in the order, tells us that "imprisonment and irons were the two normal methods of restricting movement, but references also occur to house arrest, which did not allow an individual to go beyond the door of his residence."[119] It seems obvious that Sir Thomas Malory must have suffered something like this kind of imprisonment, for, as Richard Griffith has reminded us, some form of house arrest is the only context in which Malory's confinement makes any sense. In arguing for his Cambridgeshire candidate for author, Griffith makes the point, "Since assiduous search by three generations of scholars has turned up no hint that a man named Thomas Malory was accused, charged, arrested, tried, convicted, fined, sentenced, or committed to prison at any time during the 1460s, it is a fair inference that he was not actually 'in prison,' in an official sense, at all." Of course this point holds true for Malory of Yorkshire as well as for Malory of Cambridgeshire. Griffith goes on to say that "if Malory was not writing his book in prison, then he must have been taken prisoner at some place where his manuscript was accessible to him, which probably means his own home" (Griffith, 169–170). True.

There has never been, to my knowledge, a specific suggestion made by any scholar as to how, when, where, or why Sir Thomas Malory was imprisoned. Of course, there was that keen excitement among scholars when Hicks and others unearthed the felony records of Sir Thomas Malory of Newbold Revel, but all of that lasted only until it was evident that this Malory's imprisonment ended in 1461, when he used a pardon to get out of jail; no new charges were ever brought against him after that date, and the *Morte* was written by someone who was a prisoner in 1469–1470.

[119] Alan Forey, "Judicial Processes in the Military Orders: The Use of Imprisonment and Chaining," in ed. Alan Forey, *The Military Orders from the Twelfth to the Early Fourteenth Centuries* (Toronto and Buffalo: University of Toronto, 1992), 87.

P. J. C. Field has constructed a theory that, although it is pages long, has as its premise simply that Malory of Newbold Revel was imprisoned not in a jail but in some unknown other place, for some unspecified involvement in the "London conspiracy" of 1468, whereby this Malory, who had always been a Yorkist, turned traitor to Edward and became a Lancastrian. However, Field acknowledges that Malory could not have gone to prison for the conspiracy before the conspiracy was exposed, on June 14, 1468 (Field, 143–144), and in that case Malory would have had only one year and eight and a half months to write the whole *Morte,* plus *The Wedding of Sir Gawain and Dame Ragnell.* The speed at which medieval scribes copied books is the subject of many studies, but Malory was not copying books. Sometimes he was translating, sometimes he was reducing the voluminousness, but just as often he was composing. The finished work contains enough errors in chronology, characterization, and fitting together of different stories to have drawn scholarly attention through the ages, but nevertheless *Le Morte Darthur* is one of the classics of Western literature, and it is big. The making of it undoubtedly took some unknown number of years. Field concludes that it is unlikely we shall ever know what Malory did to land himself in prison, and he leaves his argument at that (Field, 144).

It is true that most of what happened five hundred years ago is lost. However, it is possible, by way of testing a hypothesis, to construct a narrative that fits all the facts as they have come down to us. This narrative does not require altering any primary evidence. It does not demand elaborate stretches of the imagination or complicated chains of acquaintance. It does not call for any personal insults and ad hominem attacks, or claims of fraudulence in documents. It does not necessitate adding to, subtracting from, ignoring, or twisting any of the evidence. It certainly does not use a priori judgments or circular reasoning. It does not claim any scribal error, anywhere. It reasons from the evidence that we do actually have and draws tentative conclusions from it without once changing the evidence itself by even a jot or a tittle. And it points not to a Sir Thomas Malory of Newbold Revel but to a Sir Thomas Malory, Knight Hospitaller, of Yorkshire, as the author of *Le Morte Darthur.*[120]

In our story, there are two kings (Henry VI and Edward IV), two priors of the Order of St. John, Hospitallers (Prior Robert Botyl and Prior John Langstrother), and two knights (Sir Humphrey Neville and Sir Thomas Malory). In the 1460s, civil war raged without ceasing all over England, between the Lancastrian supporters of Henry VI and the Yorkist supporters of Edward IV, and it is therefore a safe bet that whatever put Malory in prison had something to do with the war; scholars have not disputed that assumption (in fact, even when they study the felon Malory of Newbold Revel, they often suggest that the war was somehow the cause of his felonious behavior). At the time when Malory was writing *Le Morte,* Edward was on the throne; the author tells us in the book that he finished it in the ninth year of Edward's reign. We can try to find whatever connections there are among the Knights Hospitaller, the warring factions, and Thomas Malory; thus maybe we can figure out what could have landed Sir Thomas in a knight prison.

Henry VI was born in 1421, and inherited the throne of England in 1422, when he was not quite nine months old, the youngest person ever to succeed to the English monarchy. During Henry's childhood, England was ruled by a regency council; he was declared of age when he was sixteen, and he officially took over the ruling of England, but in fact, the quarrelsome nobles in his court held undue influence over peaceful, pious, shy Henry. He was not

[120] For further discussion of the historical events in this story, see Baumgaertner, Charlesworthy, Dockray, Gairdner, Griffith and Sherborne, Hale, Highfield, and Smalley, Homan, King, MacGibbon, Markham, Rupert Matthews, McLean, Mercer, Miller, Wagner, Warkworth (consult bibliography), and standard histories of the Wars of the Roses. For further discussion concerning the Knights Hospitallers, see Bogdanow, Borchardt, Broun, Craft, Forey, Hodges, King, Nicholson, Nicolle, O'Malley, Phillips, Porter, Riley-Smith, Speight, Walbran, among many others; consult bibliography.

a strong ruler, and England needed a strong ruler. When Henry was twenty-three, he married fifteen-year-old Margaret of Anjou, niece to the king of France; eventually Margaret took the reins of Henry's government as his abilities declined. Henry's rule became more and more unpopular, because of his tendency to "give back" territories in France that Englishmen considered to be English property, and because of a marked disorderliness in the general conduct of government. Henry's advisors had considered a marriage to Margaret to be a path to better relations with France, but as it turned out, the English did not particularly like having a French queen, in spite, or maybe because, of her having the talent for ruling that Henry lacked. Then, on August 4, 1453, Henry's mind apparently went blank all of a sudden and remained so for over sixteen months, during which time he was completely nonresponsive. His only child, a son and heir, was born during this time, and even when the baby was brought to his father, Henry showed no response. Meanwhile, the government grew more chaotic. Then, on Christmas Day, as suddenly as it went out, Henry's mind came back into focus. But things had gone to the point where he and Margaret together could never quite get control of England again. After some jockeying among factions that coveted Henry's throne, and some killing among the nobility, King Henry was deposed and imprisoned. Then came the Battle of Towton, won by supporters of Edward of York, after which Edward was declared King Edward IV, the second king in our story, on March 4, 1461. Henry was released from prison, and he and Queen Margaret and their little son fled into Scotland. Among their entourage was Humphrey Neville, who will figure prominently in our hypothetical story of how and why Thomas Malory landed in prison.

In addition to being able to point to the miserable reign of Henry VI, Edward IV came to the throne armed with a sure confidence that he was entitled to it; he believed that his descent from his and Henry's common ancestor, Edward III, was better than Henry's, and that he was therefore the rightful king of England. Yet it took more than ten years of war, and the slaughter of most of the highest members of the English nobility, and even the murder of King Henry himself, to secure Edward's rule. The Battle of Towton was fought on Palm Sunday in March of 1461; John Sadler says that "Palmsunday Field was England's bloodiest day,"[121] and he quotes A. A. Gill: "In this valley on one savage day, a greater proportion of our population died than in a whole year of the First World War. It was by far the bloodiest battle in our history"[122] (Gill, quoted in Sadler, 5). Edward assumed after Towton that the struggle was over, and he had himself crowned on June 28. But the struggle was not over; it was not to be over until ten years later, when, on May 4, 1471, at Tewkesbury, "the last of the Lancastrian lords were annihilated — either killed in battle, or executed afterwards, including Edward Prince of Wales,"[123] the young son of King Henry VI.

There are two medieval records that mention Thomas Malory and enable us to place him in the broader picture of the wars of the 1460s between the two kings; we have looked at both of them. The first document mentions him as one of the knights who rode north with Edward in 1462 in a campaign to take three border castles that were held by Lancastrians faithful to King Henry. The other document is the general pardon issued by King Edward in 1468, which includes a list of fifteen people excepted from the king's mercy; Sir Thomas Malory is one of those. During Edward's reign such pardons and exemptions from pardon proliferated, but it is expedient to begin

121 John Sadler, *Towton: The Battle of Palmsunday Field 1461* (Barnsley, South Yorkshire, England: Pen and Sword Military, 2011), 5. Further citations of this work will be in parentheses in the text.

122 A. A. Gill, quoted in John Sadler, *Towton*, 5. A 1999 archeological find of the remains of fifty-one men, ages sixteen to fifty, at the site of the battle, showed that they all suffered "shockingly violent deaths.... Bones cannot speak, but the horror of trauma is eloquence itself. These men died horribly, killed by opponents who were afire with killing frenzy, hacked and battered and trampled, their features obliterated in blood-fury" (Sadler, 133).

123 William Baumgaertner, *Squires, Knights, Barons, Kings: War and Politics in Fifteenth Century England* (Bloomington, IN: Trafford, 2009), pages unnumbered.

our story with the general pardon late in the chronological order of things, in July of 1468,[124] because it establishes the connection between Malory and Sir Humphrey Neville, the other knight in our story. The names of those not pardoned are organized in groups according to where they resided, and the group that includes Sir Thomas Malory, Knight, names only one other person, another man from Yorkshire, Sir Humphrey Neville, Knight. As William Matthews first pointed out, these two names comprise a separate group unto themselves in the list. That being the case, we deduce that whatever Malory did that was unpardonable had something to do with Sir Humphrey Neville, and we hypothesize that it also was the cause of Malory's imprisonment.

So, we have the date before which Malory's offense was committed, the date of his and Neville's exception from the general pardon, that is, July 16, 1468. Perhaps we can discover a beginning date and thus fix a time frame during which Malory's offense must have been committed. And that turns out to be easy in the case of Neville. He was not only pardoned by King Edward but also made a knight by him in June of 1463.[125] If our hypothesis is correct, then, that Sir Thomas Malory's offense is linked to Neville's and is the reason why Edward refused to pardon these two, then their crime must have been committed after June of 1463. So now we have our time frame: between June 1463, the date of Neville's last pardon by Edward, and

[124] P. J. C. Field points out that "every issue of this pardon should have repeated this part of its terms exactly, and the known exemplars, dated 16 July, 24 August, 1 November and 1 December 1468, and 12 February 1469, do so. On 22 February 1470, Malory, Marshall, Verdon and Philip were again excepted in the model pardon at the head of the third pardon roll; but they were not excepted (no-one was) in the model pardon at the head of the fourth roll, on 25 November 1471"(31). Matthews gives us the information that the copy of July 16 is addressed to William Paston; the August 4 copy to the executors of the will of Thomas Bekkyngton; the November 1 copy to the burgesses of Nottingham; and the December 1 copy to Wells Cathedral (130).

[125] Sir Leslie Stephen, ed. *Dictionary of National Biography*, vol. 40 (London: Macmillan, 1894), 262.

July 1468, the date when Neville and Malory together were denied pardon by that king. Let us try to discover what connections there were among Edward, the Hospitallers and thus a Hospitaller knight Sir Thomas Malory, and Sir Humphrey Neville.

For background, we must step back to 1461, when Prior Robert Botyl, who up until that date had loyally supported King Henry VI and the Lancastrian effort, turned his support and the support of his Knights Hospitallers over to the Yorkist side and King Edward. There can be very little doubt that Botyl's early devotion to King Henry was sincere. He had always been Henry's man, dealing as best he could with the travel restrictions and other restraints placed upon him by Henry because he wanted Botyl near him, partly for friendship apparently and partly for nervousness over who might not be a faithful supporter. The friendship is easy to document; when Henry's mind suddenly came back into focus in 1454, after his mental blackout, Robert Botyl was one of two men invited to come into the king's presence and see this remarkable restoration for themselves. Botyl had a short conversation with King Henry and then left the room and burst into tears of joy.[126] Nevertheless, however glad he was to see his king and friend restored to his senses, the prior apparently realized, possibly gradually over the next five years, that Henry was not fit to rule England. Botyl turned his support to Edward. Unlike many who could not seem to make up their minds between the two kings, Botyl never abandoned Edward after he had embraced his cause. As prior of the Hospitallers of the English language, Botyl was the high commander of all the monk-warriors in England, and we therefore know that after he

[126] E. J. King, *The Grand Priory of the Order of the Hospital of St. John of Jerusalem in England* (Holborn: Fleetway Press, 1924), 50–52. Prior Botyl and the bishop of Winchester were the first to be admitted to the king's presence when he recovered; E. J. King tells us that they "were deeply affected by their interview with the gentle and saintly King, and as they came out from the audience chamber, they wept tears of joy, and related how the king had told them that he was in charity with all the world, and only wished that the great Lords were the same." But in 1461, when the Yorkists rode against London and Henry, Botyl rode with them.

turned his support to Edward, any Hospitallers fighting in any battle between Henry VI and Edward IV, up until Botyl's death in September of 1468, were fighting on Edward's side. In 1461, we see his contingent riding with Edward's army against London and helping to take that city for the new king. In 1462, we see the Hospitallers again riding with Edward's forces to capture the castles at Alnwick, Dunstanburgh, and Bamburgh, which were in the hands of Henry's supporters. This time, Sir Thomas Malory is specifically named on a still-extant list of soldiers on that expedition; for a full discussion of the evidence that Hospitaller knights, including the Malory listed, were part of it, see chapter 18, "Mysterious *Milites.*" So Edward had good reason to feel confident that the Knights of St. John, under the Yorkist prior, Sir Robert Botyl, would not pose any threat to his reign; on the contrary, the order was supporting him with fighting men.

However, Edward had plenty to worry him. His own kinsmen were fighting him for the crown; the war has often been called the Cousins' War. Richard Neville, Earl of Warwick, one of the cousins, supported Edward during those early years of the 1460s, but another cousin, Humphrey Neville, did not. He was a staunch Lancastrian, true to the king whose rule he had known since childhood, Henry VI. It is this Humphrey Neville who interests us. Humphrey belonged to the Lancastrian branch of the Nevilles, descended from the first wife of Ralph Neville, First Earl of Westmoreland, while Richard belonged to the Yorkist branch, descended from Westmoreland's second wife. Richard eventually became known as "the kingmaker" because he was such a powerful force in removing Henry VI from the throne and putting Edward on it, then removing Edward and reestablishing Henry, then again removing Henry and reseating Edward. After this last "crowning" of Edward, Richard again tried to unseat him, but this time he fell in battle against Edward. Humphrey Neville, although he certainly broke promises to Edward, apparently never had any uncertainty about who was the rightful king of England. Henry VI was his proper monarch and had his lifelong support, support that eventually cost Humphrey his head. Humphrey was involved with the strife over the three great border castles in Northumberland along the Scottish border. During the years 1461–1464, these became a major bone of contention between the two English armies, and Humphrey Neville was in that struggle on the Lancastrian side from start to finish.

On March 29, 1461, Edward was victorious in the Battle of Towton and assumed therefore that the castles were rightfully his, to dispose of them as he saw fit. The deputy constable of the castles, Ralph Percy, surrendered them to Edward. On October 25, 1461, Queen Margaret, who had fled to Scotland with her husband, Henry VI, after the Battle of Towton, landed at Bamburgh with an army. Ralph Percy, who had already surrendered Bamburgh, as well as Dunstanburgh and Alnwick, to Edward in September, changed his allegiance back to Lancastrian and turned the castles over to Margaret in October. When Margaret landed at Bamburgh, Humphrey Neville was either with her or waiting for her, having already arrived, together with Thomas DeRos (a common distant kinsman of Humphrey Neville and our other knight, Thomas Malory), on one of their forays into Northumberland from Scotland, where they had fled with Henry and Margaret after the Yorkist victory at Towton. A few weeks later, Thomas Malory arrived as part of Edward's force, which had come to take the castles away from the Lancastrians. His name, remember, shows up on a list of *milites* who accompanied King Edward to the north for that purpose in December of 1462. This is one of the ironic twists of our story: late in 1462, Humphrey Neville was defending the castles for King Henry, while Thomas Malory was attacking them for King Edward. And yet these two men will later be involved together in a reckless and dangerous enterprise that will join their names in an official record and in the minds of students of *Le Morte Darthur* more than five hundred years later.

It is June 25, 1464. After going back and forth between Lancastrian and Yorkist control for two years, Alnwick and Dunstanburgh have surrendered to Edward's forces, leaving Bamburgh as the only castle still holding out for King Henry. Richard Neville, the Earl of Warwick, and his brother and deputed general John Neville, Lord Montague, lead Edward's men. The Battle of Hedgeley Moor two months previously, on April 25,

1464, has shown the Yorkists victorious; the Battle of Hexham, on May 15, likewise. The lords of the north have been slaughtered, both on the field and afterwards. Michael D. Miller, in *The Wars of the Roses,* tells us that after the battle at Hexham, which had been a rout for the Yorkists,

> Whether or not John [that is, John Neville, Lord Montague, the brother of Warwick] had King Edward IV's prior authority, he certainly judged his master's wishes correctly.... Anxious to make an effect locally in several different places, John arranged the executions at different spots. Robert, Lord Hungerford and deMoleyns, Sir John Findern and Sir Thomas Roos ... were beheaded in Newcastle. The next day Sir Philip Wentworth and Sir William Penington suffered the same fate at Middleham, the Neville stronghold in Yorkshire. John kept some prisoners on hand until King Edward IV could be present. On 26th May, in York, Edward sat, stony faced, to watch his headsman's axe rise and fall on 14 necks. Their heads were sent to decorate the Micklegate and make a suitable impression.[127]

Some had tried to escape the axe. Henry Beaufort, Duke of Somerset, was found hiding in a barn; William Tailboys, Baron Kyme, had been trapped in a coal hole; both were dragged out like rabbits in a trap and beheaded, their heads displayed for the edification of the populace.

All gone now except Ralph Grey and Humphrey Neville, holding Bamburgh. Three great cannons have been brought north for this siege: the London and the Newcastle, both of iron, and the Dijon, of brass. Warwick's men roll the big guns off the boat and up the hill to the castle, and they send in a message to the two in command: Surrender and the garrison will be released and pardoned, all except Grey and Neville. The answer comes back: no. Then comes the

[127] Michael D. Miller, "The Remaining Lancastrians, the Battle of Hexham — 15th May 1464" in *The Wars of the Roses,* pages unnumbered, www.warsoftheroses.co.uk/chapter_60.html. Further citations of this source will be in parentheses in the text.

threat: His Majesty does not wish to do damage to his castles. For every shot fired at the castle from the big guns, one man will be beheaded. Surrender. And again the answer: no. The three cannons are rolled into position and fired. When the Dijon missile hits the castle, it breaks a hole in the wall of the room where Ralph Grey is standing, and great chunks of stone and mortar come flying across the room and strike him down (Wagner, 17). Grey is seriously injured and unconscious. Humphrey Neville takes command of Bamburgh, and he negotiates with the attackers: I will surrender the castle on condition that you will allow all in it to leave. This time the *no* comes from Edward's men Warwick and Montague, both of them Neville cousins of Humphrey. The cousins barter until they reach an agreement: Humphrey will surrender the castle, and he and the garrison will be pardoned and allowed to go free; only Grey will not be allowed to leave. All in the castle except Grey depart, and Humphrey Neville vanishes. No one can find him anywhere, nor is he ever found, for the next five years.

The "pardon" given to the men holding Bamburgh Castle, including Neville, was a strategic move on the part of Warwick and Montague to secure the castle for Edward, but it was not like the general pardons, covering all offenses, published from time to time by the king. Humphrey Neville knew what fate awaited Grey, and he had no reason to doubt that the same fate would be his, if he were caught. He had broken too many promises to Edward for him to trust any promises made by Edward's men to him. He had betrayed Edward's trust in him one too many times, as indeed had Ralph Grey. Moreover, Edward had published a general pardon barely two weeks before, on June 11, which excepted only two men from his mercy, Ralph Grey and Humphrey Neville. Humphrey knew also that there were searchers out already, and had been since the battle at Hexham on May 15, looking for King Henry. Rupert Matthews tells us that "all across the north of England Yorkist scouts, soldiers and agents searched for the fugitive king Henry VI, who had not been seen or heard of since leaving Bywell Castle the day after the battle at Hexham."[128] Humphrey knew the searchers would find him. They had found Somerset in a barn; they had found Tailboys in a coal cellar. It was not long before Neville heard what had happened to Ralph Grey after his own departure from Bamburgh. Edward's men had carried him on a litter to Doncaster; "There, the Constables Court, presided over by John Tiptoft . . . who was making a name for himself by his cruelty, propped the wretched man up on pillows to hear his death sentence. He had to be carried onto the scaffold so he could be beheaded in the presence of the king" (Miller, chapter "The Remaining Lancastrians," pages unnumbered). Humphrey could have had no doubt that the same fate awaited him. His ancestral home at Brancepeth Castle was not far away, but presumably that would be the first place his enemies would look for him.

But remember, Humphrey Neville was acquainted with Sir John Langstrother, the prominent knight of the Hospital of St. John. Langstrother was one of the five men who had been commissioned by Edward on April 7 of the previous year, 1463, to go and find Neville where he was participating in the Lancastrian defense of the three border castles, and to bring him to the king in court. John Langstrother, Robert Malory, Geoffrey Middleton, James Strangways, and Thomas Scawsby had duly fetched Neville and brought him back down south to Edward. But this was not an arrest to imprison or execute Humphrey Neville. Edward was trying at that stage of things to win over the Lancastrian followers of Henry and Margaret to his side. He was treating the influential members of Henry's following with generosity, in his attempt to woo them, and when Humphrey was brought to the king, Edward pardoned and knighted him. Moreover, on this embassy to fetch Humphrey Neville, it would have been strategic for Edward to send some of Neville's friends, or at least acquaintances; Humphrey was ensconced in a castle-fortress and

[128] Rupert Matthews, *Battlefield Walks in Northumberland*, Battle Walks Series (London: Frances Lincoln, 2008), thehistorymanatlarge.blogspot.com/2012/12/the-reason-for-rthe-siege-of-bamburgh.html.

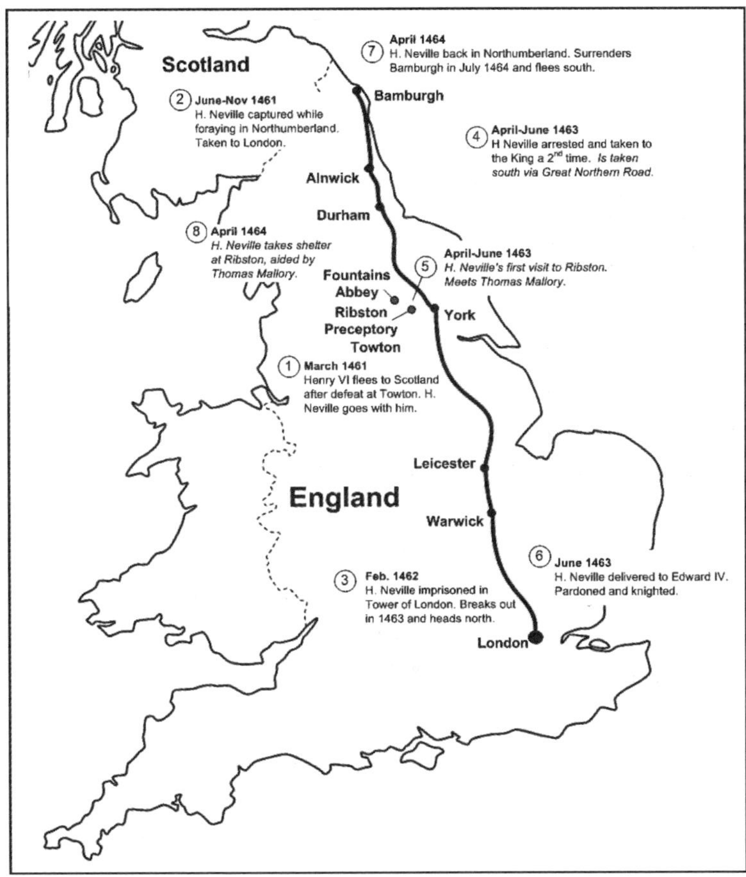

In this timeline/map, everything in italics is speculation; everything else is recorded history.

would be much more likely to cooperate and accompany them if the men who were to escort him to King Edward were known to him. This likelihood would suggest that Neville, Langstrother, Robert Malory, Middleton, Strangways, and Scawsby were already friends. At any rate, Humphrey Neville went with them, apparently readily, back to the court, and by the time they arrived, they had had days of intimate association with one another, on the road.

Humphrey Neville was the king's cousin, only about two years older than Edward. There may have been real affection between these two young men, members of the same extended family, who had grown up knowing each other well. Edward had already shown some level of patience with Humphrey regarding his stubborn support of the Lancastrian king. In 1461, for example, Humphrey had been captured and imprisoned in the Tower, granted his life on condition that he stay there. He agreed, but it was not long before he violated his agreement. He broke out of the Tower and went back to Northumberland, where he "made commotion of people against our sovereign lord the king."[129] When Langstrother brought Humphrey to Edward the next time, the king pardoned him ("took him into his grace by letters patent") for the second time and knighted him (Cal. Pat. Rolls, 511). That was in June of 1463. When Humphrey once again, ten months later, broke his promise to Edward and headed back up north to the Lancastrian enclave holding the castles, Edward had had enough. After that, there would be no more mercy for Humphrey Neville.

However, even more significant to our inquiry into the identity of the author of the *Morte* is that ride back to Edward's court alongside Sir John Langstrother, the staunchly Lancastrian Knight Hospitaller, commander of six monasteries across England including two in Yorkshire — Beverley and Ribston. During that ride Humphrey learned, if he had not known it previously, that Langstrother, despite his order's firm injunction to the Knights Hospitallers not to involve themselves in the quarrels of secular princes, and despite his vow of obedience to his superiors in the order, was a Lancastrian, a supporter of Henry VI. Humphrey learned that he could turn to the older man if necessary and count on his help; he could also count on Langstrother's firm support of King Henry. Moreover, anyone wanting to travel from Northumberland, where Bamburgh Castle was located, to London or Winchester, where King Edward was waiting, had a clear-cut choice: go over rough, unbroken ground, or use the old Roman-built Great Northern Road, which today, for most of its length, is the A1 Highway.

[129] Calendar of the Patent Rolls, Edward IV, May 1468–February 1476, last edited December 9, 2009, 511. Further citations of this work will be in parentheses in the text.

In the fifteenth century, it extended as far south as London and as far north as Edinburgh, and it still does. Common sense tells us that Langstrother's party, conducting Humphrey Neville south to deliver him to King Edward, used this road. Most travelers use it today, because it is the best one available. How much more likely to use it would be our little party of travelers when there was no other road at all available. And this road goes very close to Beverley, where Langstrother was commander of a house of Knights Hospitallers, and even closer to Ribston, where he was commander of another. Property for sale today in the village of Little Ribston advertises the appealing fact that it is only four miles away from the A1 Highway; the old monastery house was even closer, about three miles. What are the odds that, on their way south, Langstrother and his party stopped at the Hospitaller house at Ribston where Langstrother was commander, to rest, eat, care for their horses, have a respite from the concerns of war? Of course they did. And that house is where Sir Thomas Malory, Knight Hospitaller, lived — more about this presently.

That was in 1463. Now, a year later, in June of 1464, we find Humphrey Neville back in the vicinity, fleeing for his life. And there was something everybody knew about the Hospitallers of St. John: even though they were a fighting order, their first mission had always been, and still was, hospitality to the supplicant at the door. The very name of their order embodied this calling. They were known for never turning away the sick, the injured, the pauper, the fugitive. The order had had its source and beginning in this mission; the original Hospitallers provided care for those both Christian and Muslim who were injured in the Crusades, and also for pilgrims of any status who made their perilous way across seas and deserts to visit the holy places in the East. As time went by, the role of the Hospital of St. John, "whose first vow was providing hospitality for pilgrims,"[130] broadened to include the armed defense of those holy places; this in turn led gradually to fighting in the service of other causes, chosen always by

[130] John Russell, *History of France: From the Earliest Times to the Present Day* (Philadelphia, PA: Hogan and Thompson, 1837).

their superiors in the order. However, the Hospitallers never abandoned their initial vocation, hospitality. From the beginning, "all members of the order were bound by the three religious vows, together with a fourth: to be serfs and slaves of their lords the sick" (Nicolle, 10), by which name they meant the sick, the injured, the endangered, the needy, of any class or creed, who came asking for help. William Hone: "It was their vow and profession to exercise hospitality, to resist the Barbarians that should offer any injury to Pilgrims on the High Ways."[131] So strong was this duty incumbent on the Knights Hospitaller that the tradition of it was sometimes passed on to new owners of lands that had been transferred out of Hospitaller possession—"beggar's lands," they were sometimes called. Interviewed in 1811 by Richard Fenton, the owner of one such piece of land said, concerning some old documents that had come down to him with the property, that "these collections are by way of demonstration made ... having been religious lands, some still retaining the name of Beggar's land, my posterity are in that respect tyed, as it were, by a perpetual vow to maintain hospitality at Slebech as knights hospitallers formerly did, charitably relieve poor people there, not forebearing drunkards nor idle persons, who too often are the subversion of many great and noble families."[132] Simon Phillips points out that, in addition to care for the sick, "travelers should also be entertained and refreshed with meat and drink" (Phillips,

Bamburgh Castle

[131] William Hone, *The Everyday Book and Table Book, or Everlasting Calendar of Popular Amusements*, 2 vols. (London: T. Tegg, 1837), 1477. Further citations of this work will be in parentheses in the text.

[132] Richard Fenton, *A Historical Tour through Pembroke* (London: Longman, Hurst, Rees, and Orme, 1811), pages unnumbered.

8). In the fifteenth century, withdrawal of these services was not tolerated by the leaders of the order. In December of 1479, for example, "John Kendal ... informed the Pope that Prior Weston had not been maintaining hospitality at Clerkenwell, as was customary.... Weston was ordered to re-commence hospitality within two months" (Phillips, *Priors,* 8). All of this was no secret. The beggar, the person injured on the road, the sick, even the drunkard or idle person who needed help knew that if he could make it to a house of the Hospitallers he would be taken in. Moreover, Whitworth Porter tells us that "the Hospital of St. John had, from its earliest foundation, been esteemed a sanctuary, within which fugitives from justice might escape the fangs of the law" (Porter, vol. 3, 236). Humphrey Neville, desperately fleeing the severe justice of the king to whom he had broken so many promises, knew Sir John Langstrother and knew that he was commander of the monastery at Beverley and the one at Ribston, both in Yorkshire. Neville knew the house at Ribston; he had been there. Ribston was closer. Neville made for Ribston Commandery.

Castle Dunes

When we stand inside Bamburgh Castle and look out toward the sea, we see that there is a broad stretch of dunes between the great keep and the water, covered with long dune grasses; according to the Northumberland Ordinance Survey, "The dune system comprises a series of irregular parallel ridges and hummocks with a low-lying marsh and damp hollows."[133] We cannot resist imagining Humphrey Neville after the battle at Bamburgh, bereft of his horse and his knightly armor,

[133] Northumberland County Ordinance Survey Sheet 1:50 000 75, February 28, 1995.

dressed in the clothes of some humble Lancastrian soldier whose life Neville has just saved by his bargain with Edward's men, heading for the sheltering grasses and hollows of the dunes. We can speculate about Neville's mode of travel. Maybe he went on foot to the nearest Lancastrian home he could find — that part of England always predominantly supported Henry VI — and proceeded after that on a borrowed horse. But travel by boat would have been much faster and much safer from pursuit. A horse could travel fifty miles in a day and then sleep overnight; a boat could travel 120 miles in a day and required no sleep; moreover, it would be largely unobserved by people on shore. Maybe there were friendly Lancastrians who helped Humphrey to a boat. If that were so, the fugitive could have been brought over water south to the Humber, then west to its tributary the Ouse, and then farther, to the Ouse tributary the Nidd, and land safely right in the neighborhood of Ribston. Naturally, at some point, these small rivers would become unnavigable; at that point, Neville could follow their path on foot. This is speculation, of course; we do not know that Humphrey Neville headed for Ribston Commandery or how he traveled. However, no matter how we speculate about Neville's mode of travel, there is no need at all for us to speculate about whether he could have made good his escape. We know that he could: he did.

It may be that Sir Humphrey Neville and Sir Thomas Malory had always known each other, or at least known of each other, through their extended families, or they may have met for the first time the previous year, when Langstrother brought Neville to Ribston on the way south to Edward's court. Recall that alongside Langstrother in the little group of five men who fetched Neville for the king was a Robert Malory, quite likely the brother of our Thomas, but at least a relative. The two families of Humphrey Neville and Thomas Malory owned manors within two miles of each other, and they both owned property in the city of Ripon as well. And, as well as both belonging to the great Lancastrian following of Henry VI at the north, they both belonged also to a complex web of intermarried families. These connections, as family connections tend to be, were intergenerational. In due time,

Humphrey Neville's grandson Lancelot Neville was to marry Thomas Malory's cousin Anne Tempest, but in 1464, that union was in the future, and neither Thomas nor Humphrey would ever see it. However, whether Malory and Neville were lifelong friends or brand-new acquaintances, the two of them together did *something* that would link their names in an official document, Edward's general pardon of 1468, which names a handful of people who are not pardoned. And now was almost certainly the very moment when our two knights committed that offense, because the next thing that was going to happen was that Humphrey Neville would vanish from history for five years, not resurfacing until after the 1468 non-pardon. In considering what put Malory in prison, we ask the question *What did he do?* which immediately becomes the question *What could he have done?* What could a monk in a monastery, restricted by the rules of his order from "making a vagabond of himself" — in other words, going out and about in the world as ordinary people ordinarily do — do with, or for, such a swashbuckler as Humphrey Neville? And the answer comes, easy and obvious: he could have helped Neville to disappear.

Malory would have been caught in a complex decision here. First of all, there was a conflict in the Hospitaller Rule, which usually was a clear guide for him: he must offer hospitality, but at the same time, he was not to get involved in the quarrels of Christian princes. Moreover, there was a political division in 1464, within the very hierarchy of the order: even though Malory's direct superior, John Langstrother, the commander of the Ribston house, was a Lancastrian and therefore likely friendly to Humphrey Neville, still, the grand prior of all of England was Robert Botyl, a Yorkist. Recall our evidence that Malory himself, in company with a number of other Hospitallers and in accordance with the Yorkist allegiance of Botyl, had ridden out in December of 1462, to help capture for King Edward the very same castles that Neville had been defending for King Henry (chapter 18, "Mysterious *Milites*"). But in addition to the conflict in the rules and the political disagreement between Malory's superiors within the order, there was another problem: it would be misprision of treason to hide a fugitive from the king, and Malory could thereby be putting his own head on the chopping block. It is true, of course, that almost any step in the wrong direction was liable to be called treason by Edward IV, in the mood for vengeance as he was; however, this particular step would be an easy call. All around, it would have been a difficult decision.

But however difficult Malory's decision, it is not difficult at all for us to guess what he would have done. Knowing the history of Sir Humphrey's five-year invisibility, it is easy for us to posit that Malory made the merciful call: he hid Sir Humphrey. For that action, he was imprisoned. He was told, in effect, probably by both the Yorkist prior Botyl and the Lancastrian commander Langstrother, to go inside and shut the door and not to come out again until further notice. So Malory became a Knight Hospitaller prisoner. As such, he was not only enabled but encouraged and helped by his fellow Hospitallers to take on the long task of producing *Le Morte Darthur*, for he was safely secluded in his own monastery, and provided with the books necessary for his project. We know that he began that project using a French book already in Hospitaller ownership and housed in that very same house, the Ribston commandery (see chapter 7), and we find it easy to imagine that once the monks saw his work and understood what was required, they found ways of providing the needful things.

There are still some questions that our hypothetical story about Sir Thomas Malory's imprisonment must answer before we turn to other matters. The first question is this: *If Sir Thomas was obeying the rules of the order in providing hospitality and care for Humphrey Neville, and thereby of necessity involving himself in the quarrels of others — after all, he did so to save a man's life — and his more serious offense was against the king, the secular authority, then why would the Knights have been the authority that imprisoned him, rather than the king?* The answer is found in the relative smallness of Malory's infraction of Hospitaller rules, compared with the magnitude of his crime against the secular law. Both Botyl and Langstrother would have known that Malory had made the merciful choice in hiding Neville. On the other hand, his secular crime, treason, could cost him his life if he were handed over to Edward for punishment. Neither Botyl nor Langstrother could possibly have wanted Thomas Malory beheaded. Not only would that mean the loss of Malory himself, but it could mean serious diplomatic trouble in the high levels of both the Church and the state to have a member of the Order of Hospitallers beheaded for treason. So his superiors would have locked him up, put him under house arrest, to save him from the wrath of the king, who was in a killing mood.[134]

To continue our speculative story, maybe King Edward knew that Thomas Malory, the Hospitaller knight, had hidden Neville, and maybe he did not. It is possible that he, like everyone else even down to the present day, had no real information about where Neville went; he had simply vanished, and the Hospitallers kept the story to themselves. But if Edward did know that Malory had helped him disappear, then Botyl the Yorkist prior, whom Edward trusted, assured him that the Knights had ways of dealing with infractions of their rule, and he would see to it that Malory was imprisoned. The order did not have, and never had had, the authority to execute a transgressor, and the rule of the order forbade such a punishment anyway, no matter how serious his offense. King Edward knew that. Additionally, Edward did not want trouble with the order, which was supporting his claim to the throne, both diplomatically among the

[134] House arrest within the order was actually the easiest and most common punishment for infringement of rules, since its earliest beginnings. A mild transgression would result in the "Septaine," involving confinement to quarters and fasting for seven days, except that on the Wednesday and Friday bread and water were permitted. For a more serious offense, there was "Quarantaine," similar except that it lasted for forty days. Punishable rules ranged from the one forbidding members of the order to fight or break the furniture in an inn, for example, to the decree that they were never to "make vagabonds of themselves" by wandering around outside the precinct of their homes (Porter, 247–250). Even if blood were shed, capital punishment was never approved within the order; if a member was judged to deserve such treatment he would be handed over to secular authority for its enactment. One rule that was never rescinded, but over time came to be honored more in the breach than in the observance, was that a member was never to participate in the quarrels of worldly princes. Of this, obviously, Malory in our hypothetical story was guilty.

nations and, at home, with fighting men. Moreover, perhaps Neville did not seem to be very much of a threat at this point, with most of the northern recalcitrants already dead, and perhaps some old affection for his cousin Humphrey awoke in Edward. At any rate, the king contented himself with leaving Malory to the justice of the Knights. The next question that our hypothetical story must answer is *Why did King Edward wait so long—four years—before he published his intention never to pardon Sir Humphrey Neville and Sir Thomas Malory?* Again, the answer is easy to deduce from what we know of history. Like our previous answer, it is linked to Edward's trust of Sir Robert Botyl. As we have seen, it is possible that Edward did not know in 1464 that one of the Hospitaller knights had betrayed him by hiding Humphrey Neville; maybe he learned it in 1468. On the other hand, if Edward did know about Malory's crime as early as 1464, and had trusted Botyl to take care of things, he had a new reason to be nervous in 1468. The Yorkist prior Robert Botyl was dying, and the Lancastrian Sir John Langstrother was slated by the Hospitallers to take his place. Edward did not trust Langstrother at all. Gregory O'Malley details Langstrother's fall from the grace of King Edward (O'Malley, 128), from the time when Edward entrusted to him the mission of finding Humphrey Neville and bringing him to court in 1463 until Langstrother's beheading in 1472. As early as 1467, Edward seems to have been aware that the old Yorkist prior Botyl was failing, for Edward began a series of challenges directed toward the Hospitallers, who had a Lancastrian in mind for their next prior of England. In 1467, the king tried to "pack the court" against the time of Botyl's death by procuring a license for Botyl to admit five new brethren to the Hospital at royal request; apparently Edward hoped to have five new men who were loyal to himself. Then, on July 16, 1468, Edward issued another challenge to the Hospitallers: on the general pardon of that date, he named one of their knights, Sir Thomas Malory, as excepted from his mercy, and, as we guess just to make the message clear that he knew what crime Malory had committed, he listed Sir Humphrey Neville's name immediately adjacent to Malory's. This reminder of Malory's old treason could not have been misunderstood by his order.

Two months later, in September of 1468, the Yorkist prior who supported Edward, Robert Botyl, died. In unprecedented and egregious violation of the Hospitallers' protocol for choosing their new prior, and knowing well that Langstrother's "seniority, experience, and affluence virtually precluded any other candidate" (O'Malley, 128), Edward took immediate steps to block him from that powerful position. He tried to sidestep the Hospital's own time-honored method of choosing a new prior and named his young brother-in-law, Richard Wydeville, as the new prior. Not only was this boy only twenty years old; he was not even a member of the Knights Hospitallers. He was completely inexperienced and altogether unqualified, and of course Edward knew it, but Edward was through with trying to deal diplomatically with the Hospital in order to keep its support; he knew trouble was coming in the person of the Lancastrian Langstrother; let it come. At this point, although Edward, in releasing the non-pardon of our two knights, may have thought he would enjoy taking revenge on Humphrey Neville, maybe Thomas Malory was only a sort of stalking horse for Langstrother, who was Edward's real target. Simon Phillips gives us an enlightening biographical sketch of Langstrother, which suggests reasons why King Edward found him formidable:

> Born c. 1416–17, Langstrother was a member of the Order, and thus had started his military training, by the age of 17 or 18, had become a preceptor by 26, was lieutenant turcopolier by 28, castellan of Rhodes at 29, and possibly captain of St. Peter's Castle by the time he was 47. When Prior Botyl died, Langstrother (about 51 or 52 years old) was bailiff of Eagle, grand commander of Cyprus, and seneschal of the Grand Master on Rhodes. Apart from his military obligations to the Order, he also served, amongst other duties, as Hospitaller ambassador to Venice and the papal court in Rome, and as the Grand Master's

> proctor general in England, and he was entrusted as a collector of indulgence money for the defence of Rhodes. (Phillips, 53)

In addition to these offices, and more, within the order, Langstrother had also held significant secular offices, including that of treasurer of England. As prior and the high commander of all of the order's warriors in England, Langstrother would have real power, which he could be expected to use for Henry VI rather than for Edward IV. The struggle between the Hospital and the king over the selection of the new prior went on for upwards of two years; presumably Edward thought that if he could succeed in installing young Richard Wydeville, then he himself could command the Hospital in England. Finally, in 1470, Langstrother was named by bull of the grand master of the order, Jean Baptiste Orsini, as the chosen man, and accepted as such in Edward's court.

Meanwhile, until 1469, Humphrey Neville was still in hiding. And that is our next question: Where was he? The *Year Book of 4 Edward IV* has it that after surrendering the castle at Bamburgh, Neville, "flying southwards, took refuge in a cave on the banks of the Derwent, which here for some distance forms the boundary between Northumberland and Durham." And we do have reason to believe that the caves in that area could afford shelter sometimes, from the legend of the queen and the robber. The story is told that Queen Margaret of Anjou, fleeing with her young son from the field after the Battle of Hexham, encountered a cave dweller on the path. Margaret thrust the boy at the rough-looking man and implored him to save his prince, and he did, giving both his prince and his erstwhile queen a hiding place in his cave until her men found her.[135] However, the boundary between Northumberland and Durham may have been too perilously close to the Neville family seat at Brancepeth for him to stop there. On the other hand, if he left his own neighborhood, which presumably would have been very familiar to him, he would need help hiding. Matthews says that

135 "The Battle of Hexham," *The Monthly Chronicle of North-Country Lore and Legend* 2, no. 11 (January 1888): 29.

the common belief has been that he hid in a Yorkshire cave (Matthews, 135). If the tradition that Neville was in Yorkshire is correct, then it is easy to figure out who helped him find a good cave. Remember, Thomas Malory grew up at his parents' manor at Studley, adjacent to Fountains Abbey on the rocky banks of the River Skell, and he and his brothers and sisters spent their childhood with access to some of the best hiding caves in the county. Remember, too, that when the first little band of Cistercian monks arrived at Fountains in 1132, these caves, along with the spreading trees, offered them shelter for two years while they were building their monastery. Today the caves hold a great deal of charm for tourists; one of them has put her travel experience in a comment on the Internet: she went to Fountains and got caught in a rainstorm, she says, and "ended up hiding in a little cave with benches."[136] It is easy for us to believe that Neville in his desperate flight showed up at the door of Ribston Commandery and told Thomas Malory his story, and Malory said something like, "I know just the perfect place. I found it when I was a kid."

A cave beside the Skell

And then there is the question that is probably uppermost in the reader's mind at this point in our story, and it takes us firmly out of hypothesis and into historical fact: How do we know that Sir Thomas Malory was in the Ribston commandery? The first piece of direct evidence in this whole search for Malory's identity is his own statement in his book that he is one of the Chevaliers — "And here ... followyth the Most Pyteuous Tale of the Morte Arthure Saunz Gwerdon *Par le*

[136] Sandra S, "Fountains Abbey and Studley Royal Water Garden," TripAdvisor, June 27, 2011, https://www.tripadvisor.com/ShowUserReviews-g209973-d211827-r113998068-Fountains_Abbey_and_Studley_Royal_Water_Garden-Ripon_North_Yorkshire_England.html.

Shyvalere Sir Thomas Malleorre, knight"[137]—for we know that in fifteenth-century England the knights called Chevaliers were the Hospitallers. And then there is that other piece of direct evidence, which locates Malory firmly in the commandery of the Chevaliers at Ribston: the margin note in an ancient manuscript, in an old hide trunk, "Ci comence le livre que Sir Thomas Malori Chr reduce in Engloys et fuist emprente par Willm Caxton"—"Here begins the book that Sir Thomas Malory, Chevalier, reduced into English and had printed by William Caxton." So here we find ourselves at the nub. Sir Thomas Malory reduced old French books into English, and one of those books leads us to Sir Thomas Malory. We saw in chapter 7 that the fact he used the Hospitallers' *Suite du Merlin* shows he was in the Hospitallers' Ribston monastery where it was kept. And *where* he was shows us *who* he was. Why was he in a monastery? No doubt we could make up all sorts of reasons. But the obvious reason is easy: because he was a monk.[138]

[137] For discussion, see chapter 3, above.

[138] This story of who put Sir Thomas Malory in jail is more history than guess, as the reader can easily see, but it does encompass speculation; there are things in it that we cannot truly know. On the other hand, it is based on known history, and there is nothing in it that contradicts what we do know. I hope it will inspire others to speculate and to publish their hypotheses; conjecture is, after all, at the heart of human inquiry. If we are ever to know for sure who imprisoned Malory, and why, it will surely be necessary for scholars to follow their surmise, that Questing Beast, where it leads. And then, if it leads only to hypothesis, they must say so, and not fall into the trap that currently entangles the study of Malory's identity by confusing speculation with fact.

22

Still Searching for Sources

WE HAVE FOUND manuscript sources in Yorkshire for those parts of the *Morte* taken from the Ribston *Suite du Merlin*; and for the tale of the Roman War, taken from the Thornton alliterative *Morte Arthure*. We have found a good possibility for the original of the *Queste*, owned by Malory's distant cousin Richard Ros, and another for the *Mort Artu*, likewise owned by Ros. We have not found source manuscripts for the rest of *Le Morte Darthur*. But William Matthews has given us one of the best attempts to locate Malory's sources, even though he failed to notice the DeRos-Malory connection and its implications. After examining the private libraries in England and failing to find there everything Malory needed, he proposed that except for the English material, the medieval collections held in France might have supplied Malory with his source books, and he examined each of those collections. I believe Matthews was onto something significant concerning the Jacques d'Armagnac collection. His information that that library contained everything Malory needed other than the English poems; his map of the area around Armagnac; and his listing of those twenty-four place names that appear on that map and also in *Le Morte* (Matthews, 148) are impressive. I think the d'Armagnac library would be a good place to look, and now that our Malory lens has been adjusted so that we can see a Knight Hospitaller as our author, we have a new reason to look there. Remember, every knight of the Hospital was required to go directly to the Holy Land for his years of service in arms against the Turk, before he was posted to a commandery in his homeland, and the Castle d'Armagnac was located near the most direct route for English Knights traveling across France to the East. Aveyron, with historical connections to the house of Armagnac, is seventy-seven miles away. Aveyron had five Hospitaller preceptories. La Cavalerie, the most interesting to us in our search, is also the oldest of the five, all of which are still standing. *Travel France* tells us that La Cavalerie "was built at the junction of roads which led to the Mediterranean ports where the pilgrims embarked for the Holy Land."[139] We may assume that the Hospitallers as well as pilgrims used their commandery at Aveyron to embark for the Holy Land. It may well be that Sir Thomas Malory was there and saw the books and the neighborhood, both going out and coming back. Possibly he even stayed for a while. The Armagnac records are lost, Professor Matthews tells us, but he offers encouragement in case "any young scholar-adventurer should be inspired to pursue the quest into the wilderness of French archives" (Matthews, 149). I hope there is such an adventurer out there somewhere.

There is another strong possibility closer to home, the Cistercian Fountains Abbey, which had a large library before the destruction of the monasteries and is located, as we have seen, adjacent to the Malory home at Studley. Quite possibly Thomas Malory, growing up next door, was educated at the abbey school. The Cistercians and the Hospitallers, both being Bernardian orders, shared a common spirituality, and the two monasteries, Ribston Commandery and Fountains Abbey, were only about ten miles apart. It is likely that Fountains would have lent its books to a Hospitaller knight-monk at Ribston who needed them, especially if that knight were their former pupil and next-door neighbor, and a member of one of their donor families. We know that the abbey did sometimes lend its books; lending and borrowing books among themselves in order to make copies was one way that monasteries increased their collections. Moreover, in a Cistercian history of Fountains' holdings we learn that "the community might lend some of its books to

[139] "Knights Templar Commanderies in Aveyron History," Travel France Online, https://www.travelfranceonline.com/knights-templar-commanderies-in-aveyron-history/.

outsiders. To make sure that these were treated with care and returned to the monastery, there was often an *Ex libris* on the flyleaf... and sometimes also a caution or a curse upon anyone who dared to damage or retain the book."[140] If Fountains would lend books to anybody, presumably it would lend books to a house of Hospitallers.

It has been argued that a Cistercian abbey, such as Fountains, would not own romances; its library would consist entirely of sacred books. Yet among the meager handful of books that have been found, survivals of the dissolution at Fountains, are some that are not sacred — grammar, astronomy, music scores, a bestiary (which may have been used in the instruction of Abbey school children), cartularies, account books, medical tracts, a copy of Bede's *History*, and a *Brut* — and the fact that there was a *Brut* in the Fountains library encourages us to think that other Arthurian material may have been part of its collection as well. After all, monasteries did receive random donations, and a Cistercian did write the *Queste del Saint Graal*, which Malory used. Almost the whole collection, which began to be assembled with the entry of Hugh, Dean of York, into the monastery in 1132, was destroyed or dispersed by Henry VIII. George Lawton (28, n. b) says of that desecration, "Learning suffered a great loss by the neglect to provide a receptacle for the libraries of the suppressed monasteries, instead of suffering the books to be sold as waste paper." He quotes John Bale:

> A number of them which purchased these superstitious mansions (the monasteries,) reserved of those library books — some to form their jakes [that is, to be used as toilet paper] — some to scour their candlesticks, and some to rub their boots; and some they sold to grocers and soap-sellers, and some they sent over the sea to the book-binders, not in small numbers, but, at times, in ships. I know a merchant (who shall at this time be nameless,) that bought the contents of two noble libraries for

140 cistercians.shef.ac/uk/fountains/buildings/library.

> forty shillings price. A shame it is to be spoken. This stuff has been occupied instead of grey paper. Our posterity may well curse the wicked fall of our age—this unreasonable sport of England's most noble antiquities.[141]

Bale was right, of course; history does not smile on the perpetrators of this abominable violation. However, great efforts are being made today by the British National Trust to catalog whatever medieval books have survived in England. It may be that a trove of romances rescued from the destruction of Fountains Abbey will yet be found, saved by some private lover of Arthur and his lady and his knights, and kept for us all this time in some old trunk in some old house somewhere. It has been known to happen.

[141] John Bale, "Declaration upon Leland Journal, 1549," *Fuller's Church History Book VI*, 333; quoted in George Lawton, *Religious Houses of Yorkshire* (London: Simpkin, 1853), 28.

23

A Bodacious Boondoggle

THE MOST NOTICEABLE feature of the entire body of research in modern times into the identity of the author of *Le Morte Darthur* is the ardent attempt to fit the available evidence into a predetermined mold: it must be made to fit the features of Sir Thomas Malory of Newbold Revel, Warwickshire. From the time when George Lyman Kittredge, in the 1890s, stated that he had done a thorough search among fifteenth-century records and found only one Thomas Malory who could be the author, the Warwickshire man who was written up in Sir William Dugdale's history of his county, scholars have shown a definite bias in favor of that candidate, and that prejudice is not the result of any particularly convincing evidence. The only real evidence is that he had the right name, he was a knight, and he lived in the right century. Never mind that other researchers have found other Thomas Malorys whose claims seemed to be valid; never mind that William Matthews presented his meticulous research and his support for a man that Kittredge failed to find, Thomas Malory of Yorkshire, in a detailed and convincing "skeptical inquiry" over fifty years ago — the man from Newbold Revel is usually assumed to be the author. His fans are easy to recognize: they do not look at evidence and consider where it leads; they begin their discussion by assuming that the Newbold Revel man wrote the book, and if any evidence leads to another conclusion, they spin it. Advocacy of him by now displays so much twisting of original evidence and so much faulty logic that the whole case has become a tissue of imaginary things.

Medieval prison in Venice, tourist-ready

The primary obstacle to accepting this candidate as the author has been his criminal career, which is discordant with the book he is supposed to have written. There is also the problem of access to source books, which in fact is a problem for any candidate, but it was especially so when the Newbold Revel man was assumed to be a felon in jail for his crimes. Thomas Malory of Newbold Revel was in and out of prisons during a span of nine or ten years; he was imprisoned in Marshalsea, Ludgate, Newgate, and the Tower of London between 1451 and 1461. These prisons, except for parts of the Tower where kings and queens were sometimes held, were facilities for criminals.[142] Those criminals got no sympathy. Until after Dick Whittington's prison reforms, they got no running water either. They got whatever food they could get by gifts from outside or bribery inside. They certainly got no library of expensive books to while away their idle hours. Matthews describes Newgate Prison:

142 Newgate Prison was destroyed late in the nineteenth century, after having been the scene of untold misery for hundreds of years. No picture of its medieval interior is available. However, it was coeval with the Venice prison, shown above, and may have been similar. Notice, in the picture on the left, the low cell doors and the hole in the wall beside each door, which affords the only access to the small unlit room where multiple prisoners were incarcerated together, without light, plumbing, or any other facilities. The larger door shown on the right is not a cell door but the door to a corridor.

> It was a prison for criminals and traitors mainly; it was desperately overcrowded, and all but a few favored inmates were kept in darkness and chains. Food, even water, was inadequate; plague and prison fever decimated the population. Even after Dick Whittington caused the jail to be cleaned and water faucets to be supplied, it continued to be a charnel; of sixty debtors from Ludgate who asked to be transferred there as a way of escaping their debts, forty died, and in one year of the London coroner's rolls, a large part of the deaths recorded took place in this very prison. (Matthews, 59)[143]

Edward Hicks, the main discoverer of Malory's prison record, was aware of all these problems, and yet he seems to have had difficulty in acknowledging them. In trying to reconcile these facts with his advocacy of Thomas Malory of Newbold Revel as our author, he encumbered himself in a tangle of mixed-up history and bad logic. Considering Malory's access to source books, he declared that the

[143] Anne F. Sutton claimed, in "Malory in Newgate: A New Document", *The Library: The Transactions of the Bibliographical Society*, Seventh Series, 1, no. 3 (Sept. 2000), 243, that a newly found document proved Sir Thomas Malory was a prisoner in Newgate in 1468, and that he produced the *Morte* there. However, Sutton does not explain how she draws her conclusion based on the document, which is a list of twenty-one witnesses, including Malory, to a deathbed declaration held at Newgate. It gives no suggestion that any of the witnesses was an inmate; in fact, Sutton comments on eleven of the men listed, and they were not inmates; they were the keeper, five yeomen, a secretary, an administrator, a surgeon, and a priest. The document itself gives information on seven more of the witnesses, without calling them inmates: a draper, an ironmonger, a woolpacker, and four "gentlemen." That leaves only four witnesses without an identifying tag. Since no one listed is said to be an inmate, it is not clear why Sutton thinks the document proves that Malory was one. Moreover, in addition to this document, there are extant at least five records of Malory's having acted as witness to various transactions at different times and places — a sale, two property settlements, a priory grant, and a betrothal ceremony (Field, "The Malory Life-Records," in *A Companion to Malory*, 119–125); and these records are not seen as any evidence of Malory's concurrent residence. Sutton's article does not add any new information pertinent to the search for Malory's identity; the problems attending incarceration in Newgate for our author still hold.

Greyfriars library "so near at hand must have been a veritable godsend during his long detention. 'Detention,' indeed, expresses his situation much more accurately than incarceration; for had he been confined in the fetid dungeons which Newgate possessed, his life would have been as short as those of the Carthusians who, imprisoned for refusing to acknowledge the supremacy of Henry VIII, succumbed in a few weeks to their loathsome surroundings" (Hicks, 68). One must wonder what unstated assumptions Hicks was making: he acknowledged that Malory was confined in Newgate, he knew the loathsomeness of the place and its danger to life itself, yet he said that somehow Malory was not subject to its loathsomeness and perils but, on the contrary, enjoyed the convenience of the library in the neighboring monastery as he was writing his book.

In his defense of the Warwickshire Malory as the author, Hicks wandered off into various social movements that he thought might exonerate Malory for his crimes: Lollardry, hatred of monks and monasteries, even land enclosure. But all of these phenomena, as interesting as they may be, are not to be found in *Le Morte Darthur*. Arthur and all of his knights are nothing if not faithful Catholics; monasteries are seen as refuges of kindness and healing; and land enclosure was in the future for Thomas Malory; he knew nothing about it. Hicks knew that, but he tried to use it nevertheless: "The practice of land enclosure, which caused so much discontent in England, was just beginning at this time; but the monks of Coombe Abbey [that is, the abbey besieged and vandalized by Malory and his gang] are not among the offenders named at the Parliamentary Inquiry of 1517" (Hicks, 48). Land enclosure? Inquiry of 1517? How far afield Hicks was inspired to go to exonerate his favorite Malory, and only to be forced in the end to concede that Coombe Abbey was not one of the "bad" monasteries. There are passages in *Le Morte Darthur* where Lancelot (that is, Malory) inveighs against violence to women; moreover, Arthur requires all of his knights to renew their oath yearly never to "enforce" women but always to come to their aid. Reasonably, anyone might interpret those passages to mean that the rapist Sir Thomas of Newbold Revel did not write the *Morte*. When Edward Hicks looked at those passages, however, he took them as proof, not that his man did not write the book but that the double rape of Joan Smyth for which this Malory was put in prison never took place (Hicks, 55)! This was the crime to which Kittredge was referring when he said that "the double charge of rape was manifestly absurd — a mere legal formula if the woman of the house was present and had been forcibly removed from her dwelling while it was ransacked" (Kittredge, viii). Again, to what lengths this Malory's fans will go in twisting the evidence to support him.

There are a few exceptions, of course, but not many. Larry Benson, for example, found Matthews's skeptical inquiry to be valid and summed up his own position in reaction to it: "We know that Malory was a knight, that he was imprisoned, and that he delighted in hunting, in chivalric practice, and in Arthurian literature. William Matthews has shown us that we cannot go beyond that. Our Sir Thomas Malory was almost certainly not the colorful jailbird who enlivened so many classroom lectures on the *Morte Darthur*."[144] But voices like Benson's are drowned in the general acclamation of the colorful jailbird.

Eventually, the world of Malory scholarship realized that the author was probably not incarcerated as a felon in a prison for felons; he was probably a prisoner of war or a political prisoner. This conclusion is satisfactory for a number of reasons, not the least of which is that the Warwickshire Malory's record of imprisonment as a criminal ends in 1461, years before the book was written. However, the proponents of Malory of Newbold Revel still cling to the old criminal and spin his criminal record in whatever ways they think fit. In arguing for their candidate, they seem not to have noticed that claiming for him house arrest in some castle or monastery somewhere, where he could comfortably write his book, renders completely irrelevant the fact that Thomas Malory of Newbold Revel is the only candidate

[144] Larry D. Benson, *Malory's* Morte Darthur (Cambridge, MA: Harvard University Press, 1976), ix.

with a prison record. Any man called Thomas Malory, designated a knight, could have been in prison for political reasons in 1469 and written *Le Morte Darthur*. Any Sir Thomas Malory could have been a prisoner of war. Logically, the claim of political arrest completely removes the advantage formerly held by the man with a known prison record, the man of Newbold Revel, in our contest for authorship. But logic is not a strong point in the argument favoring him.

Edward Hicks wrote his biography of the Newbold Revel man in 1928. That was a long time ago. But even today, many years after William Matthews demonstrated that there is a better candidate, we still see the dodging and spinning. For example, Sue Ellen Holbrook clearly does not notice that her evidence leads away from Newbold Revel. She says this:

> In Warwickshire, Malory had inimical relations with both the alien priory of Carthusian Monks Kirby in 1450 and also the Cistercian Coombe Abbey in 1451. Even seven years later when he was "detained" in the Marshalsea, it was "for surety of the place ... especially towards the Abbot of Coombe." Yet the landscape of his *Morte Darthur* includes only congenial religious establishments, some modest, others rich, that provide knights, ladies, and their companions with good counsel, confession, last rites, interment, even adventures, and above all both medical care and, as Lancelot expects in the stanzaic *Morte*, lodging. (Holbrook, 30)

Then, after giving us two examples of the monks' kind hospitality, she goes on with her discussion of Guenevere as abbess, still assuming that Malory of Newbold Revel wrote the book. Apparently, it never even dawns on her that all this friendly treatment of houses of religion in *Le Morte* is good evidence that its author was not that renowned breaker of monasteries, Sir Thomas Malory of Warwickshire; he must have been somebody else.

Even the consideration of dialect, which would seem to be a straightforward and unbiased enterprise, is affected by this assumption that the Warwickshire Malory authored *Le Morte*. Jeannette Marshall Denton has written a study of Malory's dialect; she pronounces early that "Sir Thomas Malory was likely born around 1416 [she cites P. J. C. Field for that date] to a prominent family on the estate of Newbold Revel in what is now northeastern Warwickshire. We can surmise from these facts [*sic*] that he likely grew up speaking an upper-class form of the local Warwickshire dialect."[145] We see immediately that Denton will run into trouble, because the dialect of the *Morte Darthur* is not that of Warwickshire. She comes up to the challenge, however, by positing that this upper-class Warwickshire man probably had a wide acquaintance and therefore could have learned the right dialect somewhere, somehow. Then she goes on with her discussion of "Malory's" dialect. She does not question whether maybe somebody else is the author, rather than the Newbold Revel man. And she does not seem to know the weakness of Field's argument for a birth date for that man of about 1416 (chapter 17, "Dugdale Defended").

Denton is not alone, by any means. Helen Cooper makes the same assumptions when she — with plenty of company, it must be said — claims that Malory appears to have been working from a copy of the alliterative *Morte Arthure* different from the only copy that exists today, the Thornton (Cooper, 537). She bases that judgment partly on the belief that our author was the Warwickshire man: "The dialect in which the poem is written," she tells us, is "more northern than Malory's own," referring to Malory of Newbold Revel. Presumably that Malory would not have been able to supply the additional alliteration in his adaptation of the poem that the author did, in fact, supply. But Cooper does not therefore consider the possibility that the Newbold Revel man may not be the author. No. She assumes that there must have been a copy of the alliterative poem other than the

[145] Jeannette Marshall Denton, "An Historical Linguistic Description of Sir Thomas Malory's Dialect," in *Arthuriana* 13, no. 4 (Winter 2003): 15.

Thornton, which Malory used. But William Matthews firmly dealt with that argument, fifty years ago. He demonstrated that our author could not have used another copy of the *Morte Arthure* without making changes to whole lines and thus changing larger patterns and meanings within the poem (Matthews, 213). However, there is no reason why Malory could not have used the Thornton with changes less radical if he knew northern dialect, as he did if he was a man from Yorkshire. It appears that Cooper does not notice that a man from Yorkshire would be familiar and comfortable with the northern ways of poetry, and thus able to add to the alliteration and northern vocabulary himself, because she is assuming that Malory was the Newbold Revel man.

Sally Shaw's treatment of dialectal features in Malory is another good example of this type of failure to see the evidence clearly. In her brief (three pages) linguistic evaluation of the two texts of *Le Morte*, Caxton and Winchester, she offers examples of nonstandard forms she finds in them, often making such comments as "May be northern.... Spellings found in the north and east Midlands which derive from Scandinavian forms.... Hint of a more northerly origin for the MS.... The northern ... appear more often in the MS.... Definitely northern or north Midland.... Influence of the alliterative *Morte Arthure*, with its markedly northern language.... A few northern -and(e) endings ... a northern characteristic." But she tells us that "Malory was himself a Warwickshire man," and therefore the origin of his manuscript couldn't have been very far north; it was "certainly not beyond the Midlands, or the variations would have been more numerous and striking."[146] She does not tell us how many northern variations she would have considered numerous and striking enough to be significant. She doesn't mention the hundreds of such variations detailed by William Matthews. She believes Malory was from Warwickshire, and that belief apparently colors her judgment about the dialect of the *Morte*.

[146] Sally Shaw, "Caxton and Malory," in *Essays on Malory*, 123.

We have already examined the way P. J. C. Field deals with records, changing what he thinks should be changed, claiming scribal error, obfuscating. He attempts to deflect anything that seems negative about Thomas Malory of Newbold Revel to some other cause: the Wars of the Roses, the persecution by government officials, the lies of the chroniclers. When there is a blank spot in the records, he often fills it with his own speculation and then on a subsequent page uses that same speculation as the first premise in a further syllogism, just as though it had been universally acknowledged truth. The most egregious example of this method is Field's opinion that Thomas Malory of Yorkshire was the "byblow of a country squire" and therefore could not have been the author of *Le Morte Darthur*. This is pure fabrication, but once postulated it is assumed in Field's book to be proven and incontrovertible. Hyonjin Kim is referring to just this sort of thing when he complains of Field's "predetermined … will to advance the claim of his beloved candidate. His frequent recourse to the process of chain guessing, which is often conducted with unjustified confidence, makes some of his conclusions very hard to swallow" (Kim, 2, n. 5). "Chain guessing" is the perfect term for Field's technique.

As we have seen, each proponent of the Warwickshire Malory finds his or her own method of sidestepping. This chapter began by stating that the most remarkable feature of this entire body of research is the attempt to fit the evidence into the features of Sir Thomas Malory of Newbold Revel. Throughout this book, we have seen how that attempt works: if the knights named on a list of those who went with King Edward IV on his 1462 march north to capture three castles were Yorkists, then the Thomas Malory on the list was obviously a Yorkist, and therefore the Newbold Revel man. On the other hand, since the Thomas Malory whose name appears on a 1468 list of those to whom the same king denied his pardon was of course a Lancastrian, then we see that Malory of Newbold Revel had obviously changed his allegiance and become a Lancastrian. If Sir William Dugdale, the historian of Warwickshire, says that Thomas Malory was a valiant soldier who served his county in Parliament later in his life, and was buried under a grand memorial, then we are pleased to see that he was the very knight of Newbold Revel. But if Dugdale says that this knight was old enough to be a soldier in 1415, then Dugdale must have been mixed up, because in that case the Newbold Revel man would have been too old in 1469 to be writing *Le Morte Darthur*. If the great dialectician Angus McIntosh pronounces that the dialect of the *Morte* is not from Warwickshire, then we remain silent on McIntosh's pronouncement. If McIntosh gives his opinion that the dialect is not exactly northern but "northerly," we sidestep that pronouncement and say that he decisively rejected Yorkshire as its locale. There are countless other examples.

The capstone of this structure comes from Professor Field, who manages to combine two fallacies, the argument from silence and the argument from circular reasoning, in a sort of double whammy that simply takes the breath away. He and many others have searched for some evidence that Sir Thomas Malory of Newbold Revel was in some sort of prison somewhere in 1469–1470. There isn't any. Malory was granted a pardon on October 24, 1461, and after that time the records never mention him as any kind of prisoner, either criminal or political, again. Field acknowledges this; he says, "Repeated scholarly searches of the legal records have found no trace of arrest, charge, trial, or verdict" (131). But then, in an amazing acrobatic leap of logic, he takes this complete absence of evidence to mean not that Malory was not in jail but that his "enemies" had put him there and deliberately kept no record (131)! But that is not all. He assures us that we know his candidate was in prison, because he said so in his book—"the *Morte Darthur* shows that he was in prison at about this time" (131)—and apparently truly believes that he has presented us with unanswerable proof. He seems not to notice the circularity of his argument, that he is assuming what he is trying to prove—that is, that Malory of Newbold Revel was our author—for the *Morte* does not say that the Newbold Revel man was in prison; it says that the author was.

The world of Malory scholarship seems to have bought Malory of Newbold Revel lock, stock, and barrel by ignoring the fact that the only factor in his favor over all the other Thomas Malorys in England when *Le Morte Darthur* was written is that he was an acknowledged knight during the ninth year of the reign of Edward IV. Everything else is fabricated by eagerness to have an answer to the mystery. In fact, the whole case for Sir Thomas Malory of Newbold Revel currently consists of a small collection of facts held together precariously with a thin tissue of bad logic.

And that is where the contest has stood until today.

But today, for the first time, we are examining the plethora of evidence, both circumstantial and direct, that the author of *Le Morte Darthur* was not, after all, Malory of Newbold Revel. He was, in fact, the person he said he was when he signed his book, telling us it was written "Par le Shyvalere Sir Thomas Malleore, knyght": he was one of the Chevaliers, the Knights Hospitaller. It is remarkable that all the pieces of evidence for this identification fit together easily in a framework of solid logic that requires no bending, stretching, spinning, or ignoring of the facts. But even more remarkable, even astonishing, is that there is nothing new here. There is no discovery of a new text, for example, like the Winchester Malory, or anything else not previously known. Everything in the case for the Yorkshireman has been available to scholars all the time, but we simply have not had eyes to see it. The paradigm, meaning the by-now ingrained acceptance of the Newbold Revel man, has overpowered us. Still, there remains a gnawing uneasiness emanating from that acceptance. We have been instructed at length that it doesn't necessarily take a good man to write a good book, and we know it well. But there is still that marked and insistent malocclusion between this particular man and this particular book. It does not sit well with us.

A perennial question concerning King Arthur has been *Who was he, a man or only a myth?* The mist of time blurs our view of him, even though every now and then a new scholarly article attempts to inform us who the real Arthur was. But chances are we would have no particular interest in him anyway if it had not been for Thomas Malory. It was he who gave to the English-speaking world King Arthur and the whole panoply of medieval Romance, which has had and continues to have immeasurable influence not only on our literature but on our culture in general. From Tennyson to Twain, from Rossetti to Monty Python, from *Camelot* to proliferating online interactive games, from the pint-sized Lancelot standing under the porch light on Halloween decked out in shining armor made of aluminum foil, with one hand holding his bag of treats and the other holding Excalibur, to you, Gentle Reader — Malory's influence is everywhere, even in this cynical age, even when it serves merely as a temple against which to throw bricks. And what a story is here, that this Malory, this real man, has over centuries been subject to the ironic injustice of being almost as shadowy as his Arthur. The great question concerning Sir Thomas Malory has been *Who was he?* Who could possibly have done what he did?

But he told us himself who he was. He was "the servaunt of Jesu bothe day and nyght."

APPENDIX A

DIALECT MATTERS CONTINUED

MATTHEWS'S STUDY OF Malory's dialect is vital to our search for his identity. However, the format of Matthews's presentation of linguistic variants, in closely packed prose, seems as likely to discourage readers as to enlighen them. This is an attempt to make things easier, following Matthews's lead in the use of an appendix, but spreading examples out for easier reading. Readers should be aware that what they see here is only a brief sample and summary of Matthews's findings, for the purpose of suggesting how extensive his dialect study actually is. They are urged to read Matthews's full analysis.

That analysis begins after three appendices devoted to other matters and labeled by Matthews respectively A, B, and C. Appendices D through H comprise his study of Malory's dialect; D is labeled Winchester Text Excluding Roman War. I retain here Matthews's designations of appendices, and begin my summary with Appendix D, which starts on page 337.

Appendix D, the Winchester Text Not Including the Roman War

Matthews offers in appendix D a sixteen-page analysis of the Winchester text, but not including the Roman War episode (he examines that episode separately), in order to discover whether there are any northern usages in parts of the *Morte* other than the Roman War; we would expect to see heavily northern influence in that part, since it has as its source the northern alliterative poem *Morte Arthure*. Appendix D divides the elements of dialect into morphology, syntax, spelling, and vocabulary and gives us a detailed description of each as detected in both Caxton and Winchester versions of the *Morte*. Here is a sample from the Vocabulary section of Matthews's appendix D:

> IV. Vocabulary. The following words that appear in the Winchester text of *Le Morte Darthur* (excluding Book V) [Book V contains the Roman War episode, which is studied separately in appendix G] seem to have been northernisms either absolutely or comparatively. Except for their use by Malory, many are recorded mainly—even solely—in northern alliterative poems. The evidence for their status is provided by specific statements in Rolf Kaiser's study of Middle English dialect vocabulary and in the *Oxford English Dictionary* (OED) and the Michigan *Middle English Dictionary* (MED), by the locales of the Middle English documents cited by the dictionaries, and by the distribution in modern dialects recorded in Wright's *English Dialect Dictionary* (EDD).
>
> AFONNED, doting, madly in love, 647.8: OED *fond,* these senses only in Nthn documents; MED slightly wider usage; EDD, Nthn, NMid. ANGRE, anger, 8.8: OED, mainly Nthn citations; MED, somewhat wider; EDD, Sc. Nthn, Dev. AR, ere, 168.10 and six other usages (against normal or): OED, Nthn use from ON *ar,* Sthn use from unstressing of OE *aer;* MED, similar; EDD Sc. *air.* AWKE, crosswise, perverse, 415.7: OED, prob. from ON, rare and most examples Nthn; MED, same; EDD, Yks, eAng. SCys. (Matthews, 183)

This excerpt shows only the entries for vocabulary words beginning with A. The list goes through the whole alphabet. Matthews's summary of appendix D:

> Allowing for repetitions, the total of these northern and northernish words is about **550** [emphasis mine].... Malory's memory of these two poems [that is, the two northern poems in English, the alliterative *Morte Arthure* and the stanzaic *Le Morte Arthur*] might explain some of his northernisms; but it could only be a very limited explanation, for of the nearly two hundred different northern words that he used in sections that *he translated from French* [emphasis mine], only seventy-five occur in the alliterative poem, and only twenty-two in the stanzaic one. (Matthews, 192)

Remember, this particular appendix concerns itself with only those parts of the *Morte* outside the Roman War episode, which is based upon the English alliterative *Morte Arthure*. Medieval French poetry was not based on alliteration, as was northern English poetry. It is impossible to explain why Malory would use difficult and unusual words from northern, North Midland, Yorkshire, and Scottish dialects to translate French documents, unless he himself was from the northern part of England, and therefore so comfortable with these words that he hardly noticed that he was doing so.

Appendix E, Comparison of Winchester and Caxton Texts

Next comes, in appendix E, a five-page linguistic comparison of the Winchester (W) and Caxton (C) texts, with the view of trying to discover whatever changes Caxton may have made to the *Morte*, as compared with the version embodied in the Winchester manuscript, which is generally believed to be closer to Malory's own text than is the Caxton. Again, Matthews presents alphabetically, going through the whole alphabet, all those words of interest because either C or W uses a northern form while the other version does not. This time, Matthews sets out the corresponding forms side-by-side for us to examine; here is a small sample:

> In the following cases, the Winchester text (represented by the form in capital letters) is northern or old-fashioned while the corresponding Caxton form (in lower-case letters) is standard or more familiar; numbers are page numbers.
>
> ADREMED, dretched 1169
> AFONNED, assoted 647
> AR, ere 982, 1079, 1200
> ARSTE, erst 969, 1013, 1079
> AT UNHAPPIS, by unhap 389
> AWGHE, owe 610
> AWNE, owne 763. (Matthews, 193–194)

These are the words that begin with A, in which the Winchester form, given first, is northern or old-fashioned, while the Caxton uses the standard form. The list goes on to study the entire alphabet, for a total of *ninety-two* comparisons. Then Matthews turns to the reverse position. In the second group, the Caxton text has the northern form while the Winchester has the more familiar standard form. Again, Matthews goes through the whole alphabet, presenting comparisons of words of this status; he gives us a total of *eighty-eight* comparisons. His conclusion is this:

> The conclusion must be that both Winchester and Caxton are standardized texts, Caxton more so than Winchester. The fact that, despite this standardization, Caxton has some fifty words and a sprinkling of forms that are matched by standard usages in Winchester must mean that the text from which they both derive ultimately (and which must be akin to Malory's own) was considerably more northern in its language than even the Winchester text. (Matthews, *Inquiry*, 197)

Appendix F, Other Middle English Documents

Next, in appendix F, we are given eight pages of tightly packed comparisons with other Middle English documents, with known dialectal provenance. Matthews introduces this appendix by telling us that the central and most frequently mentioned area connected with the northernisms in Malory is Yorkshire; he then begins his analysis with the Wakefield plays:

> The *Wakefield Plays* represent the language of the West Riding, about 30 miles south of Ripon, in the early fifteenth century. The following words and forms used by Malory appear in the glossary to A.C. Cawley's selection, *The Wakefield Pageants* (Manchester, 1958). *als, anger, are* "before," *at* "that," *awne, byr* "rush," *bowne, brast, breme* "fierce." *busk, bustuw, can* "did," *can thank, carl, cast* and *kest, clater, crak, dede* "death," *dyke, doughtys, dre, endlang, fellys, flyt, fond, gate, gar, gart, gnast, grete, grym, haill, how, hap, hope, hundreth, ill, keyle* "cool," *ken, kyrk, lad, layn, leyne* "give," *lig, loft* "high," *lowsyd, make* "compose, make," *masterman, mekill, mell* "speak," *mon* "must," *nerehand, nowder, or, overtwhart, rayse, rake, rase, renk, sekir, syn, skar, slo, spar, spyrd, steven, sty, tane, tene, thole, thrang, thrife, till, tray, trane, untill, wake, walteryng, war, wark, wars, wawghs, Yoyll* "Yule": also spellings and grammatical forms such as *betokyns, carpys, gyftys, gyf* "give," *lyffand, leyfe* "leave." (Matthews, 199)

Matthews lists here those words from the Wakefield plays that are found in the *Morte*; he lists in appendix F as well those words in the following works, also of northern composition, that appear in Malory: *The English Writings of Richard Rolle of Hampole*; *The Metrical Life of St. Robert of Knaresborough*; *The Poems of Laurence Minot*; *Ywain and Gawain*; the alliterative *Morte Arthure, Sir Gawain and the Green Knight*; the *Geste Historiale of the Destruction of Troy*; and the *Plumpton Correspondence*. The result is an impressive four pages of northern words and usages, particularly from Yorkshire, that appear in Malory. Matthews tells us that "their continuance as Yorkshire dialect may also be checked in two substantial recent glossaries of the county's local vocabulary, C. Clough Robinson's *A Glossary of Words Pertaining to the Dialect of Mid-Yorkshire* (London, 1876), and Sir Alfred Edward Pease's *A Dictionary of the Dialect of the North Riding of Yorkshire* (Whitby, 1928)" (Matthews, *Works,* 202), and then he lists for us the Yorkshire words that Robinson and Pease glossed. Here they are:

> *angery, antered, at, awe, awne, bait* "feed," *bank, boun, breeks, brigg, brast, bray* "beat," *busk, carl, clave, cleg* "stick to," *cleugh, click* "seize," *crack* "talk," *daftish, deead* "death," *dike, dwine, eam* "uncle," *egg* "incite," *endlang, fell, fill,* "fell," *flang, flit, fond* "foolish," *frack* "bold," *frind* "friend," *gain* "direct," *gait* "way," *gainest, gap, gar, gate* "way," *gert* "great," *gif* "if," *grutch* "begrudge," *hale* "call," *hap, hapment, harbour,* "lodging," *hawse* "neck," *hilling* "coverlet," *howsomever, ill, intil, keeal, kemp, ken, kest, kirk, lig, lith, lope, lowse, make* "friend," *marrish, mickle, moun, nearhand, nesh, nowther, ony, or, owther, raase, rome* or *raum* "shout," *rous* "rush," *sad* "heavy," *sal* "shall," *scar* "cares," *scattert, shaffment, shent ower, sidelang, sikker, sine, slack* "valley," *slee* "slay," *sly* "clever," *speir* "ask," *sprent* "sprinkled," *stakker, stale* "stole," *steven* "shout," *stour* "commotion," *strake* "struck," *sty* "path," *swang, swarth* "turf," *suld* "should," *taen* "taken," *thrang* "crowd," *throof* "thrived," *thrumble* "tease," *til* "to," *trade* "trod," *umbethink, unheppen* "unpractical," *until, walt* "overturn," *wan* "won," *wantin* "deficient," *wap* "blow," *war, waur* "worse," *wark, warse, wayk, whatsomever, whensomever, wheresomever, whuther, wrang, yat* "gate," *yon.* (Matthews, 202–203)

Altogether, Matthews gives us a meticulously researched and reliably documented case for the northern influence in the vocabulary of the *Morte.*

He then turns the same assiduous search to Malory's word usage in the documents of Warwickshire and London, explaining that "the foregoing comparisons establish that almost all Malory's apparent northernisms were used by Yorkshiremen and alliterative poets in the late Middle English period, but a further check is necessary to discover whether they may have also been used elsewhere" (Matthews, 203). For Malory the two significant areas are Warwickshire and London, because those are the known addresses of Sir Thomas Malory of Newbold Revel, Warwickshire, Kittredge's candidate for authorship of the *Morte*. So Matthews studies in detail the *Coventry Leet Book* and two Coventry Corpus Christi plays, representing the language of Warwickshire near Newbold Revel; Stephen Scroope's translation of *The Dictes and Sayings of the Philosophers*; some short pieces published by Caxton; and an anonymous translation of *The Book of the Knight of La Tour-Landry*, all of which represent the language of London in the fifteenth century. He faithfully studies the variations from standard in words in these works, classifying them as to spelling, grammar, and vocabulary, and gives us *123* as examples. Then he tells us which of them are found in *Le Morte Darthur, fifteen* in all: *con, stonde, honde, londe, dud, hit, yate, yiven, yaf, shaftmond, cast, looe, fryth, tyll, untyll,* and he comments that "these, however, are the least significant items in the list, for they may sometimes be found in documents from London and other dialect areas: they are all found in northern documents, for instance. On the other hand, the most striking dialect features in the list do not appear in Malory at all" (Matthews, 205).

Then he gives us his conclusion: "From this, and also from the fact that almost none of the many northernisms in Malory's text appear in these Warwickshire documents, the conclusion must be that by far the greatest part of the forms and words that have been listed from *Le Morte Darthur* reflect an origin other than Warwickshire. A comparison with modern Warwickshire dialect emphasizes this conclusion. The only words in the Malory list that appear in G.F. Northall's *A Warwickshire Word-Book,* EDS (London, 1896), are: *egg* 'to incite,' *girt* 'great,' *howsumdever, mun* 'must,' *slade* 'tract of land,' *yon*'" (Matthews, 205).

Interestingly, Matthews's conclusion matches that of Angus McIntosh, that the dialect of the *Morte* is not the dialect of Warwickshire.

Matthews concludes appendix F with a brief look at Chaucer, who of course wrote in the century previous to Malory's, and he notes that "in the imitation of northern (probably north-Yorkshire) dialect used by the clerks in the Reeve's Tale there are more northernisms than in all the rest of Chaucer's writing, and that several of them are items similar to those listed from *Le Morte Darthur*," offering as illustration *thirty-one* words: *fares, has, falles, bringes, says, tydes, awen, na, swa, banes, waat, sal, taa, wrang, als, ay, dawe, daf, fonne, gif, hethen, ille, ill-hayl, los, y-mel, sin, til, wagges, wanges, whilk,* and *wight.*

Appendix G, the Roman War Episode

Appendix G consists of a fifteen-page linguistic analysis of the Roman War episode in the *Morte,* which is known to have as its source the northern English poem designated the alliterative *Morte Arthure,* known to have been copied, in the only existing copy, by the Yorkshire scribe Robert Thornton. No one will be surprised to see that this tale leans heavily toward northern dialect and prosody, particularly alliteration, and is, in Matthews's words, "formidably difficult"; he goes on: "The consequent problems relating to Malory's prosing, therefore, are the degree of his understanding of the poem, particularly in the details of its language, and the extent to which his northernisms are taken from the poem" (Matthews, 207). Matthews proceeds by "making a close and full comparison of Malory's prosing, as it is represented in W, with the poem as it is represented in the Thornton MS" (Matthews, 207). The analysis is divided into the classifications grammar, spelling, and vocabulary. The Roman War episode, not surprisingly, contains a larger proportion of northernisms than Malory uses elsewhere.

But an even more interesting observation is that many of the northern words and forms that Malory uses in this part of *Le Morte* do not appear in the alliterative source poem. Matthews discusses the various categories of northernisms with which Malory was obviously familiar enough to use them freely, independently of his source. The most striking example, found in the analysis of grammar usage, is this:

> For the third person singular, the episode has thirty-nine examples of the standard *-th* inflection: *greyth* 188, *longyth* 191, *metyth* 239, etc. But it has far more examples of northern *ys*; there are *117* all told, and of these, *sixty-eight* are not matched in the poem, but appear in Malory's substitute synonyms or in passages that he apparently added or paraphrased radically. (Matthews, 208)

Malory also appropriately uses vocabulary of the north that does not appear in the poem. Matthews classifies "northern words which Malory transferred directly from the poem or used with different measures of independence from the poem. Characterization of the words as northernism," he tells us, is based upon specific statements or the nature of the citations in the OED, MED, EDD, Rolf Kaiser's 1937 study,[147] and the glossaries of Yorkshire dialect compiled by Robinson and Pease. Here is the tally for the different classifications.

Simple Transferals. "*Thirty* words, representing *forty-one* uses, are simply transferred from the poem, occurring at exactly the same points in the narrative and in the same contexts." Matthews lists the thirty words for us and gives their standard equivalents (Matthews, 210).

Possible Transferals. "The following *forty-five* northern words, representing some *sixty-nine* uses, also occur in the poem. But they do not

[147] Rolf Kaiser, *Zur Geographie des mittelenglischen Wortschatzes,* Palaestra 205 (Leipzig: Mayer and Müller, 1937), page numbers not given.

occur at the same points as Malory has them" (210). Matthews lists the forty-five words and describes the position of each and how it is used in the poem (Matthews, 210–212).

Non-transferals. "The fact that Malory's uses of over half the words in the foregoing subsection are so far removed from the places where they occur in the poem makes it probable that they were part of his own vocabulary. This possibility is strengthened by the fact a considerable number of northern words in Malory's version do not appear in the poem at all" (Matthews, 212). Matthews lists in this section *nineteen* words, with their standard English equivalents, for a total of vocabulary entries in appendix G, analysis of the Roman War episode solely, of *ninety-four* words.

But that is not all. The analysis goes on, with a list of "an accounting of those usages which may be regarded as translation"; this accounting runs to four closely packed pages, and a total of *219* words or phrases, by my count.

Matthews gives us this list of the words in question, and a discussion of this skill in our author, and then he deals with the theory held by some scholars who notice these discrepancies and cannot believe that Malory himself could have handled the dialect so well, possibly because they are unaware that there was a Thomas Malory of Yorkshire available to write the *Morte*. Possibly thinking of Sir Thomas of Warwickshire, they propose that Malory must have had a source of the poem other than the Thornton manuscript, which is the only one in existence today. In answer to their proposal, Matthews says this:

> This explanation, usually applied to a few isolated words, does not face the large number of such words that is listed in this Appendix; and it therefore takes no account of the extensive textual differences that such a theory would entail if it were to account for the *eighteen* words (and more usages) listed above in subsection (c) and the still more numerous words in subsection (b) which occur in the poem only at

> points remote from those where Malory used them. To assume that these *fifty* or so forms were in the text of the poem that Malory used would usually entail altering the alliterative patterns of the lines in which the words occurred, and therefore changing the phrasing not only of those lines but of contiguous lines too. Since the poem as we have it usually reads satisfactorily in these places, a consistent application of this explanation would necessitate postulating a text which differed frequently and extensively from the Thornton text, but apparently without any recognizable reason in meaning or poetics. A simpler explanation is that the differences are Malory's doing. (Matthews, 213)

Indeed. However, some scholars appear to dislike simple explanations, particularly if those simple explanations challenge their pet theories. In this case, the pet theory in point is that Malory of Newbold Revel wrote the *Morte*. However, as a Warwickshire man, he probably would not have been able to understand, let alone write, the dialect of the north. The simplest glance can tell us even today that that dialect was much different from other medieval dialects. Therefore, say these critics, Malory of Newbold Revel, Warwickshire, must have been using a source poem different from the Thornton as he wrote *Le Morte*, and that source poem has since vanished. Matthews disagrees.

Matthews's analysis of the language in the Roman War episode is long, detailed, and compelling. He concludes that "Malory's command of the difficult vocabulary of the alliterative *Morte Arthure* was remarkably competent" (Matthews, 221). Malory was undoubtedly familiar with northern dialect and with other alliterative poems than this one. Obviously, the most likely way to gain such a command of a dialect obscure to other English speakers, even those contemporary with our author, was to learn it by growing up in the North Country.

Appendix H, Alliteration

Alliterative verse originated in the Germanic poetry that is ancestor to English poetry; in other words, it originated in the north and continued into Malory's time to be associated with northern poetry. Malory was apparently fond of alliteration. He used it here and there throughout the *Morte,* without reference to any such thing in his sources, which of course are largely French. Appendix H in Matthews gives us sixteen pages of discussion and examples of Malory's alliteration in the *Morte,* outside the Roman War episode, which was copied from the alliterative *Morte Arthure.* Matthews divides his analysis of alliteration outside the Roman War into several categories; I give one example from each category from the many that Matthews gives. Malory's version is given in the left column; the source poem's reading is in the right.

First category: Sometimes, Matthews says, we find Malory "taking over a line without any change except those demanded by prose syntax" (Matthews, *Inquiry,* 226); he gives *four examples, saying that they are so numerous that a few will suffice*; here is one of them:

into the vale of Vyterbe, and there to vytayle my knyghtes 189.28	In the Vale of Viterbe vetaile my knyghttes 353

Second category: Then there is Malory's "taking over a line from the poem but replacing one or more of its dialectal or unusual words with familiar words that retain the alliteration" (Matthews, 226); here is one of Matthews's *twenty-four* examples:

and syth ryde unto Roome with my royallyst knyghtes 190.22	Ryde all thas rowme landes with ryotous knyghttes 432

Third category: Sometimes Malory "employs more complete or more conventional alliteration than the corresponding lines of the poem"; I give one of Matthews's *ten* examples:

I make myne avow unto mylde Mary 188.2	And I salle make myne awowe devotly to Criste 294

Fourth category: Sometimes Malory independently expresses the same meaning as a line in the source poem but with different words and letter-rhymes; here is one example of the *seven* offered by Matthews:

And of all the soveraynes that we sawe 192.13	Of all the wyes thate I watte in this werlde ryche 533

Fifth category: "Malory often changed the meaning slightly or added small details" (Matthews *Inquiry* 231) expressed in alliteration; this example is one of the *twenty-four* offered by Matthews:

dame Elyneys son of Ingelonde was Emperour of Roome 188.10	That ayere was of Ynglande and emperour of Rome 283

Sixth category: Matthews tells us that "there remain … alliterative passages, half-lines, full-lines, and two extended sequences, which have no parallels at all in the Thornton text" (Matthews, 233); I give here three of the *forty-three* examples given by Matthews:

I complayned me to the Potestate the Pope hymself 189.16
they helde Irelonde and Argayle and all the Oute Iles 189.24
Sir, sayde the senatours, lette be suche wordis 192

Seventh category: Matthews tells us that "in the last section of his book, the story of Arthur's death, Malory worked from two sources simultaneously: a version of the French *Mort Artu* and an English poem entitled *Le Morte Arthure*. The poem was composed not far from the Humber in the late fourteenth century [extant today in a unique manuscript, British Museum Harley 2252]; it is written in rhymed stanzas, but its phraseology is strongly influenced by alliterative verse. This fact explains the abundance of alliteration in Malory's narrative at this point" (Matthews, 236). I give here one example out of Matthews's *eleven*:

Than had sir Gawayne suche a grace and gyffte that an holy man had given hym 1216.32	Than had syr Gawayne such a grace An holy man had boddyn that bone. *Le Morte Arthure* 2802–2803

Matthews concludes his appendix H by saying that Malory was perfectly capable of writing alliterative phrases and whole lines for himself; there is no necessity for postulating that he was copying since-vanished sources when he wrote such passages. In fact,

> He used some alliterations throughout his writing, *even when translating from French* [emphasis mine].... In the full analysis of Malory's northern dialect words and forms, it was necessary to conclude that he added northernisms to his version of his northern sources and that this must have been because he was familiar with northern dialect and northern alliterative verse. The conclusion about his alliteration must be much the same. (Matthews, 237)

Following this study is a sixteen-page examination of alliteration in the *Morte,* which is useful in determining the dialect in that work because alliteration is universally acknowledged to be a strong feature of northern composition, descending from the old Germanic alliterative tradition of the north.

All of this adds up to eighty-five densely packed pages of Matthews's 238-page book. Yet scholars have largely overlooked or ignored this significant body of work. Of course, there are critics who ignore it because they believe so truly that Thomas Malory of Newbold Revel, Warwickshire, is the author of *Le Morte Darthur.* They do not consider it necessary to look at Matthews's facts, because they are so completely convinced that they already know the answer to the identity question. Perhaps, because they have not looked, they are not even aware that Matthews's dialectal study is so extensive. On the other hand, I think it is possible that some scholars, perhaps most, have not given due consideration to

Matthews's work simply because it is so hard to read. Except for parts of pages 226 to 233, which offer some side-by-side comparisons of certain alliterative passages, the linguistic examination is largely set out in continuous prose, with the forms under scrutiny simply imbedded in paragraphs. Thus, we have passages like this one on page 205:

> III. *Comparison with London documents.* Checking of the words in the Malory list with the glossaries in EETS editions of some London and standard texts composed in the fifteenth century yield these results: (*a*) Stephen Scrope's lengthy translation of *The Dictes and Sayings of the Philosophers,* done in 1450, is a collection of anecdotes and tales; it contains only these items from the list: *carle, keel, plite, unbethinke* (*ynge*). (*b*) Caxton's short prose romance, *Paris and Vienne,* which he published in the same year as *Le Morte Darthur,* contains only *happe*; his *Fayttes of Armes,* 1489, lists only *brenne, lovyng* "praise," *or, syn*; and the translation of the long romance, *The Four Sons of Aymon,* which he issued shortly after he printed Malory, contains: *an-angred, are* "ere," *brenne, conne* "know," *gare* "cause," *happed, heeled* "covered," *laddes, lene* "give," *mykyll, overhwarte, scathe, sin, spered* "asked," *stoure* "noise." (*c*) The anonymous translation of *The Book of the Knight of La Tour-Landry,* an earlier fifteenth-century work, lists only: *kiste* "cast," *lyge* "lie," *overthwartly, steven, taches* "blemishes."

Or this one, on page 214:

> The following list provides an accounting of those usages which may be regarded as translation. The capitalized words are those in the poem; the lowercase equivalents are Malory's. The asterisks distinguish words which seem to have been poetical, obsolescent, or dialectal in Malory's time.

> *ABOWNE "above" 3072, *abovyn* 243.6. ALFYNE "bishop in chess" 1343, *elffe* 207.20. *ANLACE 1148, *a shorte dagger* 2041. ASKRYEDE "shouted" 2773, *had grete care* 236.16. *AWKWARDE 2247, *overthwarte* 223.17. *AYERE "go" 455, *ryde* 191.3.
>
> *BALE "sorrow" 1054, *sorow* 202.15. BALEFULLE 1029, *fayre* 202.1. BALE FYRE "signal" 1048, *bryght fyre* 202.11. *BEDGATT "going to bed" 1030, *go to his bed* 202.16. BELYFE "quickly" 1263, *blythe* 206.12. *BYERNS "warriors" 1391, 2785, 2656, *felowys* 209.4, *barowne* 236.25, *kingez* 233.5. *BIRDEZ "girls" 1029, 1136, *maydens* 202.1, 203.21. *BLONKES "horses" 615, 895, 2518, 2672, *horsys* 194.4, 196.2, 199.24, 228.22, 233.20. *BLYSCHIT "glanced" 116, *loked up* 185.12. *BOWES "goes" 2310, *were brought* 225.15. *BOWNEZ "goes to ground" 1136, *kneled* 203.22. BOURDEZ "jests" 1170, *lough* 204.16. *BRAYEDEZ "drives" 3126, *rode unto* 243.3. *BREDE "roast meat" 1052, 2716, *birdis* 202.13, *byrdys* 234.23. *BRENES "cuirasses" 1413, *helmys* 209.14 (cp *buskede in brenyes* 2517), *armed* 228.20. BRYNNEZ "burns" 1241, *destroyed* 206.2. *BRYTTENYD, BRITTENES "destroy(s)" 802, 823, 1067, 1242, *rentyth* 197.9, *slowe* 197.21, *mourtheryng* 202.21, *made grete slaughtir* 206.2. *BROTHELY "fiercely" 1408, *on both sydys* 209.11. BRUSTENE "break" 2772, BRISTE 2808, *brake* 236.15, 237.8. *BUS "behoves" 2576, *bade hym* 230.14. *BUSKES "goes, hurries" 1223, 1378, 2068, *remevyth* 205.19, turned to 208.18, *gyred thorowoute* 220.19. BUSTOUS "rough" 775, *grymly* 196.22.

The reader will easily see that this format for the presentation of variations is hard on the eyes and the understanding. Quoted above is a section setting out those thirty words beginning with A and B (capitalized), along with their variants; Matthews continues with this format through the whole alphabet, for a total of *218* (capitalized) expressions, for which he states variants. The material above is only a sample, all found on one page of appendix D. Few could continue to pay close and comprehending attention for the whole alphabetical presentation of this highly significant portion of his book devoted to dialectal analysis. In the following examples, I have expanded on the page a section of appendix D, "Linguistic Analysis of *Le Morte Darthur*: Winchester Text Excluding Roman War," in order to illustrate that Matthews packs a great deal of information into very few lines in his book. All of the visually expanded material below appears on two pages (177–179) of continuous paragraphing in Matthews. He begins by explaining:

> This present appendix does not contain a complete account of the language of Malory's work. It is concentrated on the Winchester text, it ignores Book V, and the Caxton text is cited only in relation to details in Winchester. The reasons for these limitations are that Winchester and Caxton are both predominantly written in fifteenth-century standard English. Winchester, however, has a considerable number of variations, almost all of them northern (sampling reveals no significant differences in the work of the two copyists). Most of these are represented by standard forms or words in Caxton, but with some very significant variations, in which Caxton has northern forms which are represented by standard forms in Winchester. The analysis is therefore directed toward the northern element in both texts, and to their bearing upon the linguistic texture of Malory's original text. (Matthews, 177)

Then Matthews continues, in the same tight paragraphing, to analyze the following variations, which I have expanded for easier reading.

Matthews: "Analysis of Book V is deferred to Appendix E because it presents the special problem of an episode derived from a northern poem" (Matthews, 177).

Matthews sets out the analysis of Winchester in four categories: **Morphology, Syntax, Spelling,** and **Vocabulary** (177ff).

Morphology

Personal Pronouns Common Gender

In the fifteenth century, there was widespread use of two separate sets of third-person plural personal pronouns: those inherited from Old Norse, which eventually predominated in Modern English (*they, their, them*), and the native English forms *hir/her*. As would be expected from their Norse origin, the *they/their/them* forms began with adoption in the northern dialect area and in time spread over the whole of England.

In both C and W:

the *th* forms predominate;

they is regular in both texts.

Winchester:

their/there are about twice as frequent as *hir/her*;

them is approximately as frequent as *hem*.

Example; on pages 21–36 W, occurrences:

their 28

hir 13

them 21

hem 21

Caxton:

"agrees broadly" with W;

rather more *h*-forms,

but

some *th*-forms where W has *h*-forms.

Feminine Pronouns

C and W: normally the standard *she,*

but

one possible variant: C *she,* W *so* (948); probably represents northern form *sho.*

Neuter Pronouns

W: normally *hit/hyt*; occasionally *yt/it.*

C: roughly the reverse of W.

Matthews: "In pronouns, therefore, the usage is standard, such as might be found in a document from almost any area at this time" (178), except for the *so* for *sho,* in W, pointed out above.

Inflections of Present Indicative Verbs

Generally standard, in C and W,

but

in W, many northern inflections.

Third person singular:

W standard *yth*

C standard *eth*

but

in W:

me repentys 33 examples

methynkes 8 examples

me semys 501

repentis me 119

marvaylles me 303

me forthynkes 429

me wantis 116

us thynkis 1172

she gretys 140

he gretys 268
lyggys 402
what ayles 1128
she sendis 142
repentys 1128
hauntys 269
dystresses 269
growys 255
hongys 255
longis 174
worchys 1238
rydys 1127
lovys 1136
betokyns 1237
she shrekys and wepys 324
regnys 545

Matthews: "Although this inflection may occasionally be found in East-Anglian writings in Malory's time and in London documents a little later, it was originally northern; and in Malory's day it was still essentially a North-Midland and northern usage.... In the C text all but three of these constructions are replaced by the standard *-eth* ... [but these three are significantly] close together: me *repentis* 1219, *betokyns* 1237, *worchys* 1238. No less significant is it that C once uses an *-s* inflection where W has *-th*: *has* 1135 (W *hath*); and that a grammatical error in C: *that me repentest* 258 (W *repentis*), confirms the W reading" (Matthews, 178).

Plural Inflections

W: usually *-th*; sometimes *-e/-en*
C: usually *e/en*, sometimes *-th*
Standard forms;
but in two instances,

W: northern *-ys*:
soddeyn adventures befallys 147
their shyldys hongys 268
C uses *-en* in these cases,
but in one instance,
C: *says his bretheren* 269
W: *seyde*

Present Participial Inflection
C and W: standard *-ing*, in various spellings
but
W, once: northern *-ande*: *dryvande* 305

By contrast with this northern form,
W, and sometimes C, “perhaps a score” of *y-* prefix participles; thus,

in W and C:
ipurveyed 22
yfared 28
ityed 481

in W only:
i-armed 20
ibrought 552
ygyffyn 363
ihorsed 29
isette 1196

in C only:
y-hurte 1072
y-barryd 1130

This *y-* prefix is usually found in western or southern, and sometimes in standard, texts.

W: second person singular preterites, especially

was

were

had

are often uninflected, "a northernism."

Past Tenses

In the following sample of those most often used, W employs northern or North Midland forms, Caxton the same or the standard form:

W: *faught* C: *fought*
W: *flange* 263 C: *flange*
W: *hylde* 296 C: *helde*
W: *hynge* 158 C: *henge*
W: *lepe* 1049 C: *lepte*
W: *stake* 48 C: *stack*
W: *stange* 1235 C: *stonge*
W: *stale* 1243 C: *stale*
W: *strake* 112 C: *stroke*
W: *swall* 1049 C: *swalle*
W: *swange* 395 C: *swange*
W: *sware* 274 C: *swore*
W: *thanke* 142 C: *thanked*
W: *thrange* 351 C: *thrange*
W: *throoff* 263 C: *throfe*
W: *trade* 1134 C: *trade*
W: *wan* 314 C: *wanne*
W: *wysshe* 715 C: *wasshe*
W: *wrange* 528 C: *wrange*

Noun Plural Inflections

W: *-ys/-is*

C: *-ys,-is*; also frequently *es*

Matthews: “except for the standard *-en* plurals in *brethren, chyldyrn, eyen,* ‘eyes’ and a single use of *kyne* ‘cows,’ both texts are remarkably free of the *-en* inflexion.”

I offer here a brief summary and sample of Matthews’s findings, for the purpose of giving readers a sense of how extensive is the dialect study that is presented fully in his appendices. Wherever a subtotal of the variant forms is provided by Matthews, I have highlighted it with bold type; this emphasis is my own, intended to help readers comprehend the large numbers of northern forms found in the *Morte* by Professor Matthews.

APPENDIX B

EPILOGUE: THE REST OF THE STORY

THROUGHOUT THE SPRING of 1469, Thomas Malory's kinsman and neighbor, Sir John Conyers, who had somehow acquired the nickname Robin of Redesdale, gathered all the hotheads young and old from the north of England who were willing to go and fight for their deposed king Henry against the usurper Edward, and they headed south. They joined their forces with "Kingmaker" Warwick as he rode against Edward to capture him.

William Malory, the brother of our Thomas, fought with Robin of Redesdale and was killed. William Malory, the father of our Thomas and of William Junior, also fought but survived. Robert Malory, another kinsman, possibly another brother of our Thomas, fought and survived. Sir John Langstrother, prior-elect of the Hospitallers, and his retinue of knights, fought in the rebellion, and Langstrother survived. Sir Humphrey Neville came out of his hiding place after five years and joined the Robin of Redesdale rebellion. He survived.

Warwick, who was at that time trying to make King Edward obey him, allied with Conyers's followers. Early in the summer, they captured Edward in what came to be called the Battle of Edgecote. The Redesdale (Conyers) forces went home.

On August 12, 1469, Jaquetta, Duchess of Bedford, King Edward's mother-in-law, accused Sir John Langstrother, Robert Malory, and thirty-three others of murdering her husband and son, who had been beheaded at Edgecote, apparently on Warwick's orders.

No judicial charges were ever brought. Warwick tried to rule England with King Edward as his puppet but without much success.

Humphrey Neville had apparently believed that Warwick's plan had been to overthrow Edward and restore Henry. When it became apparent that Warwick had no intention to restore Henry, Humphrey Neville gathered his own forces and staged his own rebellion against Warwick and Edward. In order to get men to follow him against Humphrey Neville, Warwick was obliged to free Edward. Under King Edward, Humphrey was captured and, on September 29, 1469, beheaded in the presence of the king.

The struggle went on. On April 14, 1471, Warwick was killed at the Battle of Barnet. On May 4, 1471, the young Edward, Prince of Wales, son of Henry VI and Margaret of Anjou, was killed at the Battle of Tewkesbury. Supporters of Henry who survived that battle, including Hospitaller Prior John Langstrother, took sanctuary in the nearby Tewkesbury Abbey. At first, Edward agreed to honor the sanctuary, but then he broke his promise. On May 7, 1471, Prior Langstrother, along with others, was dragged out of sanctuary and beheaded. Shortly thereafter, Henry VI died in captivity in the Tower, apparently murdered. Margaret of Anjou, having lost her husband and her son, faded from history.

The death date of the Chevalier Sir Thomas Malory, Knight, is not known.

Bibliography

Adams, Alison, et al., eds. *The Changing Face of Arthurian Romance: Essays on Arthurian Prose Romances in Memory of Cedric E. Pickford*. Cambridge: Boydell Press, 1986.

Altick, Richard Daniel. *The Scholar Adventurers*. Athens, Ohio: Ohio State University Press, 1987.

Archibald, Elizabeth, and A. S. G. Edwards, eds. *A Companion to Malory*. Cambridge: D. S. Brewer, 1996.

Archibald, Elizabeth, and David F. Johnson, eds. *Arthurian Literature 26*. Woodbridge, Suffolk: D. S. Brewer, 2009.

Armstrong, Dorsey. *Gender and the Chivalric Community in Malory's* Morte D'Arthur. Gainesville: University Press of Florida, 2003.

Atkinson, Stephen B. "Malory's Lancelot and the Quest of the Grail." In *Studies in Malory*, edited by James Spisak, 129–152. Kalamazoo, MI: Medieval Institute, 1985.

Bale, John. "Declaration upon Leland Journal, 1599," in *Fuller's Church History Book VI*; quoted in George Lawton, *Religious Houses of Yorkshire*. London: Simpkin, 1853.

———. "Chivalry, Cistercianism, and the Grail." *Arthurian Studies*. Cambridge: Boydell and Brewer, 2003.

Barber, Richard. "Malory's *Le Morte Darthur* and Court Culture under Edward IV." *Arthurian Literature* 12 (1993):133–155.

Baugh, A. C. "Documenting Sir Thomas Malory." *Speculum* 8, no. 1 (January 1933): 3–29.

Baumgaertner, William. *Squires, Knights, Barons, Kings: War and Politics in Fifteenth Century England*. Bloomington, IN: Trafford, 2009.

Bennett, J. A. W., ed. *Essays on Malory*. Oxford: Clarendon Press, 1963.

Benson, Larry D., ed. *Malory's* Morte Darthur. Cambridge, MA: Harvard University Press, 1976.

Benson, Larry D., and Edward E. Foster, eds. *King Arthur's Death: The Middle English Stanzaic* Morte Arthur *and Alliterative* Morte Arthure. Middle English Texts. Kalamazoo, MI: Medieval Institute, 1994.

Bernard of Clairvaux. *In Praise of the New Knighthood: A Treatise on the Knights Templar and the Holy Places of Jerusalem.* Translated by M. Conrad Greenia, O.C.S.O., with an introduction by Malcolm Barber. Cistercian Fathers Series 19B. Kalamazoo, MI and Spencer, MA: Cistercian 2003.

Boddie, John Bennett. *Historical Southern Families.* Vol. 10. Referenced in "Mallory/Palmer." Southern-Style. www.southern-style.com/Mallory.htm.

———. *Virginia Historical Genealogies.* Redwood City, CA: Clearfield, 1954. Reprint Baltimore: Genealogical, 1990, 1996, 1999, 2005.

Bogdanow, Fanni. *The Romance of the Grail.* Manchester: Manchester University Press; New York: Barnes and Noble, 1966.

———. "An Interpretation of the Meaning and Purpose of the Vulgate *Queste del Saint Graal* in the Light of the Mystical Theology of St Bernard." In *The Changing Face of Arthurian Romance: Essays on Arthurian Prose Romances in Memory of Cedric E. Pickford,* edited by Alison Adams et al, 23–46. Cambridge: Boydell Press, 1986.

Borchardt, Karl, et al., eds. *The Hospitallers, the Mediterranean and Europe: Festschrift for Anthony Luttrell.* Burlington, VT: Ashgate,

Braddock, Robert C. Review of *The Knights Hospitaller of the English Langue 1460–1565,* by Gregory O'Malley. *Renaissance Quarterly* 59, no. 4 (Winter 2006): 1286–1287.

Bradford, Ernle. *The Shield and the Sword.* New York: Barnes and Noble, 1972. New York: Open Road Media, 2014.

Bredero, Adriaan H. *Christendom and Christianity in the Middle Ages.* Translated by Reinder Bruinsma. Grand Rapids, MI: William B. Eerdmans, 1994.

British Library Catalog of Additions to the Manuscripts. BL Add. MS 62129, from Fountains Abbey. Listed in Kristeller, IV:83b: New Series 1981–1985, Part II, Index. London: The British Library 377, 1994.

British National Trust. https://www.nationaltrust.org.

Broun, Richard. *Synoptical Sketch of the Illustrious and Sovereign Order of Knights Hospitallers of St. John of Jerusalem, and of the Venerable Langue of England.* London: Printed for the Order, 1857.

Browne, Charles. *Transactions of the St. Paul's Ecclesiastical Society* 2 (February 1884): 197. London: Alabaster, Passmore, and Sons.

Bruce, Phillip, ed. *Virginia Magazine of History and Biography* 13 (1893).

Bruun, Mette Birkedal, ed. *The Cambridge Companion to the Cistercian Order.* Cambridge, MA: Cambridge University Press, 2012.

Chambers, E. K. "Sir Thomas Malory." *The English Association Pamphlet* 51 (January 1922).

Charlesworth, Dorothy. "The Battle of Hexham 1464." *Archaeologia Aeliana,* Fourth Series, vol. 30 (1952).

Check, Christopher. "The Sad History of the Knights Templar." Catholic Answers. February 1, 2009. https://www.catholic.com/magazine/print-edition/the-sad-history-of-the-knights-templar.

Cherewatuk, Karen. "Malory's Launcelot and the Language of Sin and Confession." *Arthuriana* 16, no. 2 (Summer 2006): 68–72.

Chrétien de Troyes. *Lancelot: The Knight of the Cart.* Translated with an introduction by William W. Comfort. London: Dent; New York: Dutton, 1914, 1970.

Clark, David, et al., eds. *Arthurian Literature* 28. Cambridge: D. S. Brewer, 2011.

Clark, Laura. "But Ayenste Deth May No Man Rebell: Death Scenes as Tools for Characterization in Thomas Malory's *Morte D'Arthur.*" Master's thesis, Southern Methodist University, 2008. ProQuest (AAT 1453248).

Comfort, William W. Introduction to *The Quest of the Holy Grail,* translated by W. W. Comfort. Cambridge, Ontario: In Parentheses 2000.

Cooper, Helen, ed. "The Lancelot-Grail Cycle in England: Malory and His Predecessors." *Arthurian Studies.* Cambridge: Boydell and Brewer, 2003.

———. "M. For Merlin." In *Medieval Heritage: Essays in Honour of Tadahiro Ikegami,* edited by M. Kanno et al., 93–105. Tokyo: Yushodo Press, 1997.

———. *Sir Thomas Malory*: Le Morte Darthur: *The Winchester Manuscript.* New York: Oxford University Press, 1998.

Craft, Pete. "Malory's Conflicting Conception of Knighthood." April 12, 2001. vault.hanover.edu/~battles/arthur/lancelot.htm.

Crossley, F. H. *The English Abbey: Its Life and Work in the Middle Ages.* 1935. London: Batsford, 1949, 1962.

Cummins, Neil. "Lifespans of the European Elite, 800–1800." *The Journal of Economic History* 77, no. 2 (June 2017): 406–439, http://neilcummins.com/Cummins2017.pdf.

Speight, Harry. *Nidderdale and the Garden of the Nidd: A Yorkshire Rhineland. Being a Complete Account, Historical, Scientific, and Descriptive of the Beautiful Valley of the Nidd.* London: Elliot Stock,1894.

De Jong, M. B. *In Samuel's Image:* Child Oblation in the Early Medieval West. Leiden and New York: Brill, 1996.

Denton, Jeannette Marshall. "An Historical Linguistic Description of Sir Thomas Malory's Dialect." *Arthuriana* 13, no. 4 (Winter 2003): 14–47.

Derolez, Albert. *The Palaeography of Gothic Manuscript Books from the Twelfth to the Early Sixteenth Century*. Cambridge, MA: Cambridge University Press, 2006.

Dibdin, Thomas Frognall. *The Library Companion: Or, the Young Man's Guide and the Old Man's Comfort, in the Choice of a Library*. London: Harding, Triphook, and Lepard, 1825.

Dockray, K. R. "The Yorkshire Rebellions of 1469." *The Ricardian* 6, no. 82 (December 1983): 246–257. Digitized 2005, Richard III Society. https://richardiii.net/wp-content/uploads/2021/08/06-83-The-Yorkshire-Rebellions-of-1469.pdf.

Dodsworth, Roger. *Monasticon Anglicanum, a History of the Abbies and Other Monasteries, Hospitals, and Cathedral and Collegiate Churches, with Their Dependencies, in England and Wales; Also of All Such Scotch, Irish and French Monasteries, as Were in Any Manner Connected with Religious Houses in England*. 3 vols. London: Aliciae Warren, 1655–1673.

Dugdale, Sir Thomas. *The Antiquities of Warwickshire Illustrated: From Records, Leiger-Books, Manuscripts, Charters, Evidences, Tombes, and Armes, Beautified with Maps, Prospects, and Portraitures*. London: Thomas Warren, 1656.

———. *Monasticon Anglicanum, or, the History of the Ancient Abbies, and Other Monasteries, Hospitals, Cathedral, and Collegiate Churches, in England and Wales, with Divers French, Irish, and Scotch Monasteries Formerly Relating to England*. London: Sam Keble, 1692.

Edwards, A. S. G. "The Reception of Malory's *Morte Darthur*." In *A Companion to Malory*, edited by Elizabeth Archibald and A. S. G. Edwards, 241–252. Cambridge: D. S. Brewer, 1996.

Edwards, Elizabeth. "The Place of Women in the *Morte Darthur*." In *A Companion to Malory*, edited by Elizabeth Archibald and A. S. G. Edwards, 37–54. Cambridge: D. S. Brewer, 1996.

Encyclopaedia Britannica Online. "Chevalier." https://www.britannica.com/topic/chevalier.

Falknier, Caesar. "Hospital of St. John of Jerusalem in Ireland." *Proceedings of the Royal Irish Academy, Section C: Archeology, Celtic Studies, History, Linguistics, Literature* 26 (1906/1907): 301. https://breeheritage.com/2015/07/13/ballyhogue-and-the-knights-hospitallers/.

Farrer, William. *Early Yorkshire Charters, Being a Collection of Documents Anterior to the Thirteenth Century Made from the Public Records,*

Monastic Chartularies, Roger Dodsworth's Manuscripts and Other Available Sources. Edinburgh: Ballantyne and Hanson, 1914.

Fenton, Richard. *A Historical Tour through Pembrokeshire*. London: Longman, Hurst, Rees, and Orme, 1811.

Field, P.J.C. "Caxton's Roman War." In *The Malory Debate*, edited by P.J.C. Field, 127–168. Cambridge, MA: D.S. Brewer, 1998.

———. "The Malory Life-Records." In *A Companion to Malory*, edited by Elizabeth Archibald and A.S.G. Edwards, 115–130. Cambridge, MA: D.S. Brewer, 1996.

———. *The Life and Times of Sir Thomas Malory*. Cambridge, MA: D.S. Brewer, 1993.

———, ed. *The Malory Debate*. Cambridge, MA: D.S. Brewer, 2008.

———. "Malory and *The Wedding of Sir Gawain and Dame Ragnell*." *Archiv für das Studium der neueren Sprachen und Literaturen* 218 (1982): 374–381.

———. *Malory: Texts and Sources*. Cambridge, MA: D.S. Brewer, 1998.

Flower, William. *The Visitation of Yorkshire in the Years 1563 and 1564*. Edited by C.B. Norcliffe. London: n.p., 1881. Digitized via Internet Archive BookReader, June 7, 2008.

Forey, Alan. *The Military Orders from the Twelfth to the Early Fourteenth Centuries*. Toronto and Buffalo: University of Toronto Press, 1992.

Fraser's Magazine for Town and Country 14 (1876): 349.

Fries, Maureen. "Indiscreet Objects of Desire: Malory's Tristram and the Necessity of Deceit." In *Studies in Malory*, edited by James Spisak, 87–108. Kalamazoo, MI: Medieval Institute, 1985.

Gairdner, James, ed. *Three Fifteenth-Century Chronicles with Historical Memoranda by John Stowe, the Antiquary, and Contemporary Notes of Occurrences Written by Him in the Reign of Queen Elizabeth*. Westminster: J.B. Nichols and Sons, 1845, 1880. London: Forgotten Books, 2013. https://www.forgottenbooks.com/fr/books/ThreeFifteenthCenturyChronicles_10315053.

Gillard, Derek. *Education in England: A Brief History*. Derek Gillard, 2018. www.educationengland.org.uk/history/.

Gilson, Étienne. "La Mystique de la Grace dans la Queste del Saint Graal." *Romania* 51, no. 203 (1925): 321–347.

Gordon, E.V. and Eugene Vinaver. "New Light on the Text of the Alliterative *Morte Arthure*." *Medium Aevum* 6, no. 2 (1937): 81–98.

Gordon, Leff. "The Thornton Manuscript." *Speculum* 53, no. 4 (October 1978).

Greer, Germaine. *The Obstacle Race: The Fortunes of Women Painters and Their Work*. London and New York: Tauris Parke: 2001.

Griffith, Ralph, and James Sherborne, eds. *Kings and Nobles in the Later Middle Ages*. New York: St. Martin's Press, 1986.

Griffith, Richard R. "The Authorship Question Reconsidered: A Case for Thomas Malory of Papworth St Agnes, Cambridgeshire." In *Aspects of Malory,* edited by Toshiyuki Takamiya and Derek Brewer, 159–177. Woodbridge, Suffolk: D. S. Brewer, 1981.

———. "The Political Bias of Malory's 'Morte Darthur.'" *Viator* 5 (1974): 365–386.

Grovier, Kelly. *The Gaol: The Story of Newgate, London's Most Notorious Prison*. London: John Murray, 2009.

Hahn, Thomas, ed. *Sir Gawain: Eleven Romances and Tales*. Kalamazoo, MI: Medieval Institute, 1995.

Hale, J., J. Highfield, and B. Smalley, eds. *Europe in the Late Middle Ages*. London: Faber and Faber, 1965.

Hamel, Mary, ed. *Morte Arthure: A Critical Edition*. New York and London: Garland, 1984.

———. *Rewriting the Chronicle Tradition: The Alliterative "Morte Arthure" and Arthur's Sword of Peace.* Berkeley: University of California Press, 1960.

Hanks, D. Thomas, and Janet Jesmok, eds. *Malory and Christianity: Essays on Sir Thomas Malory's Morte Darthur.* Kalamazoo, MI: Medieval Institute, 2013.

Hanks, D. Thomas, and Jessica G. Grogdon, eds. *The Social and Literary Contexts of Malory's Morte Darthur*. Arthurian Studies 42. Cambridge, MA: D. S. Brewer, 2000.

Harris, E. Kay. "Evidence Against Lancelot and Guenevere in Malory's *Morte Darthur*: Treason by Imagination." *Exemplaria* 7, no. 1 (1995): 179–208.

Hellinga, Lotte. *Caxton in Focus: The Beginning of Printing in England*. London: The British Library, 1982.

Hellinga, Lotte, and Hilton Kelliher. "The Malory Manuscript." *The British Library Journal* 3, no. 2 (Autumn 1977): 91–113.

Henty, G. A. *A Knight of the White Cross: A Tale of the Siege of Rhodes* (New York: Charles Scribner's Sons, 1895). Online via Project Gutenberg, April 13, 2009.

Hibbert, Christopher. *The English: A Social History 1066–1945*. New York and London: Norton, 1987.

Hicks, Edward. *Sir Thomas Malory, His Turbulent Career*. Cambridge, MA: Harvard University Press, 1928.

Hills, Tim. "The Fountains Abbey Yews." Ancient Yew Group. https://www.ancient-yew.org/pdfs/Fountains%20Abbey.pdf..

Hodges, George. *Fountains Abbey: The Story of a Mediaeval Monastery*. London: John Murray, 1904.

Holbrook, Sue Ellen. "Guenevere: The Abbess of Amesbury and the Mark of Reparation." *Arthuriana* 20, no. 1 (Spring 2010): 25–51.

Holler, Dennis. *A New History of French Literature*. Cambridge, MA: Harvard University Press, 1994.

Homan, Helen Walker. "Cistercian Order of the Common Observance." In *Knights of Christ*, 25–41. Englewood Cliffs, NJ: Prentice-Hall, 1957. Catholic Culture. https://www.catholicculture.org/culture/library/view.cfm?recnum=4425.

Hone, William. *The Everyday Book and Table Book, or Everlasting Calendar of Popular Amusements*. 2 vols. London: T. Tegg, 1837.

Hynes-Berry, Mary. "A Tale Breffly Drawyne oute of Freynsche." In *Aspects of Malory*, edited by Toshiyuki Takamiya and Derek Brewer, 93–106. Woodbridge, Suffolk: D. S. Brewer and Roman Littlefield, 1980.

Ihle, Sandra Ness. *Malory's Grail Quest: Invention and Adaptation in Medieval Prose Romance*. Madison, WI: University of Wisconsin Press, 1983.

Ingham, R. "Multilingualism in the Middle Ages." Lecture at Birmingham City University, Birmingham, England, 2007.

Jefferson, Judith Ann, and Ad Putter. "Alliterative Patterning in the *Morte Arthure*." *Studies in Philology* 102, no. 4 (Fall 2005): 415–433.

Jones, Nigel. *Tower: An Epic History of the Tower of London*. London: Hutchinson, 2011.

Kaeuper, Richard. *Chivalry and Violence in Medieval Europe*. Oxford: Oxford University Press, 1999.

Kaiser, Rolf. *Zur Geographie des mittelenglischen Wortschatzes*. Palaestra 205. Leipzig: Mayer and Müller, 1937.

Kato, Tomomi. *A Concordance to "The Works of Sir Thomas Malory."* Tokyo: University of Tokyo Press, 1974.

Kaufman, Amy S. "'For This Was Drawyn by a Knyght Presoner': Sir Thomas Malory and *Le Morte Darthur*." In *Prison Narratives from Boethius to Zana*, edited by P. E. Phillips, 35–55. New York: Palgrave Macmillan, 2014.

Keiser, George R. "More Light on the Life and Milieu of Robert Thornton." *Studies in Bibliography* 36 (1983): 111–119.

Kelliher, Hilton, and Lotte Hellinga. "The Malory Manuscript and Caxton." *The British Library Journal* 3, no. 2 (Autumn 1977): 91–113.

Kelly, Robert L. "Wounds, Healing, and Knighthood in Malory's 'Tale of Launcelot and Guenevere.'" In *Studies in Malory*, edited by James W. Spisak, 173–192. Kalamazoo, MI: Medieval Institute, 1985.

Kendrick, Robert L. "William Matthews on Caxton and Malory." *Arthuriana* 7, no. 1 (Spring 1997): 3–133.

Kennedy, Beverly. "Adultery in Malory's *Le Morte d'Arthur*." *Arthuriana* 7, no. 4 (Winter 1997): 63–91.

———. *Knighthood in the Morte Darthur*. Arthurian Studies 11. Woodbridge, Suffolk, and Rochester, New York: D. S. Brewer, 1985, 1992.

Kennedy, E. D. "John Hardyng and the Holy Grail." In *Arthurian Literature VIII*, ed. Richard Barber. Cambridge, MA: Boydell and Brewer, 1989.

Ker, N. R., ed. *Medieval Libraries of Great Britain: A List of Surviving Books*. 2nd ed. London: Royal Historical Society, 1964.

———, ed. *The Winchester Malory: A Facsimile*. London: Early English Text Society, 1976; London: Scolar Press, 1976. Reproduced in facsimile from the copy in the Pierpont Morgan Library, New York.

Kibler, William W. "The Lancelot-Grail Cycle: Texts and Transformations." *Speculum* 72, no. 1 (January 1997): 189–191.

Kim, Hyonjin. *The Knight without the Sword: A Social Landscape of Malorian Chivalry*. Arthurian Studies 45 Cambridge: D. S. Brewer, 2000.

King, E. J., and Major General Earl of Scarborough. *The Grand Priory of the Order of the Hospital of St. John of Jerusalem in England*. Holborn: Fleetway Press, 1924.

Kittredge, George Lyman. "Who Was Thomas Malory?" In *Harvard Studies and Notes in Philology and Literature*. Vol. 5. Boston: Ginn, 1896.

"Knights Templar Commanderies in Aveyron History." Travel France Online. https://www.travelfranceonline.com/knights-templar-commanderies-in-aveyron-history/.

Kraemer, Alfred Robert. *Malory's Grail Seekers and Fifteenth-Century English Hagiography*. Studies in the Humanities, Literature, Politics, Society 44. New York: P. Lang, 1999.

Larking, Lambert B, ed. *Knights Hospitallers in England*. Cambridge, England: Camden Society, 1857.

Lawrence-Mathers, Anne. *Manuscripts in Northumbria in the Eleventh and Twelfth Centuries*. Woodbridge, Suffolk, and Rochester, New York: Boydell and Brewer, 2003.

Lawton, George. *The Religious Houses of Yorkshire*. London: Simpkin, 1853.

Levy, Bernard S., and Paul E. Szarmach, eds. *The Alliterative Tradition in the Fourteenth Century*. Kent, OH: Kent State University Press, 1981.

Lewis, C. S. "The English Prose *Morte*." *Times Literary Supplement*. June 7, 1947. 274.

Linton, Cecelia Lampp. "Another of the Works of Thomas Malory?" Address to the Annual Conference of the Southeastern Medieval Association, Marymount University, Arlington, VA, 1995.

———. "Malory, [Sir] Thomas." In *The Continuum Encyclopedia of British Literature,* edited by Steven R. Serafin and Valerie Grosvenor Myer. New York and London: Continuum, 2003. 632–633.

———. "Monasticism, Malory, and *Le Morte Darthur*." Address to the Annual Conference of the Southeastern Medieval Association, Wofford College, Spartanburg, SC, 2021.

———. "Resisting the Paradigm: Sir Thomas Malory, Knight Hospitaller." Address to the Annual Conference of the Southeastern Medieval Association, University of North Carolina at Greensboro, NC, 2019.

Lord, Victoria. "The Medieval Scribe and the Art of Writing." Ultimate History Project. www.ultimatehistoryproject.com/the-medieval-scribe.html.

Lumiansky, R. M. "Sir Thomas Malory's *Le Morte Darthur*, 1947–1987: Author, Title, Text." *Speculum* 62, no. 4 (October 1987): 878–897.

MacGibbon, David. *Elizabeth Woodville 1437–1492: Her Life and Times*. 1938. Digital publication: Amberley, August 19, 2014.

Madden, Thomas F. *The New Concise History of the Crusades*. New York: Barnes and Noble, 2007.

Mahoney, Dhira B. "The Truest and Holiest Tale: Malory's Transformation of *La Queste del Saint Graal*." In *Studies in Malory,* edited by James W. Spisak,109–28. Kalamazoo, MI: Medieval Institute, 1985.

Malory, Sir Thomas. *The Works of Sir Thomas Malory*. Edited by Eugene Vinaver. 3 vols. 2nd ed. Oxford: Oxford University Press, 1967.

———. *The Works of Sir Thomas Malory*, ed. Eugene Vinaver. 1 vol. 2nd ed. Oxford: Oxford University Press, 1971.

Mann, Jill. *Life in Words: Essays on Chaucer, the Gawain-Poet, and Malory*. Toronto: University of Toronto Press, 2014.

———. "Malory and the Grail Legend." In *A Companion to Malory,* edited by Elizabeth Archibald and A. S. G. Edwards, 203–220. Cambridge: D. S. Brewer, 1996.

———. "Taking the Adventure: Malory and the *Suite du Merlin*." In *Aspects of Malory*, edited by Toshiyuki Takamiya and Derek Brewer, 71–91. Woodbridge, Suffolk: D. S. Brewer and Roman Littlefield, 1981.

Markham, Clements B. "The Battle of Towton." *The Yorkshire Archeological Journal* 10 (1889):1–34.

Martin, A. T. "The Identity of the Author of the *Morte Darthur*." *Archeologia* 56 (1898):165–182.

———. *The Redemption of Chivalry: A Study of the* Queste del Saint Graal. Geneva: Droz, 1979.

Matheson, Lister M. *The Prose Brut: The Development of a Middle English Chronicle*. Tempe, AZ: Medieval and Renaissance Texts and Studies, 1998. Vol. 180.

Matthews, Rupert. *Battlefield Walks in Northumberland*. Battlefield Walks Series. London: Frances Lincoln, 2008. http://thehistorymanatlarge.blogspot.com/2012/12/the-reason-for-rthe-siege-of-bamburgh.html.

Matthews, William. "Caxton and Malory — a Defense." In *Medieval Literature and Folklore Studies: Essays in Honour of Francis Lee Utley*, edited by Jerome Mandel and Bruce A. Rosenberg, 75–95. New Brunswick, NJ: Rutgers University Press, 1970.

———. *The Ill-Framed Knight: A Skeptical Inquiry into the Identity of Sir Thomas Malory*. Berkeley and Los Angeles: University of California Press, 1966.

———. *The Tragedy of Arthur: A Study of the Alliterative "Morte Arthure."* Berkeley and Los Angeles: University of California Press, 1960.

McCarthy, Terence. "Malory and the Alliterative Tradition." In *Studies in Malory*, edited by James Spisak, 53–85. Kalamazoo, MI: Medieval Institute, 1985.

McCorkell, Edmund J., C.S.B. "The Cistercian Influence in *The Quest of the Holy Grail*." *The Pamphlet* 29. Toronto: The Institute of Medieval Studies, University of Toronto, 1934.

McIntosh, Angus, M. L. Samuels, and Margaret Laing, eds. *Middle English Dialectology: Essays on Some Principles and Problems*. Aberdeen, Scotland: Aberdeen University Press, 1989.

———. Review of *The Ill-Framed Knight*, by William Matthews. *Medium Aevum* 37, no. 3 (1968): 346–348.

McLean, Will. "Buying Power of 14th Century Money." A Commonplace Book. July 3, 2008. willscommonplacebook.blogspot.com/2008/07/buying-power-of-14th-century-money.html.

Meale, Carol M. "Manuscripts, Readers and Patrons in Fifteenth-Century England: Sir Thomas Malory and Arthurian Romance'. *Arthurian Literature* 4 (1985): 93–126.

Mercer, Malcolm. *The Medieval Gentry: Power, Leadership and Choice during the Wars of the Roses*. New York: Continuum, 2010.

Michelet, F. L. "East and West in Malory's Roman War The Implications of Arthur's Travel on the Continent." *Multilingua* 18, no. 2–3 (1999): 123–286.

Miller, Michael D. "The Remaining Lancastrians, the Battle of Hexham — 15th May 1464." In *The Wars of the Roses*. www.warsoftheroses.co.uk/chapter_60.html.

Moeller, Charles. "Chivalry." In *The Catholic Encyclopedia*. Vol. 3 (New York: Robert Appleton, 1908), https://www.newadvent.org/cathen/03691a.htm.

Moorman, Charles. "Desperately Defending Winchester." *Arthuriana* 7, no. 1 (Spring 1997): 24–30.

Muhammad ibn Umar al-Waqidi. *Kitab, al-Maghazi*, vol. 3 (London: Oxford University Press, 1966)

Mulberger, Stephen. "Religion in Fifteenth-Century England." ORB: Online Reference Book for Medieval Studies. https://the-orb.arlima.net/textbooks/muhlberger/15c_religion.html.

Murrin, Michael. *History and Warfare in Renaissance Epic*. Chicago: University of Chicago Press, 1994.

New World Encyclopedia. "Courtly Love." https://www.newworldencyclopedia.org/entry/Courtly_Love#:~:text=Courtly%20love%20was%20a%20medieval,end%20of%20the%20eleventh%20century.

New World Encyclopedia. "Knights Hospitaller." https://www.newworldencyclopedia.org/entry/Knights_Hospitaller.

Nicholson, Helen. "The Knights of Christ? The Templars, Hospitallers and Other Military Orders in the Eyes of their Contemporaries, 1128–1291." ORB: Online Reference Book for Medieval Studies. https://the-orb.arlima.net/encyclop/religion/monastic/knights.html.

Nicolle, David. *Knight Hospitaller*. Vol. 2. Oxford: Osprey, 2002.

Nolan, Barbara. "The Tale of Sir Gareth and the Tale of Sir Lancelot." In *A Companion to Malory*, edited by Elizabeth Archibald and A. S. G. Edwards, 153–182. Cambridge, MA: D. S. Brewer, 1996.

Norris, Ralph. *Malory's Library: The Sources of the* Morte Darthur. Arthurian Studies 71. Cambridge, MA: D. S. Brewer, 2008.

———. "Sir Gawain and Dame Ragnell Reconsidered." *Arthuriana* 19, no. 2 (Summer 2009): 82–102.

Oakeshott, Walter. "The Finding of the Manuscript." In *Essays on Malory,* edited by J. A. W. Bennett, 6. Oxford: Clarendon Press, 1963.

O'Loughlin, J. L. N. "The Middle English Alliterative *Morte Arthure.*" *Medium Aevum* 4 (1935): 159.

O'Malley, Gregory. *The Knights Hospitaller of the English Langue 1460–1565.* Oxford: Oxford University Press, 2005.

Order of St. John of Jerusalem, Knights Hospitallers, Malta, The Americas Priory. Website: https://www.saintjohn.org/.

Page, William. "Hutton Conyers." In *A History of the County of York North Riding,* edited by William Page, vol. 1, 403–405. London, 1914.

Parins, Marilyn, ed. *Sir Thomas Malory, the Critical Heritage.* London: Routledge, 1987, 2002.

Passaro, Jonathan. "Malory's Text of the *Suite du Merlin.*" In *Arthurian Literature XXVI,* edited by Elizabeth Archibald and David F. Johnson. Woodbridge, Suffolk: D. S. Brewer 2009.

Pearsall, Derek. "The Origins of the Alliterative Revival." In *The Alliterative Tradition in the Fourteenth Century,* edited by B. S. Levy and P. E. Szarmach. Kent, OH: Ohio State University Press, 1981.

Phillips, Philip Edward, ed. *Prison Narratives from Boethius to Zana.* New York: Palgrave Macmillan, 2014.

Phillips, Simon. *The Prior of the Knights Hospitallers in Late Medieval England.* Woodbridge: Boydell Press, 2009.

———. "Walking a Thin Line: Hospitaller Priors, Politics, and Power in Late Medieval England." In *The Military Orders.* Vol. 5, *Politics and Power,* edited by Peter W. Edbury. Hampshire, England, and Burlington, VT: Ashgate, 2009.

Porter, Whitworth. *A History of the Knights of Malta or the Order of St. John of Jerusalem.* 2 vols. London: Longman, Brown, Green, Longmans, and Roberts, 1858.

Powlett, Catherine Lucy Wilhelmina, Duchess of Cleveland. *The Battle Abbey Roll with Some Account of the Norman Lineages.* In 3 vols. Vol 1. London: John Murray, 1889.

Pratt, Karen. "The Cistercians and the *Queste del Saint Graal.*" *Reading Medieval Studies* 21 (1995): 69–96.

Pyles, Thomas. *The Origins and Development of the English Language.* 2nd ed. New York: Harcourt, Brace, Jovanovich, 1971.

Ralls, Karen. *The Templars and the Grail: Knights of the Quest.* Wheaton, IL: Quest Books, 2003.

Rawlings, Gertrude Burford. *The Story of Books.* New York: D. Appleton, 1906.

Ribston and the Old Knight Monks. www.goodrickfamilyhistory.co.uk/420218910.

Rickard, J. "Sir Humphrey Neville of Brancepeth (c. 1439–1469)." History of War. March 26, 2014. http://www.historyofwar.org/articles/people_neville_humphrey_brancepeth.html.

Rhys, John. Preface to *Le Morte D'Arthur,* edited by John Rhys. London: J. M. Dent and Sons, 1906.

Riddy, Felicity. "Contextualizing *Le Morte Darthur*: Empire and Civil War." In *A Companion to Malory,* edited by Elizabeth Archibald and A. S. G. Edwards, 55–74. Cambridge, MA: D. S. Brewer, 1996.

Riley-Smith, Jonathan. *The Knights Hospitallers in the Levant c. 1070–1309.* New York: Palgrave Macmillan, 2012.

———. *Templars and Hospitallers as Professed Religious in the Holy Land.* Notre Dame, IN: University of Notre Dame Press, 2010.

Royal Australian Historical Society. "History of the Templars." Website. www.osj-nsw.org.au/Historical%20Summary%20nsw.htm.

Rumble, T. C. "The First *Explicit* in Malory's *Morte D'arthur.*" *Modern Language Notes* 71, no. 8 (December 1956): 564–566.

Russell, John. *History of France: From the Earliest Times to the Present Day.* Philadelphia, PA: Hogan and Thompson, 1837.

S., Sandra. "Fountains Abbey and Studley Royal Water Garden." TripAdvisor. June 27, 2011. https://www.tripadvisor.com/ShowUserReviews-g209973-d211827-r113998068-Fountains_Abbey_and_Studley_Royal_Water_Garden-Ripon_North_Yorkshire_England.html.

Sadler, John. *Towton: The Battle of Palmsunday Field 1461.* Barnsley, South Yorkshire, England: Pen and Sword Military, 2011.

Sands, Donald B, ed. *Middle English Verse Romances.* New York: Holt, Rinehart, and Winston, 1966.

Scudder, Vida Dutton. *Le Morte Darthur of Sir Thomas Malory and Its Sources.* New York: E. P. Dutton; London: J. M. Dent and Sons, 1917.

Seaton, Ethel. *Sir Richard Roos, c. 1410–1482: Lancastrian Poet.* London: Rupert Hart-Davis, 1961.

Selwood, Dominic. *The Knights Hospitallers in England: Being the Report of Prior Philip de Thames to the Grand Master Elyan de Villanova, AD 1338.* Cambridge, England: Camden Society, 1999.

Shaw, Sally. "Caxton and Malory." In *Essays on Malory,* edited by J. A. W. Bennett, 114–145. Oxford: Clarendon Press, 1963.

Shepherd, Stephen H. A., ed. *Le Morte Darthur, or The Hoole Book of Kyng Arthur and of his Noble Knyghtes of the Round Table*. Norton Critical Edition. New York, London: W. W. Norton, 2004.

Shictman, Martin B. and James P. Carley, eds. *Culture and the King: The Social Implications of the Arthurian Legend.* New York: SUNY Press, 1994.

Sir Thomas Malory, Preface to *The Works of Sir Thomas Malory.* Edited by Eugene Vinaver. 3 vols. Oxford: Clarendon Press, 1970.

———. *The Works of Sir Thomas Malory*. Edited by Eugene Vinaver. 3 vols. 2nd ed. Oxford: Oxford University Press, 1967.

———. *The Works of Sir Thomas Malory.* Edited by Eugene Vinaver. 1 vol. 2nd ed. Oxford: Oxford University Press, 1971.

Smalley, Justin. "St. Bernard of Clairvaux and the New Knighthood". October 10, 2000–March 25, 2001. http://www2.hanover.edu/battles/arthur/bernard.htm.

Sommer, H. Oskar, ed. *Le Morte Darthur: Studies on the Sources.* 3 Vols. London: D. Nutt, 1891.

Speight, Harry. *Nidderdale and the Garden of the Nidd: A Yorkshire Rhineland. Being a Complete Account, Historical, Scientific, and Descriptive of the Beautiful Valley of the Nidd.* London: Elliot Stock,1894.

Spisak, James W. "Malory's 'Lost' Source." In *Studies in Malory,* edited by James W. Spisak, 227–230. Kalamazoo, MI: Medieval Institute, 1985.

———. *Caxton's Malory: A New Edition of Sir Thomas Malory's "Le Morte D'Arthur."* Berkeley and Los Angeles, CA: University of California Press, 1983.

———. *The Malory Debate on the Texts of* Le Morte Darthur. Arthurian Studies 47. Cambridge, MA: D. S. Brewer, 2000.

Stanley, Jennifer. *"The French Book Saith": Malory's Adaptation of His Sources*. Ph.D. diss., Vanderbilt University, Nashville, TN, 2012.

Stephen, Sir Leslie, ed. *Dictionary of National Biography*. Vol. 40. London: Macmillan, 1894.

Steve Weidenkopf, *The Glory of the Crusades*. El Cajon, CA: Catholic Answers Press, 2014.

Stones, Alison. "The Lancelot-Grail Story: Summary of the Branches." University of Pittsburgh. https://www.lancelot-project.pitt.edu/LG-web/TheStory-Summary.htm.

Storer, James Sargant, and Henry Sargant Storer. *Delineations, Graphical and Descriptive, of Fountains' [sic] Abbey in the West Riding of the County of York*. London: Longman, Rees, and C. Tilt, 1820.

Strutt, Jacob George. *Sylva Britannica; Or, Portraits of Forest Trees Distinguished for Their Antiquity, Magnitude, or Beauty, Drawn from Nature and Etched by Jacob George Strutt.* London: Henry G. Bohn, 1822–1826.

Suite du Merlin Manuscript. Cambridge University Library Add. MS 7071.

Sumner, Laura, ed. *The Weddynge of Sir Gawen and Dame Ragnell.* Smith College Studies in Modern Languages 5, no. 4 (July 1924). Northampton, MA: Smith College, 1924.

Sutton, Anne F. "Malory in Newgate: A New Document." *The Library: The Transactions of the Bibliographical Society*, Seventh Series, 1, no. 3 (September 2000): 243–262.

Szarnicki, Henry A. *The Monastic Child-Oblate, a History of the Institution to the Carolingian Period, with a Translation of the* Liber de Oblatione Puerorum *by Rabanus Maurus.* Ph.D. diss., The Catholic University of America, Washington, DC, June 1965.

Takamiya, Toshiyuki, and Derek Brewer, eds. *Aspects of Malory.* Woodbridge: D. S. Brewer and Roman Littlefield, 1981.

The Quest of the Holy Grail. Translated by Pauline Matarasso. Middlesex: Penguin Books, 1969.

"Knights Templar Commanderies in Aveyron History." Travel France Online. https://www.travelfranceonline.com/knights-templar-commanderies-in-aveyron-history/.

Travis, Charles Clay, and Diana E. Greenway, eds. *Early Yorkshire Families.* Cambridge: Cambridge University Press, 1973.

Trimnell, Karen. " 'And Should Have Been Oderwyse Understond': The Disenchanting of Sir Gromer Somer Joure." *Medium Aevum* 71, no. 2 (2002): 294–301.

Tucker, P. E. "Chivalry in the *Morte.*" In *Essays on Malory,* edited by J. A. W. Bennett, 64–103. Oxford: Clarendon Press, 1963.

Wagner, John A. *Encyclopedia of the Wars of the Roses.* Santa Barbara, CA: ABC-CLIO, 2001.

Waite, Arthur Edward. *The Vulgate Cycle of the Holy Grail.* Whitefish, MT: Kessinger, 1993. Extract from Arthur Edward Waite, *The Holy Grail: The Galahad Quest in the Arthurian Literature.*

Walbran, John. *A Guide to Ripon, Harrogate, Fountains Abbey, Bolton Priory and Several Places of Interest.* London: A. Johnson; Bell and Daldy, 1856.

———. *Memorials of the Abbey of St Mary of Fountains, including a Genealogical Account of the Lords of Studley Royal, 1841.* Vol. 2, part 1. The Publications of the Surtees Society, vol. 57. Ripon: William Harrison, 1876.

Walsh, John Michael. "Malory's 'Very Mater of La Cheualer du Charyot': Characterization and Structure." In *Studies in Malory,* edited by James W. Spisak, 199–223. Kalamazoo, MI: Medieval Institute, 1985.

Warkworth, John. *A Chronicle of the First Thirteen Years of the Reign of King Edward the Fourth*. London: Camden Society, 1835.

Weidenkopf, Steve. *The Glory of the Crusades.* El Cajon, CA: Catholic Answers Press, 2014.

Wheeler, Bonnie, et al., eds. *The Malory Debate: Essays on the Texts of Le Morte Darthur*. Arthurian Studies 47. Cambridge, England and Rochester, New York: Boydell and Brewer, 2000.

Wheeler, Kip. "Common Religious Texts: The *Pater Noster, Credo,* and *Ave Maria* in the Late Medieval Period (1281 AD–1400 AD)." Dr. L. Kip Wheeler. Carson-Newman University. https://web.cn.edu/kwheeler/lords_prayer_1400.html.

Whetter, K. S. "Genre as Context in the Alliterative *Morte Arthure*." *Arthuriana* 20, no. 2 (Summer 2010): 45–65.

Whitteridge, Gweneth. "The Identity of Sir Thomas Malory, Knight-Prisoner." *The Review of English Studies,* New Series 24, no. 95 (August 1973): 257–265.

Williams, T. Letter to the editor. *The Athenaeum*. July 1896.

Wilson, R. H. "The Rebellion of the Kings in Malory and in the Cambridge *Suite du Merlin*." *The University of Texas Studies in English* 31 (1952): 13–26.

Wright, M. R. "Designing the End of History in the Arming of Galahad." *Arthuriana* 5, no. 4 (Winter 1995): 45–55.

Year Book of 4 Edward IV.

Index of Names

About the Author

DR. CECELIA LAMPP LINTON credits her detection of a religious vocation in the author of *Le Morte Darthur* to the fact that she was educated by nuns—they are attuned to such things—in parish schools and then in the venerable St. Vincent's Academy in Savannah, Georgia, which has been enlightening girls since 1845. Higher education and a long career on the other side of the desk have never overshadowed that early encounter with the rigors of her formation by the teaching nuns. When she began reading P. J. C. Field's work concerning Sir Thomas Malory's identity, Linton knew before the end of Chapter 1 that this book had to be written, and so she has written it, with great joy along the way. She can be found at home, usually with some part of her numerous family, in a certain old house in Manassas, Virginia, or else in another one, even older, in Savannah.